Understanding Automotive Electronics

Understanding Automotive Electronics

Sixth Edition

By: William B. Ribbens, Ph.D.

With Contributions to Previous Editions by:

Norman P. Mansour
Gerald Luecke
Charles W. Battle
Edward C. Jones
Leslie E. Mansir

Newnes

An Imprint of Elsevier Science
Amsterdam Boston London New York Oxford Paris
San Diego San Francisco Singapore Sydney Tokyo

Newnes is an imprint of Elsevier Science.

Library of Congress Cataloging-in-Publication Data
Ribbens, William B.
    Understanding automotive electronics / William B. Ribbens ; with contributions to previous editions by Norman P. Mansour ... [et al.] — 6th ed.
      p. cm
    Includes index.
    ISBN 0-7506-7599-3 (pbk. : alk. paper)
    1. Automobiles—Electronic equipment.   I. Mansour, Norman P.   II. Title.

TL272.5 .R45 2002
629.2′7—dc21

                           2002034651

British Library Cataloguing-in-Publication Data
A catalogue record for this book is available from the British Library.

The publisher offers special discounts on bulk orders of this book.

For information, please contact:

Manager of Special Sales
Elsevier Science
200 Wheeler Road
Burlington, MA 01803
Tel: 781-313-4700
Fax: 781-313-4882

For information on all Newnes publications available, contact our World Wide Web home page at: http://www.newnespress.com

10 9 8 7 6 5 4 3 2 1

Printed in the United States of America

To Katherine

Contents

Preface

Since the introduction of electronics for emission control on engines, the evolution of electronics in automobiles has advanced rapidly. The pace of development has inspired five revisions of this book in roughly twenty years to avoid obsolescence. Rarely in history have technical developments moved at such a pace.

Electronics have become standard implementation for control on all modern vehicles impacting virtually all automotive subsystems. Such features as powertrain control, vehicle motion control, antilock braking systems, and airbags could only be achieved practically through the use of electronics. These features have become standard features in the highly competitive North American automotive market.

The first edition of this book was devoted primarily to electronic engine control because this was the chief application at that time. A number of automotive systems which were discussed in the chapter on the future of automotive electronics in the second, third, fourth, and fifth editions are now in production. These systems are presented in the appropriate chapters of this fifth edition. This latest edition covers the automotive subsystems incorporating electronics except for entertainment systems. These systems have been omitted partly due to space limitations and because automotive entertainment systems are closely related to home entertainment systems, which are discussed in many excellent publications.

In its revised form, this book explains automotive electronics as of 2001. It should prepare the reader for an understanding of present as well as future developments in this field into at least the early part of the twenty-first century.

William B. Ribbens

Automotive Fundamentals

Picture yourself in the not-too-distant future driving your new car along a rural interstate highway on a business trip. You are traveling along one of the new automated highways in which individual cars are controlled electronically to maintain a fixed spacing in a lane at a preferred speed. Typically, these cars are traveling at 70 mph and are spaced about 25 ft apart. The cars are computer controlled via a digital communication link, including a cable buried in the center of the "cruise" lane and follow one another in a pattern known as platooning. Your car will automatically remain in this cruise control lane until you approach your destination exit.

You press a button on the steering column and an image of a road map appears faintly visible (so as not to obscure the road ahead) on the windshield in front of you. This map shows your present position and the position of the destination city. The distance to your destination and the approximate arrival time are displayed on the digital instrument cluster.

You are talking on your cellular phone to your office about some changes in a contract that you hope to negotiate. You are wearing a lightweight headset that enables you to use the cell phone "hands free" to drive. Dialing is accomplished by voice command using voice recognition software in your cell phone controller. After the instructions for the contract changes are completed, a printer in your car generates a copy of the latest contract version.

Your spouse (in the passenger seat) is sending e-mail messages using the on-board computer that is linked by radio to the Internet. Your son (in the rear seat) is watching a movie via an interactive digital link, while your daughter (also in a rear seat) is doing a math lesson from an education center with an interactive video link.

After you finish your phone call, the onboard entertainment system starts playing music for you at a comfortable level relative to the low-level wind and road noise in the car. After completing your phone conversation, you press another button on the steering wheel and the music is replaced by a recorded lesson in French verb conjugation, which you have been studying. Suddenly, the French lesson is interrupted by a message delivered in natural-sounding synthesized speech. "You have fuel remaining for another 50 miles at the present speed. Your destination is 23 miles away. Recommend refueling after exiting the highway. There is a station that accepts your electronic credit near the exit (you know, of course, that the electronic credit is activated by inserting the fuel nozzle into the car). Also, the left rear tire pressure is low and the engine control system reports that the mass air flow sensor is intermittently malfunctioning and should be serviced soon." After this message has been delivered, the French lesson returns.

modern engines are 4-stroke/cycle, gasoline fueled, spark ignited, normally aspirated, and water cooled. By illustrating the fundamentals of engine operation using the example engine of Figure 1.2, we can thus explain the differences that have occurred with modern electronic controls.

The major components of the engine include the following:

1. Engine block
2. Cylinder
3. Crankshaft
4. Pistons
5. Connecting rods
6. Camshaft
7. Cylinder head
8. Valves
9. Fuel control system
10. Ignition system
11. Exhaust system
12. Cooling system
13. Electrical system

Electronics play a direct role in all aspects of controlling engine operation, including the fuel and air flow control, ignition, exhaust and evaporative emission systems, and diagnostic and maintenance operations as well as many other secondary functions. It will be shown in Chapters 5, 6, and 7 that in order to meet government regulations for exhaust emissions and fuel economy, these systems combine to optimize performance within regulatory requirements. In the earliest days of government regulation, electronic controls were applied to existing engine designs. However, as electronic technology evolved, the engine mechanical configuration was influenced (at least indirectly) by the electronic controls that were intended to be applied. The evolution of engine control electronics is explained in Chapters 5, 6 and 7 of this book.

Engine Block

Conventional internal combustion engines convert the movement of pistons to the rotational energy used to drive the wheels.

Mechanical rotary power is produced in an engine through the combustion of gasoline inside cylinders in the engine block and a mechanism consisting of pistons (in the cylinders) and a linkage (connecting rod) coupled to the crankshaft. Mechanical power is available at the crankshaft.

The cylinders are cast in the engine block and machined to a smooth finish. The pistons fit tightly into the cylinder and have rings that provide a tight sliding seal against the cylinder wall. The pistons are connected to the

Automotive Fundamentals

Picture yourself in the not-too-distant future driving your new car along a rural interstate highway on a business trip. You are traveling along one of the new automated highways in which individual cars are controlled electronically to maintain a fixed spacing in a lane at a preferred speed. Typically, these cars are traveling at 70 mph and are spaced about 25 ft apart. The cars are computer controlled via a digital communication link, including a cable buried in the center of the "cruise" lane and follow one another in a pattern known as platooning. Your car will automatically remain in this cruise control lane until you approach your destination exit.

You press a button on the steering column and an image of a road map appears faintly visible (so as not to obscure the road ahead) on the windshield in front of you. This map shows your present position and the position of the destination city. The distance to your destination and the approximate arrival time are displayed on the digital instrument cluster.

You are talking on your cellular phone to your office about some changes in a contract that you hope to negotiate. You are wearing a lightweight headset that enables you to use the cell phone "hands free" to drive. Dialing is accomplished by voice command using voice recognition software in your cell phone controller. After the instructions for the contract changes are completed, a printer in your car generates a copy of the latest contract version.

Your spouse (in the passenger seat) is sending e-mail messages using the on-board computer that is linked by radio to the Internet. Your son (in the rear seat) is watching a movie via an interactive digital link, while your daughter (also in a rear seat) is doing a math lesson from an education center with an interactive video link.

After you finish your phone call, the onboard entertainment system starts playing music for you at a comfortable level relative to the low-level wind and road noise in the car. After completing your phone conversation, you press another button on the steering wheel and the music is replaced by a recorded lesson in French verb conjugation, which you have been studying. Suddenly, the French lesson is interrupted by a message delivered in natural-sounding synthesized speech. "You have fuel remaining for another 50 miles at the present speed. Your destination is 23 miles away. Recommend refueling after exiting the highway. There is a station that accepts your electronic credit near the exit (you know, of course, that the electronic credit is activated by inserting the fuel nozzle into the car). Also, the left rear tire pressure is low and the engine control system reports that the mass air flow sensor is intermittently malfunctioning and should be serviced soon." After this message has been delivered, the French lesson returns.

A short time later, the French lesson is again interrupted by the electronic voice message system: "Replace the disk in the Navigation CD player with disk number 37 for detailed map and instructions to your destination, please." Then the French lesson returns.

You insert the correct disk in the Navigation CD player as requested and the map display on the windshield changes. The new display shows a detailed map of your present position and the route to your destination. As you approach the city limits, the car speed is automatically reduced to the legal limit of 55 mph. The voice message system speaks again: "Leave the highway at exit 203, which is one-half mile away. Proceed along Austin Road to the second intersection, which is Meyer Road. Turn right and proceed 0.1 mile. Your destination is on the right-hand side of the road. Don't forget to refuel."

This scenario is not as farfetched as it sounds. All of the events described are technically possible. Some have even been tested experimentally. The electronic technology required to develop a car with the features described exists today. The actual implementation of such electronic features will depend on the cost of the equipment and the market acceptance of the features.

USE OF ELECTRONICS IN THE AUTOMOBILE

For most people, the automobile has come to be an appliance. It is arguably the most cost effective, most user friendly of appliances available today. The personal computer industry likes to refer to its products as user friendly. However if the automobile had the same user friendliness as a PC, it would arrive in six or more large boxes and require the owner to install the engine wheels and seats and load the programs into its various electronic systems and the documentation would be unreadable. Moreover, in use it would break down every 100 or so miles. This comparison is offered tongue in cheek, but it does illustrate the relatively high reliability of modern automobiles with their various electronic subsystems. Although its utility is primarily for transportation, the new automobile electronics can give it a broad range of auxiliary capabilities, as will be illustrated in this book.

EVOLUTION OF AUTOMOTIVE ELECTRONICS

Microelectronics will provide many exciting new features for automobiles.

Electronics have been relatively slow in coming to the automobile primarily because of the relationship between the added cost and the benefits. Historically, the first electronics (other than radio) were introduced into the commercial automobile during the late 1950s and early 1960s. However, these features were not well received by customers, so they were discontinued from production automobiles.

Environmental regulations and an increased need for economy have resulted in electronics being used within a number of automotive systems.

Two major events occurred during the 1970s that started the trend toward the use of modern electronics in the automobile: (1) the introduction of government regulations for exhaust emissions and fuel economy, which required better control of the engine than was possible with the methods being used; and (2) the development of relatively low cost per function solid-state digital electronics that could be used for engine control and other applications.

Electronics are being used now in the automobile and probably will be used even more in the future. Some of the present and potential applications for electronics are

1. Electronic engine control for minimizing exhaust emissions and maximizing fuel economy
2. Instrumentation for measuring vehicle performance parameters and for diagnosis of on-board system malfunctions
3. Driveline control
4. Vehicle motion control
5. Safety and convenience
6. Entertainment/communication/navigation

Many of these applications of electronics will be discussed in this book.

CHAPTER OVERVIEW

This chapter will give the reader a general overview of the automobile with emphasis on the basic operation of the engine, thus providing the reader with the background to see how electronic controls have been and will be applied. The discussion is simplified to provide the reader with just enough information to understand automotive mechanics. Readers who want to know the mechanics of an automobile in more detail are referred to the many books written for that purpose.

THE AUTOMOBILE PHYSICAL CONFIGURATION

The earliest automobiles consisted of carriages (similar to those drawn by horses) to which a primitive engine and drivetrain and steering controls were added. Typically, such cars had a strong steel frame that supported the body of the car. The wheels were attached to this frame by a set of springs and shock absorbers that permitted the car to travel over the uneven road surfaces of the day while isolating the car body from many of the road irregularities. This same general configuration persisted in most passenger cars until some time after World War II, although there was an evolution in car size, shape, and features as technology permitted. Beginning in the late 1960s, government regulations imposed severe design constraints on automobiles that led (as will be shown) to an evolution of electronic systems in automotive design. It is this evolution that is the primary focus of this book.

For the remainder of this chapter, the basic automobile components and systems are reviewed as they pertained to the post–World War II, preemissions-control era. This review provides a framework within which the present day automobile with its extensive use of electronics can be understood. In this sense, the motivation for applying electronics to solve regulatory problems imposed on the industry can readily be seen. Readers with a solid background in basic automotive systems may want to skip the remainder of the present chapter.

This early configuration is depicted in Figure 1.1, in which many of the important automotive systems are illustrated. These systems include the following:

1. Engine
2. Drivetrain (transmission, differential, axle)
3. Suspension
4. Steering
5. Brakes
6. Instrumentation
7. Electrical/electronic
8. Motion control
9. Safety
10. Comfort/convenience
11. Entertainment/communication/navigation

In Figure 1.1 the frame or chassis on which the body is mounted is supported by the suspension system. The brakes are connected to the opposite end of the suspension components. The steering and other major mechanical systems are mounted on one of these components and attached as necessary through mechanical components to other subsystems.

This basic vehicle configuration was used from the earliest cars through the late 1960s or 1970s, with some notable exceptions. The increasing importance of fuel efficiency and government-mandated safety regulations led to major changes in vehicle design. The body and frame evolved into an integrated structure to which the power train, suspension, wheels, etc., were attached.

Once again with a few notable exceptions, most cars had an engine in a front configuration with the drive axle at the rear. There are advantages in having the engine located in the front of the vehicle (e.g., crash protection, efficient engine cooling). Until recently, the so-called drive wheels through which power is delivered to the road have been the rear wheels (as depicted in Figure 1.1). This configuration is known as rear wheel drive. For safety and stability the front wheels are used to steer the vehicle.

This rear wheel drive configuration is not optimal from a traction standpoint since the relatively large weight of the engine/transmission is

Figure 1.1
Systems of the Automobile

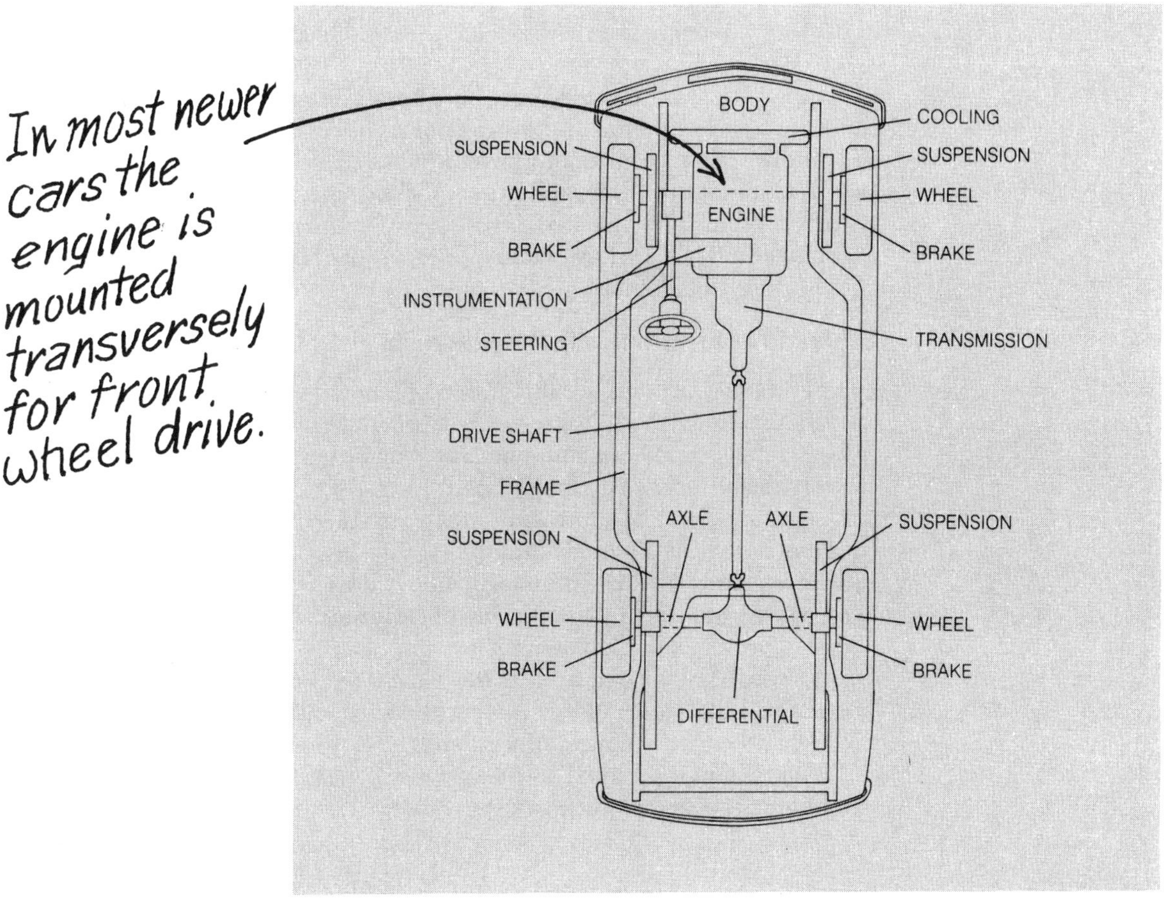

In most newer cars the engine is mounted transversely for front wheel drive.

primarily on the front wheels. In order to take advantage of the engine weight for traction, many present-day cars combine steering and drive wheels in the front (i.e., so-called front wheel drive cars). In achieving front wheel drive, certain compromises must be made with respect to complexity and steering radius. Moreover, there is a tendency for the torque applied to the front wheels to adversely affect steering through a phenomenon known as "torque steer." Nevertheless, the technology of front engine front wheel steering is quite mature and has become commonplace in modern cars.

In front wheel drive cars the engine is mounted transversely (i.e., with the rotation axis orthogonal to the vehicle axis as opposed to along the vehicle axis). In automotive parlance the traditional engine orientation is referred to as *North-South,* and the transverse orientation as *East-West.* The transmission is mounted adjacent to the engine and oriented with its axis parallel to the engine axis. The differential and drive axle configuration is normally mounted in the transmission; the combined unit is thus called the *transaxle.*

All of the systems listed above have been impacted by the introduction of electronics. The evolution of these electronics has been so rapid that a book such as this requires continuous revision to have any hope of reflecting the latest state of the art. New applications of electronics to each of the above systems continually supplement those already in use resulting in an environment in which electronics represents something of the order of 20% of the cost of a modern car.

Evolution of Electronics in the Automobile

This book explores the application of modern solid-state electronics to the various automotive subsystems described above. In order to give the evolution of electronics in automobiles a suitable perspective, it is helpful to consider the history of automotive electronics. Apart from auto radios, some turn signal models, and a few ignition systems, there was very little use of electronics in the automobile until the early 1970s. At about this time, government-mandated emission regulations, fuel economy, and safety requirements motivated the initial use of electronics. The dramatic performance improvements and relatively low cost of electronics have led to an explosive application of electronics in virtually every automotive subsystem. The relative cost/benefit of electronic subsystems in automobiles is largely affected by the production volume. (Some 15 to 16 million new cars and light trucks are sold in the United States each year.) Such a large production volume significantly lowers the unit cost for any electronic system relative to aerospace volumes.

SURVEY OF MAJOR AUTOMOTIVE SYSTEMS

We will be exploring these electronic systems in great detail later in this book, but first it is helpful to review the basic mechanical configurations for each component and subsystem. Modern automotive electronics were first applied to control the engine in order to reduce exhaust emissions and somewhat later to improve fuel economy. Consequently, we review the engine configuration first in this survey.

THE ENGINE

The engine in an automobile provides all the power for moving the automobile, for the hydraulic and pneumatic systems, and for the electrical system. A variety of engine types have been produced, but one class of engine is used most: the internal combustion, piston-type, 4-stroke/cycle, gasoline-

**Figure 1.2
Cutaway View of a 6-
Cylinder, Overhead-
Valve, Inline Engine
(*Source:* Crouse)**

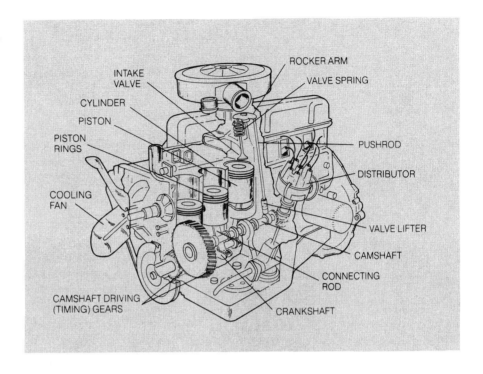

fueled, spark-ignited, liquid-cooled engine. This engine will be referred to in this book as the spark-ignited, or SI, engine.

Although rapid technological advances in the control of the SI engine have been achieved through the use of electronics, the fundamental mechanical configuration has remained unchanged since this type of power plant was first invented. In addition, the introduction of modern materials has greatly improved the packaging, size, and power output per unit weight or per unit volume. In order that the reader may fully appreciate the performance improvements that have been achieved through electronic controls, we illustrate the engine fundamentals with an example engine configuration from the pre-electronic era.

Figure 1.2 is a partial cutaway drawing of an SI engine configuration commonly found in the period immediately following World War II. The engine there illustrated is a 6-cylinder, overhead-valve, inline engine. Alternate engine configurations today are either a 4-cylinder inline or a V-type engine with either 6 or 8 cylinders (although there are exceptions). Moreover, the materials found in present-day engines permit greatly reduced weight for a given engine power.

Nevertheless, modern electronically controlled engines have much in common with this example configuration. For example, the vast majority of modern engines are 4-stroke/cycle, gasoline fueled, spark ignited, normally aspirated, and water cooled. By illustrating the fundamentals of engine operation using the example engine of Figure 1.2, we can thus explain the differences that have occurred with modern electronic controls.

The major components of the engine include the following:

1. Engine block
2. Cylinder
3. Crankshaft
4. Pistons
5. Connecting rods
6. Camshaft
7. Cylinder head
8. Valves
9. Fuel control system
10. Ignition system
11. Exhaust system
12. Cooling system
13. Electrical system

Electronics play a direct role in all aspects of controlling engine operation, including the fuel and air flow control, ignition, exhaust and evaporative emission systems, and diagnostic and maintenance operations as well as many other secondary functions. It will be shown in Chapters 5, 6, and 7 that in order to meet government regulations for exhaust emissions and fuel economy, these systems combine to optimize performance within regulatory requirements. In the earliest days of government regulation, electronic controls were applied to existing engine designs. However, as electronic technology evolved, the engine mechanical configuration was influenced (at least indirectly) by the electronic controls that were intended to be applied. The evolution of engine control electronics is explained in Chapters 5, 6 and 7 of this book.

Engine Block

Conventional internal combustion engines convert the movement of pistons to the rotational energy used to drive the wheels.

Mechanical rotary power is produced in an engine through the combustion of gasoline inside cylinders in the engine block and a mechanism consisting of pistons (in the cylinders) and a linkage (connecting rod) coupled to the crankshaft. Mechanical power is available at the crankshaft.

The cylinders are cast in the engine block and machined to a smooth finish. The pistons fit tightly into the cylinder and have rings that provide a tight sliding seal against the cylinder wall. The pistons are connected to the

Figure 1.3
Piston Connection to Crankshaft (*Source:* Crouse)

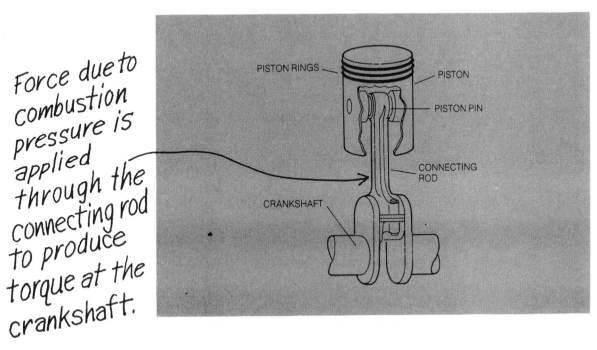

Force due to combustion pressure is applied through the connecting rod to produce torque at the crankshaft.

crankshaft by connecting rods, as shown in Figure 1.3. The crankshaft converts the up and down motion of the pistons to the rotary motion and the torque needed to drive the wheels.

Cylinder Head

The cylinder head contains an intake and exhaust valve for each cylinder. When both valves are closed, the head seals the top of the cylinder while the piston rings seal the bottom of the cylinder. During combustion, high pressure is devoloped in the cylinder which, in turn, produces a force on the piston that creates the torque on the crankshaft.

The valves are operated by off-center (eccentric) cams on the camshaft, which is driven by the crankshaft as shown in Figure 1.4. The camshaft rotates at exactly half the crankshaft speed because a complete cycle of any cylinder involves two complete crankshaft rotations and only one sequence of opening and closing of the associated intake and exhaust valves. The valves are normally held closed by powerful springs. When the time comes for a valve to open, the lobe on the cam forces the pushrod upward against one end of the rocker arm. The other end of the rocker arm moves downward and forces the valve open. (*Note:* Some engines have the camshaft above the head, eliminating the pushrods. This is called an *overhead cam* engine.)

Figure 1.4
Valve Operating
Mechanism (*Source:*
Crouse)

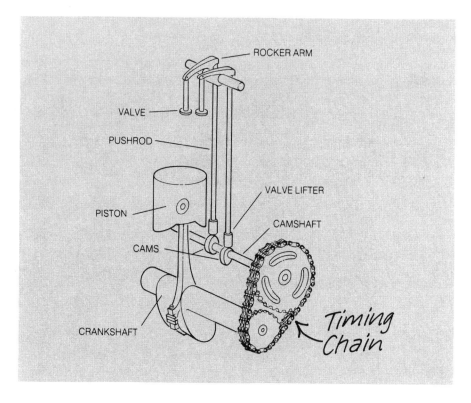

The 4-Stroke Cycle

Conventional SI engines operate using four "strokes," with either an up or down movement of each piston. These strokes are named *intake, compression, power,* and *exhaust.*

   The operation of the engine can be understood by considering the actions in any one cylinder during a complete cycle of the engine. One complete cycle in the 4-stroke/cycle SI engine requires two complete rotations of the crankshaft. As the crankshaft rotates, the piston moves up and down in the cylinder. In the two complete revolutions of the crankshaft that make up one cycle, there are four separate strokes of the piston from the top of the cylinder to the bottom or from the bottom to the top. Figure 1.5 illustrates the four strokes for a 4-stroke/cycle SI engine, which are called:

1. Intake
2. Compression
3. Power
4. Exhaust

   There are two valves for each cylinder. The left valve in the drawing is called the *intake valve* and the right valve is called the *exhaust valve.* The intake valve is normally larger than the exhaust valve. Note that the crankshaft is assumed to be rotating in a clockwise direction. The action of the engine during the four strokes is described in the following sections.

**Figure 1.5
The Four Strokes of a
Typical Modern
Gasoline-Fueled,
Spark-Ignition Engine**

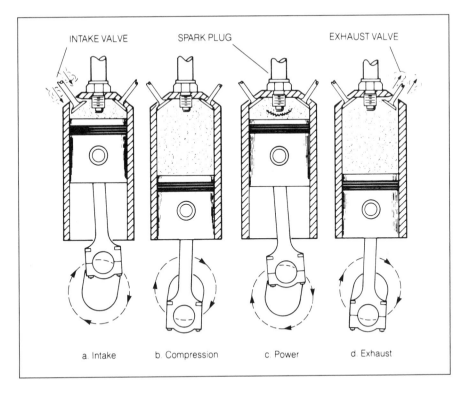

a. Intake   b. Compression   c. Power   d. Exhaust

Intake

During the intake stroke (Figure 1.5a), the piston is moving from top to bottom and the intake valve is open. As the piston moves down, a partial vacuum is created, which draws a mixture of air and vaporized gasoline through the intake valve into the cylinder.

It will be shown in Chapters 5, 6, and 7 that, in modern, electronically controlled engines, fuel is injected into the intake port and is timed to coincide with the intake stroke. The intake valve is closed after the piston reaches the bottom. This position is normally called *bottom dead center* (BDC).

Compression

During the compression stroke (Figure 1.5b), both valves are closed, and the piston moves upward and compresses the fuel and air mixture against the cylinder head. When the piston is near the top of this stroke, the ignition system produces an electrical spark at the tip of the spark plug. (The top of the stroke is normally called *top dead center*—TDC.) The spark ignites the air–fuel mixture and the mixture burns quickly, causing a rapid rise in the pressure in the cylinder.

Power

During the power stroke (Figure 1.5c), the high pressure created by the burning mixture forces the piston downward. The cylinder pressure creates the force on the piston that results in the torque on the crankshaft as described above. It is only during this stroke that actual usable power is generated by the engine.

Exhaust

During the exhaust stroke (Figure 1.5d), the piston is again moving upward. The exhaust valve is open and the piston forces the burned gases from the cylinder through the exhaust port into the exhaust system and out the tailpipe into the atmosphere.

Each piston on a 4-stroke SI engine produces actual power during just one out of four strokes.

This 4-stroke cycle is repeated continuously as the crankshaft rotates. In a single-cylinder engine, power is produced only during the power stroke, which is only one-quarter of the cycle. Modern automotive engines have multiple cylinders, each of which contributes power during its associated power stroke. In a multicylinder engine, the power strokes are staggered so that power is produced during a larger fraction of the cycle than for a single-cylinder engine. In a 4-cylinder engine, for example, power is produced almost continually by the separate power strokes of the four cylinders. The shaded regions of Figure 1.6 indicate which cylinder is producing power for each 180 degrees of crankshaft rotation. (Remember that one complete engine cycle requires two complete crankshaft rotations of 360 degrees each, for a total of 720 degrees.)

ENGINE CONTROL

Control of the engine in any car means regulating the power that it produces at any time in accordance with driving needs. The driver controls

**Figure 1.6
Power Pulses from a
4-Cylinder Engine**

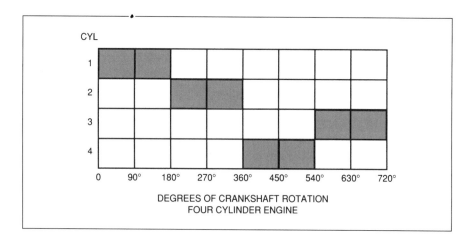

**Figure 1.7
Intake Manifold and
Fuel Metering**

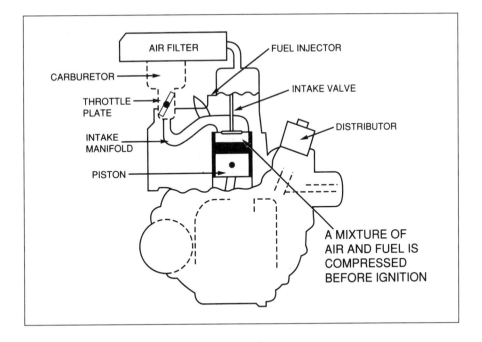

engine power via the accelerator pedal, which, in turn, determines the setting of the throttle plate via a mechanical linkage system. The throttle plate is situated in the air intake system and is, in effect, a rotary valve that impedes the air flowing past it (Figure 1.7). The intake system is an assembly of pipes or passageways through which the air flows from outside into each cylinder. The air flowing into the engine flows past the throttle plate, which, in fact, controls the amount of air being drawn into the engine during each intake stroke.

As we will show in later chapters, the power produced by the engine is proportional to the mass flow rate of air into the engine. The driver then controls engine power directly by controlling this air mass flow rate with the throttle plate. As the accelerator pedal is depressed, the throttle plate rotates, permitting air to flow at an increased rate.

Of course, the power produced by the engine depends on fuel being present in the correct proportions. Fuel is delivered to each cylinder at a rate that is proportional to air flow. The fuel flow rate is determined by fuel injectors (one for each cylinder), which are operated by an electronic engine control system as explained in Chapters 5 and 7. There it is shown that fuel flow rate is regulated so as to minimize exhaust gas pollutant concentration. It should be noted that before the advent of electronic engine controls fuel flow was regulated by a device known as a carburetor (as depicted in Figure 1.7).

IGNITION SYSTEM

To produce power, the gasoline engine must not only have a correct mixture of fuel and air, but also some means of initiating combustion of the mixture. Essentially the only practical means is with an electric spark produced across the gap between a pair of electrodes of a spark plug. The electric arc or spark provides sufficient energy to cause combustion. This phenomenon is called *ignition.*

Once a stable combustion has been initiated, there is no further need for the spark during any engine cycle. Typically, the spark must persist for a period of about a millisecond (one thousandth of a second). This relatively short period makes spark ignition possible using highly efficient pulse transformer circuits in which a circuit having a relatively low average current can deliver a very high-voltage (high peak power) pulse to the spark plug.

The ignition system itself consists of several components: the spark plug, one or more pulse transformers (typically called *coils*), timing control circuitry, and distribution apparatus that supplies the high-voltage pulse to the correct cylinder.

Spark Plug

The spark is produced by applying a high-voltage pulse of from 20 kV to 40 kV (1 kV is 1,000 volts) between the center electrode and ground. The actual voltage required to start the arc varies with the size of the gap, the compression ratio, and the air–fuel ratio. Once the arc is started, the voltage required to sustain it is much lower because the gas mixture near the gap becomes highly ionized. (An ionized gas allows current to flow more freely.) The arc is sustained long enough to ignite the air–fuel mixture.

A typical spark plug configuration is shown in Figure 1.8. The spark plug consists of a pair of electrodes, called the *center* and *ground electrodes,* separated by a gap. The gap size is important and is specified for each engine. The gap may be 0.025 inch (0.6 mm) for one engine and 0.040 inch (1 mm) for another engine. The center electrode is insulated from the ground electrode and the metallic shell assembly. The ground electrode is at electrical ground potential because one terminal of the battery that supplies the current to generate the high-voltage pulse for the ignition system is connected to the engine block and frame.

High-Voltage Circuit and Distribution

The ignition system provides the high-voltage pulse that initiates the arc. Figure 1.9 is a schematic of the electrical circuit for the ignition system as it existed before electronic control systems. The high-voltage pulse is generated by inductive discharge of a special high-voltage transformer commonly called an *ignition coil.* The high-voltage pulse is delivered to the appropriate spark plug at the correct time for ignition by a distribution circuit. In a modern

**Figure 1.8
Spark Plug
Configuration**

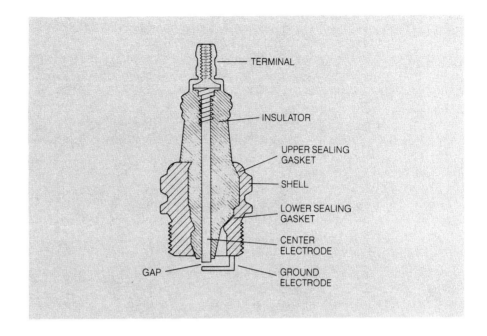

**Figure 1.9
Schematic of the
Ignition Circuit**

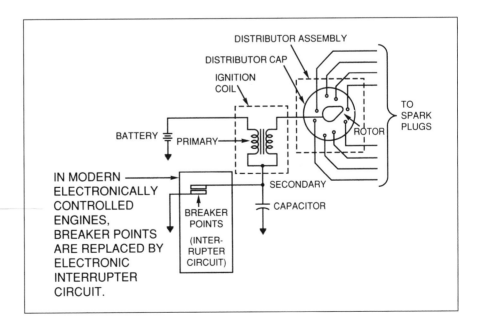

**Figure 1.10
Distributor**

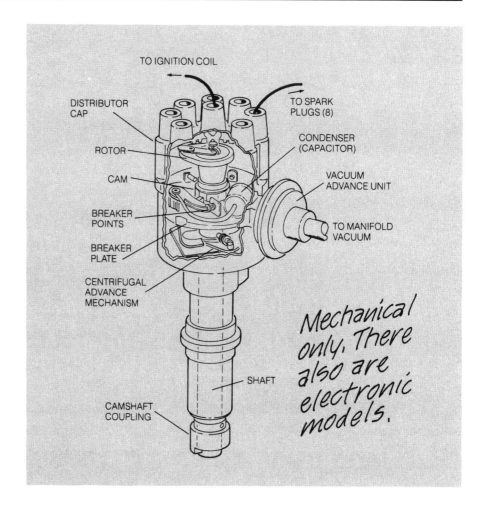

engine, the breaker points have been replaced with an electronic control module in which a power transistor controls the coil current as explained in Chapter 5.

Before the advent of modern electronic controls, the distribution of high-voltage pulses was accomplished with a rotary switch called the *distributor*. Figure 1.9 shows a schematic of a typical distributor; Figure 1.10 is a typical physical layout. The center electrode is mechanically driven by the camshaft (via gears) and rotates synchronously at camshaft speed (i.e., one-half of crankshaft speed). The distributor is an obsolete means for distribution of the spark to the appropriate spark plug, and is being replaced by multiple coils, typically one each for a pair of cylinders (or one for each cylinder), as explained in Chapter 7.

Once again, as in the case of fuel delivery, we explain spark distribution in terms of the distributor and spark initiation in terms of breaker points in order to provide a framework for the discussion of the modern distributorless ignition systems. In this way the reader can see the benefits of the electronic controls.

A set of electrical leads, commonly called *spark plug wires,* is connected between the various spark plug center terminals and the individual terminals in the distributor cap. The center terminal in the distributor cap is connected to the ignition coil secondary.

Spark Pulse Generation

The actual generation of the high-voltage pulse is accomplished by switching the current through the primary circuit (see Figure 1.9). The mechanism in the distributor of a traditional ignition system for switching the primary circuit of the coil consists of opening and closing the breaker points (of a switch) by a rotary cam in the distributor (explained later). During the intervals between ignition pulses (i.e., when the rotor is between contacts), the breaker points are closed (known as *dwell*). Current flows through the primary of the coil, and a magnetic field is created that links the primary and secondary of the coil.

At the instant the spark pulse is required, the breaker points are opened. This interrupts the flow of current in the primary of the coil and the magnetic field collapses rapidly. The rapid collapse of the magnetic field induces the high-voltage pulse in the secondary of the coil. This pulse is routed through the distributor rotor, the terminal in the distributor cap, and the spark plug wire to the appropriate spark plug. The capacitor absorbs the primary current, which continues to flow during the short interval in which the points are opening, and limits arcing at the breaker points.

The waveform of the primary current is illustrated in Figure 1.11. The primary current increases with time after the points close (point *a* on waveform). At the instant the points open, this current begins to fall rapidly. It is during this rapid drop in primary current that the secondary high-voltage pulse occurs (point *b*). The primary current oscillates (the "wavy" portion; point *c*) because of the resonant circuit formed between the coil and capacitor.

It will be shown in Chapter 7 that in electronic ignition systems the breaker points are replaced by a solid-state switch (in the form of a transistor). In Chapter 3 it will be shown that a transistor in saturation is equivalent to a closed switch, and a cutoff transistor is equivalent to an open switch. It is further explained in Chapter 7 that the transistor state (i.e., saturation or cutoff) is controlled electronically in order to set dwell and spark timing.

The distributor in a conventional ignition system uses a mechanically activated switch called *breaker points.* The interruption of ignition coil current when the breaker points open produces a high-voltage pulse in the secondary.

**Figure 1.11
Primary Current
Waveform**

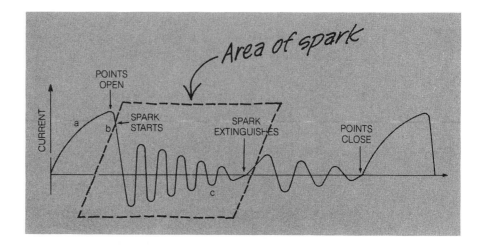

A multisurfaced cam, mounted on the distributor shaft, is used to open and close the breaker points.

The mechanism for opening and closing the breaker points of a conventional distributor is illustrated in Figure 1.12. A cam having a number of lobes equal to the number of cylinders is mounted on the distributor shaft. As this cam rotates, it alternately opens and closes the breaker points. The movable arm of the breaker points has an insulated rubbing block that is pressed against the cam by a spring. When the rubbing block is aligned with a flat surface on the cam, the points are closed (i.e., dwell period), as shown in Figure 1.12a. As the cam rotates, the rubbing block is moved by the lobe (high point) on the cam as shown in Figure 1.12b. At this time, the breaker points open (corresponding to point b of Figure 1.11) and spark occurs.

The rotary switch that connects the coil to the appropriate spark plug wire is connected to the same shaft as the cam, thereby synchronizing the actions of spark creation with the switching of the high-voltage pulse to each spark plug. The distributor shaft is coupled to the camshaft and rotates at the same speed and is positioned relative to the camshaft so that the spark occurs at the correct time during each engine cycle to produce optimum combustion. This relative position of distribution and camshaft is known as "ignition timing."

IGNITION TIMING

The point at which ignition occurs, in relation to the top dead center of the piston's compression stroke, is known as ignition timing.

Ignition occurs some time before top dead center (BTDC) during the compression stroke of the piston. This time is measured in degrees of crankshaft rotation BTDC. For a modern SI engine, this timing is typically 8 to 10 degrees for the basic mechanical setting with the engine running at low speed (low rpm). This basic timing is set by the design of the mechanical coupling between the crankshaft and the distributor. The basic timing may be adjusted slightly in many older cars by physically rotating the distributor housing, during routine maintenance.

**Figure 1.12
Breaker Point
Operation**

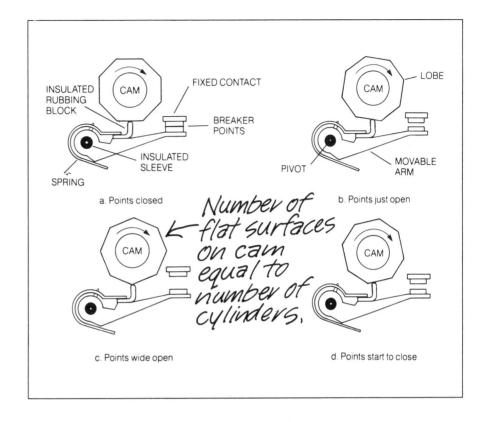

INSULATED
RUBBING
BLOCK

CAM

FIXED CONTACT

BREAKER
POINTS

INSULATED
SLEEVE

SPRING

a. Points closed

LOBE

CAM

MOVABLE
ARM

PIVOT

b. Points just open

Number of flat surfaces on cam equal to number of cylinders.

CAM

c. Points wide open

CAM

d. Points start to close

As the engine speed increases, the angle through which the crankshaft rotates in the time required to burn the fuel and air mixture increases. For this reason, the spark must occur at a larger angle BTDC for higher engine speeds. This change in ignition timing is called *spark advance.* That is, spark advance should increase with increasing engine rpm. In a conventional ignition system, the mechanism for this is called a *centrifugal spark advance.* It is shown in Figure 1.10. As engine speed increases, the distributor shaft rotates faster, and the weights are thrown outward by centrifugal force. The weights operate through a mechanical lever, so their movement causes a change in the relative angular position between the rubbing block on the breaker points and the distributor cam, and advances the time when the lobe opens the points.

In addition to speed-dependent spark advance, the ignition timing needs to be adjusted as a function of intake manifold pressure. Whenever the throttle is nearly closed, the manifold pressure is low (i.e., nearly a vacuum). The combustion time for the air–fuel mixture is longer for low manifold pressure conditions than for high manifold pressure conditions (i.e., near atmospheric pressure). As a result, the spark timing must be advanced for low pressure conditions to maintain maximum power and fuel economy. The mechanism to do this is a vacuum-operated spark advance, also shown in Figure 1.10. The vacuum advance mechanism has a flexible diaphragm connected through a rod to the plate on which the breaker points are mounted. One side of the diaphragm is open to atmospheric pressure; the other side is connected through a hose to manifold vacuum. As manifold vacuum increases, the diaphragm is deflected (atmospheric pressure pushes it) and moves the breaker point plate to advance the timing. Ignition timing significantly affects engine performance and exhaust emissions; therefore, it is one of the major factors that is electronically controlled in the modern SI engine.

The performance of the ignition system and the spark advance mechanism has been greatly improved by electronic control systems. Because ignition timing is critical to engine performance, controlling it precisely through all operating conditions has become a major application of digital electronics, as explained in Chapter 7.

It will be shown in Chapter 7 that ignition timing is actually computed as a function of engine operating conditions in a special-purpose digital computer known as the electronic engine control system. This computation of spark timing has much greater flexibility for optimizing engine performance than a mechanical distributor and is one of the great benefits of electronic engine control.

ALTERNATIVE ENGINES

The vast majority of automobile engines in North America are SI engines. Alternative engines such as the diesel have simply not been able to compete effectively with the SI engine in the United States. Diesel engines are used mostly in heavy-duty vehicles such as large trucks, ships, railroad locomotives, and earth-moving machinery. However, there is some use of these engines in light-duty trucks and some passenger cars. These engines are being controlled electronically, as explained later in this book.

Diesel Engine

Physically, the diesel engine is nearly identical to the gasoline engine and can be either 4 stroke or 2 stroke/cycle. It consists of cylinders cast into a block with pistons, connecting rods, crank shaft, camshaft, and valves (4-stroke engine). Torque and power are produced during the 4 strokes as in the case of the 4-stroke gasoline engine. The diesel engine fuel is supplied via a fuel injection system that injects fuel either directly into the cylinder (direct injection system) or into the intake port during the intake stroke (indirect injection system).

Diesel engines are subject to exhaust emission regulations similar to those applied to gasoline engines. Emissions are influenced by the timing of fuel injection relative to the compression and power strokes. The evolution of electronic control of diesel engines is explained in Chapters 5, 6, and 7.

Another alternative to the SI engine has been the Wankel, or rotary, engine. As in the case of the diesel engine, the number of Wankel engines has been very small compared to the SI engine. One limitation to its application has been somewhat poorer exhaust emissions relative to the SI engine.

Still another potential competitor to current automotive engines is the 2-stroke/cycle engine. This engine, which is similar in many respects to the traditional engine, is a gasoline-fueled, spark-ignited, reciprocating engine. It has achieved widespread use in lawnmowers, small motorcycles, and some outboard marine engines. It had (at one time) even achieved limited automotive use, though it suffered from poor exhaust emissions.

Just as in the case of the 4-stroke/cycle engine, electronic controls have significantly improved 2-stroke/cycle engine performance relative to mechanical controls. At the present time, it does not appear likely that the 2-stroke/cycle engine will have sufficient passenger car application in the foreseeable future to justify its discussion in this book.

An alternative to the internal combustion engine as an automotive power plant is electric propulsion in which the mechanical power required to move the car comes from an electric motor. Electric propulsion of automobiles is not new. Electric motors were used to propel cars in the early part of the twentieth century. The necessary electric energy required was supplied by storage batteries. However, the energy density (i.e., the energy per unit weight) of storage cells has been and continues to be significantly less than gasoline or diesel fuel. Consequently, the range for an electrically powered car has been much less than that for a comparably sized IC engine-powered car.

On the other hand, the exhaust emissions coming from an electrically powered car are (theoretically) zero, making this type of car very attractive from a pollution standpoint. At the time of this writing, only a handful of relatively expensive electrically powered cars are in operation, and generally their performance and range are inferior to those of gasoline-fueled cars.

One attractive option for electrically powered cars is a combination of a gasoline-fueled engine with an electric propulsion system. Such cars are known as hybrid cars and can be operated either as purely electric propulsion (with energy supplied by storage cells) or as a combination of an engine driving a generator to supply the electric power for the motor.

A hybrid car can be operated with electric propulsion in urban areas where exhaust emissions are required to be low (or zero) and as a gasoline-fueled, engine-driven car in rural areas where the range advantage of the gasoline-fueled option is superior to the electric propulsion and where exhaust emissions are somewhat less of an issue.

The efficiency of electric propulsion is improved by raising the operating voltage from the present-day 14-volt systems (i.e., using 12-volt-rated batteries). This efficiency gain is responsible in part for the evolution of car electrical systems from the present 14-volt to 42-volt systems.

In the early years following the introduction of cars with 42-volt electrical systems, there will be two separate electrical buses, one at 14 volts and the other at 42 volts. The 14-volt bus will be tied to a single 12-volt (nominal) battery. The 42-volt electrical bus will be tied to three 12-volt batteries connected in series. The 14-volt bus will supply power to those components and subsystems that are found in present-day vehicles including, for example, all lighting systems and electronic control systems. The 42-volt bus will be associated with the electric drive system of the hybrid car where it can provide more efficient propulsion than would be possible with a 14-volt system.

The hybrid vehicle is capable of operation in three modes in which power comes from: (a) the engine only; (b) the electric motor only; and (c) the combined engine and electric motor. In achieving these modes of operation, the engine and electric motor must be coupled to the drivetrain. It is beyond the scope of this book to discuss all of the mechanical configurations for coupling the engine and the motor. The two major types of coupling methods are known as a series or parallel hybrid electric car.

Rather, we consider one system that has proven effective for this coupling in which the electric motor rotor is constructed on an extended crankshaft of the engine. The motor stator is constructed in a housing that is part of or attached to the engine case. The electric motor in this configuration is the starting motor for the engine, as well as the generator/alternator for electric power as well as the motor for the electric propulsion. Under mode (a), the motor rotates freely and neither produces nor absorbs any power. In modes (b) and (c), the motor receives electric power from an electronic control system and delivers the required power to the drivetrain.

Although many electric motor types have the potential to provide the mechanical power in a hybrid vehicle, the brushless d-c motor seems to be the preferred type in practical application. This type of motor is described in Chapter 6, which deals with automotive sensors and actuators.

A schematic depiction of a hybrid vehicle power train is shown in Figure 1.13. There are a variety of hybrid vehicle configurations, and the type shown in Figure 1.13 is a representative one illustrating the main features of such a configuration.

The power to move the vehicle can come from the engine alone, from the battery via electric power to the motor/generator (motor in this case), or by both acting together. The motor generator/rotor is connected on the shaft between the crankshaft and the transaxle assembly. The engine is connected to the transaxle by a mechanism that permits the modes of operation stated above.

In Figure 1.13, this mechanism is denoted C and can be one of many possible devices. In some configurations, it is an electrically activated clutch

**Figure 1.13
Example of Hybrid
Vehicle Configuration**

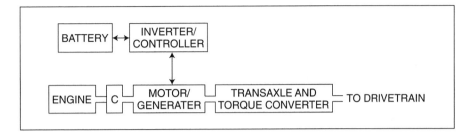

that disconnects the engine from the transaxle when it is switched off for electric propulsion but connects the engine to the transaxle for engine-only power or for combined engine electric motor operation. In other vehicles, the engine and motor are coupled to the drivetrain via a power-splitting device capable of controlling the power split between IC engine and electric motor.

In a typical hybrid vehicle, the relative power from the IC engine and the electric motor is adjusted to give optimum performance during normal driving. In those exhaust emission-sensitive geographic areas, the vehicle can be powered solely by the electric propulsion. The distribution of power as well as the generation of power for both systems are electronically controlled.

Yet another option for electric propulsion involves the use of fuel cells to generate the electric power to drive the associated motors. As will be shown in the last chapter of this book, a fuel cell uses hydrogen and oxygen to directly generate electric power, with exhaust consisting only of water. A great many technical problems must be solved before the fuel-cell-powered car can become a practical reality, but this type of car has great potential for reducing automobile-generated pollution. A detailed discussion of fuel cells for automotive propulsion appears in the final chapter of this book.

DRIVETRAIN

The engine drivetrain system of the automobile consists of the engine, transmission, drive shaft, differential, and driven wheels. We have already discussed the SI engine and we know that it provides the motive power for the automobile. Now let's examine the transmission, drive shaft, and differential in order to understand the roles of these devices.

Transmission

The transmission is a gear system that adjusts the ratio of engine speed to wheel speed. Essentially, the transmission enables the engine to operate within its optimal performance range regardless of the vehicle load or speed. It provides a gear ratio between the engine speed and vehicle speed such that the engine provides adequate power to drive the vehicle at any speed.

The transmission provides a match between engine speed and vehicle speed.

To accomplish this with a manual transmission, the driver selects the correct gear ratio from a set of possible gear ratios (usually three to five for passenger cars). An automatic transmission selects this gear ratio by means of an automatic control system.

The configuration for an automatic transmission consists of a fluid-coupling mechanism, known as a torque converter, and a system of planetary gear sets. The torque converter is formed from a pair of structures of a semitoroidal shape (i.e., a donut-shaped object split along the plane of symmetry). Figure 1.14a is a schematic sketch of a torque converter showing the two semitoroids. One of the toroids is driven by the engine by the input shaft. The other is in close proximity and is called the turbine. Both the pump and the turbine have vanes that are essentially in axial planes. In addition, a series of vanes are fixed to the frame and are called the reactor. The entire structure is mounted in a fluid, tight chamber and is filled with a hydraulic fluid (i.e., transmission fluid). As the pump is rotated by the engine, the hydraulic fluid circulates as depicted by the arrows in Figure 1.14a. The fluid impinges on the turbine blades, imparting a torque to it. The torque converter exists to transmit engine torque and power to the turbine from the engine. However, the properties of the torque converter are such that when the vehicle is stopped corresponding to a nonmoving turbine, the engine can continue to rotate (as it does when the vehicle is stopped with the engine running).

The planetary gear system consists of a set of three types of gears connected together as depicted in Figure 1.14b. The inner gear is known as the sun gear. There are three gears meshed with the sun gear at equal angles, which are known as planetary gears. These three gears are tied together with a cage that supports their axles. The third gear, known as a ring gear, is a section of a cylinder with the gear teeth on the inside. The ring gear meshes with the three planetary gears.

In operation, one or more of these gear systems are held fixed to the transmission housing via a set of hydraulically actuated clutches. The action of the planetary gear system is determined by which set or sets of clutches are activated. For example, if the ring gear is held fixed and input power (torque) is applied to the sun gear, the planetary gears rotate in the same direction as the sun gear but at a reduced rate and at an increased torque. If the planetary gear cage is fixed, then the sun gear drives the ring gear in the opposite direction as is done when the transmission is in reverse. If all three sets of gears are held fixed to each other rather than the transmission housing, then direct drive (gear ratio = 1) is achieved.

A typical automatic transmission has a cascade connection of a number of planetary gear systems, each with its own set of hydraulically actuated clutches. In an electronically controlled automatic transmission, the clutches are electrically or electrohydraulically actuated.

Most automatic transmissions have three forward gear ratios, although a few have two and some have four. A properly used manual transmission

**Figure 1.14a
Schematic Cross
Section of a Torque
Converter**

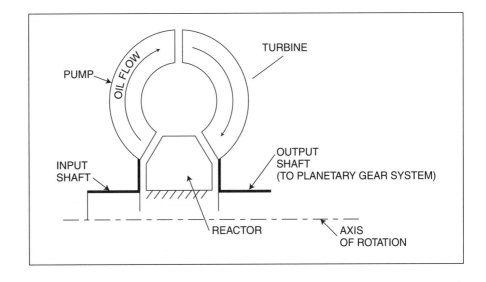

**Figure 1.14b
Planetary Gear
System**

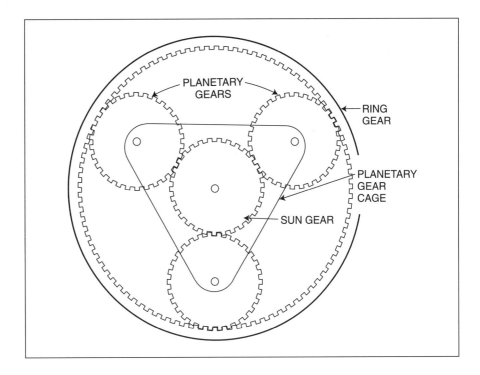

**Figure 1.14c
Schematic of a
Differential**

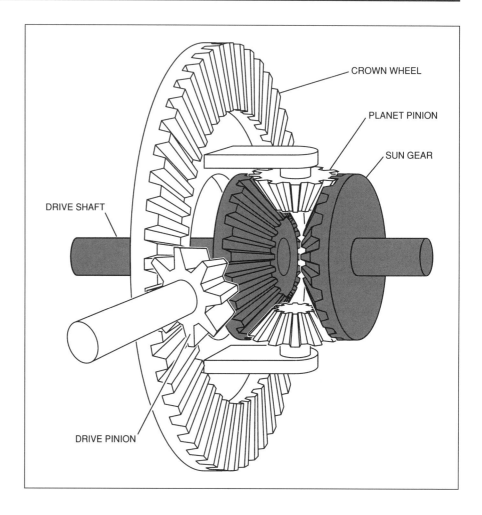

CROWN WHEEL

PLANET PINION

SUN GEAR

DRIVE SHAFT

DRIVE PINION

normally has efficiency advantages over an automatic transmission, but the automatic transmission is the most commonly used transmission for passenger automobiles in the United States. In the past, automatic transmissions have been controlled by a hydraulic and pneumatic system, but the industry is moving toward electronic controls. The control system must determine the correct gear ratio by sensing the driver-selected command, accelerator pedal position, and engine load.

The proper gear ratio is actually computed in the electronic transmission control system. Once again, as in the case of electronic engine control, the electronic transmission control can optimize transmission control. However, since the engine and transmission function together as a power-producing unit, it is sensible to control both components in a single electronic controller.

Drive Shaft

The drive shaft is used on front-engine, rear wheel drive vehicles to couple the transmission output shaft to the differential input shaft. Flexible couplings, called *universal joints*, allow the rear axle housing and wheels to move up and down while the transmission remains stationary. In front wheel drive automobiles, a pair of drive shafts couples the transmission to the drive wheels through flexible joints known as constant velocity (CV) joints.

Differential

The combination of drive shaft and differential completes the transfer of power from the engine to the rear wheels.

The differential serves three purposes (see Figure 1.14c). The most obvious is the right angle transfer of the rotary motion of the drive shaft to the wheels. The second purpose is to allow each driven wheel to turn at a different speed. This is necessary because the "outside" wheel must turn faster than the "inside" wheel when the vehicle is turning a corner. The third purpose is the torque increase provided by the gear ratio. This gear ratio can be changed in a repair shop to allow different torque to be delivered to the wheels while using the same engine and transmission. The gear ratio also affects fuel economy. In front wheel drive cars, the transmission differential and drive shafts are known collectively as the *transaxle assembly*.

SUSPENSION

Another major automotive subsystem is the suspension system, which is the mechanical assembly that connects each wheel to the car body. The primary purpose of the suspension system is to isolate the car body from the vertical motion of the wheels as they travel over the rough road surface.

The suspension system can be understood with reference to Figure 1.15, which illustrates the major components. Notice that the wheel assembly is connected through a movable assembly to the body. The weight of the car is supported by springs. In addition, there is a so-called *shock absorber* (sometimes a *strut*), which is in effect a viscous damping device. There is a similar assembly at each wheel, although normally there are differences in the detailed configuration between front and rear wheels.

The mass of the car body is called the *sprung mass*, that is, the mass that is supported by springs. The mass of the wheel assemblies at the other end of the springs is called *unsprung mass*.

All springs have the property that the deflection of the spring is proportional to the applied axial force. The proportionality constant is known as the *spring rate*. The springs are selected for each car such that the car body height is as desired for the unloaded car. Typically, the weight on the front wheels is greater than on the rear wheels, therefore, the front springs normally have a higher spring rate than the rear.

**Figure 1.15
Major Components of
a Suspension System**

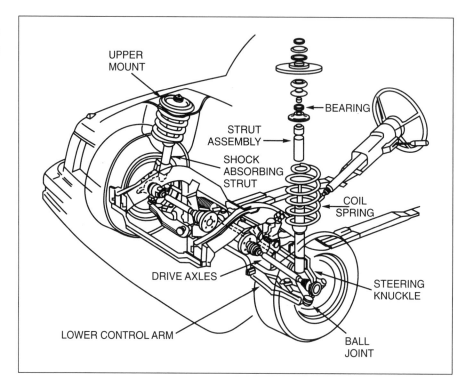

Similar to the springs, the shock absorbers (struts) also produce a force that acts to support the weight of the car. However, unlike the springs, the shock absorbers produce a force in response to the motion of the wheel assembly relative to the car body. Figure 1.16 is an illustration of a typical shock absorber.

The shock absorber consists of a cylinder and piston assembly. The cylinder is filled with a viscous oil. There are small oil passages through the piston through which the oil can flow. As the wheel assembly moves up and down, the piston moves identically through the cylinder. The oil (which is essentially incompressible) flows through the oil passages. A force is developed in response to the piston motion that is proportional to the piston velocity relative to the cylinder. This force acts in combination with the spring force to provide a damping force. The magnitude of this force for any given piston velocity varies inversely with the aperture of the oil passages. This aperture is the primary shock absorber parameter determining the damping effect and influencing the car's ride and handling. In Chapter 2, the influence of the shock absorber damping on wheel motion is explained. In Chapter 8, the mechanism for varying the shock absorber characteristics under electronic control to provide for variable ride and handling is explained.

**Figure 1.16
Shock Absorber
Assembly**

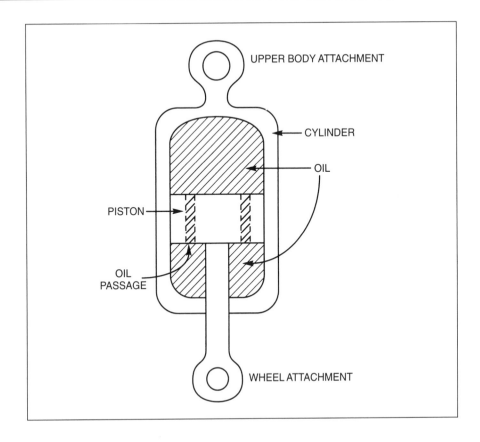

BRAKES

Brakes are as basic to the automobile as the engine drivetrain system and are responsible for slowing and stopping the vehicle. Most of the kinetic energy of the car is dissipated by the brakes during deceleration and stopping (with the other contributions coming from aerodynamic drag and tire rolling resistance).

There are two major types of automotive brakes: drum and disk brakes. Drum brakes are an extension of the types of brakes used on early cars and horsedrawn wagons. Increasingly, automobile manufacturers are using disk brakes. Consequently, it is this type that we discuss here.

Disk brakes are illustrated in Figure 1.17. A flat disk is attached to each wheel and rotates with it as the car moves. A wheel cylinder assembly (often called a *caliper*) is connected to the axle assembly. A pair of pistons having brakepad material are mounted in the caliper assembly and are close to the disk.

Under normal driving conditions, the pads are not in contact with the disk, and the disk is free to rotate. When the brake pedal is depressed,

Figure 1.17
Disk Brake System

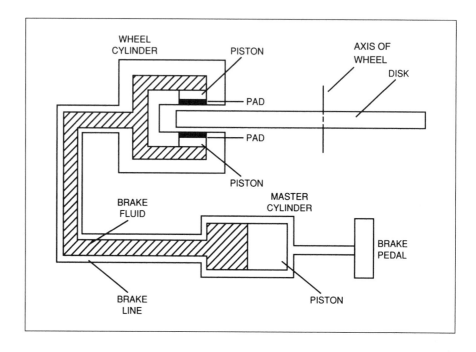

hydraulic pressure is applied through the brake fluid to force the brake pads against the disk. The braking force that decelerates the car results from friction between the disk and the pads.

Electronic control of braking benefits safety by improving stopping performance in poor or marginal braking conditions. Chapter 8 explains the operation of the so-called *antilock braking system* (ABS).

STEERING SYSTEM

A steering system is one of the major automotive subsystems required for operation of the car (see Figure 1.18). It provides the driver control of the path of the car over the ground. Steering functions by rotating the plane of the front wheels in the desired direction of the turn. The angle between the front wheel plane and the longitudinal axis of the car is known as the *steering angle*. This angle is proportional to the rotation angle of the steering wheel.

Traditionally, automotive steering systems have consisted solely of mechanical means for rotating the wheels about a nominally vertical axis in response to rotation of the steering wheel. The inclination of this axis gives rise to a restoring torque that tends to return the wheels to planes that are parallel to the vehicle's longitudinal axis so that the car will tend to travel straight ahead. This restoring torque provides a steering stability for the car.

When steering the car, the driver must provide sufficient torque to overcome the restoring torque. Because the restoring torque is proportional to

**Figure 1.18
One Type of Steering
Mechanism**

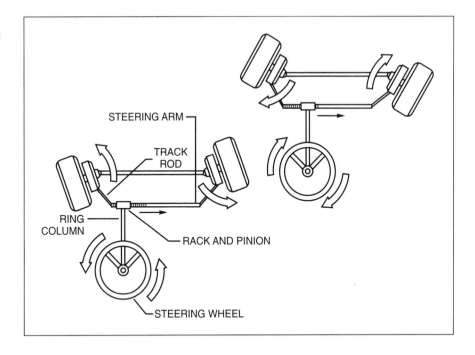

the vehicle weight for any given steering angle, considerable driver effort is required for large cars, particularly at low speeds and when parking.

In order to overcome this effort in relatively large cars, a power steering system is added. This system consists of an engine-driven hydraulic pump, a hydraulic actuator, and control valve. Whenever the steering wheel is turned, a proportioning valve opens, allowing hydraulic pressure to activate the actuator. The high-pressure hydraulic fluid pushes on one side of the piston. The piston, in turn, is connected to the steering linkage and provides mechanical torque to assist the driver in turning. This hydraulic force is often called steering *boost*. The desired boost varies with vehicle speed, as depicted in Figure 1.19.

This graph shows that the available boost from the pump increases with engine speed (or vehicle speed), whereas the desired boost decreases with increasing speed. In Chapter 8, we discuss an electronic control system that can adjust the available boost as a function of speed to desirable levels.

In addition to the automotive systems described above, electronics is involved in the implementation of cruise control systems, heating and air conditioning systems, as well as entertainment and some safety systems. Moreover, electronics is responsible for introducing new systems that could, in fact, not exist without electronics, such as navigation systems, communication systems, and electronic diagnostic systems.

Once electronics had achieved successful application in engine control, the ball was rolling, so to speak, for the introduction of electronics in a variety

**Figure 1.19
Desired Boost Versus
Speed**

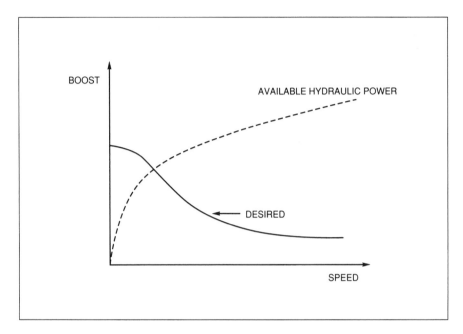

of systems in the automobile. It will be seen that the very high cost-effectiveness of electronics has strongly motivated their application to various other systems.

SUMMARY

In this chapter, we have briefly reviewed the major systems of the automobile and discussed basic engine operation. In addition, we have indicated where electronic technology could be applied to improve performance or reduce cost.

The next few chapters of this book are intended to develop a basic understanding of electronic technology. Then we'll use all this knowledge to examine how electronics has been applied to the major systems. In the last chapter, we'll look at some ideas and methods that may be used in the future.

Quiz for Chapter 1

1. The term *TDC* refers to
   a. the engine exhaust system
   b. rolling resistance of tires
   c. crankshaft position corresponding to a piston at the top of its stroke
   d. the distance between headlights

2. The distributor is
   a. a rotary switch that connects the ignition coil to the various spark plugs
   b. a system for smoothing tire load
   c. a system that generates the spark in the cylinders
   d. a section of the drivetrain

3. The air–fuel ratio is
   a. the rate at which combustible products enter the engine
   b. the ratio of the mass of air to the mass of fuel in a cylinder before ignition
   c. the ratio of gasoline to air in the exhaust pipe
   d. intake air and fuel velocity ratio

4. Ignition normally occurs
   a. at BDC
   b. at TDC
   c. just after TDC
   d. just before TDC

5. Most automobile engines are
   a. large and heavy
   b. gasoline-fueled, spark-ignited, liquid-cooled internal combustion type
   c. unable to run at elevations that are below sea level
   d. able to operate with any fuel other than gasoline

6. An exhaust valve is
   a. a hole in the cylinder head
   b. a mechanism for releasing the combustion products from the cylinder
   c. the pipe connecting the engine to the muffler
   d. a small opening at the bottom of a piston

7. Power is produced during
   a. intake stroke
   b. compression stroke
   c. power stroke
   d. exhaust stroke

8. The transmission
   a. converts rotary to linear motion
   b. optimizes the transfer of engine power to the drivetrain
   c. has four forward speeds and one reverse
   d. automatically selects the highest gear ratio

9. The suspension system
    a. partially isolates the body of a car from road vibrations
    b. holds the wheels on the axles
    c. suspends the driver and passengers
    d. consists of four springs

10. The camshaft
    a. operates the intake and exhaust valves
    b. rotates at the same speed as the crankshaft
    c. has connecting rods attached to it
    d. opens and closes the breaker points

11. An SI engine is
    a. a type of internal combustion engine
    b. a Stirling engine
    c. always fuel injected
    d. none of the above

12. The intake system refers to
    a. the carburetor
    b. a set of tubes
    c. a system of valves, pipes, and throttle plates
    d. the components of an engine through which fuel and air are supplied to the engine

The Systems Approach to Control and Instrumentation

Generally speaking, electronic systems function to control, measure, or communicate. Automotive electronic systems fall generally into these same three application areas. The major categories of automotive electronic systems include

1. Engine/power train control
2. Ride/handling control
3. Cruise control
4. Braking/traction control
5. Instrumentation (instrument panel)
6. Power steering control
7. Occupant protection
8. Entertainment
9. Comfort control
10. Cellular phones

Historically, automotive electronics was confined primarily to communications, with the incorporation of AM radios and police-car two-way radio systems. These remained the only significant electronics applications throughout the 1930s and 1940s. This was an era in which vacuum tubes were the only important active electronic devices.

The development of solid-state electronics, beginning with the transistor in the late 1940s and evolving through high-performance integrated circuits, provided a technology that was compatible with the evolution of other automotive electronic systems such as ignition systems, turn signals, instrumentation, and a variety of other automotive subsystems. Perhaps the biggest evolutionary jump occurred in the 1970s with the advent of electronic fuel control systems, a step motivated primarily by government regulations (as we will show later). Since then the evolution of electronic systems in automobiles has seen spectacular growth, such that automotive electronics is now estimated to account for 10% to 25% of the cost of the vehicle, depending on feature content.

CHAPTER OVERVIEW

This book will discuss the application of electronics in automobiles, from the standpoint of electronic systems and subsystems. In a sense, the systems approach to describing automotive electronics is a way of organizing the subject into its component parts based on functional groups. This chapter will lay the foundation for a discussion by explaining the concepts of a system and a subsystem, and how such systems function. The means for characterizing the performance of any system will be explained so that the reader will understand some of the relative benefits and limitations of automotive electronic systems. This chapter will explain generally what a system is and, more precisely, what an electronic system is. In addition, basic concepts of electronic systems that are applicable to all automotive electronic systems, such as structure (architecture) and quantitative performance analysis principles, will be discussed.

This chapter contains a few mathematical expressions. It is not necessary to be familiar with the relevant mathematics to understand the material presented in this chapter. The mathematics is included to supplement the associated discussion with details for those who have an appropriate background.

Two major categories of electronic systems—analog or continuous time and digital or discrete time—will be explained. In most cases, it is theoretically possible to implement a given electronic system as either an analog or digital system. The relatively low cost of digital electronics coupled with the high performance achievable relative to analog electronics has led modern automotive electronic system designers to choose digital rather than analog realizations for new systems.

CONCEPT OF A SYSTEM

A *system* is a collection of components that function together to perform a specific task. Various systems are encountered in everyday life. It is common practice to refer to the bones of the human body as the skeletal system. The collection of highways linking the country's population centers is known as the interstate freeway system.

Electronic systems are similar in the sense that they consist of collections of electronic and electrical parts interconnected in such a way as to perform a specific function. The components of an electronic system include transistors, diodes, resistors, and capacitors, as well as standard electrical parts such as switches and connectors among others. All of these components are interconnected with individual wires or with printed circuit boards. In addition, many automotive electronic systems incorporate specialized components known as *sensors* or *actuators* that enable the electronic system to interface with the appropriate automotive mechanical systems.

Systems can often be broken down into subsystems. The subsystems also consist of a number of individual parts.

Any electronic system can be described at various levels of abstraction, from a pictorial description or a schematic drawing at the lowest level to a block diagram at the highest level. For the purposes of the present discussion, this higher-level abstraction is preferable. At this level, each functional subsystem is characterized by inputs, outputs, and the relationship between input and output. Normally, only the system designer or maintenance technician would be concerned with detailed schematics and the internal workings of the system. Furthermore, the only practical way to cover the vast range of automotive electronic systems is to limit our discussion to this so-called system level of abstraction. It is important for the reader to realize that there are typically many different circuit configurations capable of performing a given function.

BLOCK DIAGRAM REPRESENTATION OF A SYSTEM

The designer of a system often begins with a block diagram, in which major components are represented as blocks.

At the level of abstraction appropriate for the present discussion, an electronic system will be represented by a block diagram. Depending on whether a given electronic system application is to (a) control, (b) measure, or (c) communicate, it will have one of the three block diagram configurations shown Figure 2.1.

In block diagram architecture, each functional component or subsystem is represented by an appropriately labeled block. The inputs and outputs for each block are identified. In electronic systems, these input and output variables are electrical signals, except for the system input and system output. One benefit of this approach is that the subsystem operation can be described by functional relationships between input and output. There is no need to describe the operation of individual transistors and components within the blocks.

Figure 2.1a depicts the architecture or configuration for a control application electronic system. In such a system, control of a physical subsystem (called the *plant*) occurs by regulating some physical variable (or variables) through an actuator. An actuator has an electrical input and an output that may be mechanical, pneumatic, hydraulic, chemical, or so forth. The plant being controlled varies in response to changes in the actuator output. The control is determined by electronic signal processing based on measurement of some variable (or variables) by a sensor in relationship to a command input by the operator of the system (i.e., by the driver in an automotive application).

In an electronic control system, the output of the sensor is always an electrical signal (denoted e_1 in Figure 2.1). The input is a physical variable in the plant being controlled. The electronic signal processing generates an output electrical signal (denoted e_2 in Figure 2.1) that operates the actuator. The signal processing is designed to achieve the desired control of the plant in relation to the variable being measured by the sensor. The operation of such a control system is described later in this chapter. At this point, we are interested only in describing the control system architecture. A detailed explanation of electronic control is presented later in this chapter.

The architecture for electronic measurement (also known as instrumentation) is similar to that for a control system in the sense that both structures incorporate a sensor and electronic signal processing. However, instead of an actuator, the measurement architecture incorporates a display

Figure 2.1
Block Diagrams for Various System Applications

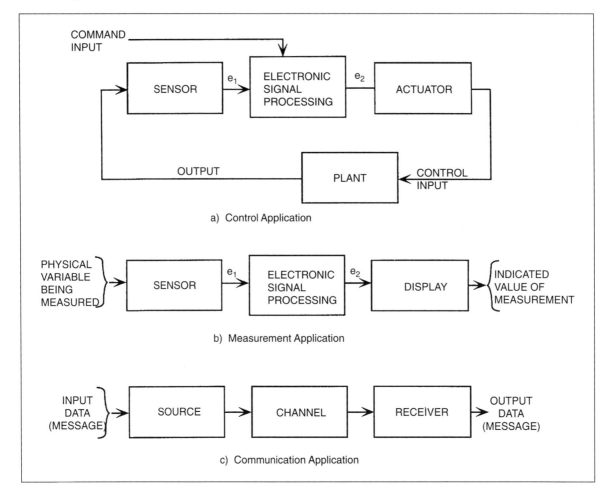

a) Control Application

b) Measurement Application

c) Communication Application

device. A display is an electromechanical or electro-optical device capable of presenting numerical values to the user (driver). In automotive electronic measurement, the display is sometimes simply a warning light with a fixed message rather than a numeric display. Nevertheless, the architecture is as shown in Figure 2.1b. It should be noted that both control and instrumentation electronic systems use one or more sensors as well as electronic signal processing.

Figure 2.1c depicts a block diagram for a communication system. In such a system, data or messages are sent from a source to a receiver over a communication channel. This particular architecture is sufficiently general that it can accommodate all communication systems, from ordinary car radios to digital data buses between multiple electronic systems on cars. Communication systems are described in greater detail later in this chapter.

ANALOG SYSTEMS

Although digital electronic systems are rapidly replacing analog systems in automotive electronics, it is simpler to describe analog systems first since they can generally be understood more intuitively than digital systems. Considering control and instrumentation applications, the sensor converts the input variable to a proportional electrical signal continuously. That is, as the input quantity varies, the sensor output voltage varies proportionately. In mathematical terms, letting x be the amplitude of the input quantity (e.g., pressure, displacement, or temperature), the output voltage of an ideal sensor (denoted v) is continuously proportional to x:

$$v = k_s x$$

In this expression, k_s represents the so-called *transducer gain* of the sensor.

Figure 2.2 illustrates the operation of an ideal pressure sensor, in which x is the pressure of a fluid and v is the sensor output voltage. The graph seen in Figure 2.2a shows this pressure as it varies with time; Figure 2.2b shows the corresponding ideal sensor output voltage. In this example, at every instant of time the sensor output voltage is a multiple of the input pressure; the transducer gain is .02 volts/kPa.

In a control system using this sensor, the signal processing component should perform an operation on this voltage and generate an output e_2 to drive the actuator. The signal processing is designed to create the correct actuator voltage at each instant to achieve the desired control. There are many examples of such a system in automotive electronic systems. One of the most important points of this analog system is that the system functions continuously with time.

An Example Analog System

Perhaps the most familiar example of an analog electronic system is the home audio entertainment system. Figure 2.3 depicts such a system that includes a phonograph record. This example system incorporates a sensor, an electronic signal processor, and an actuator. Although the phonograph has been replaced by other recording means, it is common enough to be familiar to most readers. Moreover, it is, perhaps, more easily understood than other recording media such as magnetic tape or compact discs.

In this system, the input is the mechanical vibration of the phonograph needle as it tracks along the groove in the record. The sensor is the phonograph cartridge that converts these mechanical vibrations to an analog electrical signal. This electrical signal, which is too weak to drive the loudspeakers (the actuators in the present example) at an acceptable audio level, is amplified in

Figure 2.2
Ideal Pressure Sensor

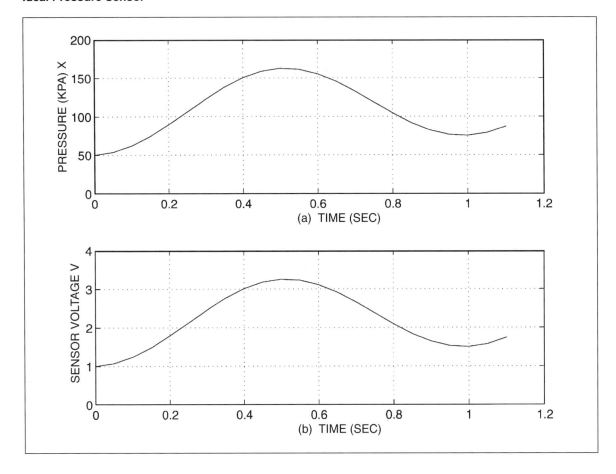

(a) TIME (SEC)

(b) TIME (SEC)

the stereo amplifier. The amplifier increases the power level to a point at which it can drive the loudspeakers. In mathematical terms, if the power level input to the amplifier is P_i, then the power output to the speakers (denoted P_o) is an amplified version of the input:

$$P_o = GP_i$$

where G is the power gain of the amplifier. That is, the input power is continuously amplified by the amplifier by a factor of G.

CHARACTERISTICS OF A DIGITAL ELECTRONIC SYSTEM

In contrast to an analog electronic system that operates in continuous time, a digital system operates in discrete instants of time. This process of

**Figure 2.3
Example of an
Electronic System**

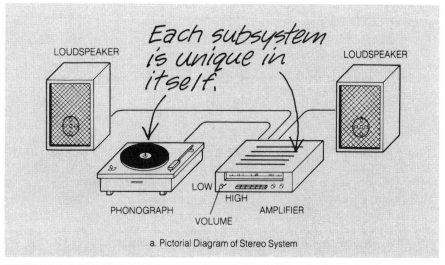

Each subsystem is unique in itself.

LOUDSPEAKER

LOUDSPEAKER

LOW

HIGH

PHONOGRAPH

VOLUME

AMPLIFIER

a. Pictorial Diagram of Stereo System

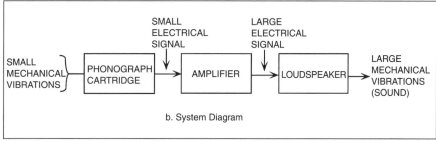

SMALL
ELECTRICAL
SIGNAL

LARGE
ELECTRICAL
SIGNAL

SMALL
MECHANICAL
VIBRATIONS

PHONOGRAPH
CARTRIDGE

AMPLIFIER

LOUDSPEAKER

LARGE
MECHANICAL
VIBRATIONS
(SOUND)

b. System Diagram

representing a continuous-time quantity at specific discrete times is called *sampling* and is illustrated in Figure 2.4.

Conceptually, a sample of a continuously varying quantity is obtained by connecting a switch between the output of a suitable sensor and the input to the digital electronic system. This hypothetical switch is periodically closed for a very brief instant (e.g., 1 microsecond) and then opened for a longer period (e.g., 1 millisecond). During the brief time the switch is closed, the input to the digital system is the value of the sensor output, which represents a sample of the quantity being measured. In practice, this switch is implemented by fast-acting solid state components (discussed later).

Figure 2.4a illustrates a continuously varying quantity that is denoted x (which might, for example, be intake manifold pressure). This continuous-time quantity is sampled electronically at times that are multiples of a basic sample period. Figure 2.4a depicts the sample points of the continuous

Figure 2.4
Sampling of a Continuous Variable

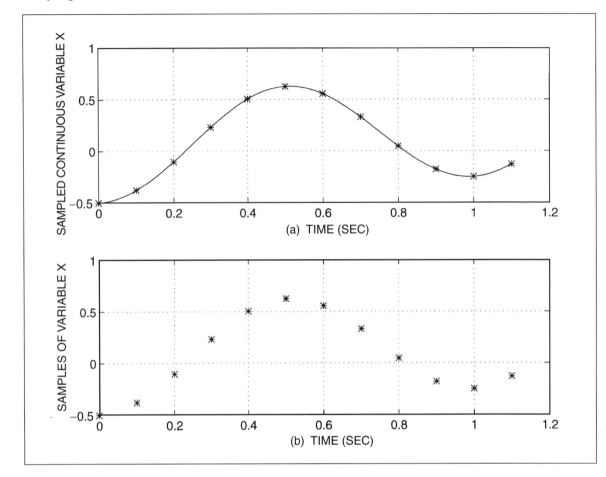

pressure as asterisks. Each sample is the value of the continuous variable at a specific (discrete) time. A sequence of samples is presented to the signal processor at the corresponding sample times. The sequence of samples is shown in Figure 2.4b. In a digital electronic system, the signal processing is performed by some form of digital computer. This computer requires time to perform its computations. The time between samples provides an interval in which the necessary computations are performed.

The time between any successive samples is normally a constant known as *sample time*. The reciprocal of the sample time is the rate at which samples are taken (i.e., the number of samples/second) and is known as the *sample frequency*.

Sample time is a critically important parameter for any digital system and is chosen with great care by the system designer. It must be sufficiently long to enable the computer to perform its computations on any given sample before the next sample is taken, or the computer cannot keep up with the data stream in real time. On the other hand, if the sample time is too long, then the input might change too much for the sampled data to adequately represent the continuous quantity being sampled. The time required for computation on each sample is influenced in part by the processor speed and by the efficiency of the program being used to perform the computations. This aspect of performance is discussed in greater detail in Chapter 4.

The sampled data illustrated in Figure 2.4b are in a sampled analog format. This format is not compatible with a digital system. One more step, called *quantization*, is required to convert the sampled analog data into data that can be read by the computer. In a digital electronic system, each sample is represented numerically by its magnitude. For example, a sequence of samples of a continuous quantity might be {0.9, 1.1, 1.6, 2.3, 1.5, 1.2, . . .}. However, computers don't use decimal number systems since there is no practical way to represent decimal digits. Rather, computers use a binary number system that is based on 2 rather than 10. In a binary number system, each numerical value is represented by a combination of ones or zeros. For example, the decimal number 11 is represented by 1011. This system will be described in greater detail in Chapter 3, but for the present, it is sufficient to understand that each sample is converted to a binary number in the form of combinations of one or zero. Chapter 3 will explain that this binary system is appropriate for a computer, in which ones and zeros correspond to transistors that are either "on" or "off," respectively. By having a sufficient number of transistors, it is possible to represent any possible numerical value.

The circuit that converts sampled analog data to binary values is called an *analog-to-digital converter* (ADC). It is also sometimes called a *quantizer*. When the computer has finished calculations on a given sample, it outputs a numerical value to an external device in the form of a binary number. If that device is analog, as in the case of an actuator for a control system, the output binary number must be reconverted to analog format. This conversion is done in a device known as a *digital-to-analog converter* (DAC). The two types of converters are explained in detail in Chapter 4. Not all digital electronic systems require converters, because some sensors and actuators are digital already. Except for these cases, a digital electronic system for either control or instrumentation has a block diagram as depicted in Figure 2.5.

ELECTRONIC SYSTEM PERFORMANCE

The performance of an electronic system is evaluated by quantitative descriptions of how well it performs its intended task and inherently uses numerical representation (e.g., parameters and graphs). The home audio

Figure 2.5
Digital Control (a) or Measurement (b) System Configuration

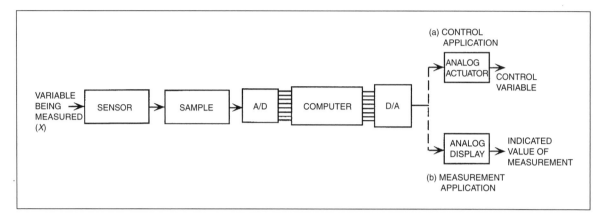

system, which has been mentioned previously as a familiar example of an electronic system, will serve as an example for performance analysis.

The performance of a high-fidelity home audio system is described by such characteristics as frequency response, maximum power level, harmonic distortion, and linearity (as well as other characterizations that are specific to an audio system). The "fidelity" of an audio system, which expresses how well it reproduces the sounds from the source, is best given by its frequency response. Unwanted distortion of the sound is characterized by harmonic distortion and linearity. Similar measures are also appropriate and useful for characterizing an electronic system.

The performance of any electronic system (analog or digital) is determined by its various components—transistors, resistors, capacitors, sensors, actuators, displays, and so forth—as well as by the system architecture or interconnections of its components. For a digital electronic system, performance is further determined by the computer program (software) that is running in the associated computer. The system designer makes careful choices for the system structure as well as for the parameter values (e.g., resistance or capacitance) to tailor the specific system performance to the specifications of a given task.

Just as in the case of a hi-fi audio system, the fidelity of an automotive electronic system to dynamically changing inputs is given by its frequency response. Specifically, this is the response of the system to a standard input called a *sinusoid.* The standard input is a smoothly varying periodic quantity as illustrated by the graph in Figure 2.6.

The input fluctuates through a complete cycle beginning at zero, increasing positively to a maximum, then moving symmetrically negatively

Figure 2.6
Sinusoidal Signal

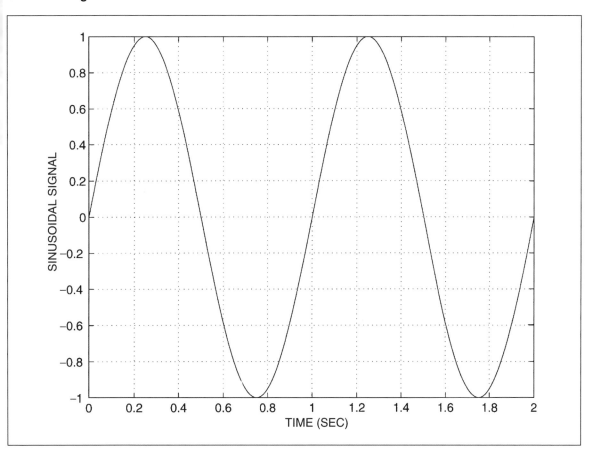

back to zero in T seconds. It then repeats periodically in intervals of T seconds. The frequency f of the input is the number of cycles in one second, or

$$f = 1/T$$

In mathematical terms, a sinusoidal input $x(t)$ is given by the following equation:

$$x(t) = X \sin(2\pi ft)$$

where

X = amplitude of the input
f = frequency
t = time

Figure 2.7
Illustration of Steady-State Input and Output of a System

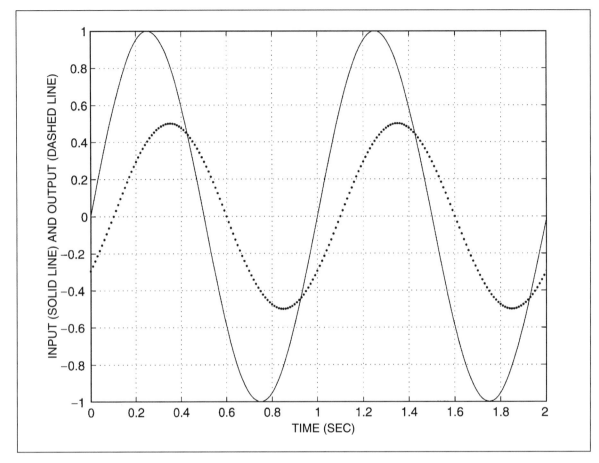

The output of an electronic system from a sinusoidal input is also sinusoidal at the same frequency, as depicted by the graphs in Figure 2.7, in which the solid curve is the input and the dashed curve the output.

The *frequency response* of an electronic system is defined as the ratio of the peak amplitude of the output (denoted Y) to the peak amplitude of the input (denoted X). Notice that there is a time delay in the response of the system relative to the input, corresponding to the difference in zero crossing of the input and output.

In formal mathematical terms, the output $y(t)$ is given by

$$y(t) = Y \sin[2\pi f(t - d)]$$

where

Y = amplitude of the output
d = time delay

The system frequency response, denoted H, is formally defined as follows:

$$H = Y/X$$

The delay is expressed as a fraction of the period, called the *phase*, and is usually denoted by the Greek letter phi (ϕ):

$$\phi = 2\pi\, d/T$$
$$= 2\pi f d$$

For an electronic system that is ideal with respect to its dynamic performance, the frequency response is a constant for all frequencies. In practice, the frequency response varies with frequency. A graph of the frequency response of a typical electronic system is shown in Figure 2.8.

In this example, the frequency response is close to ideal (i.e., constant) over a range of frequencies from frequency f_1 to f_2. For frequencies below f_1 or above f_2, the response drops off. In the example of a hi-fi amplifier, f_1 might be about 20 Hz and f_2 might be about 20 kHz. The range of frequencies over which the frequency response is nearly constant is called the system *bandwidth*. The frequency response is said to be "flat" over this bandwidth. For example, in Figure 2.8 the frequency response is nearly constant from 10^2 (100) Hz to about 10^4 (10,000) Hz. In automotive electronic systems, this range of frequencies is determined by the system designer to be compatible with the corresponding range of input frequencies in normal systems operation. There are numerous references to the bandwidth of automotive electronic systems in later chapters.

The performance of any system can be evaluated from the response of the output to a sinusoidal input. Important properties of the system can be determined from this response, such as resonance, bandwidth, and response to rapid input changes.

To illustrate this performance analysis method, consider the suspension system, which is an important automotive system. Figure 2.9 is a simplified representation of the suspension system at one wheel on a car. The car body (sprung mass M_s) is supported by a spring (depicted as K in Figure 2.9) and shock absorber (denoted as D in Figure 2.9). The unsprung mass (wheel and axle assembly) is displaced by force f, which is transmitted by the tire in response to a rough road. The response of this system is the displacement x of the unsprung mass relative to its rest position. The input to this system is a force that in mathematical terms we denote $F(t)$.

Perhaps the most important input for characterizing system performance is the sinusoid. In our example, we consider a sinusoidal force such as might occur on a so-called washboard gravel road. The force transmitted by the tire

Figure 2.8
Frequency Response of an Example System

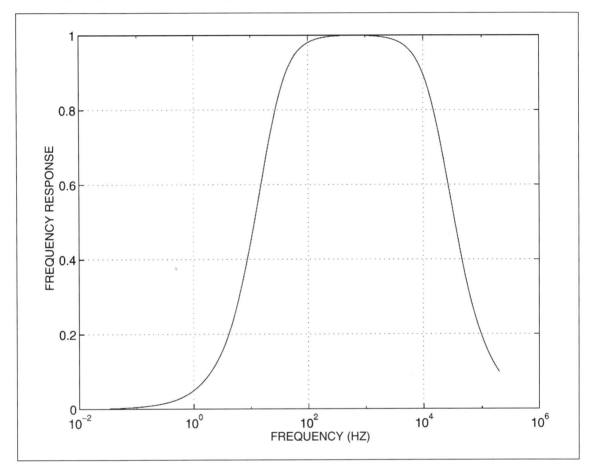

to the unsprung mass, depicted by the solid curve in Figure 2.10, is represented by

$$F(t) = F_0 \sin \omega t$$

where

F_0 = amplitude of the force
w = $2\pi f$
f = frequency or $(1/T)$
T = period

**Figure 2.9
Simplified
Suspension System**

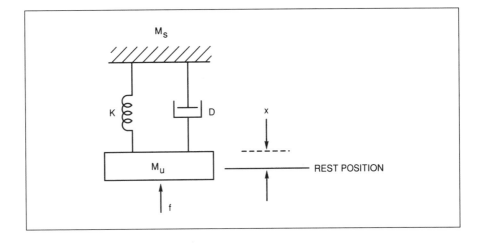

The displacement of the unsprung mass is represented by x (relative to the rest position) and is depicted by the dashed curve in Figure 2.10. This displacement is given mathematically by

$$x = X \sin(\omega t - \phi)$$

where ϕ equals phase, or $2\pi d/T$.

The performance of the example suspension system is given by the sinusoidal frequency response. For any system, the sinusoidal frequency response is the ratio of the amplitude of the response to the amplitude of the input. In our example, the response amplitude is X and the input amplitude is F, yielding

$$H = \frac{X}{F}$$

The sinusoidal frequency response of any system is a function of (i.e., depends on) frequency. In our example, the frequency of the rough road force due to the washboard road is proportional to the speed at which the car travels over the road. For the example suspension system, frequency response is depicted in Figure 2.11. In this illustration, four separate responses are shown for four different shock absorber damping constants. For very low damping coefficient D (weak damping or defective shock absorber), the response becomes very large for frequencies near the resonant frequency (i.e., f_0):

$$f_0 = \sqrt{\frac{M_u}{K}}$$

The resonant frequency is the "natural frequency" of oscillation at which the unsprung mass vibrates. If the car were to be suspended so that the wheel

Figure 2.10
Graph of Force Transmitted by the Tire

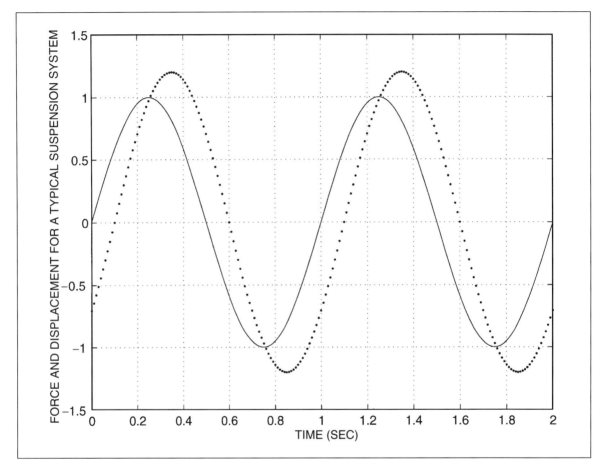

assembly were to be off the ground and if this assembly were displaced and then released, it would vibrate at the resonant frequency. For a typical car, this frequency will be of the order of 1 Hz. This situation is depicted by the uppermost dotted curve in Figure 2.11.

For a somewhat larger damping, the response is large enough near resonance to absorb the road force, transmitting relatively little of this force to the car body. A car with a so-called soft suspension yields relatively good ride characteristics. Unfortunately, a soft suspension tends to have relatively poor handling. The situation is depicted by the next highest dotted curve in Figure 2.11.

On the other hand, for very high damping coefficient, the response decreases sharply for frequencies greater than f_0. This circumstance

Figure 2.11
Frequency Response for Four Different Shock Absorber Damping Constants

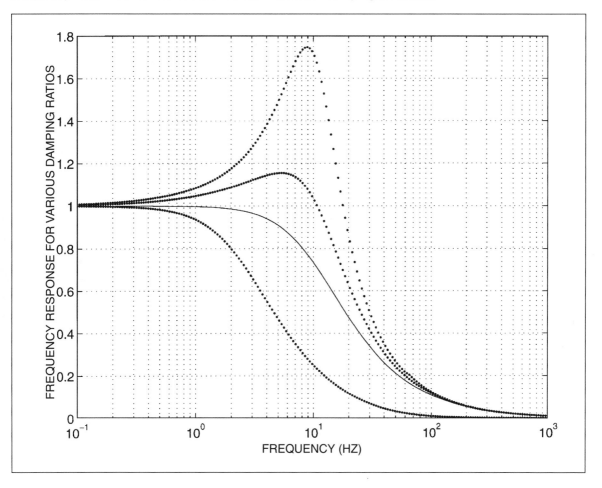

corresponds to a very stiff suspension in which much of the road force is transmitted by the shock absorber to the car body, making for a rather rough ride. This situation is depicted by the lowest dotted curve in Figure 2.11.

The response that is often optimum for many applications is called *critical damping* D_c:

$$D_c = \sqrt{M_u K}$$

Critical damping gives the most uniform response for the greatest range of frequencies. This situation (which is normally the most desirable) is depicted by the solid curve in Figure 2.11.

Figure 2.12
Step Response of a
System

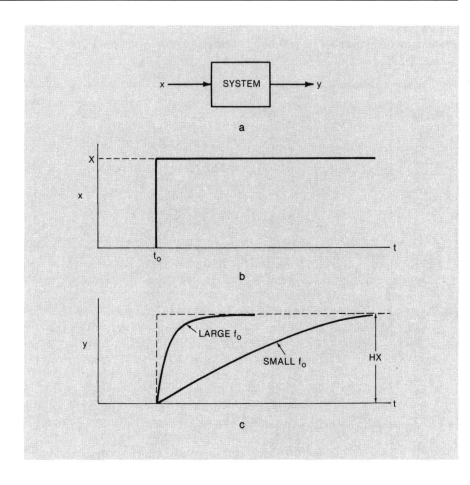

Step Response

The step response
characterizes the
performance of a
system.

The performance of a system is also represented by its time response which is closely related to its frequency response. Perhaps the most meaningful method of assessing the time response of a system is to examine its response to an input step. Figure 2.12 is a graph of a step input to the example system as well as the system response. The step input is an abrupt change occurring at time t_0. However, the output change is gradual relative to the input. The output asymptotically approaches a steady value HX.

The rate at which the output approaches the final value varies inversely with bandwidth, as illustrated in Figure 2.12 (where bandwidth is denoted f_0). Although the actual response of the system depends on the characteristics of the system, the response time of any system generally varies inversely with its bandwidth.

INSTRUMENTS

Instrumentation systems, whether electrical, mechanical, or a combination of both, measure a physical quantity and provide a report of that measurement.

An instrument (or instrumentation system) is a device for measuring some specific quantity. Automotive instruments have traditionally been mechanical, pneumatic, hydraulic, electrical, or combinations of these. However, modern automotive instrumentation is largely electronic. These electronic instruments or instrumentation systems are used to measure a variety of physical quantities, including

1. Vehicle speed
2. Total distance traveled
3. Engine angular speed (rpm)
4. Fuel quantity and/or flow rate
5. Oil pressure
6. Engine coolant temperature
7. Alternator charging current

For an understanding of measurement instrumentation, it is helpful to review a definition of measurement.

Measurement

A *measurement* is defined as a numerical comparison of an unknown magnitude of a given physical quantity to a standard magnitude of the same physical quantity. In this sense, the result of a measurement is normally a numerical value expressing the indicated value of the measurement as a multiple of the appropriate standard. However, other display devices are possible in which simple messages are given. Automotive instrumentation does not always display measured quantities. Rather, a warning lamp (or buzzer) is activated whenever a given quantity falls outside of allowed limits. For example, it is common practice not to provide a display of measured values for engine oil pressure or coolant temperature. Warning lamps are activated by the electronic instrumentation system whenever oil pressure is too low or coolant temperature is too high.

Issues

In any measurement made with any instrument there are several important issues, including

1. Standards
2. Precision
3. Calibration
4. Accuracy
5. Errors
6. Reliability

Each of these issues has an important impact on the performance of the instrumentation.

The *standard* magnitudes of the physical variables measured by any instrument are maintained by the National Institute of Standards & Technology in the United States. These standard magnitudes and the fundamental relationships between physical variables determine the units for each physical quantity.

The *precision* of any instrument is related to the number of significant figures that is readable from the display device. The greater the number of significant figures displayed, the greater the precision of the instrument.

Calibration is the act of setting the parameters of an instrument such that the indicated value conforms to the true value of the quantity being measured.

The *accuracy* of any measurement is the conformity of the indicated value to the true value of the quantity being measured. *Error* is defined as the difference between true and indicated values. Hence, accuracy and error vary inversely. The required accuracy for automotive electronic systems varies with application, as will be shown in later chapters. In general, those instruments used solely for driver information (e.g., fuel quantity) have lower accuracy requirements than those used for such applications as engine control or diagnosis.

The errors in any measurement are generally classified as either systematic or random. *Systematic* errors result from known variations in instrument performance, for which corrections can be made if desired. There are many sources of systematic error, including temperature variations in calibration, loading, and dynamic response. Since virtually any component in an instrument is potentially susceptible to temperature variations, great care must be exercised in instrument design to minimize temperature variations in calibration. As will be seen later in this book, most automotive instruments have relatively low precision requirements, so that temperature variations in calibration are negligible. *Random* errors are essentially random fluctuations in indicated value for the measurement. Most random measurement errors result from noise.

Systematic *loading* errors are due to the energy extracted by an instrument when making a measurement. Whenever the energy extracted from a system under measurement is not negligible, the extracted energy causes a change in the quantity being measured. Wherever possible, an instrument is designed to minimize such loading effects. The idea of loading error can be illustrated by the simple example of an electrical measurement, as illustrated in Figure 2.13. A voltmeter M having resistance R_m measures the voltage across resistance R. The correct voltage (v_c) is given by

> Systematic errors in the accuracy of instruments are due to known imperfections in an instrument; random errors are caused by outside disturbances.

$$v_c = V\left(\frac{R}{R + R_1}\right)$$

However, the measured voltage v_m is given by

**Figure 2.13
Illustration of Loading
Error**

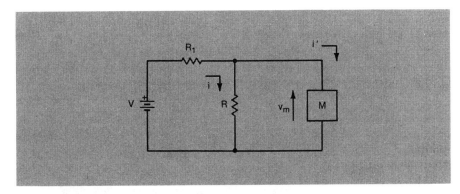

**Figure 2.14
Instrument Dynamic
Error**

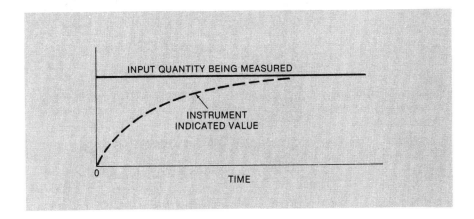

$$v_m = V\left(\frac{R_p}{R_p + R_1}\right)$$

where R_p is the parallel combination of R and R_m:

$$R_p = \frac{RR_m}{R + R_m}$$

Loading is minimized by increasing the meter resistance R_m to the largest possible value. For conditions where R_m approaches infinite resistance, R_p approaches resistance R, and v_m approaches the correct voltage. Loading is similarly minimized in measurement of any quantity by minimizing extracted energy. Normally, loading is negligible in modern instrumentation.

Another significant systematic error source is the *dynamic response* of the instrument. Any instrument has a limited response rate to very rapidly changing input, as illustrated in Figure 2.14. In this illustration, an input quantity to the instrument changes abruptly at some time. The instrument begins responding, but cannot instantaneously change and produce the new value. After a time, the indicated value approaches the correct reading (presuming correct instrument calibration). The greater the bandwidth of an instrument or instrumentation system, the more quickly it can follow rapid changes in the quantity being measured.

In many automotive instrumentation applications the bandwidth is purposely reduced to avoid rapid fluctuations in readings. For example, the type of sensor used for fuel quantity measurements actually measures the height of fuel in the tank with a small float. As the car moves, the fuel sloshes in the tank, causing the sensor reading to fluctuate randomly about its mean value. The signal processing associated with this sensor has an extremely low bandwidth so that only the average reading of the fuel quantity is displayed, thereby eliminating the undesirable fluctuations in fuel quantity measurements that would occur if the bandwidth were not restricted.

The *reliability* of an instrumentation system refers to its ability to perform its designed function accurately and continuously whenever required, under unfavorable conditions, and for a reasonable amount of time. Reliability must be designed into the system by using adequate design margins and quality components that operate both over the desired temperature range and under the applicable environmental conditions.

BASIC MEASUREMENT SYSTEM

The basic block diagram for an electronic instrumentation system has been given in Figure 2.1b. That is, each system has three basic components: sensor, signal processing, and display. Essentially, all electronic measurement systems incorporated in automobiles have this basic structure regardless of the physical variable being measured, the type of display being used, or whether the signal processing is digital or analog.

Understanding automotive electronic instrumentation systems is facilitated by consideration of some fundamental characteristics of the three functional components. Again it should be noted that the trend in automotive electronic systems is toward digital rather than analog realization. However, because both realizations are used, both types of components are discussed below.

Sensor

Sensors convert one form of energy, such as thermal energy, into electrical energy.

A *sensor* is a device that converts energy from the form of the measurement variable to an electrical signal. An ideal analog sensor generates an output voltage that is proportional to the quantity q being measured:

$$v_s = K_s q$$

where K_s is the sensor calibration constant.

By way of illustration, consider a typical automotive sensor—the throttle-position sensor. The quantity being measured is the angle (theta) of

**Figure 2.15
Digial Sensor
Configuration**

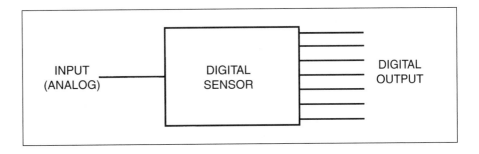

the throttle plate relative to closed throttle. Assuming for the sake of illustration that the throttle angle varies from 0 to 90 degrees and the voltage varies from 0 to 5 volts, the sensor calibration constant K_s is

$$K_s = \frac{5}{90°} = .056 \, \text{volt}/\text{degree}$$

Alternatively, a sensor can have a digital output, making it directly compatible with digital signal processing. For such sensors, the output is an electrical equivalent of a numerical value, using a binary number system as described earlier in this chapter. Figure 2.15 illustrates the output for such a sensor. There are N output leads, each of which can have one of two possible voltages, representing a 0 or 1. In such an arrangement, 2^N possible numerical values can be represented. For automotive applications, N ranges from 8 to 16, corresponding to a range of 64 (2^8) to 256 (2^{16}) numerical values.

Of course, a sensor is susceptible to error just as is any system or system component. Potential error sources include loading, finite dynamic response, calibration shift, and nonlinear behavior. Often it is possible to compensate for these and other types of errors in the electronic signal processing unit of the instrument. If a sensor has limited bandwidth, it will introduce errors when measuring rapidly changing input quantities. Figure 2.16 illustrates such dynamic errors for an analog sensor measuring an input that abruptly changes between two values (this type of input is said to have a *square wave* waveform). Figure 2.16a depicts a square wave input to the sensor. Figure 2.16b illustrates the response that the sensor will have if its bandwidth is too small. Note that the output doesn't respond to the instantaneous input changes. Rather, its output changes gradually, slowly approaching the correct value.

Signal processing can be used to compensate for systematic errors of sensors.

An ideal sensor has a *linear transfer characteristic* (or transfer function), as shown in Figure 2.17a. Thus, some signal processing is required to linearize the output signal so that it will appear as if the sensor has a straight line (linear) transfer characteristic, as shown in the dashed curve of Figure 2.17b. Sometimes a nonlinear sensor may provide satisfactory operation without

Figure 2.16
Sense Error Caused by Limited Dynamic Response of Sensor

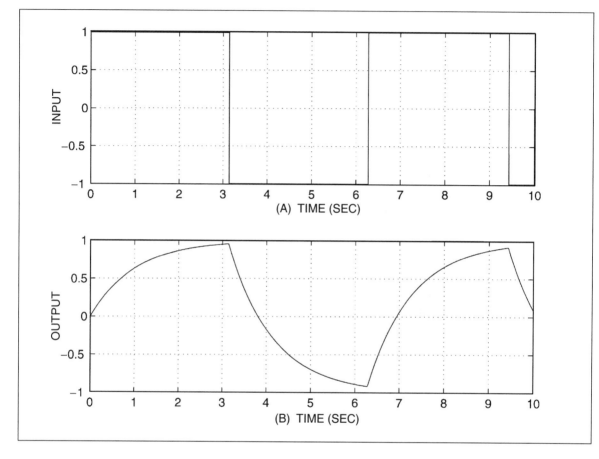

linearization if it is operated in a particular "nearly" linear region of its transfer characteristic (Figure 2.17b). Moreover, signal processing can be used to "correct" any nonlinearities of a given sensor, yielding a correct value of the variable being measured. This signal processing would perform the nonlinear correction by suitable calculation on the data from the sensor output.

Sensors are subject to random errors such as heat, electrical noise, and vibrations.

    Random errors in electronic sensors are caused primarily by internal electrical noise. Internal electrical noise can be caused by molecular vibrations due to heat (thermal noise) or random electron movement in semiconductors (shot noise). In certain cases, a sensor may respond to quantities other than the

**Figure 2.17
Sensor Transfer
Characteristics**

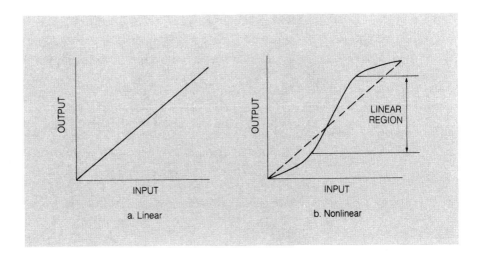

a. Linear

b. Nonlinear

quantity being measured. For example, the output of a sensor that is measuring pressure may also change as a result of temperature changes. An ideal sensor responds only to one physical quantity or stimulus. However, real sensors are rarely perfect and will generally respond in some way to outside stimuli. Signal processing can potentially correct for such defects.

Displays and Actuators

Automotive display devices, typically analog or digital meters, provide a visual indication of the measurements made by the sensors.

To be useful for measurement purposes, an electronic instrumentation system must somehow make the results of measurement available to the user. This is done through the display, which yields numerical values to the user. As in other aspects of electronic systems, the display can be analog or digital. Both types of displays are described in detail in Chapter 9. In automotive applications, a "display" is often just a warning (e.g., lamp) to the driver of an out-of-tolerance value for a given variable or parameter.

Displays, like sensors, are energy conversion devices. They have bandwidth, dynamic range, and calibration characteristics, and, therefore, have the same types of errors as do sensors. As with sensors, many of the shortcomings of display devices can be reduced or eliminated through the imaginative use of signal processing.

Actuators convert electrical inputs to an action such as a mechanical movement.

An *actuator* is an energy conversion device having an electrical input signal and an output signal that is mechanical (e.g., force or displacement). Automotive actuators include electric motors and solenoid-controlled valves and switches. These are used, for example, in throttle positioners for cruise control.

Signal Processing

Signal processing, as defined earlier, is any operation that is performed on signals traveling between the sensor and the display. Signal processing converts the sensor signal to an electrical signal that is suitable to drive the display. In addition, it can increase the accuracy, reliability, or readability of the measurement. Signal processing can make a nonlinear sensor appear linear, or it can smooth a sensor's frequency response. Signal processing can be used to perform unit conversions such as converting from miles per hour to kilometers per hour. It can perform display formatting (such as scaling and shifting a temperature sensor's output so that it can be displayed on the engine temperature gauge either in centigrade or in Fahrenheit), or process signals in a way that reduces the effects of random system errors.

Signal processing can be accomplished with either a digital or an analog subsystem. The trend in automotive electronic systems toward fully digital instrumentation means that the majority of automotive electronic signal processing is accomplished with a digital computer.

DIGITAL SIGNAL PROCESSING

The block diagram of a digital instrumentation system is shown in Figure 2.5. In this figure the sensor is assumed to be analog and is measuring a physical variable (which we call x in this figure). This continuously varying quantity is sampled (as described earlier) and quantized, yielding a sequence of binary-valued numbers (which we call x_n when $n = 1, 2, 3, \ldots$). In more formal mathematical terms, this sequence is given by

$$x_n = x(nT) \qquad n = 1, 2, 3, \ldots$$

where T is the sample period. That is, each x_n is the value of the input at discrete time nT. This sequence is the input to a digital computer that performs the digital signal processing (DSP). The output from the computer (which we call y_n) is a sequence of digital data that is input to the display. The display is assumed to be digital since such display devices are commonplace in automotive electronic instrumentation systems. It should be noted that in the event the sensor is digital, the sample and quantizer (ADC) are not required because the digital sensor output is in a form that can be read directly by the computer.

The actual signal processing computation is specific to a given application. Perhaps the most general statement that can be made concerning the DSP operation is that each output from the computer is made by a series of computations performed by the computer on one or more input samples. The mathematical formula or rule for these computations is called an *algorithm*. The number of inputs used to compute each output is specific to a given algorithm, which, in turn, is specific to a given application.

The DSP operates on the samples x_n under program control to perform arithmetic and logical operations (as explained in Chapter 4) and generate an output y_n for each input x_n. The set of steps performed on x_n to yield y_n is determined by the desired processing algorithm. Although there are a great many algorithms used in automotive electronics, it is possible to illustrate an important class of DSP algorithms with the following recursive digital filter algorithm:

$$y_n = \sum_{k=0}^{K} a_k x_{n-k} - \sum_{j=1}^{J} b_j y_{n-j}$$

In this algorithm, the coefficients a_k and b_j are constants. The variables x_{n-k} are previous inputs, beginning with the most recent (x_n) and ending with the oldest input used to find y_n (that is, x_{n-k}). Similarly y_{n-j} are previously computed outputs, beginning with y_{n-1} (the most recent) and ending with y_{n-j}. The microcomputer calculates each product (that is, $a_k x_{n-k}$ and $b_j y_{n-j}$) and sums the products for each k from 0 to K and for each j from 1 to J.

As an example of DSP application, consider a low pass filter. The digital equivalent of such a filter has a very simple algorithm,

$$y_n = ax_n - by_{n-1}$$

where a and b are constants that determine the dynamic response of the digital filter.

Throughout the remainder of this book, there will be specific examples given of DSP systems in which the signal processing operations are performed by computation in a microcomputer. The trend for virtually the entire spectrum of automotive electronics is for digital implementation of signal processing.

ANALOG SIGNAL PROCESSING

Although signal processing is mostly digital today, it is worthwhile to explain certain aspects of analog signal processing, as it is occasionally used for low-cost signal processing involving simple functional operations.

The operational amplifier is the predominant analog signal processing building block.

The primary building block of analog signal processing is the operational amplifier, which is depicted symbolically in Figure 2.18. An operational amplifier is a very high gain differential amplifier; that is, it amplifies the difference between the two input voltages. These voltages (relative to ground) are denoted v_1 and v_2. The input labeled + in Figure 2.18 is known as the *noninverting* input, and the one labeled – is called the *inverting* input. The output voltage v_o, relative to ground, is given by the following equation:

$$v_o = A(v_1 - v_2)$$

where A is the *open-loop gain*. For an ideal operational amplifier, the open-loop gain should be infinite. In practice it is finite, though very large (e.g., more than 100,000 typically).

**Figure 2.18
Operational Amplifier
Diagram**

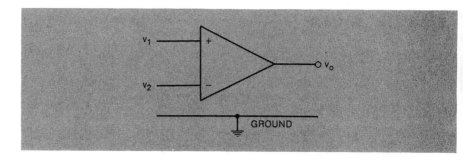

**Figure 2.19
Example Sensor
Frequency Response**

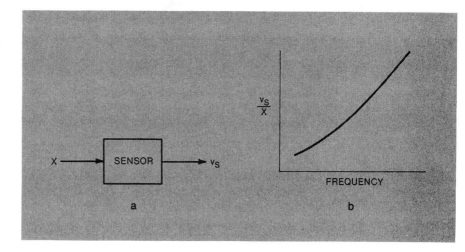

As an example of the signal processing application of the operational amplifier, consider an instrument using a sensor that has an imperfect response. For the purpose of illustration, assume that the frequency response H for the sensor is as shown in Figure 2.19. The output voltage for a fixed-amplitude input increases linearly with frequency, as shown in the graph. An example of this type of frequency response is a magnetic angular speed sensor, described in Chapter 6.

A signal processing circuit that can compensate for the undesirable frequency response is shown in Figure 2.20. In this circuit, a parallel resistance–capacitance (R_fC) combination is connected in a so-called feedback path from the output to the inverting input. The frequency response for this circuit ($H_{sp} = v_0/v_s$) is shown graphically in Figure 2.21. Also shown in this illustration is the frequency response for the combination sensor and signal processor. For frequencies above about 2 Hz, the frequency response ($H = v_0/x$) for the combination is flat, as is desired. The characteristics and applications of operational amplifiers are discussed in greater detail in Chapter 3.

**Figure 2.20
Operational Amplifier
Circuit Used to
Compensate for the
Poor Frequency
Response of a Sensor**

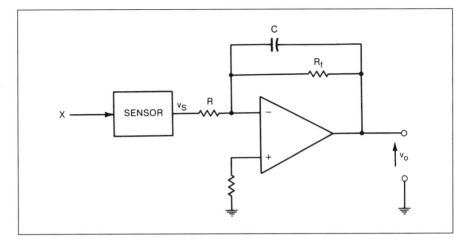

CONTROL SYSTEMS

Control systems are systems that are used to regulate the operation of other systems. For this discussion, the system being controlled is known as the *system plant.* The controlling system is called an *electronic controller.*

In preparation for discussing the many electronic control systems in automobiles it is worthwhile to explain in detail what a control system is. A control system is described by its fundamental elements, which are the objectives of control, system components, and results or outputs. The objectives of a control system are the quantitative measures of the tasks to be performed by the system. These describe the desired values of a variable or of multiple variables and are normally specified by the user. The results are called outputs (or controlled variables). Typically, the objective of a control system is to regulate the values of the outputs in a prescribed manner by the (operator-determined) inputs through the elements (or components) of the control system.

A control system should

Control systems, which are used to control the operation of other systems, are measured in terms of accuracy, speed of response, stability, and immunity from external noise.

1. Perform its function accurately.
2. Respond quickly.
3. Be stable.
4. Respond only to valid inputs (noise immunity).

A control system's accuracy determines how close the system's output will come to the desired output, with a constant-value input command. Quick response determines how closely the output of the system will track or follow a changing input command. A system's stability describes how a system behaves

Figure 2.21
Frequency Response for Operational Amplifier Circuit

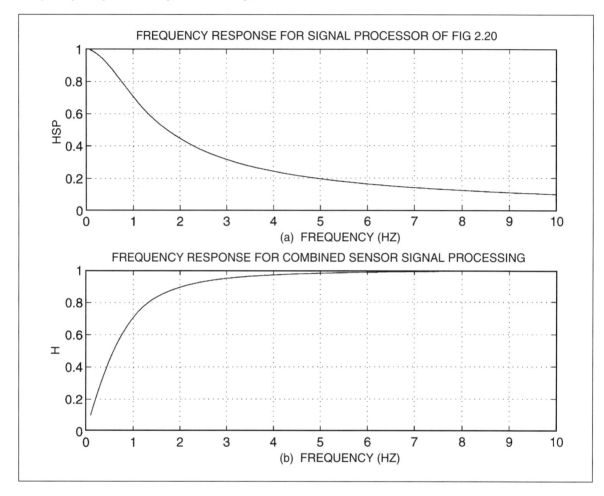

when a change, particularly a sudden change, is made by the input signal. The output of an unstable control system will diverge from its intended value based on its input. For any automotive application, a control system must be stable and controllable over the entire desired operating range. A good controller design will minimize the chance of unstable operation under even extreme operating conditions. A system should maintain its accuracy by responding only to valid inputs. When noise or other disturbances threaten to change the system plant's output, good design will eliminate response to such inputs from system performance as much as possible. A control system having small (ideally zero) response to noise inputs is said to have good noise immunity. Accuracy, quick response, stability, and noise immunity are all determined by the control system configuration and parameters chosen for a particular plant.

The purpose of a control system is to determine the output of the system (plant) being controlled in relation to the input and in accordance with the operating characteristics of the controller. The relationship between the controller input and the desired plant output is called the *control law* for the system. The desired value for the plant output is often called the *set point.*

The output of an electronic control system is an electrical signal that must be converted to some mechanical (or other) action in order to regulate the plant. A device that converts the electrical signal to the desired mechanical action is called an *actuator.* Looking ahead to our discussion of automotive electronics, a specific actuator will be introduced, namely, an electrically activated fuel injector. Generally speaking, an actuator has input electrical terminals that receive electrical power from the control electronics. By a process of internal electromechanical energy conversion, a mechanical output is obtained that operates to control the plant. In the case of the fuel injector, the air–fuel mixture is controlled, which, in turn, controls the engine output.

Although electronic controllers can, in principle, be implemented with either analog or digital electronics, the trend in automotive control is digital. Since the purpose of this chapter is to discuss fundamentals of electronic systems, both continuous-time (analog) and discrete-time (digital) control systems are presented.

There are two major categories of control systems: open-loop (or feedforward) and closed-loop (or feedback) systems. There are many automotive examples of each, as we will show in later chapters. The architecture of an open-loop system is given in the block diagram of Figure 2.22.

Open-Loop Control

The components of an open-loop controller include the electronic controller, which has an output to an actuator. The actuator, in turn, regulates the plant being controlled in accordance with the desired relationship between the reference input and the value of the controlled variable in the plant. Many examples of open-loop control are encountered in automotive electronic systems, such as fuel control in certain operating modes.

An open-loop control system never compares actual output with the desired value.

In the open-loop control system of Figure 2.22, the command input is sent to the electronic controller, which performs a control operation on the input to generate an intermediate electrical signal (denoted i in Figure 2.22). This electrical signal is the input to the actuator which generates a control input (denoted u in Figure 2.22) to the plant that, in turn, regulates the plant output to the desired value. This type of control is called open-loop control

Figure 2.22
Open-Loop Control System Block Diagram

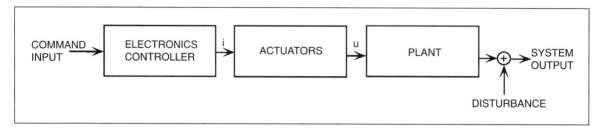

because the output of the system is never compared with the command input to see if they match.

The operation of the plant is directly regulated by the actuator (which might simply be an electric motor). The system output may also be affected by external disturbances that are not an inherent part of the plant but are the result of the operating environment.

One of the principal drawbacks to the open-loop controller is its inability to compensate for changes that might occur in the controller or the plant or for any disturbances. This defect is eliminated in a closed-loop control system, in which the actual system output is compared to the desired output value in accordance with the input. Of course, a measurement must be made of the plant output in such a system, and this requires measurement instrumentation.

Closed-Loop Control

It is the potential for change in an open-loop system that led to feedback, or closed-loop, control. In a closed-loop control system a measurement of the output variable being controlled is obtained via a sensor and fed back to the controller, as illustrated in Figure 2.23.

The measured value of the controlled variable is compared with the desired value for that variable based on the reference input. An error signal based on the difference between desired and actual values of the output signal is created, and the controller generates an actuator signal u that tends to reduce the error to zero. In addition to reducing this error to zero, feedback has other potential benefits in a control system. It can affect control system performance by improving system stability and suppressing the effects of disturbances in the system. Later chapters will include numerous examples of closed-loop control, such as idle speed control.

The generic closed-loop control system illustrated in Figure 2.23 has some of the components found in an open-loop control system, including the plant to be controlled, actuator(s), and control electronics. In addition, however, this system includes one or more sensors and some signal-

**Figure 2.23
Closed-Loop Control
Configuration**

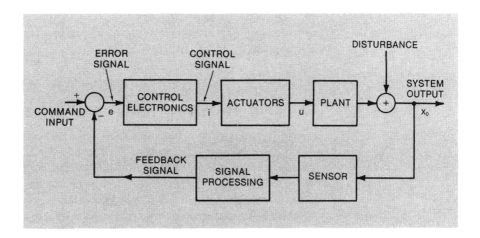

conditioning electronics. The signal conditioning used in a closed-loop control system plays a role similar to that played by signal processing in measurement instrumentation. That is, it transforms the sensor output as required to achieve the desired measurement of the plant output. Compensation for certain sensor defects (e.g., limited bandwidth) is possible, and in some cases necessary, to allow for the comparison of the plant output with the desired value. Electronic control systems are classified by the way in which the error signal is processed to generate the control signal. The major control systems include proportional, proportional-integral, and proportional-integral-differential controllers.

PROPORTIONAL CONTROLLER

The component at the left of the block diagram of Figure 2.23 is the element in which the output is actually compared to the input. An error signal is obtained by electrically subtracting the feedback signal from the command input. The error signal is the input to the control electronics system, which, in turn, generates an output called a *control signal.* The control signal is applied to the actuator, and the actuator moves in such a direction as to reduce the error between the actual and desired output to zero.

In Figure 2.23, the sensor provides a measurement x_o of the plant output. The error signal e is obtained by subtracting x_o from the desired value x:

$$e = x - x_o$$

In a proportional control system, the error signal is amplified by an amplifier to yield an output v_c, which is the control signal:

$$v_c = Ge$$

where G is the amplifier gain.

The actuator causes the plant output y to increase in proportion to v_c. The operation of this control system is as follows. Assume arbitrarily that the plant output (x_o) is larger than its desired value. In this case the error signal e is negative. The amplified error signal is applied to the actuator, causing the plant output to decrease. Thus, x_o will decrease until $x_o = x$, at which point e is zero and the output remains fixed at the desired value. A controller that generates a control signal proportional to the error signal is called a *proportional controller*.

Disturbance Response

Any purely proportional control system has poor response to a disturbance. Typically, a disturbance is caused by factors that are outside of the plant or the control system. For example, in Chapter 8 in a discussion of cruise control, we introduce an example of a disturbance in which cruise control is activated on a level road. When the car encounters a hill, the change in load on the engine is a disturbance.

The dotted curve in Figure 2.24 shows the response of a proportional control system to a disturbance d at time $t = 1$ sec. Instead of remaining at the set point x_o following disturbance d, the system response changes to a steady error e, which is given by

$$e = \frac{d}{G}$$

In principle, the error for any given disturbance can be made as small as desired by raising the feedback gain. Unfortunately, the control system dynamic response is also affected by G. Raising the gain too far will cause the system response to become oscillatory. Often if the gain is too large, the system becomes unstable. This property of having a steady error in response to a steady disturbance is fundamental to all control systems incorporating a proportional controller, but can be eliminated by use of a proportional integral controller.

Concept of Integration

Before beginning the discussion of proportional integral (PI) control, it is worthwhile to discuss the concept of integration briefly. Of course those readers having a background in and familiarity with integral calculus can skip this discussion. The concept of an integrator can perhaps best be understood with reference to the block diagram of Figure 2.25a. In mathematical terms this system is denoted:

$$y = \int x\, dt$$

and the output y is said to be the integral of the input x with respect to time. In more practical terms the integrator can be thought of as a device that

Figure 2.24
Response of a Proportional Control System to a Disturbance

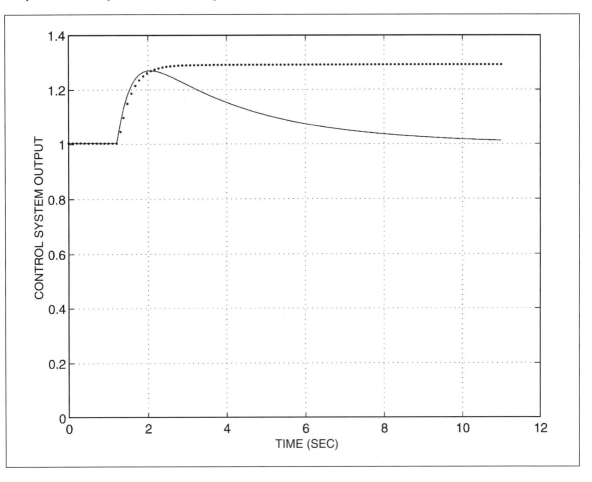

continuously "adds" or accumulates the input such that the input is the rate of change of the output.

A good practical example of an integrator is depicted in Figure 2.25b. In this figure the integrator is a storage tank into which fluid is flowing. The output for this example is the total volume of fluid that has accumulated at any time (until the tank is full). The input to this integrator is the volume flow rate x of fluid flowing into the tank. For example, if the volume flow rate into a tank were 10 gal/min then every minute the volume of fluid in the tank (y) would increase by 10 gallons, that is to say, the volume of fluid in the tank would be 10 multiplied by the time (from empty) that the fluid flows into the

**Figure 2.25
Concept of Integration**

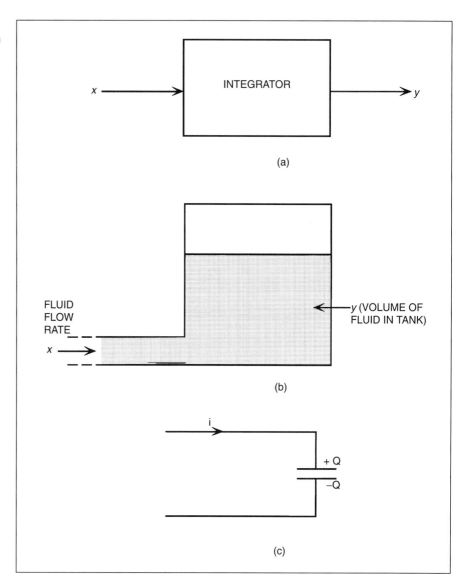

tank. This is a rather straightforward concept when the input is constant. However, if the input volume flow rate changes continuously, then the volume of fluid is given by the integral (with respect to time) of the input flow rate.

Another device that acts as an integrator is a capacitor into which a current is flowing, as depicted in Figure 2.25c. The charge stored in the capacitor Q is the integral with respect to time of the current:

$$Q = \int i\,dt$$

Figure 2.26
Block Diagram for Proportional Integral Controller

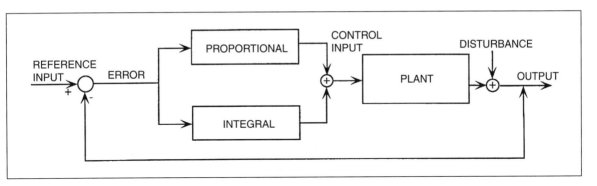

This property of a capacitor is used to implement the integral part of an analog proportional integral control system. (See the discussion in Chapter 3 of operational amplifiers.)

PROPORTIONAL INTEGRAL CONTROLLER

One way of avoiding the steady disturbance response error of a proportional (P) controller is to use a controller that is called a proportional integral (PI) controller. The proportional integral control corrects for a serious defect in a purely proportional controller. In the latter type, any steady disturbance leads to a steady error in the output regulation. The configuration for a PI controller is shown in Figure 2.26. This controller combines a term proportional to the error with the integral of the error.

The error signal for a PI controller is generated the same way as for the P controller. That is, the error e is the difference between the desired and actual values:

$$e = x - x_o$$

The controller then generates the integral of the error,

$$\int e \, dt$$

electronically. The control signal that is applied to the plant includes a part that is proportional to the error as well as a part that is proportional to the integral of the error. The resulting control signal is the sum of these two parts

$$v_c = Ge + k \int e \, dt$$

where G is the proportional gain and k is the integral gain. The proportional part of the control signal acts the same as in a P controller, that is, it drives the plant so as to reduce the error to zero.

However, consider the case of a disturbance to the system that tends to produce a steady error in a P controller. In a PI controller, the integral part continues to increase (since the integral of a steady error continuously increases until the error itself is zero). This integral part of the control signal drives the plant in a direction to reduce the error due to disturbance to zero.

The disturbance rejection of a PI and P controller is illustrated in Figure 2.24. Here a steady disturbance occurs at time $t = 0$. The P controller response is shown in the dotted curve, which depicts the steady error. The PI controller response is shown by the solid curve, for which the error eventually is reduced to zero. This ability to reduce errors due to disturbance to zero is a fundamental property of PI controllers.

In principle a PI controller could be implemented in a purely mechanical control system. However, in practice the only feasible implementation of an integral is electronic (where integration can be implemented by means of a capacitor in a simple electronic circuit). Integrals can also be implemented with digital controllers. The relative ease and low cost of implementing PI controllers is part of the motivation for the trend toward electronic control in automotive systems.

A good example of the performance of a PI controller is given in Chapter 8. The accuracy of speed regulation for a PI controller in the presence of disturbance (hills) is superior to that of a P controller. It is worthwhile to summarize that a PI controller will, in general, reduce the error in response to disturbances to exactly zero, whereas the P controller will always have a residual output error.

Digital PI Controller

A PI controller can also be implemented via a digital control system in which the control signal is generated with a special-purpose digital computer. Such a system operates in discrete time by representing the variables at sample times.

In a digital PI controller, the control electronics samples the error signal at multiples of the sample period. The control signal includes two parts: a proportional part and an integral part. The proportional part is proportional to the most recent sample of the error. The integral part includes a sum of several previous samples. If there is no disturbance to the system, the sum is zero (or at least very small). If there is a disturbance, the sum of previous errors can become very large. The sum of previous errors in the control signal is applied to the actuator in such a way as to force the controlled system to reduce the error caused by disturbance toward zero.

In mathematical terms, the control signal at sample time t_k, which we denote v_k, is given by

$$v_k = -Ge_k - K\sum_{m=1}^{M}e_{k-m}$$

where

e_k is the most recent sample

e_{k-m} is the mth oldest sample ($m = 1, 2, \ldots, M$)

G is proportional gain

K is integral gain

The dynamic properties of a PI controller with the above control law are determined by the sizes of the proportional (G) and integral (K) gains as well as the number (M) of error samples included in the sum (Σ).

PROPORTIONAL INTEGRAL DIFFERENTIAL CONTROLLER

Still another control type that finds wide application in practice is the proportional integral differential (PID) controller. In a PID controller, the control signal is given by

$$v_k = -Ge_k - K\sum_{m=1}^{M}e_{k-m} - D[(e_k - e_{k-1})/T]$$

The final term in this expression for the control signal involves the difference between the two most recent samples of the error. This term represents the rate of change of the error, and its inclusion in the control law often improves dynamic response greatly. For the corresponding analog (continuous-time) controller, the control signal is given by

$$v_c = Ge_k + K\int e\,dt + D\frac{de}{dt}$$

In this discussion of the general properties of a control system, negative signs have arbitrarily been chosen for the coefficients in the digital control algorithms and positive signs for analog control. The actual signs for G, K, D must be chosen to yield a stable control system.

CLOSED-LOOP LIMIT-CYCLE CONTROL

In a proportional control system the control signal is proportional to the error between desired and actual output.

The control electronics in the previous example provided what is called proportional control because the control signal is proportional to the error signal. Other combinations of control electronics are possible, and it is a challenge to the system designer to develop imaginative types of control electronics to improve the performance of a given plant.

Another type of control that is used in automotive applications is limit-cycle control. Limit-cycle control is a type of feedback control that monitors the system's output and responds only when the output goes beyond preset

**Figure 2.27
Limit-Cycle Controller
to Control Oven
Temperature**

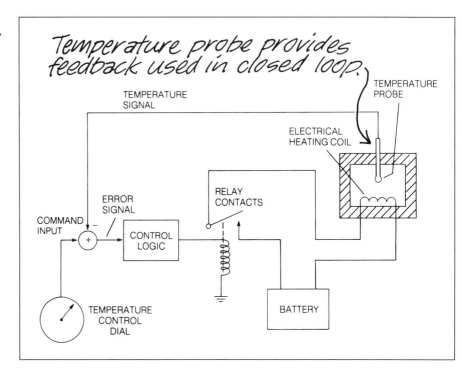

limits. Limit-cycle controllers often are used to control plants with nonlinear or complicated transfer functions.

An example of a limit-cycle controller is the temperature-controlled oven depicted in Figure 2.27. The temperature inside the oven is controlled by the length of time the heating coil is energized. The temperature of the oven is measured with a temperature probe, and the corresponding electrical signal is fed back to the command to obtain an error signal. The control electronics checks the error signal against the temperature control dial to determine if one of the following two conditions exists:

Limit-cycle control responds only when the error is outside a pair of limits.

1. Oven temperature is below minimum setting of command input.
2. Oven temperature is above maximum setting of command input.

The control electronics responds to error condition 1 by closing the relay contacts to energize the heating element. This causes the temperature in the oven to increase until the temperature rises above a maximum limit, producing error condition 2. In this case, the control electronics opens the relay contacts and the heat is turned off. The oven gradually cools until condition 1 again occurs and the cycle repeats. The oven temperature varies between the upper and lower limit, and the variations can be graphed as a function of time, as shown in Figure 2.28.

**Figure 2.28
Oven Temperature
Graph**

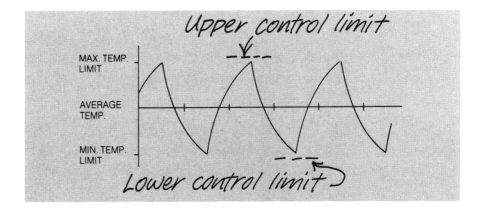

The amplitude of the temperature variations, called the *differential,* can be decreased by reducing the difference between the maximum and minimum temperature limits. As the limits get closer together, the temperature cycles more rapidly (frequency increases) to hold the actual temperature much closer to the desired constant temperature. Thus, the limit-cycle controller controls the system to maintain an average value close to the command input. This type of controller has gained popularity due to its simplicity, low cost, and ease of application. Fuel control, one of the most important automotive electronic control systems is, at least partially, a limit-cycle control system (see Chapter 5).

Quiz for Chapter 2

1. Which of the following are examples of systems?
   a. clock
   b. electric dishwasher
   c. communication network
   d. society
   e. all of the above

2. Block diagrams are developed in what type of analysis?
   a. physical
   b. quantitative
   c. qualitative

3. Specific system parameters are determined in what type of analysis?
   a. physical
   b. quantitative
   c. qualitative

4. What is a sensor used for?
   a. to convert a nonelectrical input to an electrical output
   b. to convert an electrical input to a mechanical output
   c. to reduce the effects of noise and other disturbances on the measured quantity
   d. all of the above

5. What does an actuator do?
   a. converts a nonelectrical input to an electrical output
   b. converts an electrical input to an action
   c. reduces the effects of noise and other disturbances on the measured quantity
   d. all of the above

6. What does signal processing do?
   a. converts a mechanical input to an electrical output
   b. converts an electrical input to a mechanical output
   c. reduces the effects of noise and other disturbances on the measured quantity
   d. all of the above

7. An error amplifier is used to compare which of the following two signals?
   a. the output of a sensor and the input to a signal processor
   b. the output of a system and the command input of a system
   c. the output of a signal processor and the output of a system
   d. none of the above

8. A basic instrumentation system consists of which of the following components?
   a. sensor
   b. actuator
   c. signal processor
   d. all of the above

9. A control system may contain which of the following components?
   a. error amplifier
   b. control logic
   c. plant
   d. all of the above

10. Which of the following are examples of a plant?
   a. automotive drivetrain
   b. high-temperature oven
   c. an airplane navigation system
   d. all of the above

Electronics Fundamentals

This chapter is for the reader who has little knowledge of electronics. It is intended to provide an overview of the subject so that discussions in later chapters about the operation and use of automotive electronics control systems will be easier to understand.

The chapter discusses electronic devices and circuits having applications in electronic automotive instrumentation and control systems. Topics include semiconductor devices, analog circuits, digital circuits, and fundamentals of integrated circuits.

SEMICONDUCTOR DEVICES

All of the active circuit devices (e.g., diodes and transistors) from which electronic circuits are built are themselves fabricated from so-called semiconductor materials. A semiconductor material in pure form is neither a good conductor nor a good insulator. The ability of a material to conduct electric current is characterized by a property called conductivity. A metal such as copper, which is a good conductor, has a relatively high conductivity. An insulator such as mica has relatively low conductivity. A semiconductor material has conductivity somewhere between that of a good conductor and that of a good insulator. Therefore, this material (also called semiconductor material) and devices made from it are semiconductor devices (also called solid-state devices).

There are many types of semiconductor devices, but transistors and diodes are two of the most important in automotive electronics. Furthermore, these devices are the fundamental elements used to construct nearly all modern integrated circuits. Therefore, the discussion of semiconductor devices will be centered on these two.

Semiconductor devices are made from silicon or germanium that is purposely contaminated with impurities that change the conductivity of the material. Transistors are semiconductor devices that are used as active devices in electronic circuits.

The earliest transistors were made from germanium, but today silicon is by far the most commonly used semiconductor material for making diodes, transistors, and other semiconductor devices. The conductivity of a pure semiconductor can be varied in a predictable manner by diffusing precisely controlled amounts of very specific impurities into it. Boron and phosphorus often are used as impurity source materials to alter the conductivity of silicon. When boron is used, the semiconductor material becomes a so-called p-type semiconductor. When phosphorus is used, the semiconductor material becomes an n-type semiconductor. It is not necessary for the purposes of this book to understand the differences between p-type and n-type semiconductors. However, the interested reader can consult any of the standard introductory references on the theory of semiconductor devices for further information.

Semiconductor devices such as diodes and transistors are quite different from common linear components such as resistors, capacitors, inductors, and transformers. The following discussion presents an explanation of the operation of these devices.

Although it is not a physically correct model, an n-type semiconductor can be thought of as a semiconductor having excess electrons that flow whenever an external voltage is applied. Similarly, a p-type material behaves functionally as though it had excess positively charged particles called "holes." Various combinations of n-type and p-type semiconductor materials make up all solid-state devices used to make up a modern electronic system. In actual fact, all current flow is via the motion of electrons.

Throughout this book, current flow is taken to be conventional current in which the direction of flow is from positive to negative, whereas in reality current consists of electron motion from negative to positive. This choice of current is merely convenient for notational purposes and has no effect on the validity of any circuit analysis or design.

Diodes

A diode acts much like a one-way valve, allowing current to flow in only one direction.

A diode is a two-terminal electrical device having one electrode that is called the *anode* (a p-type semiconductor) and another that is called the *cathode* (an n-type semiconductor). A solid-state diode is formed by the junction between the anode and the cathode. In practice, a p-n junction is formed by diffusing p-type impurities on one side of the intended junction and n-type impurities on the other side. Diodes can be thought of as one-way resistors or current check valves because they allow current to flow through them in only one direction, depending on the polarity of voltage (bias) across the anode and cathode. When current flows in the forward (conducting) direction with a plus voltage on the anode, diodes have low resistance (typically a few ohms). This is called the *forward biased condition*. (The conventional current flow direction of positive to negative is used in this book.) When the current flows in the reverse (nonconducting) direction with a plus voltage on the cathode, diodes have a very high resistance (typically a few million ohms). This is called the *reverse biased condition*.

Figure 3.1a shows the schematic symbol for a diode, and Figure 3.1b is a graph of the actual and ideal voltage and current transfer characteristics for a typical diode. Notice on the ideal curve that the diode doesn't start conducting until the voltage across it exceeds V_d volts; then, for small increases in voltage, the current increases very rapidly. For silicon diodes, V_d is about 0.7 volt. For germanium diodes, V_d is about 0.3 volt. Even for the actual curve, the change in current is quite steep for 0.1 volt changes in the voltage across the diode after V_d has been exceeded.

**Figure 3.1
Diode Characteristics**

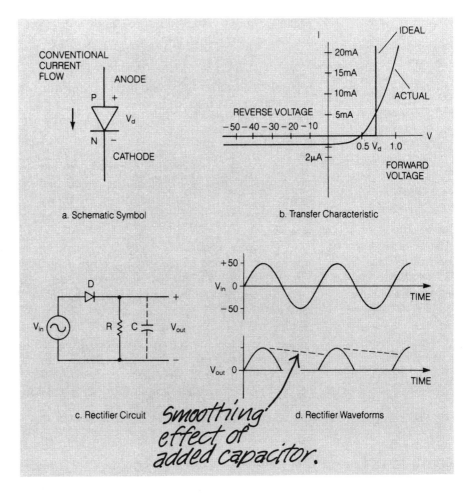

a. Schematic Symbol

b. Transfer Characteristic

c. Rectifier Circuit

Smoothing effect of added capacitor.

d. Rectifier Waveforms

When designing or analyzing circuits, V_d is often ignored in relatively high-voltage circuits in which V_d is a very small percentage of the total voltage; however, in low-voltage and low-level signal circuits, V_d may be a significant factor.

Rectifier Circuit

A diode has low resistance when forward biased and high resistance when reverse biased.

The circuit in Figure 3.1c, a very common diode circuit, is called a *half-wave rectifier circuit* because it effectively cuts the ac (alternating current) waveform in half. Consider the circuit first without the dotted-in capacitor. The alternating current voltage source is a sine wave with a peak-to-peak amplitude of 100 volts (50 volt positive swing and 50 volt negative swing). Waveforms of the input voltage and output voltage plotted against time are shown as the solid lines in Figure 3.1d. Notice that the output never drops below 0 volts. The diode is reverse biased and blocks current flow when the input voltage is negative, but when the input voltage is positive, the diode is forward biased and permits current flow. If the diode direction is reversed in the circuit, current flow will be permitted when the input voltage is negative and blocked when the input voltage is positive.

The half-wave rectifier is used to convert an ac voltage into a dc (direct current) voltage that stays either above 0 volts or below 0 volts, depending on which way the diode is installed. Rectifier circuits are commonly used to convert the ac voltage into a dc voltage for use with automotive alternators to provide dc current for battery charging and to supply electrical power to the vehicle.

The use of a capacitor to store charge and resist voltage changes smooths the rippling or pulsating output of a half-wave rectifier.

The input voltage V_{in} of Figure 3.1c is ac; the output voltage V_{out} has a dc component and a time-varying component, as shown in Figure 3.1d. The output voltage of the half-wave rectifier can be smoothed by adding a capacitor, which is represented by the dotted lines in Figure 3.1c. Since the capacitor stores a charge and opposes voltage changes, it discharges (supplies current) to the load resistance R when V_{in} is going negative from its peak voltage. The capacitor is recharged when V_{in} comes back to its positive peak and current is supplied to the load by the V_{in}. The result is V_{out} that is more nearly a smooth, steady dc voltage, as shown by the dotted lines between the peaks of Figure 3.1d. The amplitude of the ripples in the output voltage can be made insignificant by choosing a capacitor having sufficiently large capacitance.

Transistors

Transistors are useful as amplifying devices.

Diodes are static circuit elements; that is, they do not have gain or store energy. Transistors are active elements because they can amplify or transform a signal level. Transistors are three-terminal circuit elements that act like current-controlled current valves. There are two common bipolar (i.e., consisting of n-type and p-type semiconductors) types. Figure 3.2a shows the schematic symbol for an NPN transistor, and Figure 3.2b shows the schematic symbol for a PNP transistor. P represents p-type semiconductor material; N represents n-type material. The area where the p-type and n-type materials join is called a *PN junction* (or simply a junction). Current flows into the base and collector of an NPN transistor and out of the emitter. The currents in a PNP transistor flow exactly opposite to those in the NPN transistor; that is, current flows into the emitter and out of the base and collector. In fact, this is the only difference between the PNP transistor and NPN transistor. Their functions as amplifiers and switches are the same.

**Figure 3.2
Transistor Schematic
Symbols**

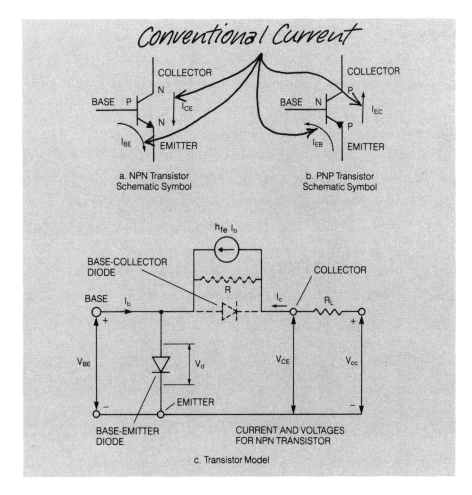

a. NPN Transistor
Schematic Symbol

b. PNP Transistor
Schematic Symbol

c. Transistor Model

During normal operation, current flows from the base to the emitter in an NPN transistor. The collector-base junction is reverse biased, so that only a very small amount of current flows between the collector and the base when there is no base current flow.

The base-emitter junction of a transistor acts like a diode. Under normal operation for an NPN transistor, current flows forward into the base and out the emitter, but does not flow in the reverse direction from emitter to base. The arrow on the emitter of the transistor schematic symbol indicates the forward direction of current flow. The collector-base junction also acts as a diode, but supply voltage is always applied to it in the reverse direction. This junction does have some reverse current flow, but it is so small ($1 \cdot 10^{-6}$ to $1 \cdot 10^{-12}$ amperes) that it is ignored except when operated under extreme conditions, particularly temperature extremes. In some automotive applications, the extreme temperatures may significantly affect transistor operation. For such applications, the circuit may include components that automatically compensate for changes in transistor operation.

**Figure 3.2
Continued**

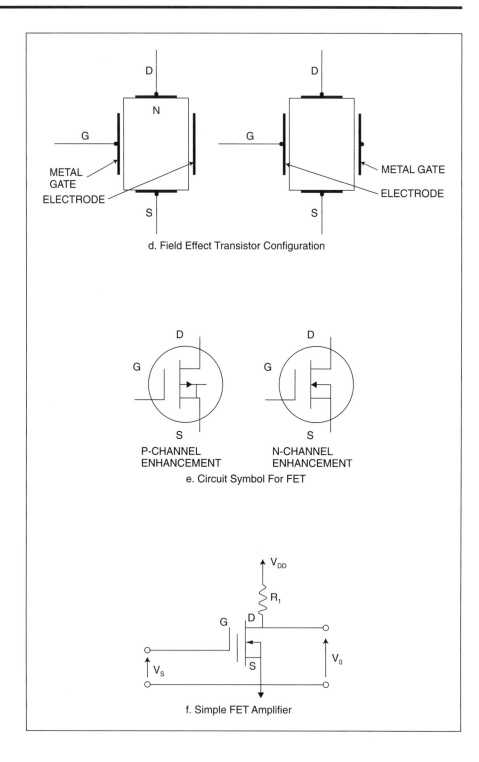

d. Field Effect Transistor Configuration

P-CHANNEL
ENHANCEMENT

N-CHANNEL
ENHANCEMENT

e. Circuit Symbol For FET

f. Simple FET Amplifier

Under normal linear (analog) circuit operation, the collector-base junction is reverse biased as mentioned previously; however, when used as a switch in the on condition, the collector-base junction can become forward biased. In normal operation, the current that flows through the collector-emitter terminals is controlled by the current flowing through the base terminal. Relatively small base currents control relatively large collector currents through a complicated physical process that is beyond the scope of this book. However, for the purposes of the present discussion, it is correct to think of the transistor as a current-amplifying device in which the base current controls the collector current. The current amplification of a typical transistor is on the order of 100. That is, a base current controls a collector current that is about 100 times larger.

Field Effect Transistors

The types of transistors discussed above are known as bipolar transistors because they operate by conduction via both electrons and holes. As explained earlier, they amplify relatively weak base currents yielding relatively large collector-emitter output currents. They are in effect current-controlled current amplifiers.

Another type of transistor operates as a voltage-controlled amplifier and is called a field effect transistor (FET). There are many variations of FETs, and it is beyond the scope of this book to discuss them all.

Unlike the bipolar transistor which is fabricated with two p-n junctions, the field effect transistor consists of a slab of either n-type or p-type semiconductor as depicted in Figure 3.2d. The symbol for an FET is depicted in Figure 3.2e, and a typical amplifying circuit is shown in Figure 3.2f. An FET is known either as an n-channel or p-channel FET depending upon whether the semiconductor is n-type or p-type material, respectively.

An FET is a three-terminal active circuit element having a pair of electrodes connected at opposite ends of the slab of semiconductor and called source (denoted S) and drain (denoted D). A third electrode, called the gate (denoted G), consists of a thin layer of conductor that is electrically insulated from the semiconductor slab.

The example-amplifying circuit shown in Figure 3.2f depicts the current path from power supply V_{DD} through a load resistor R_L and through the transistor from D to S and then to ground. A signal voltage V_S applied at the ground electrode controls the current flow through the FET and thereby through the load resistance.

Functionally, the FET operates like a voltage-controlled current source. A relatively weak signal applied to the gate can yield a relatively large voltage V_O across the load resistance.

There are many types of FETs characterized by fabrication technology, material doping (i.e., n-channel or p-channel), and whether the gate voltage tends to increase the number of charge carriers (called enhancement mode) or decrease the number of charge carriers (depletion mode). Perhaps the most common gate fabrication involves a metal with an oxide layer placed against the semiconductor in the sequence metal-oxide-semiconductor (MOS). The oxide layer insulates the metal from the semiconductor so that no current flows through the gate electrode. Rather, the voltage applied to the gate creates an electric field that controls current flow from source to drain. The terminology for an FET having this type of gate structure is n-MOS or p-MOS, depending on whether the FET is n-channel or p-channel. Often, circuits are fabricated using both in a complementary manner, and the fabrication technology is known as complementary-metal-oxide-semiconductor (CMOS). Regardless of the fabrication technology or the type of semiconductor, an FET functions as a voltage-controlled current source.

The operation of transistor amplifiers is illustrated using bipolar-type transistors. To aid in circuit analysis, Figure 3.2c shows the diagram of a commonly used transistor model for an NPN transistor. The base-emitter diode is shown in solid lines in the circuit, while the collector-base diode is shown in dotted lines because generally it can be ignored.

The base-emitter diode does not conduct (there is no transistor base current) until the voltage across it exceeds V_d volts in the forward direction. If the transistor is a silicon transistor, V_d equals 0.7 volt just as with the silicon diode. The collector current I_c is zero until the base-emitter voltage V_{BE} exceeds 0.7 volt. This is called the *cutoff condition*, or the off condition when the transistor is used as a switch.

When V_{BE} rises above 0.7 volt, the diode conducts and allows some base current I_b to flow. The collector current I_c is equal to the base current I_b times the transistor current gain h_{fe}. The current gain (h_{fe}) can range from 10 to 200 depending on the transistor type. It is represented by a current generator in the collector circuit of the model. This condition is called the *active region* because the transistor is on and amplifying. It also is called the *linear region* because collector current is (approximately) linearly proportional to base current. The dotted resistance in parallel with the collector-base diode represents the leakage of the reverse biased junction, which is normally neglected, as discussed previously.

A transistor is saturated when a large increase in the base-to-emitter current results in only a small increase in the collector current.

A third condition known as the *saturation condition* exists under certain conditions of collector-emitter voltage and collector current. In the saturation condition, large increases in the transistor base current produce little increase in collector current. When saturated, the voltage drop across the collector-emitter is very small, usually less than 0.5 volt. This is the on condition for a transistor switching circuit. This condition occurs in a switching circuit when the collector of the transistor is tied through a resistor R_L to a supply voltage V_{cc} as shown in Figure 3.2c. Enough base current is supplied to the transistor to drive the transistor into the saturated condition, in which the output voltage (voltage drop from collector to emitter) is very small and the collector-base diode may become forward biased. Having briefly described the behavior of transistors, it is now possible to discuss circuit applications for them.

TRANSISTOR AMPLIFIERS

In a transistor amplifier, a small change in base current results in a corresponding larger change in collector current.

Figure 3.3 shows a transistor amplifier. The ac voltage source, V_{in}, supplies a signal current to the base-emitter circuit. The transistor is biased to operate in the linear region at some steady state I_b and I_c. The voltage source, V_{cc}, supplies the steady-state base and collector dc currents I_b and I_c, respectively, and any signal current change i_c to the collector-emitter circuit. The small signal voltage V_{in} varies the base current around the steady dc operating point. This small current change is i_b, and it causes a corresponding but larger change in collector current i_c around the steady-state operating current I_c. The small signal current change causes a V_{out} change across the load resistor R_c. The small signal voltage gain of the circuit is as shown in Figure 3.3:

$$A = \frac{V_{out}}{V_{in}} = h_{fe}\frac{R_c}{R_b}$$

This is found by using the model and the equations $V_{out} = i_c R_c$, $i_c = h_{fe} i_b$, and $i_b = V_{in}/R_b$, where h_{fe} is the small signal current gain.

Transistor amplifiers are commonly used in analog circuits, including those in automotive systems.

Circuits such as those depicted in Figure 3.3 are combined to make many types of amplifiers that are used in a variety of applications. Such circuits, especially when made in one package with integrated circuit technology (to be discussed later), are called *linear circuits* or *analog circuits*.

OPERATIONAL AMPLIFIERS

An op amp is a very high-gain differential amplifier.

An operational amplifier (op amp) is another standard building block of integrated circuits and has many applications in analog electronic systems. It is normally connected in a circuit with external circuit elements (e.g., resistors and capacitors) that determine its operation. An op amp typically has a very

**Figure 3.3
Transistor Amplifier
Circuit**

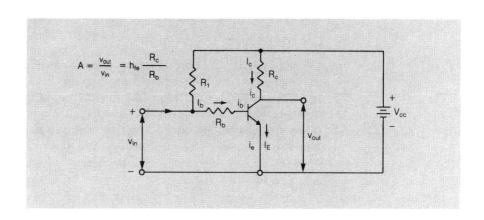

**Figure 3.4
Operational Amplifier
Circuit**

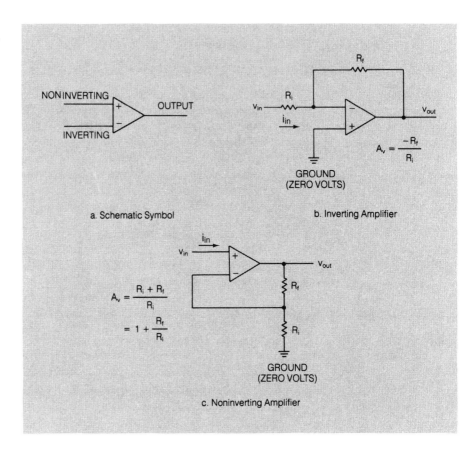

a. Schematic Symbol

b. Inverting Amplifier

c. Noninverting Amplifier

high voltage gain of 10,000 or more and has two inputs and one output (with respect to ground), as shown in Figure 3.4a. A signal applied to the inverting input (−) is amplified and inverted at the output. A signal applied to the noninverting input (+) is amplified but is not inverted at the output.

Use of Feedback in Op Amps

The op amp is normally not operated at maximum gain, but feedback techniques can be used to adjust the gain to the value desired, as shown in Figure 3.4b. Some of the output is connected to the input through circuit elements (resistors, capacitors, etc.) to oppose the input changes. In the example of Figure 3.4b, the feedback path consists of resistor R_f. The gain is adjusted by the ratio of the two resistors and is calculated by the following equation:

$$A_v = -\frac{R_f}{R_i} = \frac{V_{out}}{V_{in}}$$

As indicated by applying the signal to the (–) terminal, the minus sign in the equation means signal inversion from input to output; that is, if the input goes positive, the output goes negative.

Since the op amp amplifies the voltage difference between its two inputs, it can be used as a differential amplifier as well as a single-input amplifier.

It is interesting to consider the inputs to the op amp in the inverting mode configuration (Figure 3.4b). The output voltage v_o is given by

$$v_o = A(v_1 - v_2)$$

where

v_1 is the noninverting input voltage
v_2 is the inverting input voltage

or

$$v_1 - v_2 = \frac{v_o}{A}$$

For an ideal op amp, the open-loop gain should approach infinity. In this case, the input voltages should become equal. That is, $v_1 - v_2 = 0$ for the ideal case, or $v_1 = v_2$.

The inverting amplifier of Figure 3.4b has the noninverting input at ground potential, that is, $v_1 = 0$. Consequently, the inverting input is (ideally) also at ground potential. In fact, the feedback path provides a current that holds the inverting input at so-called virtual ground. Furthermore, as the inverting input is held at ground potential, the input impedance of the op amp circuit of Figure 3.4b presented to input voltage V_{in} is the resistance of R_i:

$$\frac{V_{in}}{i_{in}} = R_i$$

By contrast, the input impedance presented to the input voltage V_{in} by the noninverting op amp configuration (Figure 3.4c) is ideally infinite. This very high input impedance is one of the primary features of the noninverting op amp configuration.

A noninverting amplifier is also possible, as shown in Figure 3.4c. The input signal is connected to the noninverting (+) terminal, and the output is connected through a series connection of resistors to the inverting (–) input terminal. The gain, A_v, in this case is

$$A_v = \frac{V_{out}}{V_{in}} = 1 + \frac{R_f}{R_i}$$

Besides adjusting gain, negative feedback also can help to correct for the amplifier's nonlinear operation and distortion.

Summing Mode Amplifier

One of the important op amp applications is summing of voltages. Figure 3.5 is a schematic drawing of a summing mode op amp circuit. In this circuit, a pair of voltages v_a and v_b (relative to ground) are connected through resistances R to the inverting input. The output voltage v_o is proportional to the sum of the input voltages:

$$v_o = \frac{-R_f(v_a + v_b)}{R}$$

For example, a compatible stereo broadcast system incorporating a right channel and a left channel characterized by voltages v_R and v_L, respectively, transmits the sum v_S of the channel voltages:

$$v_S = v_R + v_L$$

At the same time, the difference voltage v_D is transmitted on a subcarrier:

$$v_D = v_R - v_L$$

The right-channel voltage can be separated from the sum and difference voltages using the circuit of Figure 3.5. Replacing voltages v_a and v_b by v_S and v_D, respectively, yields an output:

$$v_o = \frac{-R_f}{R}(v_R + v_L + v_R - v_L)$$

$$= \left(\frac{-2R_f}{R}\right)v_R$$

Figure 3.5
Summing Amplifier

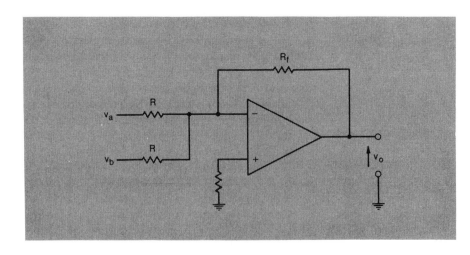

A simple extension of this circuit permits similar separation of the left-channel voltage.

Analog Computers

Analog computers, like those used to simulate the performance of automotive systems, are constructed with operational amplifiers.

The op amp is the basic building block for analog computers. Analog computers are used to simulate the behavior of other systems. Virtually any system that can be described in a block diagram using standard building blocks can be duplicated on an analog computer. If a control system designer is building an automotive speed controller and does not want to waste a lot of time and money testing prototypes on a real car, he or she can program the analog computer to simulate the car's speed electronically. By varying amplifier gains, frequency responses, and resistor, capacitor, and inductor values, system parameters can be varied to study their effect on system performance. Such system studies help to determine the parts needed for a system before any hardware is built.

The main problem with analog circuits and analog computers is that their performance changes with changes in temperature, supply voltage, signal levels, and noise levels. While most of these problems are eliminated when digital circuits are used, analog computers are much more cost effective when dealing with relatively simple systems. However, analog computers have effectively been replaced in all practical applications by a corresponding digital computer.

DIGITAL CIRCUITS

Binary circuits can operate in only one of two states (on or off).

Digital circuits, including digital computers, are formed from binary circuits. Binary digital circuits are circuits whose output can be only one of two different states. Each state is indicated by a particular voltage or current level. An example of a simple binary digital system is a door-open indicator on a car. When a car door is opened, a light comes on. When it is closed, the light goes out. The system's output (the light from the bulb) is either on or off. The on state means the door is open; the off state means it is shut.

Digital circuits also can use transistors. In a digital circuit, a transistor is in either one of two modes of operation: on, conducting at saturation; or off, in the cutoff state.

In electronic digital systems, a transistor is used as a switch. Remember that the transistor has three operating regions: cutoff, active, and saturation. If only the saturation or cutoff regions are used, the transistor acts like a switch. When in saturation, the transistor is on and has very low resistance; when in cutoff, it is off and has very high resistance. In digital circuits, the control input to the transistor switch must be capable of either saturating the transistor or turning it off without allowing operation in the active region. In Figure 3.2c, the on condition is indicated by a very low collector-to-emitter voltage and the off condition by a collector-to-emitter voltage equal to the supply voltage.

Just as a bipolar transistor has three operating modes, the FET transistor has three modes; cutoff, linear, and saturation. The FET can be used as a binary (switching) device by operating in only cutoff or saturation modes. Digital circuits made from FET's are designed so that they are in one of these two states.

Binary Number System

Combinations of digital circuits are capable of representing numbers in a binary number system.

Digital circuits function by representing various quantities numerically using a binary number system. In a binary number system, all numbers are represented using only the symbols 1 (one) and 0 (zero) arranged in the form of a place position number system. Electronically, these symbols can be represented by transistors in either saturation or cutoff. Before proceeding with a discussion of digital circuits, it is instructive to review the binary number system briefly.

The binary number system uses only two digits, 0 or 1, and is called a base 2 system. The decimal system uses 10 digits, 0 through 9, and is called a base 10 system. In the decimal system, numbers are grouped from right to left with the first digit representing the ones place (10^0), the second digit the tens place (10^1), the third digit the hundreds place (10^2), and so on. Each place increases in value by a power of 10.

In the binary system, numbers are also grouped from right to left. The rightmost digit is in the ones place (2^0) and, because only the numbers 0 and 1 can be represented, the second digit must be the twos place (2^1), the third digit the fours place (2^2), the fourth digit the eights place (2^3), and so on. Each place increases in value by a power of 2. Table 3.1 shows a comparison of place values.

Table 3.2 shows the binary equivalent for some decimal numbers. For example, the binary number 0010 is read as "zero, zero, one, zero"—not "ten."

To convert from binary to decimal, just multiply each binary digit by its place value and add the products. For instance, the decimal equivalent of the binary number 1010 is given by

**Table 3.1
Comparison of
Place Values**

	Decimal (Base 10)				Binary (Base 2)				
Place (also called digit position)	4	3	2	1	5	4	3	2	1
Value	1,000	100	10	1	16	8	4	2	1
Power of base	3	2	1	0	4	3	2	1	0

**Table 3.2
Comparison of
Numbers in
Different Bases**

Decimal (Base 10)	Binary (Base 2)
0	0000
1	0001
2	0010
3	0011
4	0100
5	0101
6	0110
7	0111
8	1000
9	1001
10	1010
11	1011
12	1100
13	1101
14	1110
15	1111
16	10000
255	11111111
256	100000000

$$(1010)_2 = (1 \times 8) + (0 \times 4) + (1 \times 2) + (0 \times 1)$$
$$= 8 + 2$$
$$= 10_{10}$$

1010_2 means that the number is a base 2, or binary, number. 10_{10} means the number is a base 10, or decimal, number. Normal notation eliminates the subscripts 2 and 10 if the number system is clear from the context.

Converting from decimal to binary can be accomplished by finding the largest number that is a power of 2 (divisor) that will divide into the decimal number (dividend) with a 1 as a quotient, putting a 1 in its place, and subtracting the divisor (the number used to divide with) from the decimal number (dividend) to get a remainder. The operation is repeated by dividing with the next lower number that is a power of 2 until the binary ones place has been tested. Any time the dividend is less than the divisor, a 0 is put in that place and the next power of 2 divisor is tried. For instance, to find the binary equivalent for the decimal number 73, the largest number that is a power of 2 and that will divide into 73 with a quotient of 1 is 64 (2^6):

$$(2^6) \quad 73/64 \quad = 1 \text{ remainder } (73 - 64) = 9$$
$$(2^5) \quad 9/34 \quad = 0$$
$$(2^4) \quad 9/16 \quad = 0$$
$$(2^3) \quad 9/8 \quad = 1 \text{ remainder } (9 - 8) = 1$$
$$(2^2) \quad 1/4 \quad = 0$$
$$(2^1) \quad 1/2 \quad = 0$$
$$(2^0) \quad 1/1 \quad = 1$$

Therefore,

$$(\text{decimal}) \, 73 = 1001001 \, (\text{binary})$$

LOGIC CIRCUITS (COMBINATORIAL)

Digital computers can perform *b*inary dig*it* (bit) manipulations very easily by using three basic logic circuits or gates: the NOT gate, the AND gate, and the OR gate. Digital gates operate on logical variables that can have one of two possible values (e.g., true/false, saturation/cutoff, or 1/0). As was previously explained, numerical values are represented by combinations of 0 or 1 in a binary number system.

As mentioned earlier, digital circuits operate with transistors in one of two possible states—saturation or cutoff. Since these two states can be used to represent the binary numbers 1 or 0, combinations of transistors that are in one of these two states can be used to represent multiple-digit binary numbers. The input and output voltages for such digital circuits will be either "high" or "low," corresponding to 1 or 0. High voltage means that the voltage exceeds a high threshold value that is denoted V_H. Symbolically, the high-voltage condition corresponding to logical 1 is written

$$V > V_H$$

meaning V exceeds V_H. Similarly, low voltage means that voltage V is given by

$$V < V_L$$

meaning V is less than V_L, where V_L denotes the low threshold value. The actual values for V_H and V_L depend on the technology for implementing the circuit. Typical values are $V_H = 2.4$ volts and $V_L = 0.8$ volt for bipolar transistors.

Digital circuit operation is represented in terms of logical variables that are denoted here with capital letters. For example, in the next few sections A, B, and C represent logical variables that can have a value of either 0 or 1.

NOT Gate

A NOT gate inverts input 1 to 0 and input 0 to 1.

The NOT gate is a logic inverter. If the input is a logical 1, the output is a logical 0. If the input is a logical 0, the output is a logical 1. It changes zeros to ones and ones to zeros. The transistor inverting amplifier of Figure 3.3 performs the same function if operated from cutoff to saturation. A high base voltage (logical 1)[1] produces a low collector voltage (logical 0) and vice versa. Figure 3.6a shows the schematic symbol for a NOT gate. Next to the schematic symbol is what is called a *truth table*. The truth table lists all of the possible combinations of input A and output B for the circuit. The logic symbol is shown also. The logic symbol is read as "NOT A."

AND Gate

An AND gate requires all input signal levels to be high for the output signal to be high.

The AND gate is slightly more complicated. The AND gate has at least two inputs and one output. The one shown in Figure 3.6 has two inputs. The output is high (1) only when both (all) inputs are high (1). If either or both inputs are low (0), the output is low (0). Figure 3.6b shows the truth table, schematic symbol, and logic symbol for this gate. The two inputs are labeled A and B. Notice that there are four combinations of A and B, but only one results in a high output.

OR Gate

The output signal of an OR gate is high when any one of its input signal levels is high.

The OR gate, like the AND gate, has at least two inputs and one output. The one shown in Figure 3.6 has two inputs. The output is high (1) whenever one or both (any) inputs are high (1). The output is low (0) only when both inputs are low (0). Figure 3.6c shows the schematic symbol, logic symbol, and truth table for the OR gate.

NAND and NOR

NAND and NOR gates may be constructed by combining AND, OR, and NOT gates.

Other logic functions can be generated by combining these basic gates. An inverter can be placed after an AND gate to produce a NOT-AND gate. When the inverter is an integral part of the gate, the gate is called a NAND gate. The same can be done with an OR gate; the resultant gate is called a NOR gate. The truth tables and schematic symbols for both of these gates are shown in Figure 3.6. Notice that the NOT function is indicated on the schematic symbol by a small circle at the output of each gate. The small circle is the schematic symbol for NOT, whereas the overbar is the logic symbol for NOT. Notice also that the truth table outputs for the NAND and NOR gates are the reverse of those for the AND and OR gates, respectively. Where C was 1, it is now 0 and vice versa. All of these gates are available in integrated circuit

---

[1] Positive logic defines the most positive voltage as logical 1. Negative logic defines the most positive voltage as logical 0. Positive logic is used throughout this book.

**Figure 3.6
Basic Logic Gates**

Provides output conditions for all combinations of inputs.

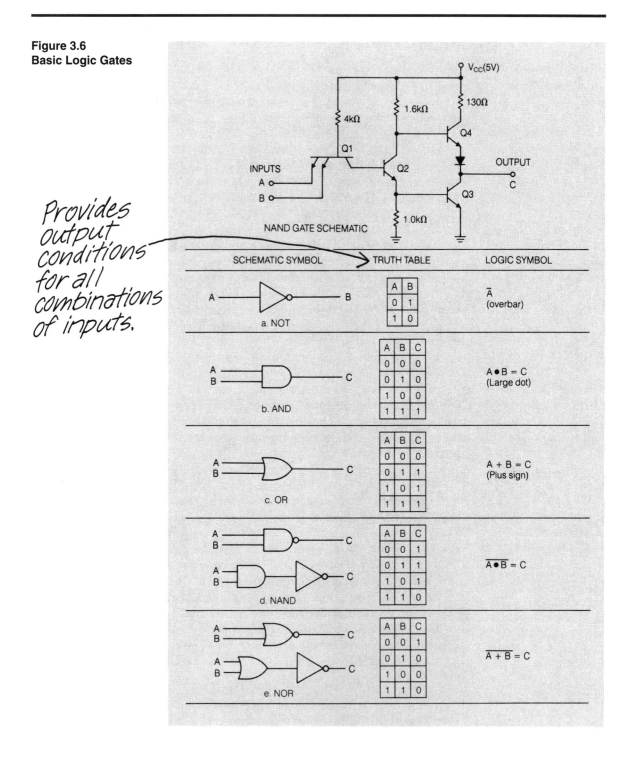

NAND GATE SCHEMATIC

SCHEMATIC SYMBOL	TRUTH TABLE	LOGIC SYMBOL

a. NOT

A	B
0	1
1	0

$\bar{A}$
(overbar)

b. AND

A	B	C
0	0	0
0	1	0
1	0	0
1	1	1

$A \bullet B = C$
(Large dot)

c. OR

A	B	C
0	0	0
0	1	1
1	0	1
1	1	1

$A + B = C$
(Plus sign)

d. NAND

A	B	C
0	0	1
0	1	1
1	0	1
1	1	0

$\overline{A \bullet B} = C$

e. NOR

A	B	C
0	0	1
0	1	0
1	0	0
1	1	0

$\overline{A + B} = C$

form with various quantities of gates in a package and various numbers of inputs per gate.

XOR and Adder Circuits

XOR gates, which output a high only when one or the other input is high, are commonly used to add binary numbers.

Another complex gate performs the exclusive OR function, abbreviated as XOR, illustrated in Figure 3.7a. The output is high only when one input is high, but not when both are high. This gate very commonly is used for comparison of two binary numbers because if both inputs are the same, the output is zero. The equivalent combination of basic gates to perform this function is shown in Figure 3.7a. The XOR gate is also available in an integral package so it is not necessary for the designer to interconnect separate gates in this manner to build the function.

All of these gates can be used to build digital circuits that perform all of the arithmetic functions of a calculator. Table 3.3 shows the addition of two binary bits in all the combinations that can occur. Note that in the case of adding a 1 to a 1, the sum is 0, and a 1, called a *carry*, is placed in the next place value so that it is added with any bits in that place value. A digital circuit designed to perform the addition of two binary bits is called a *half adder* and is shown in Figure 3.7b. It produces the sum and any necessary carry, as shown in the truth table.

A half adder circuit does not have an input to accept a carry from a previous place value. A circuit that does is called a *full adder* (Figure 3.7c). A series of full adder circuits can be combined to add binary numbers with as many digits as desired. A simple electronic calculator performs all arithmetic operations using full adder circuits and a few additional logic circuits. In such circuits, subtraction is performed as a modified form of addition by using some of the additional logic circuits. Multiplication is accomplished by repeated addition, and division is accomplished by repeated subtraction.

Of course, the addition of pairs of 1-bit numbers has no major application in digital computers. On the other hand, the addition of multiple-bit numbers is of crucial importance in digital computers. The 1-bit full adder circuit can be expanded to form a multiple-bit adder circuit. By way of illustration, a 4-bit adder is shown in Figure 3.8. Here the 4-bit numbers in place position notation are given by

Table 3.3
Addition of
Binary Bits

Bit A	0	0	1	1
Bit B	0	1	0	1
Sum	0	1	1	10

Figure 3.7
XOR and Adders

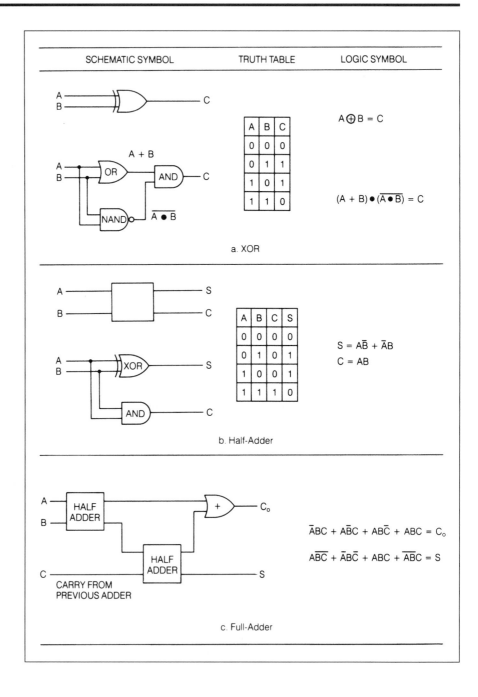

**Figure 3.8
A 4-Bit Digital Adder**

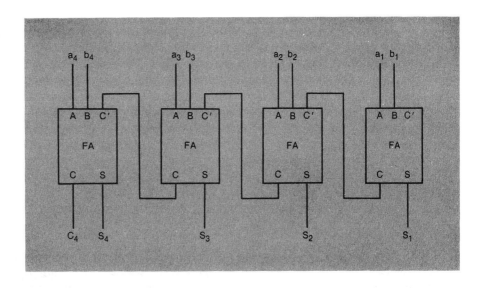

$$A = a_4 a_3 a_2 a_1$$

$$B = b_4 b_3 b_2 b_1$$

where each bit is either 1 or 0. The sum of two 4-bit numbers has a 5-bit result, where the fifth bit is the carry from the sum of the most significant bits. Each block labeled FA is a full adder. The carry out (C) from a given FA is the carry in (C') of the next-highest full adder. The sum S is denoted (in place position binary notation) by

$$S = C_4 S_4 S_3 S_2 S_1$$

LOGIC CIRCUITS WITH MEMORY (SEQUENTIAL)

Sequential logic circuits have the ability to store, or remember, previous logic states. Sequential logic circuits are the basis of computer memories.

The logic circuits discussed so far have been simple interconnections of the three basic gates NOT, AND, and OR. The output of each system is determined only by the inputs present at that time. These circuits are called *combinatorial logic* circuits. There is another type of logic circuit that has a memory of previous inputs or past logic states. This type of logic circuit is called a sequential logic circuit because the sequence of past input values and the logic states at those times determine the present output state. Because *sequential logic* circuits hold or store information even after inputs are removed, they are the basis of semiconductor computer memories.

R-S Flip-Flop

An R-S flip-flop circuit can be set into either state. It will remain latched in that state until it is set to the opposite state by the presence of opposing logic signals on its two inputs.

A very simple memory circuit can be made by interconnecting two NAND gates, as in Figure 3.9a. A careful study of the circuit reveals that when S is high (1) and R is low (0), the output Q is set high and remains high regardless of whether S is high or low at any later time. The high state of S is said to be *latched into* the state of Q. The only way Q can be unlatched to go low is to let R go high and S go low. This resets the latch. This type of memory device is called a *Reset-Set* (R-S) *flip-flop* and is the basic building block of sequential logic circuits. The term "flip-flop" describes the action of the logic level changes at Q. Notice from the truth table that R and S must not be 1 at the same time. Under this condition, the two gates are bucking each other and the final state of the flip-flop output is uncertain.

J-K Flip-Flop

The J-K flip-flop circuit is superior to the R-S flip-flop circuit because it resolves ambiguities resulting from simultaneous inputs.

A flip-flop where the uncertain state of simultaneous inputs on R and S is solved is shown in Figure 3.9b. It is called a *J-K flip-flop* and can be obtained from an R-S flip-flop by adding additional logic gating, as shown in the logic diagram. When both J and K inputs are 1, the flip-flop changes to a state other than the one it was in. The flip-flop shown in this case is a synchronized one. That means it changes state at a particular time determined by a timing pulse, called the *clock*, being applied to the circuit at the terminal marked by a triangle. The little circle at the clock terminal means the circuit responds when the clock goes from a high level to a low level. If the circle is not present, the circuit responds when the clock goes from a low level to a high level.

Synchronous Counter

Figure 3.10 shows a four-stage synchronous counter. It is synchronous because all stages are triggered at the same time by the same clock pulse. It has four stages; therefore, it counts 2^4 or 16 clock pulses before it returns to a starting state. The timed waveforms appearing at each Q output are also shown. It is easy to see how such circuitry can be used for counting, for generating other timing pulses, and for determining timed sequences. One can easily visualize how such stages can be lined up to store the digits of a binary number. If the storage is temporary, then such a combination of stages is called a *register*. If storage is to be more permanent, it is called *memory*.

Digital counter circuits can easily be arranged to develop circuits that are used in digital clocks.

Digital clocks, as well as circuits that convert binary numbers to decimal numbers so they can be displayed and read by humans, are made up of many stages of such counting circuits.

To review what has been discussed about digital circuits:

1. They operate with signals at discrete levels rather than with signals whose level varies continuously.
2. High and low voltage levels are commonly used to represent the binary numbers 1 and 0, respectively.

**Figure 3.9
Flip-Flops**

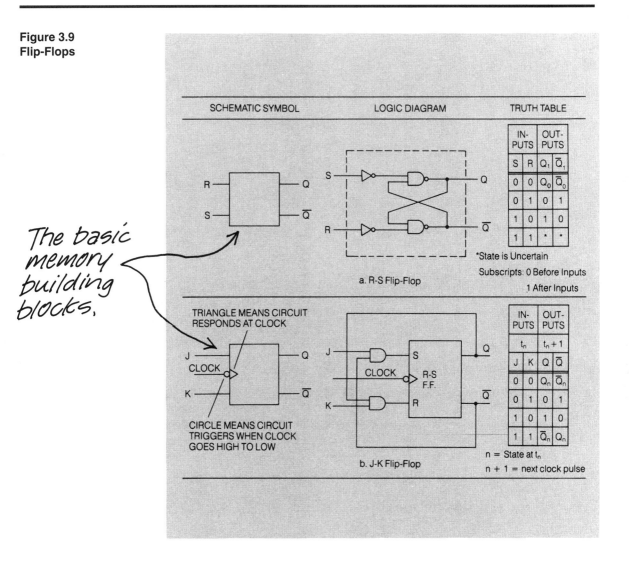

The basic memory building blocks.

SCHEMATIC SYMBOL · LOGIC DIAGRAM · TRUTH TABLE

a. R-S Flip-Flop

*State is Uncertain

Subscripts: 0 Before Inputs
1 After Inputs

IN-PUTS		OUT-PUTS	
S	R	Q_1	$\overline{Q}_1$
0	0	Q_0	$\overline{Q}_0$
0	1	0	1
1	0	1	0
1	1	*	*

TRIANGLE MEANS CIRCUIT RESPONDS AT CLOCK

CIRCLE MEANS CIRCUIT TRIGGERS WHEN CLOCK GOES HIGH TO LOW

b. J-K Flip-Flop

n = State at t_n
$n + 1$ = next clock pulse

IN-PUTS		OUT-PUTS	
t_n		$t_n + 1$	
J	K	Q	$\overline{Q}$
0	0	Q_n	$\overline{Q}_n$
0	1	0	1
1	0	1	0
1	1	$\overline{Q}_n$	Q_n

3. Combinations of ones and zeros can be used as codes to represent numbers, letters, symbols, conditions, and so forth.

4. Circuits called gates (Figures 3.6 and 3.7) can be combined to make logical decisions.

5. Circuits called flip-flops (Figure 3.9) can be used to store ones and zeros. They can be set or reset into particular binary sequences to produce or store digital information, to count, or to produce timed digital signals.

6. Transistors are used in the on and off condition in circuits to form gates and flip-flops.

**Figure 3.10
A Four-Stage
Synchronous Counter**

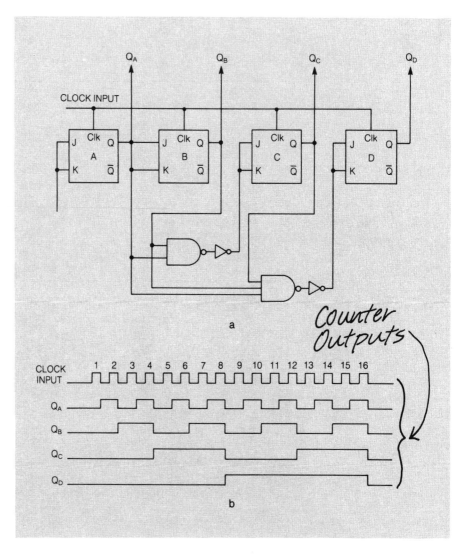

a

b

Integrated circuits are ideal for digital circuits because the digital circuits consist of many interconnected identical gates.

Digital electronic systems send and receive signals made up of ones and zeros in the form of codes. The digital codes represent the information that is moved through the digital systems by the digital circuits. Digital systems are made up of many *identical* logic gates and flip-flops interconnected to do the function required of the system. As a result, digital circuits are ideal for implementation in integrated circuits (ICs) because all components can be made at the same time on a small silicon area.

INTEGRATED CIRCUITS

By using integrated circuit technology, all of the counters, registers, and binary-to-decimal converters are produced at the same time on a tiny piece of silicon semiconductor material by the techniques of photolithography (photographic printing) and diffusion (modifying one material by combining it with another using high temperature). This is the heart of integrated circuit technology. The results are very small, high-performance circuits that use very low power and have a high reliability.

The earliest ICs appeared about 1960 and had relatively few gates, typically on the order of 10 to 12. Those devices were known as small-scale integration (SSI) integrated circuits. By 1970, medium-scale integration (MSI) ICs were available; they had on the order of 1,000 gates. The evolution of technology continued through phases of large-scale integration (LSI) ICs to very large scale integration (VLSI) ICs that had 5,000 or more gates.

One of the important consequences of IC technological progress has been that digital circuits have become available (in IC form) as electronic systems or subsystems. That is, the functional capability of digital circuits in single IC packages, or chips, has spectacularly increased in the past 30 years. One of the important digital systems that is available as an LSI IC is the arithmetic and logic unit (ALU).

Figure 3.11 is a sketch of a typical ALU showing the various connections. This 4-bit ALU has the capability of performing 16 possible logical or arithmetic operations on two 4-bit inputs, A and B.

Digital circuits are now available as electronic systems or subsystems packaged as ICs.

**Figure 3.11
ALU Circuit
Configuration**

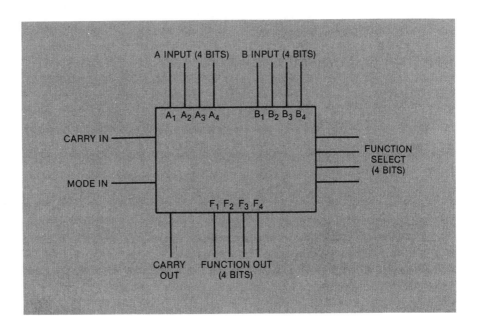

**Table 3.4
Arithmetic
Logic Functions**

Select S Input	Logic Function, $M = 1$	Arithmetic Function, $M = 0$	
		$C_n = 1$	$C_n = 0$
0000	$F = \bar{A}$ (NOT)	$F = A$	$F = A$ Plus 1
0001	$F = \overline{A + B}$ (NOR)	$F = A + B$	$F = (A + B)$ Plus 1
0010	$F = \bar{A}B$	$F = A + \bar{B}$	$F = (A + \bar{B})$ Plus 1
0011	$F = 0$	$F = $ Minus 1 (2's Complement)	$F = 0$
0100	$F = \overline{AB}$ (NAND)	$F = A + A\bar{B}$	$F = (A + A\bar{B})$ Plus 1
0101	$F = \bar{B}$ (NOT)	$F = (A + B)$ Plus $A\bar{B}$	$F = (A = B)$ Plus $A\bar{B} + 1$
0110	$F = AB + B\bar{A}$ (Exclusive OR)	$F = (A - B)$ Minus 1	$F = A$ Minus B
0111	$F = A\bar{B}$	$F = A\bar{B}$ Minus 1	$F = A\bar{B}$
1000	$F = \bar{A} + B$ (Implication)	$F = A + AB$	$F = (A + B)$ Plus 1
1001	$F = \bar{A}B + AB$ (NOT exclusive OR)	$F = A + B$	$F = (A + B)$ Plus 1
1010	$F = B$	$F = (A + \bar{B})$ Plus AB	$F = (A + \bar{B})$ Plus $A + 1$
1011	$F = AB$ (AND)	$F = AB$ Minus 1	$F = AB$
1100	$F = 1$	$F = A$ Plus A*	$F = (A + A)$ Plus 1
1101	$F = A + \bar{B}$	$F = (A + B)$ Plus A	$F = (A + B)$ Plus $A + 1$
1110	$F = A + B$ (OR)	$F = (A + \bar{B})$ Plus A	$F = (A + \bar{B})$ Plus $A + 1$
1111	$F = A$	$F = A$ Minus 1	$F = A$

*Each bit is shifted to the next more significant position.

Table 3.4 summarizes these various operations using the logical notation explained earlier in this chapter.

The Microprocessor

Perhaps the single most important digital IC to evolve has been the microprocessor (MPU). This important device, incorporating hundreds of thousands of gates in an area of about 1/4-inch square, has truly revolutionized digital electronic system development. A microprocessor is the operational core of a microcomputer and has broad application in automotive electronic systems.

The MPU incorporates a relatively complicated combination of digital circuits including an ALU, registers, and decoding logic. A typical MPU block diagram is shown in Figure 3.12. The double lines labeled "bus" are actually sets of conductors for carrying digital data throughout the MPU. Common IC MPUs use 8, 16, or 32 conductor buses.

Early twenty-first-century automobiles incorporate dozens of microprocessors that are applied for a variety of uses from advanced powertrain control to simple tasks like automatic seat and sideview mirror positioning.

A microprocessor by itself can accomplish nothing. It requires additional external digital circuitry as explained in the next chapter. One of the tasks performed by the external circuitry is to provide instructions in the form of digitally encoded electrical signals. By way of illustration, an 8-bit microprocessor operates with 8-bit instructions. There are 2^8 (or 256) possible logical combinations of 8 bits, corresponding to 256 possible MPU instructions, each causing a specific operation. A complete summary of these operations and the corresponding instructions (called microinstructions) is beyond the scope of this book. A few of the more important instructions are explained in the next chapter, which further expands the discussion of this important device. An advanced automotive microprocessor is typically at least a 32-bit device.

The microprocessor in combination with memory and other circuits under program control can accomplish very complex tasks.

Figure 3.12
MPU Block Diagram

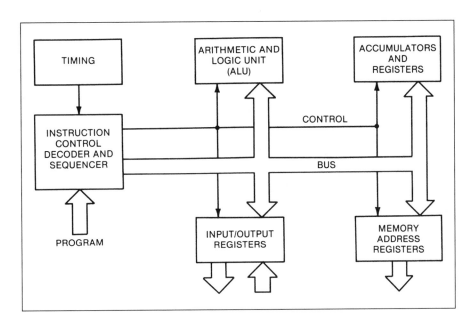

Quiz for Chapter 3

1. Forward conventional current flows in a diode circuit from
   a. anode to cathode
   b. anode to anode
   c. cathode to anode
   d. cathode to cathode

2. Forward conventional current for a PNP transistor flows from
   a. base to ground
   b. base to emitter
   c. emitter to base
   d. collector to base

3. The op amp is what type of circuit?
   a. digital
   d. analog
   c. logic gate
   d. none of the above

4. The AND gate is what type of circuit?
   a. digital
   b. analog
   c. amplifier
   d. inverter

5. Which conditions cause the output of an XOR gate to be high?
   a. both inputs are low
   b. both inputs are high
   c. either input is high but not both
   d. both inputs are zero

6. An R-S latch is what type of digital logic?
   a. combinational logic
   d. sequential logic
   c. Fortran
   d. J-K

7. Flip-flops are used in what type of logic systems?
   a. memories
   b. counters
   c. data registers
   d. all of the above

8. Integrated circuits are used in automotive electronic systems because they have excellent functional performance
   a. high reliability
   b. small size
   c. low cost
   d. all of the above

9. Digital circuits operate with voltages representing
   a. an analog of a physical quantity being measured
   b. the electrical equivalent of 1 or 0
   c. proportional currents
   d. none of the above

10. A half adder circuit can be made from
    a. an operational amplifier
    b. three NOT gates
    c. two OR gates
    d. an XOR gate in combination with an AND gate

11. A full adder can be made from
    a. a half adder with carry in
    b. two half adder circuits with carry in
    c. an R-S flip-flop
    d. all of the above

12. Which of the following devices require the use of semiconductors?
  a. transistors
  b. diodes
  c. integrated circuits
  d. all of the above

13. In which of the following circuits is a diode used?
  a. filter
  b. rectifier
  c. resistor
  d. capacitor

14. What device is used to smooth out the bumpy output of the rectifier circuit?
  a. capacitor
  b. resistor
  c. diode
  d. transistor

15. In which type of circuit are transistors used?
  a. amplifiers
  b. op amps
  c. logic gates
  d. all of the above

16. Which of the following conditions cause the output of an OR gate to be low?
  a. both inputs are high
  b. only one input is high
  c. both inputs are low

17. Which of the following conditions cause the outputs of an AND gate to be high?
  a. both inputs are low
  b. both inputs are high
  c. one input is low
  d. at least one input is low

18. What decimal number does the binary number 0110 represent?
  a. 4
  b. 3
  c. 110
  d. 6

19. What binary number does the decimal number 10 represent?
  a. 0010
  b. 0101
  c. 1010
  d. 1000

20. The binary addition of 0110 and 0010 produces what binary sum?
  a. 1000
  b. 0111
  c. 1111
  d. 1010

Microcomputer Instrumentation and Control

This chapter explains microcomputers and how they are used in instrumentation and control systems. Topics include microcomputer fundamentals, microcomputer equipment, microcomputer inputs and outputs, computerized instrumentation, and computerized control systems. The specific automotive applications of microcomputers are explained in later chapters.

MICROCOMPUTER FUNDAMENTALS

Digital versus Analog Computers

A digital computer represents each variable in terms of binary numbers.

In digital computer-based systems, physical variables are represented by a numerical equivalent using a form of the binary (base 2) number system. In the previous chapter it was shown that transistor circuits can be constructed to have one of two stable states: saturation and cutoff. These two states can be used to represent a 0 (zero) or a 1 (one) in a binary number system. To be practically useful, there must be groups of such circuits that are arranged in the form of a place position, binary number system.

By contrast, an analog system has a single lead with a voltage (relative to ground) that is proportional to the relevant physical variable. A digital system will have a group of leads, each one of which can have only two voltage levels representing 0 or 1 (as discussed in Chapter 3). It is common practice for a digital computer to have the number of voltages representing the binary digits (bits) be a multiple of 8. For example, early automotive engine control computers used 8 bits to represent data, which means that 256 (2^8) possible levels can be represented. In early twenty-first-century automotive electronic controls, 32-bit systems are commonplace.

As will be shown in subsequent chapters, digital automotive electronic systems are implemented with microprocessors in combination with other components to form a type of special-purpose digital computer or a form of digital controller having a structure very much like a computer. The later discussion of automotive digital systems can perhaps be best understood following a brief discussion of digital computer technology. In any application, including automotive, a computer performs various operations on the data. To explain the operation of a digital computer, it is helpful to first explain the operation of its various components.

Figure 4.1
Basic Computer Block
Diagram

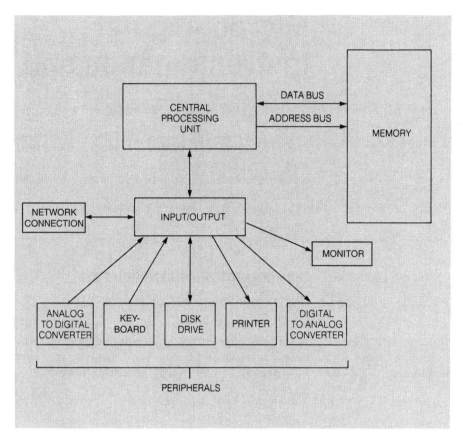

Parts of a Computer

A few of the parts of a digital computer are shown in Figure 4.1. This figure is presented only as an illustration of a representative digital computer. The actual configuration of any given computer such as might be used in an automotive application is determined by the specific tasks it is to perform. For example, an engine control computer (as described in Chapter 7) would not include disk drive, keyboard, printer, or monitor.

The *central processing unit* (CPU) is the processor that is the heart of the system. When made in an integrated circuit, it is called a microprocessor. This is where all of the arithmetic and logic decisions are made and is the calculator part of the computer. Automotive digital computers are implemented with one or more microprocessors. A more detailed description of a microprocessor is given later in this chapter.

A digital computer consists of a CPU to process information, a memory to store information, and input/output sections to communicate with the user.

The *memory* holds the program and data. The computer can change the information in memory by writing new information into memory, or it can obtain information contained in memory by reading the information from memory. Each memory location has a unique address that the CPU uses to find the information it needs.

Information (or data) must be put into the computer in a form that the computer can read, and the computer must present an output in a form that can be read by humans or used by other computers or digital systems. The input and output devices, called I/O, perform these conversions. Peripherals are devices such as keyboards, monitors, magnetic tape units, magnetic disk units, modems, and printers. The arrows on the interconnection lines in Figure 4.1 indicate the flow of data.

Microcomputers versus Mainframe Computers

Microcomputers cost less and occupy less space than the mainframe computers commonly used by governments and large businesses. However, microcomputers operate more slowly and are less accurate in mathematical operations.

With this general idea of what a computer is, it is instructive to compare a general-purpose mainframe computer and a microcomputer. A microcomputer is just a small computer, typically thousands of times smaller than the large, general-purpose mainframe computers used by banks and large corporations. At the upper end of the spectrum of computers are the very large scientific computers, many of which are made up of large numbers of computers operating in parallel. These large computers perform floating point operations (FLOPS) at something of the order of a million-billion FLOPS. On the other hand, a typical automotive digital system is of the scale of a microcomputer. Depending on feature content, a typical automobile will incorporate dozens of microcomputers. Microcomputers cost much less than mainframes, and their computing power and speed are only a fraction of those of a mainframe. A typical mainframe computer costs from tens of thousands of dollars to millions of dollars and is capable of billions of arithmetic operations per second (additions, subtractions, multiplications, and divisions). A microcomputer costs from a little less than $1,000 to a few thousand dollars and can perform several million operations per second. More important for mathematical calculations than the speed of the operation is the accuracy of the operation.

The precision and accuracy of calculations performed by a digital computer are functions of the number of bits used to represent numerical values: In order to give a numerical frame of reference, recall that an 8-bit binary number can represent 256 decimal numbers. If (as in the case of many automotive digital systems) the number is to have a sign (i.e., + or −), then only numbers from −127 to 128 can be so represented. The evolution in size and complexity has led to 32-bit computer systems. The number of signed decimal values that can be represented by an N-bit binary number is 2 to the power N–1.

Programs

A program is a set of
steps (instructions) in a
logical order. The
computer follows these
steps to perform a given
task.

A *program* is a set of instructions organized into a particular sequence to do a particular task. The first computers were little more than fancy calculators. They did only simple arithmetic and made logic decisions. They were programmed (given instructions) by punching special codes into a paper tape that was then read by the machine and interpreted as instructions. A program containing thousands of instructions running on an early model machine might require yards of paper tape. The computer would process the program by reading an instruction from the tape, performing the instruction, reading another instruction from the tape, performing the instruction, and so on until the end of the program. Reading paper tape was a slow process compared with the speed with which a modern computer can perform requested functions. In addition, the tape had to be fed through the computer each time the program was run, which was cumbersome and allowed for the possibility of the tape wearing and breaking.

To minimize the use of paper tape, and to increase computational efficiency, a method was invented to store programs inside the computer. The program is read into a large electronic memory made out of thousands of data latches (flip-flops), one for each bit, that provide locations in which to store program instructions and data. Each instruction is converted to binary numbers with a definite number of bits and stored in a memory location. Each memory location has an address number associated with it like a post office box. In fact, one could think of the computer memory bank as a large bank of post office boxes. The computer reads the binary number (instruction or data) stored in each memory location by going to the address (box number) of the information it wants to read. When the address for a particular memory location is generated, a *copy* of its information is transferred to the computer. (Note that the original information stays in its location in memory while the memory is being read.)

All modern electronic
computers have the
ability to store a
program in internal
memory and use it over
and over to accomplish
tasks.

Storing a computer program inside the computer's memory is what separates a real computer from a fancy calculator. The computer can use some of its memory for storing programs (instructions) and other memory for storing data. The program or data can be easily changed simply by loading in a different program or different data. The stored program concept is fundamental to all modern electronic computers.

MICROCOMPUTER TASKS

A microcomputer-based
engine control system
has much greater
flexibility than the early
systems which were
partly analog.

A suitably configured microcomputer can potentially perform any control or instrumentation task. For example, it will be shown in a later chapter that a microcomputer can be configured to control fuel metering and ignition for an engine. The microcomputer-based engine control system has much greater flexibility than the earliest electronic engine control systems, which, typically, used elementary logic circuits as well as analog circuits. For these early systems, changes in the performance of the control system required changes in the circuitry. With a microcomputer performing the logic functions, most changes can be made simply by reprogramming the computer. That is, the software (program) is changed rather than the hardware (logic circuits). This makes the microcomputer a very attractive building block in any digital system.

Microcomputers can also be used to replace analog circuitry. Special interface circuits can be used to enable a digital computer to input and output analog signals (this will be discussed later). The important point here is that microcomputers are excellent alternatives to hardwired (dedicated) logic and analog circuitry that is interconnected to satisfy a particular design.

In the subsequent portions of this chapter, both the computer hardware configuration and programs (software) are discussed. Because these two aspects of computers are so strongly interrelated, it is necessary for the following discussion to switch back and forth between the two.

In a modern personal computer, the program instructions and data are stored electronically in register-type circuits as described in Chapter 3. Recall that it was shown there that a register circuit consists of a sequence of flip-flop (or similar) binary circuits. Modern register-type circuits are extremely fast circuits having the capability of storing data that can be inserted or retrieved in a small fraction of a microsecond during the execution of a program. In addition, programs and data can be stored indefinitely via magnetic or optical disk media.

MICROCOMPUTER OPERATIONS

A microcomputer stores information on a temporary basis within the CPU registers. Information is transferred between the CPU registers and the memory or input/output sections by means of one or more sets of multiple wires; each set is called a *bus*.

Recall the basic computer block diagram of Figure 4.1. The central processing unit (CPU) requests information from memory (or from an input device) by generating the address for the data in memory. The address with all its bits is stored in the CPU as a binary number in a temporary data latch type memory called a *register* (see Chapter 3). The outputs of the register are sent at the same time over multiple wires to the computer memory and peripherals.

Buses

As shown in Figure 4.2, the group of wires that carries the address is called the address bus. (The word *bus* refers to one or more wires that is a common path to and from various components in the computer.) The address register used in many microcomputers holds 32 bits; these bits enable the CPU to access 2^{32} memory locations. In a microcomputer, each memory location usually contains multiples of 8 bits of data. A group of 8 bits is called a *byte* and a group of 16 bits is sometimes called a *word*.

Information is sent to or received from memory locations and input/output devices via the bidirectional data bus.

Data is sent to the CPU over a data bus (Figure 4.2). The data bus is slightly different from the address bus in that the CPU uses it to *read* information from memory or peripherals, and to *write* information to memory or peripherals. Signals on the address bus originate only at the CPU and are sent to devices attached to the bus. Signals on the data bus can either be inputs

Figure 4.2
Buses and Registers

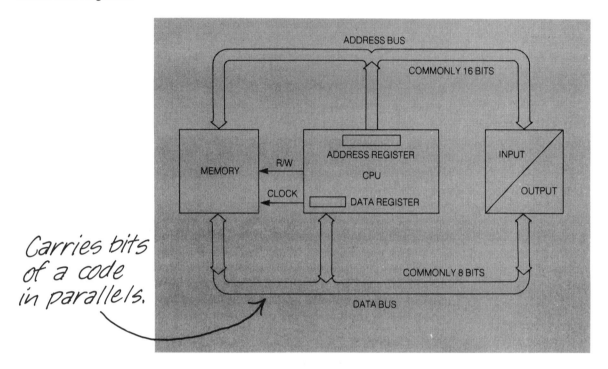

*Carries bits
of a code
in parallels.*

to or outputs from the CPU that are sent or received at the CPU by the data register. In other words, the data bus is a two-way street while the address bus is a one-way street. Another difference is that the data bus in many microcomputers might be only 16 bits wide whereas the address bus might be 32 bits wide. In addition to the address and data bus, there are sets of connections that are called the control bus. It is this control bus that sends the binary signals to the components involved in any operation at the appropriate time to cause them to perform the specific operation.

Memory Read/Write

The CPU always controls the direction of data flow on the data bus because, although it is bidirectional, data can move in only one direction at a time. The CPU provides a special read/write control signal (Figure 4.2) that tells the memory in which direction the data should flow. For example, when the read/write (R/W) line is high, the CPU reads information into a memory location.

During a memory read operation, the CPU changes the state of the read/write line and puts the appropriate address on the address bus. This causes the contents of the addressed memory location to be placed on the data bus, where they can be read by the CPU.

The timing diagram for a memory read operation is shown in Figure 4.3. Suppose the computer has been given the instruction to read data from memory location number 10. To perform the read operation, the CPU raises the R/W line to the high level to tell the memory to prepare for a read operation. Almost simultaneously, the address for location 10 is placed on the address bus ("address valid" in Figure 4.3). The number 10 in binary (0000 0000 0000 1010) is sent to the memory in the address bus. The binary electrical signals corresponding to 10 operate the specific circuits in the memory to cause the binary data at that location to be placed on the data bus. The CPU has an internal register that is activated during this read operation to receive and store the data. The data are then processed by the CPU during the next cycle of operation according to the relevant instruction.

Timing

Microcomputers use a timing signal, called a *clock*, to determine when data should be written to or read from memory.

A certain amount of time is required for the memory's address decoder to decode which memory location is called for by the address, and also for the selected memory location to transfer its information to the data bus. To allow time for this decoding, the processor waits a while before receiving the information requested from the data bus. Then, at the proper time, the CPU opens the logic gating circuitry between the data bus and the CPU data register so that the information on the bus from memory location 10 is latched into the CPU. During the memory read operation, the memory has temporary control of the data bus. Control must be returned to the CPU, but not before the processor has read in the data. The CPU provides a timing control signal, called the *clock*, that tells the memory when it can take and release control of the data bus.

Refer again to Figure 4.3. Notice that the read cycle is terminated when the clock goes from high to low during the time that the read signal is valid. This is the signal the CPU uses to tell the memory that it has read the data and the data bus can be released. The timing for a memory write operation is very similar to the memory read operation except that the R/W line is low instead of high.

The bus timing signals are very important to the reliable operation of the computer. However, they are built into the design of the machine and, therefore, are under machine control. As long as the machine performs the read and write operations correctly, the programmer can completely ignore the details of the bus timing signals and concentrate on the logic of the program.

Addressing Peripherals

In memory-mapped input/output a peripheral device is treated like a memory location by the CPU.

The reason for distinguishing between memory locations and peripherals is that they perform different functions. Memory is a data storage device, while peripherals are input/output devices. However, many microcomputers address memory and peripherals in the same way because they use a design called memory-mapped I/O (input/output). With this design, peripherals, such as

Figure 4.3
Timing Diagram for Memory Read

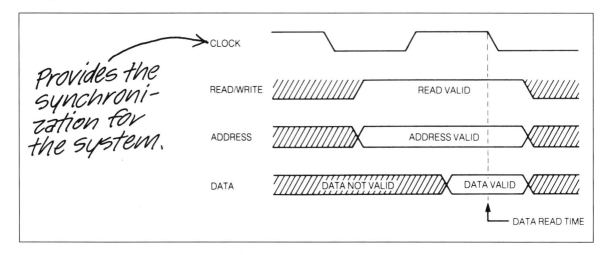

Provides the synchronization for the system.

data terminals, are equivalent to memory to the CPU so that sending data to a peripheral is as simple as writing data to a memory location. In systems where this type of microcomputer has replaced some digital logic, the digital inputs enter the computer through a designated memory slot. If outputs are required, they exit the computer through another designated memory slot.

CPU REGISTERS

The programmer (the person who writes the sequences of instructions for a particular task) uses a different model (a programming model) of the microprocessor used in a system than does the hardware designer. This model shows the programmer which registers in the CPU are available for program use, and what function the registers perform. By way of illustration Figure 4.4 shows a programming model microprocessor for a typical 8-bit (now obsolete) microcomputer. The computer has two 8-bit registers and three 16-bit registers. The 16-bit registers are discussed later; the 8-bit registers are discussed here.

Accumulator Register

The accumulator register, also called the A register, is used for arithmetic and logical operations.

One of the 8-bit registers is an *accumulator*, a general-purpose register that is used for arithmetic and logical operations. The accumulator can be loaded with data from a memory location, or its data can be stored in a memory location. The number held in the accumulator can be added to, subtracted from, or compared with another number from memory. The accumulator is the basic work register of a computer. It is commonly called the *A register*.

**Figure 4.4
Registers Available
in a Typical
Microcomputer**

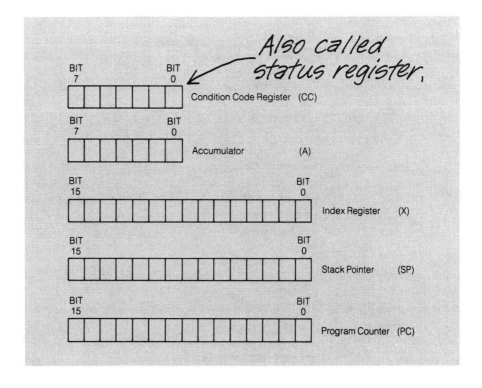

Condition Code Register

The condition code register, also called the *status register*, indicates certain conditions that take place during various accumulator operations.

The other 8-bit register, the *condition code* (CC) *register* (also called *status register*), indicates or flags certain conditions that occur during accumulator operations. Rules are established in the design of the microprocessor so that a 1 or 0 in the bit position of the CC register represents specific conditions that have happened in the last operation of the accumulator. The bit positions and rules are shown in Figure 4.5a. One bit of the CC register indicates that the A register is all zeros. Another bit, the carry bit, indicates that the last operation performed on the accumulator caused a carry to occur. The carry bit acts like the ninth bit of the accumulator. Notice what happens when we add 1 to 255 in binary:

Decimal	Binary	
255	input	11111111
+1	add +	1
256	sum	00000000
	carry	1

The condition code register can indicate if the value contained in the accumulator is negative. This gives the CPU the ability to represent a much wider range of numbers.

The eight bits in the accumulator are all zeros, but the carry bit being set to a 1 (high) indicates that the result is actually not 0, but 256. Such a condition can be checked by examining the CC register carry bit for a 1.

The condition code register also provides a flag that, when set to a 1, indicates that the number in the accumulator is negative. Most microcomputers use a binary format called *two's complement notation* for doing arithmetic. In two's complement notation, the leftmost bit indicates the sign of the number. Since one of the 8 bits is used for the sign, 7 bits (or 15 if 16 bits are used) remain to represent the magnitude of the number. The largest positive number that can be represented in two's complement with 8 bits is +127 (or +32,767 for 16 bits); the largest negative number is −128 (−32,768). Since the example accumulator is only 8 bits wide, it can handle only 1 byte at a time. However, by combining bytes and operating on them one after another in time sequence (as is done for 16-bit arithmetic), the computer can handle very large numbers or can obtain increased accuracy in calculations. Handling bits or bytes one after another in time sequence is called *serial operation*.

Branching

Instructions that direct the microcomputer to other parts of the program are called *branches*. Branches may be conditional or unconditional.

The CC register provides programmers with status indicators (the flags) that enable them to monitor what happens to the data as the program executes the instructions. The microcomputer has special instructions that allow it to go to a different part of the program. Bits of the CC register are labeled in Figure 4.5a. Typical branch-type instructions are shown in Figure 4.5b.

Program branches are either conditional or unconditional. Eight of the nine branch instructions listed in Figure 4.5b are conditional branches. That is to say, the branch is taken only if certain conditions are met. These conditions are indicated by the CC register bit as shown. The branch-always instruction is the only unconditional branch. Such a branch is used to branch around the next instruction to a later instruction or to return to an earlier instruction. Another type of branch instruction that takes the computer out of its normal program sequence is indicated for the I bit of the CC register. It is associated with an interrupt. An interrupt is a request, usually from an input or output (I/O) peripheral, that the CPU stop what it is doing and accept or take care of (service) the special request. There will be more about interrupts later in this chapter.

Microprocessor Architecture

The central component that controls and performs all operations in any microcomputer is the microprocessor, which is made up of many electronic subsystems all implemented in a single integrated circuit. As described in Chapter 3, a microprocessor consists of hundreds of thousands of transistors (on a single silicon chip) that are grouped together and interconnected to form the various subsystems, all of which are interconnected with internal address, data, and control buses.

**Figure 4.5
Use of the CC
Register**

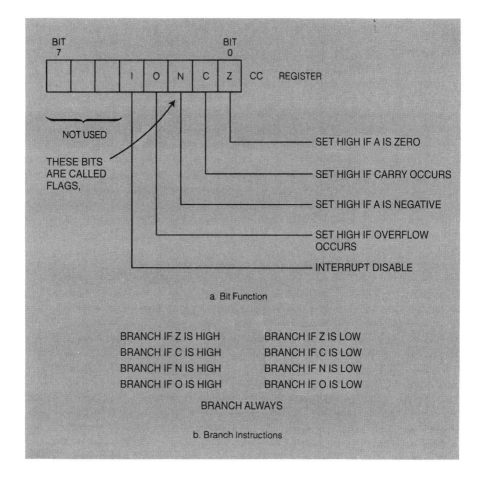

a. Bit Function

BRANCH IF Z IS HIGH   BRANCH IF Z IS LOW
BRANCH IF C IS HIGH   BRANCH IF C IS LOW
BRANCH IF N IS HIGH   BRANCH IF N IS LOW
BRANCH IF O IS HIGH   BRANCH IF O IS LOW

BRANCH ALWAYS

b. Branch Instructions

Figure 4.6 is a block diagram of a typical commercial microprocessor such as would be used in an automotive digital electronic system. The silicon chip on which the microprocessor is fabricated is mounted in a housing (usually a plastic structure) and connected to external pins that enable the microprocessor to be connected to the microcomputer. The connections to the external circuitry are depicted and labeled in Figure 4.6 and include address and data buses. In addition, external connections are made to an oscillator (clock) as well as inputs and outputs: interrupt, ready (rdy), read/write control (R/W), and data bus enable (DBE), the operation of which is explained later in this chapter.

This block diagram is divided into two main portions—a register section and a control section. The actual operations performed by the microprocessor are accomplished in the register section. The specific operations performed

**Figure 4.6
Typical
Microprocessor
Internal Architecture**

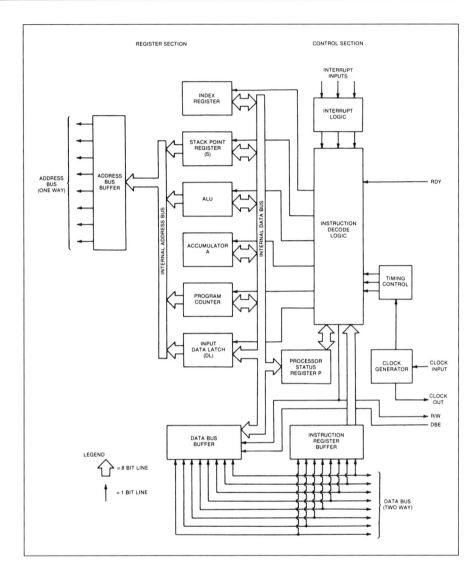

during the execution of a given step in the program are controlled by electrical signals from the instruction decoder.

During each program step, an instruction in the form of an 8 or more bit binary number is transferred from memory to the instruction register. This instruction is decoded using logic circuits similar to those presented in Chapter 3. The result of this decoding process is a set of electrical control signals that are sent to the specific components of the register section that are involved in the instruction being executed.

The data upon which the operation is performed are similarly transferred from memory to the data bus buffer. From this buffer the data are then transferred to the desired component in the register section for execution of the operation.

Note that an arithmetic and logic unit (ALU) is included in the register section of the typical microprocessor as shown in Figure 4.6. This device is a complex circuit capable of performing the arithmetic and logical operations, as explained in Chapter 3. Also included in the register section is the accumulator, which is the register used most frequently to receive the results of arithmetic or logical operation. In addition, the example microprocessor register section has an index register, stack pointer register, and program counter register. The program counter register holds the contents of the program counter and is connected through the internal address bus to the address buffer register. The address bus for the example microprocessor has 16 lines, and thereby can directly address 65,536 (i.e., 64K) of memory.

READING INSTRUCTIONS

To understand how the computer performs a branch, one must first understand how the computer reads program instructions from memory. Recall that program instructions are stored sequentially (step by step) in memory as binary numbers, starting at a certain binary address and ending at some higher address. The computer uses a register called the program counter (Figure 4.4) to keep track of where it is in the program.

Initialization

The first step in starting up a computer is initialization.

To start the computer, a small startup (boot) program that is permanently stored in the computer is run. This program sets all of the CPU registers with the correct values and clears all information in the computer memory to zeros before the operations program is loaded. This is called *initializing* the system. Then, the operations program is loaded into memory, at which point the address of the first program instruction is loaded into the program counter. The first instruction is read from the memory location whose address is contained in the program counter register; that is, the 16 bits in the program counter are used as the address for a memory read operation. Each instruction is read from memory in sequence and set on the data bus into the instruction register, where it is decoded. The instruction register is another temporary storage register inside the CPU (or microprocessor). It is connected to the data bus when the information on the bus is an instruction.

Figure 4.7
CPU Organization

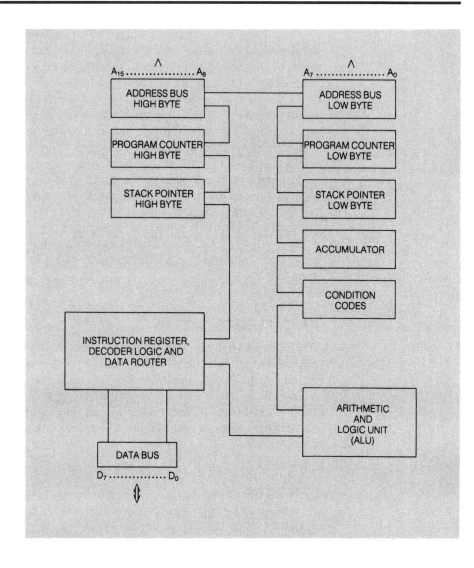

Operation Codes

The actual instructions in the program are in the form of numeric codes called operation codes (op codes).

Numeric codes called *operation codes* (or *op codes* for short) contain the instructions that represent the actual operation to be performed by the CPU. The block diagram of Figure 4.7, which illustrates part of the CPU hardware organization, should help clarify the flow of instructions through the CPU. The instruction register has a part that contains the numeric op codes. A decoder determines from the op codes the operation to be executed, and a data register controls the flow of data inside the CPU as a result of the op code instructions.

Instructions often are contained in more than one byte. In such cases, the first byte contains the op code, and succeeding bytes contain the address.

One important function of the op-code decoder is to determine how many bytes must be read to execute each instruction. Many instructions require two or three bytes. Figure 4.8 shows the arrangement of the bytes in an instruction. The first byte contains the op code. The second byte contains address information, usually the lowest or least significant byte of the address.

Program Counter

Each successive read of a memory location causes the program counter to be incremented to the address of the next byte.

The program counter is used by the CPU to address memory locations that contain instructions. Every time an op code is read (this is often called *fetched*) from memory, the program counter is incremented (advanced by one) so that it points to (i.e., contains the address of) the next byte following the op code. If the operation code requires another byte, the program counter supplies the address, the second byte is fetched from memory, and the program counter is incremented. Each time the CPU performs a fetch operation, the program counter is incremented; thus, the program counter always points to the next byte in the program. Therefore, after all bytes required for one complete instruction have been read, the program counter contains the address for the beginning of the next instruction to be executed.

Branch Instruction

In any practical computer program, there is normally the need to change the sequence of instructions as a result of some logical condition being met. An instruction of this type is called a branch instruction.

All of the branch instructions require two bytes. The first byte holds the operation code, and the second byte holds the location to which the processor is to branch.

A positive branch offset address results in a branch to a higher memory location, while a negative branch offset address results in a branch to a lower memory location.

Now, if the address information associated with a branch instruction is only 8 bits long and totally contained in the second byte, it cannot be the actual branch address. In this case, the code contained in the second byte is actually a two's complement number that the CPU adds to the lower byte of the program counter to determine the actual new address. This number in the second byte of the branch instruction is called an *address offset* or just *offset*. Recall that in two's complement notation, the 8-bit number can be either positive or negative; therefore, the branch address offset can be positive or negative. A positive branch offset causes a branch forward to a higher memory location. A negative branch offset causes a branch to a lower memory location. Since 8 bits are used in the present example, the largest forward branch is 127 memory locations and the largest backward branch is 128 memory locations.

**Figure 4.8
Instruction Byte
Arrangement**

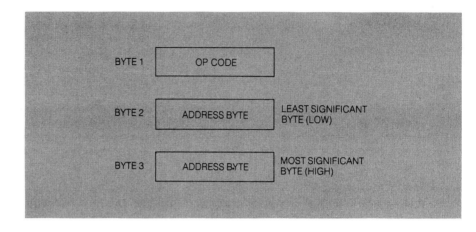

BYTE 1 — OP CODE

BYTE 2 — ADDRESS BYTE — LEAST SIGNIFICANT BYTE (LOW)

BYTE 3 — ADDRESS BYTE — MOST SIGNIFICANT BYTE (HIGH)

Offset Example

Suppose the program counter is at address 5,122 and the instruction at this location is a branch instruction. The instruction to which the branch is to be made is located at memory address 5,218. Since the second byte of the branch instruction is only 8 bits wide, the actual address 5,218 cannot be contained therein. Therefore, the difference or offset (96) between the current program counter value (5,122) and the desired new address (5,218) is contained in the second byte of the branch instruction. The offset value (96) is added to the address in the program counter (5,122) to obtain the new address (5,218), which is then placed on the address bus. The binary computation of the final address from the program counter value and second byte of the branch instruction is shown in Figure 4.9.

Jump Instruction

Branch instructions have a range of +127 or −128 (in the present 8-bit example). If the branch needs to go beyond this range, a jump instruction must be used. The jump instruction is a 3-byte instruction. The first byte is the jump op code, and the next two bytes are the actual jump address. The CPU loads the jump address directly into the program counter, and the program counter effectively gets restarted at the new jump location. The CPU continues to fetch and execute instructions in exactly the same way it did before the jump was made.

The jump instruction causes the CPU to jump out of one section of the program into another. The CPU cannot automatically return to the first section because no record was kept of the previous location. However, another instruction, the jump-to-subroutine, does leave a record of the previous instruction address.

8-bit branch operations are limited to an offset range of +127 or −128 memory locations. Thus, program branches to locations farther away must use jump instructions. These 3-byte instructions contain the entire memory address.

**Figure 4.9
Binary Computation
of Branch Address**

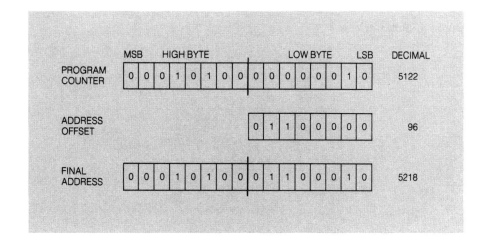

Jump-to-Subroutine Instruction

Subroutines are short programs used to perform specific tasks, particularly those tasks that must be performed several times within the same program.

A *subroutine* is a short program that is used by the main program to perform a specific function. It is located in sequential memory locations separated from the main program sequence. If the main program requires some function such as addition several times at widely separated places within the program, the programmer can write one subroutine to perform the addition, then have the main program jump to the memory locations containing the subroutine each time it is needed. This saves having to rewrite the addition program over and over again. To perform the addition, the programmer simply includes instructions in the main program that first load the numbers to be added into the data memory locations used by the subroutine and then jump to the subroutine.

The second and third bytes of a jump-to-subroutine instruction provide the address of the subroutine to be jumped to.

Refer to Figure 4.10 to follow the sequence. It begins with the program counter pointing to address location 100, where it gets the jump-to-subroutine instruction (step 1). Each jump-to-subroutine instruction (step 2) requires that the next two bytes must also be read to obtain the jump address (step 2a). Therefore, the program counter is incremented once for each byte (steps 3 and 4) and the jump address is loaded into the address register. The program counter is then incremented once more so that it points to the op-code byte of the next instruction (step 5).

Saving the Program Counter

The contents of the program counter are saved by storing them in a special memory location before the jump address is loaded into the program counter. This program counter address is saved so that it can be returned to in the main program when the subroutine is finished. This is the record that was mentioned before.

Figure 4.10
Jump-to-Subroutine

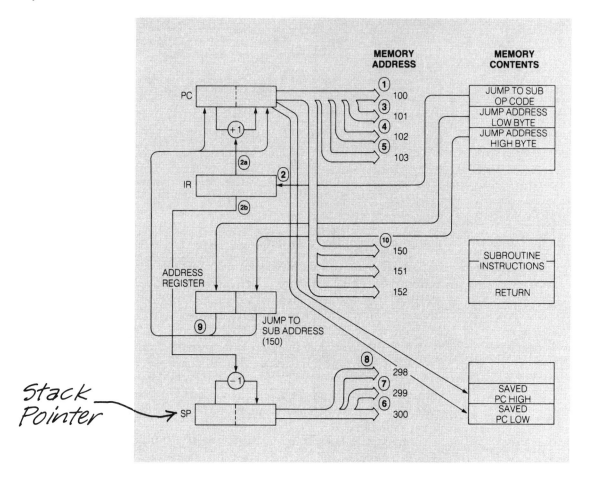

For a jump-to-subroutine, the contents of the program counter (after being incremented) are stored in two memory locations pointed to by the stack pointer. After storing them, the stack pointer value is decreased by one to prepare it for the next store.

Now refer back to Figure 4.4. There is a register in Figure 4.4 called the stack pointer (SP). The address of the special memory location used to store the program counter content is kept in this 16-bit stack pointer register. When a jump-to-subroutine op code is encountered, the CPU uses the number code contained in the stack pointer as a memory address to store the program counter to memory (step 2b of Figure 4.10). The program counter is a 2-byte register, so it must be stored in two memory locations. The current stack pointer is used as an address to store the lower byte of the program counter to memory (step 6). Then the stack pointer is decremented (decreased by one) and the high byte of the program counter is stored in the next lower memory location (step 7). The stack pointer is then decremented again to point to the next unused byte in the stack to prepare for storing the program counter again when required (step 8).

The special memory locations pointed to by the stack pointer are called stacks; if one considers memory locations as being slots stacked one atop the other, it makes sense to think of the stack pointer stacking data like plates on a shelf.

When the subroutine is completed, a return instruction retrieves the saved program counter value from the stack pointer and loads it into the program counter. Execution of the main program then resumes from the point at which the jump occurred.

After the program counter has been incremented and saved, the jump address is loaded into the program counter (step 9). The jump to the subroutine is made, and the CPU starts running the subroutine (step 10). The only thing that distinguishes the subroutine from another part of the program is the way in which it ends. When a subroutine has run to completion, it must allow the CPU to return to the point in the main program from which the jump occurred. In this way, the main program can continue without missing a step. The return-from-subroutine (RTS) instruction is used to accomplish this. It is decoded by the instruction register, and increments the stack pointer as shown in Figure 4.11, step 1. It uses the stack pointer to address the stack memory to retrieve the old program counter value from the stack (steps 2 and 4). The old program counter value is loaded into the program counter register (steps 3 and 5), and execution resumes in the main program (step 6). The return-from-subroutine instruction works like the jump-to-subroutine instruction, except in reverse.

EXAMPLE USE OF A MICROCOMPUTER

Let's look at an example of how a microcomputer might be used to replace some digital logic, and along the way learn about some more microcomputer instructions.

Microcomputers can be used in place of discrete logic circuits such as AND gates.

The digital logic to be replaced in this example is a simple AND gate circuit. Now, no one would use a microcomputer to replace only an AND gate, because an AND gate costs a fraction of what a microcomputer costs. However, if the system already has a microcomputer in it, the cost of the AND gate could be eliminated by performing the logical AND function in the computer rather than with the gate. This is a perfectly legitimate application for a microcomputer and is something that microcomputers do very well. Moreover, this example well illustrates the use of a microcomputer.

Suppose there are two signals that must be ANDed together to produce a third signal. One of the input signals comes from a pressure switch located under the driver's seat of an automobile; its purpose is to indicate whether someone is occupying the seat. This signal will be called A, and it is at logical high when someone is sitting in the seat. Signal B is developed within a circuit contained in the seat belt and is at logical high when the driver's seat belt is fastened. The output of the AND gate is signal C. It will be at logical high when someone is sitting in the driver's seat *and* has the seat belt fastened.

**Figure 4.11
Return-from-
Subroutine**

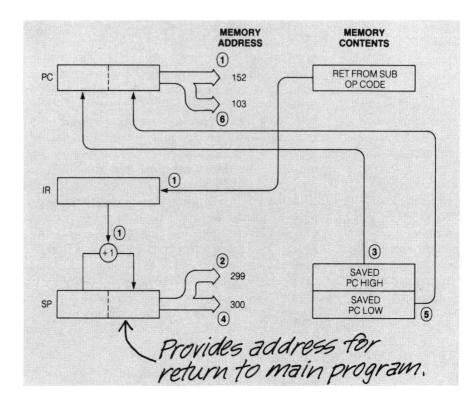

Provides address for return to main program.

Buffer

Buffers provide temporary storage for peripheral inputs and let the microcomputer treat peripherals, such as sensors, as if they were memory locations.

In order to use a microcomputer to replace the AND gate, the computer must be able to detect the status of each signal. Remember that the computer knows only what is stored in its memory. The microcomputer used here has memory-mapped I/O, in which peripherals are treated exactly like memory locations. The task is to provide a peripheral that allows the computer to look at the switch signals as if they were bits in a memory location. This can be done easily by using a device called a *buffer* (Figure 4.12). To the microcomputer, a buffer looks just like an 8-bit memory slot at a selected memory location. The 8 bits in the memory slot correspond to 8 digital signal inputs to the buffer. Each digital input controls the state of a single bit in the memory slot. The digital inputs are gated into the buffer under control of the CPU. The microcomputer can detect the state of the digital inputs by examining the bits in the buffer any time after the inputs are gated into the buffer.

In this application, signal A will be assigned to the rightmost bit (bit 0) and signal B to the next bit (bit 1). It doesn't matter that the other 6 bits are left unconnected. The computer will gate in and read the state of those lines,

Figure 4.12
Buffer

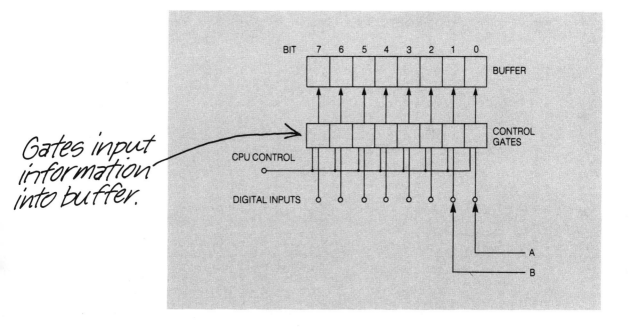

Gates input information into buffer.

but the program will be written to purposely ignore them. With the logic signals interfaced to the microcomputer, a program can be written that will perform the required logic function.

However, before writing a program, one must know the code or language in which the program is to be written. Computer languages come in various levels, including high-level language such as BASIC, assembly language that is designed for a specific microprocessor, and machine language, which is the actual language in which a program is stored in memory. For the present example, we choose the intermediate-level language (assembly language) to illustrate specific CPU operations.

Assembly Language

Microcomputer instructions are written in assembly language, a type of shorthand that uses initials or shortened words to represent microcomputer instructions.

Assembly language is a special type of abbreviated language, each symbol of which pertains to a specific microprocessor operation. Some assembly language instructions, such as branch, jump, jump-to-subroutine, and return-from-subroutine, have already been discussed. Others will be discussed as they are needed to execute an example program. Assembly language instructions have the form of initials or shortened words that represent microcomputer functions. These abbreviations are only for the convenience of the programmer because the program that the microcomputer eventually runs must be in the

Once the program has been written in assembly language, a special kind of program, called an assembler, converts the assembly language program into the binary code recognized by the microcomputer.

form of binary numbers. When each instruction is converted to the binary code that the microcomputer recognizes, it is called a machine language program. The assembly language abbreviation for the jump instruction is JMP.

Table 4.1 shows the assembly language equivalents for typical microcomputer instructions, along with a detailed description of the operation called for by the instruction. When writing a microcomputer program, it is easier and faster to use the abbreviated name rather than the complete function name. Assembly language simplifies programming tasks for the computer programmer because the abbreviations are easier to remember and write than the binary numbers the computer uses. However, the program eventually must be converted to the binary codes that the microcomputer recognizes as instructions, which is done by a special program called an *assembler*. The assembler program is run on the computer to convert assembly language to binary codes. This enables the programmer to write the program using words that have meaning to the programmer and also to produce machine codes that the computer can use.

Logic Functions

A microcomputer can AND the contents of its accumulator with a memory location to perform the logical AND function.

Microprocessors are capable of performing all of the basic logic functions such as AND, OR, NOT, and combinations of these. For instance, the NOT operation affects the accumulator by changing all ones to zeros and zeros to ones. Other logic functions are performed by using the contents of the accumulator and some memory location. All eight bits of the accumulator are affected, and all are changed at the same time. As shown in Figure 4.13, the AND operation requires two inputs. One input is the contents of the accumulator, and the other input is the contents of a memory location; thus, the eight accumulator bits are ANDed with the eight memory bits. The AND operation is performed on a bit-by-bit basis. For instance, bit 0 of the accumulator (the rightmost bit) is ANDed with bit 0 of the memory location, bit 1 with bit 1, bit 2 with bit 2, and so on. In other words, the AND operation is performed as if eight AND gates were connected with one input to a bit in the accumulator, and with the other input to a bit (in the same position) in the memory location. The resulting AND outputs are stored back into the accumulator in the corresponding bit positions. The OR logic function is performed in exactly the same way as the AND except that a 1 would be produced at the output if signal A or signal B were a 1, or if both were a 1 (i.e., using OR logic).

Shift

Using a logical operation known as a shift, a microcomputer can shift all the bits present in the accumulator to the left or right.

Instead of the AND gate inputs being switched to each bit position as shown in Figure 4.13, the microcomputer uses a special type of sequential logic operation, the shift, to move the bits to the AND gate inputs. A shift operation causes every bit in the accumulator to be shifted one bit position either to the right or to the left. It can be what is called a logical shift or it can be a circulating shift. Figure 4.14 shows the four types of shifts (logical, circulating,

**Table 4.1
Assembly Language
Mnemonics**

Mnemonic	Operand	Comment
JMP	(Address)	Jump to new program location
JSR	(Address)	Jump to a subroutine
BRA	(Offset)	Branch using the offset
BEQ	(Offset)	Branch if accumulator is zero
BNE	(Offset)	Branch if accumulator is nonzero
BCC	(Offset)	Branch if carry bit is zero
BCS	(Offset)	Branch if carry bit is nonzero
BPL	(Offset)	Branch if minus bit is zero
BMI	(Offset)	Branch if minus bit is nonzero
RTS		Retum from a subroutine

a. Program Transfer Instructions

Mnemonic	Operand	Comment
LDA	(Address)	Load accumulator from memory
STA	(Address)	Store accumulator to memory
LDA	# (Constant)	Load accumulator with constant
LDS	# (Constant)	Load stack pointer with constant
STS	(Address)	Store stack pointer to memory

b. Data Transfer Instructions

Mnemonic	Operand	Comment
COM		Complement accumulator (NOT)
AND	(Address)	AND accumulator with memory
OR	(Address)	OR accumulator with memory
ADD	(Address)	Add accumulator with memory
SUB	(Address)	Subtract accumulator with memory
AND	# (Constant)	AND accumulator with constant
OR	# (Constant)	OR accumulator with constant
SLL		Shift accumulator left logical
SRL		Shift accumulator right logical
ROL		Rotate accumulator left
ROR		Rotate accumulator right

c. Arithmetic and Logical Operations

**Figure 4.13
Microcomputer
Logical AND Function**

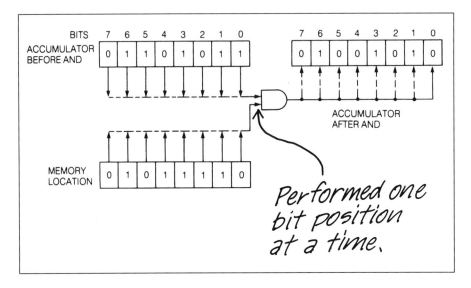

right, left) and their effects on the accumulator. In a left shift, bit 7 (the leftmost bit) is shifted into the carry bit of the CC register, bit 6 is shifted into bit 7, and so on until each bit has been shifted once to the left. Bit 0 (the rightmost bit) can be replaced either by the carry bit or by a zero, depending on the type of shift performed. Depending on the microprocessor, it is possible to shift other registers as well as the accumulator.

Programming the AND Function

It is the task of the programmer to choose instructions and organize them in such a way that the computer performs the desired tasks. To program the AND function, one of the instructions will be the AND, which stands for "AND accumulator with contents of a specific memory location," as shown in Table 4.1c. Since the AND affects the accumulator and memory, values must be put into the accumulator to be ANDed. This requires the load accumulator instruction, LDA.

The programmer often uses special names (labels) to refer to specific memory locations.

The assembly language program of Figure 4.15 performs the required AND function. The programmer must first know which memory location the digital buffer interface (Figure 4.12) occupies. This location is identified, and the programmer writes instructions in the assembler program so that the buffer memory location will be referred to by the label or name SEAT. SEAT is easier for the programmer to remember and write than the address of the buffer.

**Figure 4.14
Types of Shift
Operations**

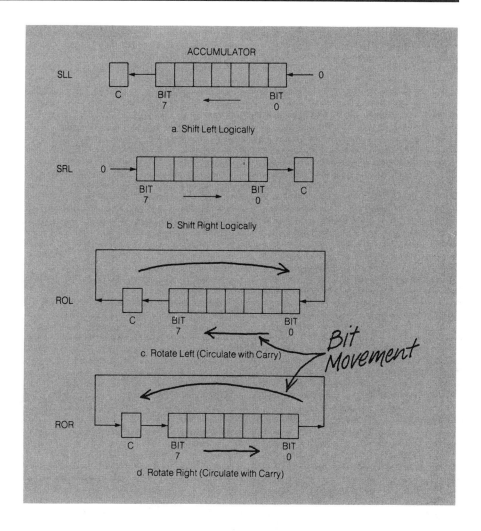

a. Shift Left Logically

b. Shift Right Logically

c. Rotate Left (Circulate with Carry)

d. Rotate Right (Circulate with Carry)

The use of a mask allows the microcomputer to separately examine two or more digital signals (bits) occupying the same 8-bit byte.

The operation of the program is as follows. The accumulator is loaded with the contents of the memory location SEAT. Note in Figure 4.12 that the two digital logic input signals, A and B, have been gated into bits 0 and 1, respectively, of the buffer that occupies the memory location labeled SEAT. Bit 0 is high when someone is sitting in the driver's seat. Bit 1 is high when the driver's seat belt is fastened. Only these two bits are to be ANDed together; the other six are to be ignored. But there is a problem because both bits are in the same 8-bit byte and there is no single instruction to AND bits in the same byte. However, the two bits can be effectively separated by using a mask.

**Figure 4.15
Assembly Language
Subroutines**

Program Label	Mnemonic	Operand
1 CHECK	LDA	SEAT
2	AND	#00000001 B
3	SLL	
4	AND	SEAT
5	RTS	

a. Subroutine CHECK

Program Label	Mnemonic	Operand
1 WAIT	JRS	CHECK
2	BEQ	WAIT
3	RTS	

b. Subroutine WAIT

Masking

During a mask operation, the accumulator contents are ANDed with the mask value, which has a zero in each bit location except for the bit(s) to be saved. The saved, or masked, bit(s) comes through unchanged, but all others are set to zero.

Masking is a technique used to allow only selected bits to be involved in a desired operation. Since the buffer contents have been loaded into the accumulator, only bits 0 and 1 have meaning, and these two bits are the only ones of importance that are to be kept in the accumulator. To do this, the accumulator is ANDed with a constant that has a zero in every bit location except the one that is to be saved. The binary constant in line 2 of Figure 4.15a (00000001) is chosen to select bit 0 and set all others to zero as the AND instruction is executed. The ANDing procedure is called *masking* because a mask has been placed over the accumulator that allows only bit 0 to come through unchanged. If bit 0 was a logical 1, it is still a logical 1 after masking. If bit 0 was a logical 0, it is still a logical 0. All other bits in the accumulator now contain the correct bit information about bit 0.

Shift and AND

During the final part of the AND operation, the shift left logical instruction is used to align the bits of signal A with the correct bits in signal B so the logical AND can be accomplished.

In our example program, the accumulator is still not ready to perform the final AND operation. Remember that SEAT contains the contents of the buffer and the conditions of signal A and signal B. The contents of the accumulator must be ANDed with SEAT so that signals A and B are ANDed together. A copy of signal A is held in the accumulator in bit 0, but it is in the wrong bit position to be ANDed with signal B in SEAT in the bit 1 position. Therefore, signal A must be shifted into the bit 1 position. To do this the shift left logical instruction is used (Figure 4.14a). With signal A in bit 1 of the accumulator and signal B in bit 1 of SEAT, the AND operation can be performed on the two bits. If both A and B are high, the AND operation will leave bit 1 of the accumulator high (1). If either is low, bit 1 of the accumulator will be low (0).

Use of Subroutines

The previous example program has been written as a subroutine named CHECK so that it can be used at many different places in a larger program. For instance, if the computer is controlling the speed of the automobile, it might be desirable to be able to detect whether a driver is properly fastened in the seat before it sets the speed at 55 miles per hour.

Since the driver's seat information is very important, the main program must wait until the driver is ready before allowing anything else to happen. A program such as that shown in Figure 4.15b can be used to do this. The main program calls the subroutine WAIT, which in turn immediately calls the subroutine CHECK. CHECK returns to WAIT with the condition codes set as they were after the last AND instruction. The Z bit (see Figure 4.5a) is set if A and B are not both high (the accumulator is zero). The BEQ instruction (see Table 4.1) in line 2 of WAIT branches back because the accumulator is zero and causes the computer to reexecute the JSR instruction in line 1 of WAIT. This effectively holds the computer in a loop rechecking signals A and B until the accumulator has a nonzero value (A and B are high).

Timing Error

A flaw in the subroutine CHECK could cause it to incorrectly perform the AND function. Notice that the logic states of A and B are sampled at different times. Signal A is first read in and masked off, then signal A and B are ANDed together. There is a possibility that during the interval between the time A is read and the time A and B are ANDed, the state of A could change. A computer is fast, but it still takes a certain amount of time for the microprocessor to execute the program instructions. For the driver's seat application, the signals have a long time between change so the time lag is not critical. However, in systems in which the timing of signals is very tight, the program would have to be rewritten to remove the lag. Even after correcting such a lag, there may be applications where variables change more rapidly than the sampling time. Special compromises must be made in such cases, or a new technique must be found to solve the problem.

MICROCOMPUTER HARDWARE

The microcomputer system electronic components are known as computer hardware. (The programs that the computer runs are called software.) The basic microcomputer parts are the CPU, memory, and I/O

The time required for the microcomputer to sample sensor inputs and perform its instructions must be taken into account during program design; otherwise, timing errors may result.

Figure 4.16
Integrated Circuit
Chip Microprocessor

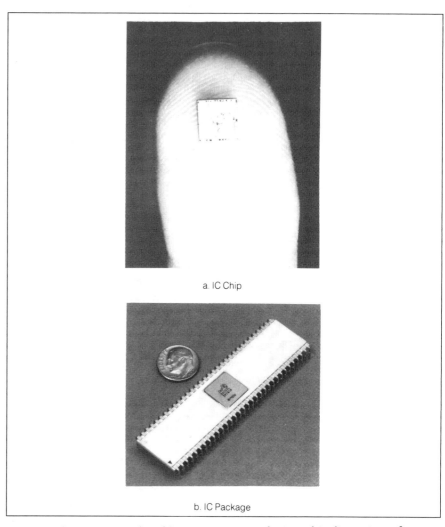

a. IC Chip

b. IC Package

(input and output peripherals). We next expand upon this discussion of important components and their associated operations.

Central Processing Unit

The central processing unit is a microprocessor. It is an integrated circuit similar to the one shown in Figure 4.16a. It contains thousands of transistors and diodes on a chip of silicon small enough to fit on the tip of a finger. It includes some form of arithmetic logic unit (ALU), as well as registers for data and instruction storage and a control section. The chip is housed in a rectangular, flat package similar to the one shown in Figure 4.16b. Newer versions of a microprocessor are packed in a flat package that has pins all the way around the perifery. The CPU gets program instructions from a memory device.

Memory: ROM

Permanent memory, called *ROM*, maintains its contents even when power is turned off. ROM is used for CPU instructions requiring permanent storage.

There are several types of memory devices available, and each has its own special features. Systems such as those found in the automobile that must permanently store their programs use a type of permanent memory called *read-only memory* (ROM). This type of memory can be programmed only one time and the program is stored permanently, even when the microcomputer power is turned off. The programs stored in ROM are sometimes called *firmware* rather than software since they are unchangeable. This type of memory enables the microcomputer to immediately begin running its program as soon as it is turned on.

Several types of ROM can be used in any microcomputer, including those found in automotive digital systems. For program storage, a ROM is used that is not alterable. The program and data storage are determined by physical configuration during manufacturing. In certain cases, it may be desirable to modify certain parameters. For example, in automotive applications it may be desirable to permit authorized persons to modify a control system parameter of a vehicle after it has been in operation for some time to improve system performance. In this case it must be possible to modify data (parameters) stored in ROM. Such modification is possible in a ROM that can be electrically erased and reprogrammed. This type of ROM is termed EEPROM (electrically erasable, programmable read-only-memory).

Memory: RAM

A form of memory that can be written to and changed, as well as read from, is commonly referred to as *RAM*.

Another type of memory, one that can be written to as well as read from, is required for the program stack, data storage, and program variables. This type of memory is called *random access memory* (RAM). This is really not a good name to distinguish this type of memory from ROM because ROM is also a random access type of memory. Random access means the memory locations can be accessed in any order rather than in a particular sequence. A better name for the data storage memory would be read/write memory (RWM). However, the term RAM is commonly used to indicate a read/write memory, so that is what will be used here. A typical microcomputer contains both ROM and RAM type memory.

It is beyond the scope of this book to discuss the detailed circuitry of all types of memory circuits. However, one example of a type of circuit that can be used for memory is the register circuit, which is implemented with flip-flop circuits as described in Chapter 3.

I/O Parallel Interface

Microcomputers require interface devices that enable them to communicate with other systems. The digital buffer interface used in the driver's seat application discussed earlier is one such device. The digital buffer interface is an example of a parallel interface because the eight buffer lines are all sampled at one time, that is, in parallel. The parallel buffer interface in the

**Figure 4.17
Digital-to-Analog
Converter Circuit
Block**

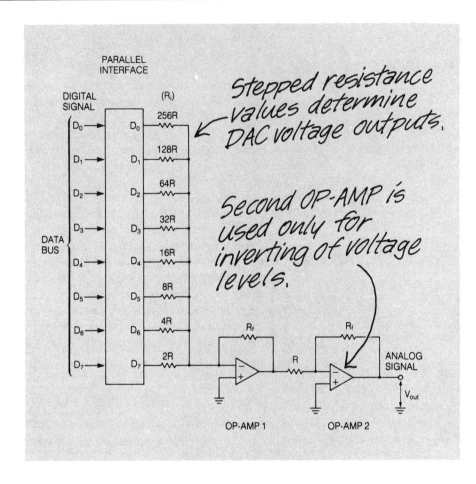

driver's seat application is an input, or readable, interface. Output, or writable, interfaces allow the microcomputer to affect external logic systems. An output buffer must be implemented using a data latch so that the binary output is retained after the microcomputer has finished writing data into it. This permits the CPU to go on to other tasks while the external system reads and uses the output data. This is different from the parallel input, in which the states could change between samples.

Digital-to-Analog Converter

A DAC converts binary signals from the microcomputer to analog voltages that are proportional to the number encoded in the input signals.

The parallel input and output interfaces are used to monitor and control external digital signals. The microcomputer can also be used to measure and control analog signals through the use of special interfaces. The microcomputer can produce an analog voltage by using a digital-to-analog converter (DAC). A DAC accepts inputs of a certain number of binary bits and produces an output voltage level that is proportional to the input number.

DACs come in many different versions with different numbers of input bits and output ranges. A common microcomputer DAC has 8-bit inputs and a 0 to 5 volt output range.

A simple 8-bit DAC is shown in Figure 4.17. This type of DAC uses a parallel input interface and two operational amplifiers. The 8 bits are written into the parallel interface and stored in data latches. The output of each latch is a digital signal that is 0 volts if the bit is low and 5 volts if the bit is high. The first op amp is a summing amplifier and has a gain of $-(R_f/R_i)$. The second op amp has a gain of -1; thus, it is only an inverter. The effect of the two amplifiers is to scale each bit of the parallel interface by a specially chosen factor and add the resultant voltages together. For instance, if only bit 0 is high and all the others are low,

$$V_{\text{out}} = 5\left[1\left(\frac{1}{256}\right) + 0\left(\frac{1}{128}\right) + 0\left(\frac{1}{64}\right) + \ldots + 0\left(\frac{1}{2}\right)\right]$$
$$= \left(\frac{5}{256}\right)$$
$$= 0.0195\,\text{v}$$

If only bits 0 and 7 are high:

$$V_{\text{out}} = 5\left[1\left(\frac{1}{256}\right) + 0\left(\frac{1}{128}\right) + 0\left(\frac{1}{64}\right) + \ldots + 1\left(\frac{1}{2}\right)\right]$$
$$= \left(\frac{645}{256}\right)$$
$$= 2.5195\,\text{v}$$

The DAC output voltage can only change in discrete steps. This causes the analog output voltage to have a staircase appearance as the binary number at the input is increased one bit at a time from minimum value to maximum value, as shown in Figure 4.18. This DAC can have any one of 256 different voltage levels. For many applications, this is a close enough approximation to a continuous analog signal.

The accuracy of the DAC's representation of the digital input signal varies with circuit design, and with the rate at which the input signal is sampled.

The DAC output voltage can change only when the computer writes a new number into the DAC data latches. The computer must generate each new output often enough to ensure an accurate representation of the changes in the digital signal. The analog output of the DAC can take only a specific number of different values and can change only at specific times determined by the sampling rate. The output of the converter will always have small discrete step changes (resolution). The designer must decide how small the steps must be to produce the desired shape and smoothness in the analog signal so that it is a reasonable duplication of the variations in the digital levels.

**Figure 4.18
Staircase Output
Voltage of the DAC in
Figure 4.17**

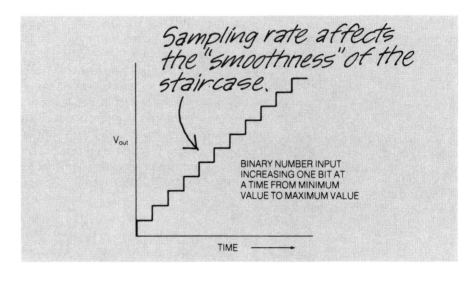

Analog-to-Digital Converter

In addition, microcomputers can measure analog voltages by using a special interface component called an analog-to-digital converter (ADC). Analog-to-digital converters convert an analog voltage input into a digital number output that the microcomputer can read.

The ADC performs a function opposite of the DAC: It converts an analog signal into digital form for processing by the microcomputer.

Figure 4.19 shows a conceptually simple, but not very practical, way of making an ADC by using a DAC and a voltage comparator. The input to the DAC is a binary number generated by the microcomputer that starts at the minimum value and increases toward the maximum value, as seen in Figure 4.18. This binary number is generated at the parallel output of the microcomputer. The output of the DAC, V_{out}, is one input to the comparator. The other input is the input voltage, V_{in}, that the ADC is measuring. When the V_{out} voltage of the DAC is less than V_{in}, the output of the comparator, V_{comp}, is a low logic level. When V_{out} is greater than V_{in}, the output of the comparator is a high level.

As soon as the binary number generated by the microcomputer causes V_{out} from the DAC to be greater than V_{in}, the comparator output goes high and stops the microcomputer from changing the binary number input further. The binary number is used by the microcomputer as the equivalent of the analog input voltage V_{in}. The microcomputer then resets and starts the binary number generation again to make another match to the V_{in} voltage. In this manner, a binary number, equivalent to a V_{in} and analog voltage, is produced at a selected sampling rate. The output of the comparator is fed back to the microcomputer through a digital input.

**Figure 4.19
Analog-to-Digital
Converter**

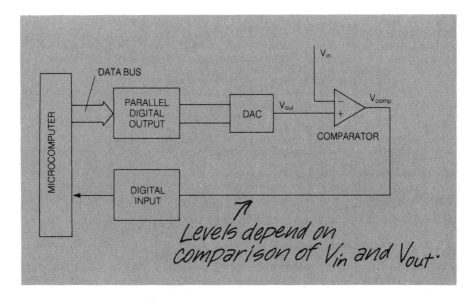

Levels depend on comparison of V_{in} and V_{out}.

Sampling

The accuracy of the DAC increases as the rate of sampling of the input signal increases.

The designer determines how quickly the microcomputer must change the DAC voltage to accurately follow the analog signal. Figure 4.20 shows a sine wave analog signal and some digital approximations with various sampling rates. Notice that Figure 4.20a with 13 samples per sine wave cycle follows the sinusoid much closer than Figure 4.20b, which only samples twice in a cycle. When the sampling rate is less than 2, as in Figure 4.20c, the staircase output doesn't follow well at all. This is because the computer didn't change the DAC input often enough to produce an output signal that closely approximates the desired signal.

The input sampling theorem states that an input signal must be sampled at least twice per cycle to be minimally accurate.

An engineer named H. Nyquist studied the sampling rate problem and determined that in order to reproduce a sinusoidal signal properly, the signal must be sampled at least twice per cycle (the Nyquist sampling theorem). Of course, more samples per cycle is better, but two samples per cycle is the minimum required.

Polling

Analog-to-digital converters that perform everything by themselves are available. The microcomputer simply tells them when to make a conversion and then waits until the conversion is done. ADCs require anywhere from a few millionths of a second to a second to complete the conversion.

Conversion time can be a serious limitation when slow converters are used. The microcomputer cannot afford to waste time waiting while the converter works. This is especially true when the microcomputer is used to

Figure 4.20
Analog Output Voltage versus Sampling Rate

Minimum to produce signal accurately.

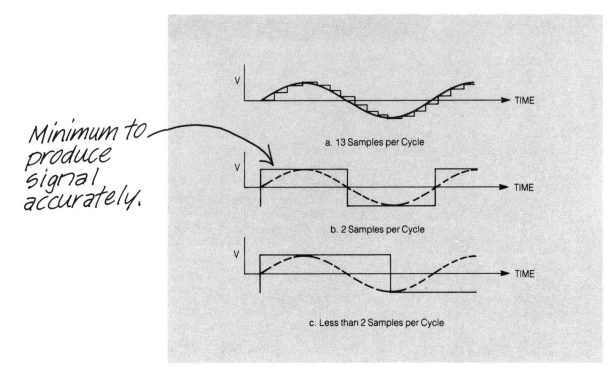

a. 13 Samples per Cycle

b. 2 Samples per Cycle

c. Less than 2 Samples per Cycle

Polling is used in some microcomputers to periodically check the ADC interface rather than waiting in an idle state for the ADC to do the conversion.

control and monitor many systems at the same time. Instead of waiting for the ADC to finish, the computer could be off running another part of the program and come back only when the conversion is done. But how will the computer know when the conversion is finished?

One way of doing this is for the microcomputer to periodically check the interface while it is running another part of the program. This method is called *polling*. A subroutine is included in the main program and is called up whenever an ADC interface is being used. This usually consists of a few lines of assembly language code that check to see if the interface is done and collect the result when it is finished. When the polling subroutine determines that the ADC is finished, the main program continues without using the polling subroutine until the ADC interface is called up again. The problem with such a scheme is that the polling routine may be called many times before the interface is finished. This can waste the computer's time and slow it down. Therefore, an evaluation must be made in certain systems to determine if polling is worthwhile.

Interrupts

Interrupts cause the CPU to jump to a specific location in the program. By signaling the microprocessor for service only when needed, interrupts are more efficient than polling.

An efficient alternative to polling uses control circuitry called an *interrupt*. An interrupt is an electrical signal that is generated outside of the CPU and is connected to an input on the CPU. The interrupt causes the CPU to temporarily discontinue the program execution and to perform some operation on data coming from an external device. A slow ADC, for instance, could use an interrupt line to tell the processor when it is finished converting. When an interrupt occurs, the processor automatically jumps to a designated program location and executes the interrupt service subroutine. For the ADC, this would be a subroutine to read in the conversion result. When the interrupt subroutine is done, the computer returns to the place where it left off in the program as if nothing had happened. (Recall the previous discussion on the jump-to-subroutine instruction.) Interrupts reduce the amount of time the computer spends dealing with the various peripheral devices.

Another important use for interrupts is in timekeeping. Suppose that a system is being used that requires things to be done at particular times; for instance, sampling an analog signal is a timed process. A special component called a timer could be used. A timer is a device that works like a digital watch. A square-wave clock signal is counted in counter registers like the one discussed in Chapter 3. The timer can be programmed to turn on the interrupt line when it reaches a certain count and then reset itself (start over). It may be inside the CPU itself or it may be contained in peripheral devices in the microcomputer system. Timers have many automotive applications (as shown later).

Such a technique is sometimes used to trigger the output of a new number to a DAC at regular intervals. The microcomputer simply programs the timer for the desired amount of time by presetting the counter to some starting value other than zero. Each time the timer counts out the programmed number of pulses, it interrupts the computer. The interrupt service subroutine then gets the new binary number that has been put into memory by the microcomputer and transfers this number to the DAC data latches at the input to the DAC.

Vectored Interrupts

All of the interrupt activity is completely invisible to the program that gets interrupted. In other words, the interrupted program doesn't know it was interrupted because its execution continues without program modification with minimum delay. Interrupts allow the computer to handle two or more things almost simultaneously. In some systems, one interrupt line may be used by more than one device. For instance, two or more ADCs may use the same interrupt line to indicate when either is ready. In this case, the computer doesn't know which device caused the interrupt. The computer could poll all the devices each time an interrupt occurs to see which one needs

Vectored interrupts tell the CPU which specific device needs service, and also may implement a priority of service scheme. Vectored interrupts allow a microcomputer to handle a number of different tasks quickly.

service, but as discussed, polling may waste time. A better way is to use vectored interrupts.

In computer parlance, a *vector* is a memory location that contains another address that locates data or an instruction. It may be a specific memory location that contains the address of the first instruction of a subroutine to service an interrupt; it may be a register that contains the same type address. In this specific case, an interrupt vector is a register that peripherals use to tell the processor which device interrupted it. When a peripheral causes an interrupt, it writes a code into the interrupt vector register so that the processor can tell which device interrupted it by reading the code. The decoder for an interrupt vector usually includes circuitry that allows each device to be assigned a different interrupt priority. If two devices interrupt at the same time, the processor will service the most important one first.

The vectored interrupt enables the microcomputer to efficiently handle the peripheral devices connected to it and to service the interrupts rapidly. Interrupts allow the processor to respond to things happening in peripheral devices without having to constantly monitor the interfaces. They enable the microcomputer to handle many different tasks and to keep track of all of them. A microcomputer system designed to use interrupts is called a *real-time computing system* because it rapidly responds to peripherals as soon as requests occur. Such real-time systems are used in digital instrumentation and control systems.

MICROCOMPUTER APPLICATIONS IN AUTOMOTIVE SYSTEMS

There is a great variety of applications of microprocessors in auto-mobiles. As will be explained in later chapters of this book, microprocessors find applications in engine and driveline control, instrumentation, ride control, antilock braking and other safety devices, entertainment, heating/air conditioning control, automatic seat position control, and many other systems. In each of these applications, the microprocessor serves as the functional core of what can properly be called a special-purpose microcomputer.

Although these applications are widely varied in operation, the essential configuration (or *architecture*) has much in common for all applications. Figure 4.21 is a simplified block diagram depicting the various components of each of the automotive systems having the applications listed previously. In this block diagram, the microprocessor is denoted MPU. It is connected to the other components by means of three buses: address bus (AB), data bus (DB), and control bus (CB). Each bus consists of a set of wires over which binary electrical signals are transmitted. By way of illustration, in early automotive application, the DB consists of 8 wires, the AB is typically 8 to 16 wires, and the control bus is a set of 3 or 4 wires.

**Figure 4.21
Architecture for
Typical Automotive
Computer**

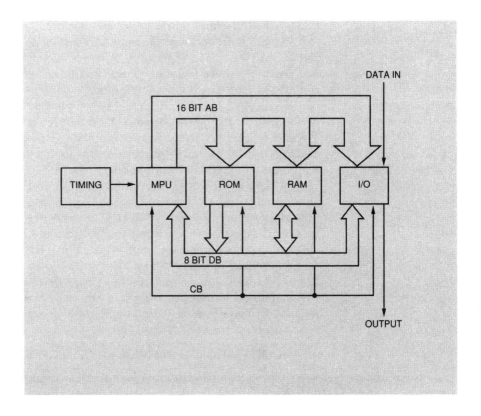

The hardware in the microcomputer remains fixed, while the programs stored in ROM can be changed as desired to perform different applications.

The operation of each special-purpose microcomputer system is controlled by a program stored in ROM. As explained earlier in this chapter, the MPU generates addresses for the ROM in sequence to obtain each instruction in corresponding sequence. The operation of each microprocessor-based automotive subsystem has a specific program that is permanently stored (electronically) in the ROM. Changes in the system operation can be achieved by replacing the ROM chip(s) with new chip(s) that contain the appropriate program for the desired operation. This feature is advantageous during the engineering development phase for any microprocessor-based system. While the hardware remains fixed, the system modifications and improvements are achieved by substituting ROM chips.

A typical automotive microprocessor-based system also incorporates some amount of RAM. This memory is used for a variety of purposes, including storing temporary results, storing the stack, and storing all of the variables, not to mention all of the other activities discussed earlier in this chapter.

The input/output (I/O) device for any given automotive microcomputer system serves as the interface connection of the microcomputer with the particular automotive system. Standard commercial I/O devices are available from the manufacturers of each microprocessor that are specifically configured to work with that processor. These I/O devices are implemented as an IC chip and are very versatile in application. A typical such I/O device has two 8-bit data ports for connecting to peripheral devices, and an 8-bit port that is connected to the data bus of the computer.

Figure 4.22 is a block diagram of a typical commercial I/O device. In this device there are two ports labeled A and B, respectively. These ports can be configured to act as either input or output, depending on the data in the data direction register. Normally the correct code for determining direction is transferred to the I/O device from the microprocessor via the system data bus.

Whenever the microprocessor is either to transfer data to the I/O device or receive data from it, a specific address is generated by the processor. This address is decoded, using standard logic, to form an electrical signal that activates the chip select inputs to the I/O. In addition, the read/write (R/W) output of the microprocessor is activated, causing data to be received (read) from a peripheral device, or transmitted (write) to a peripheral device.

This use of address lines to activate the I/O is known as *memory-mapped I/O*. In memory-mapped I/O, input or output of data is selected by reading from the I/O input address or writing to the I/O output address.

INSTRUMENTATION APPLICATIONS OF MICROCOMPUTERS

Microcomputers can convert the nonlinear output voltage of some sensors into a linear voltage representation. The sensor output voltage is used to look up the corresponding linear value stored in a table.

In instrumentation applications of microcomputers, the signal processing operations are performed numerically under program control. The block diagram of a typical computer-based instrument is depicted in Figure 4.23. In this example instrument, an analog sensor provides a continuous-time voltage, V_o, that is proportional to the quantity being measured. The continuous-time voltage is sampled at times determined by the computer. The sampled analog voltage is then converted to digital format (e.g., 8 to 16 bits) using an ADC. The digital data are connected to port A of the I/O device of the computer to be read into memory.

The ADC generates a signal when the conversion from analog to digital is completed. This signal is normally termed *end of conversion* (EOC). The EOC signal provides an interrupt signaling the computer that data are ready.

The signal processing to be performed is expressed as a set of operations that is to be performed by the microprocessor on the data. These operations are termed the *algorithm* for the signal processing operation. The algorithm is converted to a set of specific computer operations that becomes the program for the signal processing. After the signal processing is completed, the result is ready to be sent to the display device. The digital data are sent through I/O to port B to the DAC. There it is converted back to sampled analog. The sampled data are "smoothed" to a suitable continuous-time voltage by means of a special filter known as a reconstruction filter. The continuous-time output of this filter drives the continuous-time display.

**Figure 4.22
Block Diagram of a
Typical Interface
Adapter**

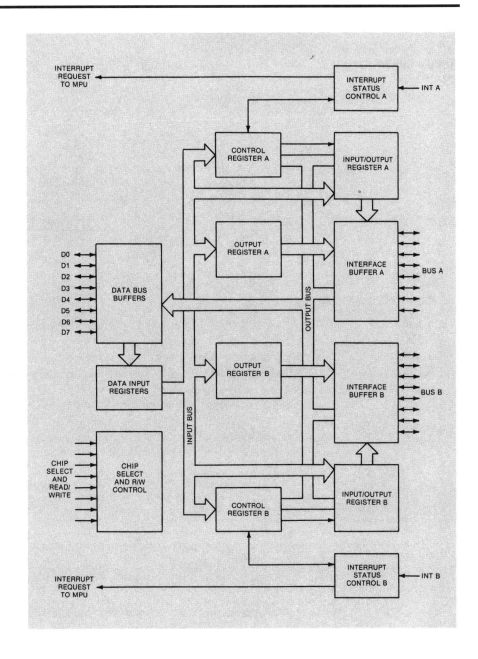

In a great many applications, the display is digital (e.g., automotive speed measurement). In this case, the conversion from digital to analog is not required, and the computer output data can directly activate the digital display.

**Figure 4.23
Typical Automotive
Instrumentation
Architecture**

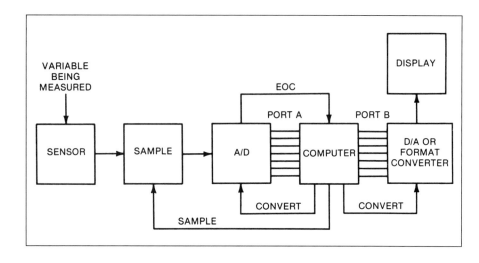

Digital Filters

Digital filters can be
programmed on a
microcomputer to reject
specific types of signals
while passing other
signals.

As an example of computer-based instrumentation signal processing
applications, consider the relatively straightforward task of filtering the
output of a sensor. Low-pass filters pass low-frequency signals but reject
high-frequency signals. High-pass filters do just the reverse: They pass high-
frequency signals and reject low-frequency signals. Bandpass filters pass
midrange frequencies but reject both low and high frequencies. Analog filters
use resistive, capacitive, and inductive components, and sometimes operational
amplifiers. Digital low-pass and bandpass filters can be programmed on a
microcomputer to perform basically the same functions as their analog
counterparts.

A digital low-pass filter could be used, for instance, to smooth the output
of an automotive fuel level sensor. The fuel level sensor produces an electrical
signal that is proportional to the height of the fuel in the center of the tank.
The level at that point will change as fuel is consumed, but it also will change
as the car slows, accelerates, turns corners, and hits bumps. The sensor's output
voltage varies widely because of fuel slosh even though the amount of fuel in
the tank changes slowly. If that voltage is sent directly to the fuel gauge, the
resulting variable indication will fluctuate too rapidly to be read.

The measurement can be made more readable and more meaningful by
using a low-pass filter to smooth out the signal fluctuations to reduce the
effects of sloshing. The low-pass filter can be implemented in a microcomputer
by programming the computer to average the sensor signal over several seconds
before sending it to the display. For instance, if the fuel level sensor signal is
sampled once every second and it is desirable to average the signal over a
period of 60 seconds, the computer saves only the latest 60 samples, averages
them, and displays the average. When a new sample is taken, the oldest sample

is discarded so that only the 60 latest samples are kept. A new average can be computed and displayed each time a new sample is taken.

Digital filtering (averaging) can be performed by a computer under the control of the software. Sometimes the section of code that performs the filtering task is simply called "the filter." Digital signal processing is very attractive because the same computer can be used to process several different signals. Also, since digital filters require no extra hardware, the filters can be made much more complex with relatively little increase in cost. In addition, the characteristics of the digital filter can be changed by changing the software. Changing the characteristics of an analog filter usually requires changing the hardware components. Another feature of digital filters (true for digital signal processing in general) is that they don't change with age or temperature, unlike analog filters.

Digital filters are implemented completely through the use of software, thus their characteristics can be easily changed. Because digital filters require no extra hardware, they are low in cost.

There are limitations to the use of digital filters, however. The frequency range of digital filters is determined by the speed of the processor. The microcomputer must be able to sample each signal at or above the rate required by the Nyquist sampling theorem. It must also be fast enough to perform all of the averaging and linearization for each signal before the next sample is taken. This is an important limitation, and the system designer must be certain that the computer is not overloaded by trying to make it do too many things too quickly.

MICROCOMPUTERS IN CONTROL SYSTEMS

Computers can also be used in control applications.

Microcomputers are able to handle inputs and outputs that are either digital or converted analog signals. With the proper software, they are capable of making decisions about those signals and can react to them quickly and precisely. These features make microcomputers ideal for controlling other digital or analog systems, as discussed in the following sections.

Closed-Loop Control System

Recall the basic closed-loop control system block diagram of Chapter 2. The error amplifier compares the command input with the plant output and sends the error signal to the control logic. The control logic uses the error signal to generate a plant control signal that causes the plant to react with a new output so that the error signal will be reduced toward zero. The control logic is designed so that the plant's output follows or tracks the command input. A microcomputer can replace the error amplifier and the control logic. The computer can compare command input and plant output and perform the computation required to generate a control signal.

Limit-Cycle Controller

The limit-cycle controller, discussed in Chapter 2, can be readily implemented with a microcomputer. Recall that the limit-cycle controller controls the plant output so that it falls somewhere between an upper and lower limit, preferably so that its average value is equal to the command input. The controller must read in the command input and the plant output and decide what control signal to send to the plant based on those signals alone.

Using a microcomputer, the upper and lower limit can be determined from the command input by using a lookup table similar to that discussed later in this chapter. The plant output is compared against these two limits. If the plant output is above the higher limit or below the lower limit, the microcomputer outputs the appropriate on/off signal to the plant to bring the output back between the two limits.

With proper software, a microcomputer can replace the error amplifier and control logic used in the closed-loop control system.

Recall that in Chapter 2 the concept of a feedback control system was introduced. There it was shown that a control system compares the value of some controlled variable with a desired value (or set point) for that variable. In such a control system, the difference between the desired and actual value is first obtained, then an electrical signal is generated. The resulting error signal is processed electronically, thereby generating a control signal that operates an actuator. The actuator changes the controlled system in such a way as to reduce the error.

A feedback control system can also be implemented using digital electronics. Figure 4.24 is a block diagram of a control system employing a computer. In this diagram, there is a physical system, or plant, that is to be controlled. The specific variable being controlled is denoted X. For example, in an automobile, the plant might be the engine and the controlled variable might be engine speed.

The desired value for X is the set point S. An error signal e is obtained:

$$e = S - X$$

The error signal is sampled, yielding samples e_n (where n represents sample number; i.e., $n = 1, 2, \ldots$). In a typical digital control system, the computer generates an output y_n for each input sample:

$$y_n = y_0 + Pe_n + I(e_n + e_{n-1} + e_{n-2})\Delta T + D\frac{(e_n - e_{n-1})}{\Delta T}$$

where

P is the proportional gain
I is the integral gain
D is the differential gain
T is the time between successive samples

The previous equation represents an example of an algorithm for the particular control strategy. The example algorithm is a form of a PID (proportional integral differential) control strategy.

After computing y_n for each input sample, a digital version of y_n is transmitted through the I/O to the DAC. There it is converted to analog format, providing a control signal to the actuator (A), which is presumed here

**Figure 4.24
Typical Digital Control
System**

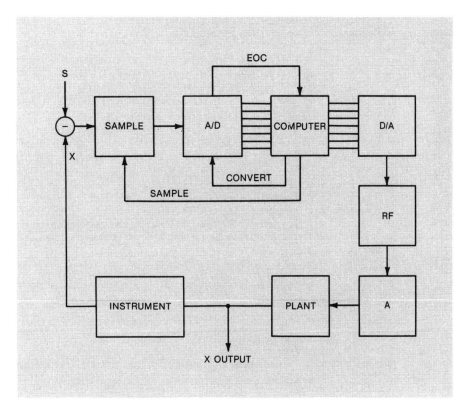

to be analog. The actuator controls the plant in such a way as to cause the error to be reduced toward zero. Many examples of the application of computer-based electronic control systems in automobiles are presented in later chapters of this book.

Multivariable Systems

With the appropriate control program, microcomputers have the ability to sample and control multiple inputs and outputs independently. This type of control is much more difficult to design when using analog circuitry.

A very important feature of microcomputer control logic is the ability to control multiple systems independently and to control systems with multiple inputs and outputs. The automotive applications for microcomputer control involve both of these types of *multivariable* systems. For instance, the automobile engine controller has several inputs (such as mass airflow rate, throttle angle, and camshaft and/or crankshaft angular position). All of the outputs must be controlled simultaneously because some inputs affect more than one output. These types of controllers can be very complicated and are difficult to implement in analog fashion. The increased complexity (and cost) of a multivariable microcomputer system is not much higher than for a single-variable microcomputer system, presuming the microcomputer has the

**Figure 4.25
Illustration of Table
Lookup and
Interpolation**

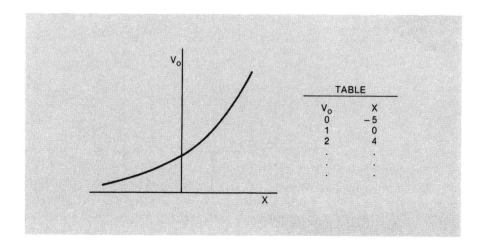

capacity to do the task. It only affects the task of programming the appropriate control scheme into the microcomputer. This type of control is discussed in a later chapter.

Table Lookup

One of the important functions of a microcomputer in automotive applications is table lookup. These applications include:

1. Linearization of sensor data
2. Multiplication
3. Calibration conversion

These applications are explained in detail in later chapters where appropriate. In this chapter, we explain the basic principle using a specific example.

The concept of table lookup is illustrated in Figure 4.25, in which a pair of variables, V_o and X, are related by the graph depicted therein. Also shown in Figure 4.25 is a table listing certain specific values for the relationship. The functional relationship between V_o and X might, for example, be the output voltage of a nonlinear sensor V_o for measuring a quantity X. If the value for V_o is known, then the corresponding value for X can theoretically be found using the graph or the tabulated values. In the latter case, the nearest two tabulated values for V_o are located, and the corresponding values for X are read from the table. Denoting V_1 and V_2 as the nearest values and X_1, X_2 as the corresponding tabulated values, the value for X corresponding to V_o is found by linear interpolation

$$X = X_1 + (X_2 - X_1)(V_O - V_2)/(V_1 - V_2)$$

**Figure 4.26
Architecture Involved
in Table Lookup**

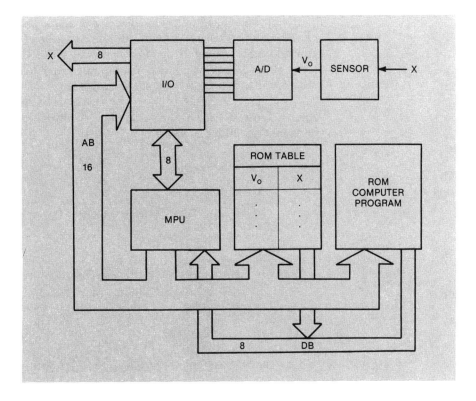

A microcomputer can perform the same operation using tabulated values for the relationship between V_o and X (i.e., $V_o(X)$ in correct mathematical notation). This method is illustrated using a specific example of the measurement of a variable X using a sensor output voltage, and variable X is assumed to be that which is illustrated in Figure 4.24. A microcomputer is to obtain the value for X using a table lookup operation.

The portion of the microcomputer that is involved in the table lookup process is illustrated in Figure 4.26. The relationship $V_o(X)$ is stored in ROM for representative points along the curve. These data are stored using V_o values as addresses, and corresponding values of X as data. For example, consider a point (V_1, X_1). The data X_1 are stored at memory location V_1 in binary format.

The operation of the table lookup is as follows. The sensor S has output voltage V_o. The computer reads the values of V_o (using an ADC to convert to digital format) through the I/O device. Then the MPU under program control (program ROM) calculates the addresses for the two nearest values to V_o, which are V_1 and V_2 ($V_1 < V_o < V_2$). The computer, under program control, reads values X_1 and X_2 and then calculates X using the preceding formula.

Repeated reference will be made to the table lookup function in later chapters. In particular, Chapter 7 will discuss how a typical digital engine control system frequently obtains data using table lookup.

After a chapter on basics of automotive engine control and a chapter on sensors and actuators, this book will deal more specifically with particular microcomputer automotive instrumentation and control systems to show how these systems are used in the automobile to control the engine and drivetrain and many auxiliary functions.

Quiz for Chapter 4

1. The parts of a computer include
   a. CPU
   b. memory
   c. input/output
   d. all of the above

2. What does a microcomputer use to interface with other systems?
   a. parallel interface
   b. analog-to-digital converter
   c. digital-to-analog converter
   d. all of the above

3. Which control line do peripherals use to get the computer's attention?
   a. power line
   b. read/write line
   c. interrupt line
   d. clock line

4. What is a data bus?
   a. a set of wires that carries bits to or from the processor and memory or peripherals
   b. a large yellow vehicle for carrying data
   c. a bus carrying addresses
   d. a set of wires for control signals

5. What are computers used for in instrumentation systems?
   a. signal processing
   b. sensor, actuator, and display linearization
   c. display formatting
   d. filtering
   e. all of the above

6. According to the Nyquist sampling theorem, a signal must be sampled at
   a. the highest frequency in the signal
   b. at least twice the highest frequency in the signal
   c. less than half the lowest frequency in the signal
   d. more than half the lowest frequency in the signal

7. What Advantages does digital signal processing have over analog signal processing?
   a. digital is more precise
   b. digital doesn't drift with time and temperature
   c. the same digital hardware can be used in many filters
   d. all of the above

8. What advantage does analog signal processing have over digital signal processing?
   a. analog is always less expensive
   b. the same analog hardware can be used for many filters
   c. analog is sometimes less expensive
   d. high-frequency signals can only be filtered with analog filters

9. What type of memory is used to permanently store programs?
   a. RAM
   b. ROM
   c. MAP
   d. RPM

10. What type of memory is used to temporarily store data and variables?
   a. RAM
   b. ROM
   c. MAP
   d. RPM

11. What distinguishes a computer from a fancy calculator?
   a. add, subtract, multiply, and divide
   b. stored program
   c. the calculators can read paper tape
   d. digital circuits

12. What part of the computer performs the arithmetic and logic functions?
   a. peripherals
   b. memory
   c. CPU
   d. address bus

13. Which computer register is the main work register?
   a. program counter
   b. stack pointer
   c. condition code register
   d. accumulator

14. A short initialization program is called what kind of program?
   a. subroutine
   b. boot program
   c. main program
   d. branch

15. Which register keeps track of program steps?
   a. program counter
   b. stack pointer
   c. condition code register
   d. accumulator

16. A programmer uses what type of statements in an assembly language program?
   a. op codes
   b. mnemonics
   c. machine code

17. Most microcomputers use how many bits to address memory?
   a. 16
   b. 32
   c. 4
   d. 6

18. Most automotive engine control microcomputers use how many bits in arithmetic?
   a. 1
   b. 6
   c. 4
   d. 32

19. Which of the following is a short program that ends with an RTS instruction?
   a. main program
   b. interrupt
   c. boot
   d. subroutine

The Basics of Electronic Engine Control

Engine control in the vast majority of engines means regulating fuel and air intake as well as spark timing to achieve desired performance in the form of torque or power output. Until the late 1960s, control of the engine output torque and RPM was accomplished through some combination of mechanical, pneumatic, or hydraulic systems. Then, in the 1970s, electronic control systems were introduced.

This chapter is intended to explain, in general terms, the theory of electronic control of the automotive engine. Chapter 7 explains practical control methods and systems. The examples used to explain the major developments and principles of electronic control have been culled from the techniques used by various manufacturers and are not necessarily representative of any single automobile manufacturer at the highest level of detail.

MOTIVATION FOR ELECTRONIC ENGINE CONTROL

The motivation for electronic engine control came in part from two government requirements. The first came about as a result of legislation to regulate automobile exhaust emissions under the authority of the Environmental Protection Agency (EPA). The second was a thrust to improve the national average fuel economy by government regulation.

Exhaust Emissions

The combustion of gasoline in an engine results in exhaust gases including CO_2, H_2O, CO, oxides of nitrogen, and various hydrocarbons.

The engine exhaust consists of the products of combustion of the air and gasoline mixture. Gasoline is a mixture of chemical compounds that are called *hydrocarbons*. This name is derived from the chemical formation of the various gasoline compounds, each of which is a chemical union of hydrogen (H) and carbon (C) in various proportions. Gasoline also contains natural impurities as well as chemicals added by the refiner. All of these can produce undesirable exhaust elements.

During the combustion process, the carbon and hydrogen combine with oxygen from the air, releasing heat energy and forming various chemical compounds. If the combustion were perfect, the exhaust gases would consist only of carbon dioxide (CO_2) and water (H_2O), neither of which is considered harmful to human health in the atmosphere. In fact, both are present in a human's breath.

Unfortunately, the combustion of the SI engine is not perfect. In addition to the CO_2 and H_2O, the exhaust contains amounts of carbon monoxide (CO), oxides of nitrogen (chemical unions of nitrogen and oxygen that are denoted NO_x), unburned hydrocarbons (HC), oxides of sulfur, and other compounds. Some of the exhaust constituents are considered harmful and have come under the control of the federal government. The exhaust emissions controlled by government standards are CO, HC, and NO_x.

Automotive exhaust emission control requirements started in the United States in 1966 when the California state regulations became effective. Since then, the federal government has imposed emission control limits for all states, and the standards became progressively tighter throughout the remainder of the twentieth century and will continue to tighten in the twenty-first century. Auto manufacturers found that the traditional engine controls could not control the engine sufficiently to meet these emission limits and maintain adequate engine performance at the same time, so they turned to electronic controls.

Fuel Economy

Everyone has some idea of what fuel economy means. It is related to the number of miles that can be driven for each gallon of gasoline consumed. It is referred to as miles per gallon (MPG) or simply *mileage*. Just like it improves emission control, another important feature of electronic engine control is its ability to improve fuel economy.

Electronic engine control is used to reduce exhaust emissions and improve fuel economy, both of which have limits set by the government.

It is well recognized by layman and expert alike that the mileage of a vehicle is not unique. It depends on size, shape, weight, and how the car is driven. The best mileage is achieved under steady cruise conditions. City driving, with many starts and stops, yields worse mileage than steady highway driving. In order to establish a regulatory framework for fuel economy standards, the federal government has established hypothetical driving cycles that are intended to represent how cars are operated on a sort of average basis.

The government fuel economy standards are not based on just one car, but are stated in terms of the average rated miles per gallon fuel mileage for the production of all models by a manufacturer for any year. This latter requirement is known in the automotive industry by the acronym CAFE (corporate average fuel economy). It is a somewhat complex requirement and is based on measurements of the fuel used during a prescribed simulated standard driving cycle.

FEDERAL GOVERNMENT TEST PROCEDURES

For an understanding of both emission and CAFE requirements, it is helpful to review the standard cycle and how the emission and fuel economy measurements are made. The U.S. federal government has published test procedures that include several steps. The first step is to place the automobile on a chassis dynamometer, like the one shown in Figure 5.1.

**Figure 5.1
Chassis
Dynamometer**

Government test procedures use a chassis dynamometer to simulate actual driving conditions in a controlled environment.

A *chassis dynamometer* is a test stand that holds a vehicle such as a car or truck. It is equipped with instruments capable of measuring the power that is delivered at the drive wheels of the vehicle under various conditions. The vehicle is held on the dynamometer so that it cannot move when power is applied to the drive wheels. The drive wheels are in contact with two large rollers. One roller is mechanically coupled to an electric generator that can vary the load on its electrical output. The other roller has instruments to measure and record the vehicle speed. The generator absorbs all mechanical power that is delivered at the drive wheels, and the horsepower is calculated from the electrical output. (746 watts of electrical output equals 1 horsepower.) The controls of the dynamometer can be set to simulate the correct load (including the effects of tire rolling resistance and aerodynamic drag) and inertia of the vehicle moving along a road under various conditions. The conditions are the same as if the vehicle actually were being driven except for wind loads.

Emission samples are collected and measured during a simulated urban trip containing a high percentage of stop-and-go driving.

The vehicle is operated according to a prescribed schedule of speed and load to simulate the specified trip. One is an urban trip and one is a highway trip. Over the years, the hypothetical driving cycles for urban and rural trips have evolved. Figure 5.2 illustrates sample driving cycle trips (one for each) that demonstrate the differences in those hypothetical test trips. It can be seen that the urban cycle trip involves acceleration, deceleration, stops, starts, and steady cruise such as would be encountered in a "typical" city automobile trip of 7.45 miles (12 km). The highway schedule takes 765 seconds and simulates 10.24 miles (16.5 km) of highway driving.

During the operation of the vehicle in the urban test, the exhaust is continuously collected and sampled. At the end of the test, the absolute mass of each of the regulated exhaust gases is determined. The regulations are stated in terms of the total mass of each exhaust gas divided by the total distance of the simulated trip.

Fuel consumption also is measured during the tests. Emission and MPG requirements have grown increasingly stringent since 1968.

In addition to emission measurement, each manufacturer must determine the fuel consumption in MPG for each type of vehicle and must compute the corporate average mileage for all vehicles of all types produced in a year. Fuel consumption is measured during both an urban and a highway test, and the composite fuel economy is calculated.

Table 5.1 is a summary of the exhaust emission requirements and CAFE standards for a few representative years. It shows the emission requirements and increased fuel economy required, demonstrating that these regulations have become and will continue to become more stringent with passing time. Not shown in Table 5.1 is a separate regulation on non-methane hydrocarbon (NMHC). Because of these requirements, each manufacturer has a strong incentive to minimize exhaust emissions and maximize fuel economy for each vehicle produced.

**Table 5.1
Emission and MPG
Requirements**

Year	Federal HC/CO/NO$_x$	California HC/CO/NO$_x$	CAFE MPG
1968	3.22/33.0/–	—	—
1971	2.20/23.0/–	—	—
1978	1.50/15.0/2.0	0.41/9.0/1.5	18.0
1979	1.50/15.0/2.0	0.41/9.0/1.5	19.0
1980	0.41/7.0/2.0	0.41/9.0/1.5	20.0
.	.	.	.
.	.	.	.
.	.	.	.
1989	0.31/4.1/1.0	0.31/4.1/1.0	27.5

**Figure 5.2
Federal Driving
Schedules (*Title 40
United States Code of
Federal Regulations*)**

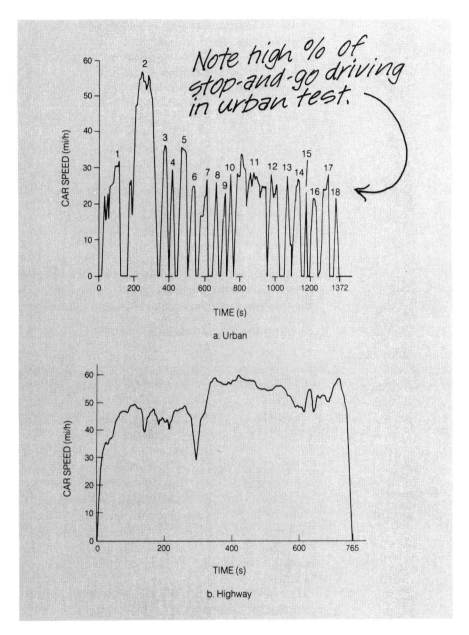

a. Urban

b. Highway

New regulations for emissions have continued to evolve and encompass more and more vehicle classes. Present-day regulations affect not only passenger cars but also light utility vehicles and both heavy- and light-duty trucks. Furthermore, regulations apply to a variety of fuels, including gasoline, diesel, natural gas, and alcohol-based fuels involving mixtures of gasoline with methanol or ethanol.

Standards have been written for the vehicle half-life (5 years or 50,000 miles—whichever comes first) and full life cycle (10 years or 100,000 miles). The standards are:

HC	0.31 g/mi
CO	4.20 g/mi
NO_x	0.60 g/mi (nondiesel)
	1.25 g/mi (diesel)

These regulations were phased in according to the following schedules:

Model year 1994:   40%
Model year 1995:   80%
Model year 1996: 100%

There are many details to these regulations that are not relevant to the present discussion. However, the regulations themselves are important in that they provided motivation for expanded electronic controls.

Meeting the Requirements

Engines using mechanical, hydraulic, or pneumatic controls cannot meet government regulations, but engines using electronic engine controls can.

Unfortunately, as seen later in this chapter, meeting the government regulations causes some sacrifice in performance. Moreover, attempts to meet the standards exemplified by Table 5.1 using mechanical, electromechanical, hydraulic, or pneumatic controls like those used in pre–emission control vehicles have not been cost effective. In addition, such controls cannot reproduce functions with sufficient accuracy across a range of production vehicles, over all operating conditions, and over the life of the vehicle to stay within the tolerance required by the EPA regulations. Each automaker must verify that each model produced will still meet emission requirements after traveling 100,000 miles. As in any physical system, the parameters of automotive engines and associated peripheral control devices can change with time. An electronic control system has the ability to automatically compensate for such changes and to adapt to any new set of operating conditions and made electronic controls a desirable option in the early stages of emission control.

The Role of Electronics

The use of digital electronic control has enabled automakers to meet the government regulations by controlling the system accurately with excellent tolerance. In addition, the system has long-term calibration stability. As an added advantage, this type of system is very flexible. Because it uses microcomputers, it can be modified through programming changes to meet a variety of different vehicle/engine combinations. Critical quantities that describe an engine can be changed easily by changing data stored in the system's computer memory.

Additional Cost Incentive

Dropping costs of microprocessors and other very large scale integrated circuits have made electronic engine control an increasingly attractive system for automobile manufacturers.

Besides providing control accuracy and stability, there is a cost incentive to use digital electronic control. The system components—the multifunction digital integrated circuits—are decreasing in cost, thus decreasing the system cost. From about 1970 on, considerable investment was made by the semiconductor industry for the development of low-cost, multifunction integrated circuits. In particular, the microprocessor and microcomputer have reached an advanced state of capability at relatively low cost. This has made the electronic digital control system for the engine, as well as other on-board automobile electronic systems, commercially feasible.

As pointed out in Chapter 3, as multifunction digital integrated circuits continue to be designed with more and more functional capability through very large scale integrated circuits (VLSI), the costs continue to decrease. At the same time, these circuits offer improved electronic system performance in the automobile.

In summary, the electronic engine control system duplicates the function of conventional fluidic control systems, but with greater precision. It can optimize engine performance while meeting the exhaust emission and fuel economy regulations and can adapt to changes in the plant.

CONCEPT OF AN ELECTRONIC ENGINE CONTROL SYSTEM

In order to understand electronic engine control it is necessary to understand some fundamentals of how the power produced by the engine is controlled. Any driver understands intuitively that the throttle directly regulates the power produced by the engine at any operating condition. It does this by controlling the air flow into the engine.

In essence the engine is an air pump such that at any RPM the mass flow rate of air into the engine varies directly with throttle plate angular position (see Figure 5.3).

As the driver depresses the accelerator pedal, the throttle angle (θ in Figure 5.3) increases, which increases the cross-sectional area through which the air flows, reducing the resistance to air flow and thereby allowing an increased air flow into the engine. The role of fuel control is to regulate the fuel that is mixed with the air so that it increases in proportion to the air flow. As we will see later in this chapter, the performance of the engine is affected strongly by the mixture (i.e., by the ratio of air to fuel). However, for any given mixture the power produced by the engine is directly proportional to the mass flow rate of air into the engine. In the U.S. system of units, an air flow rate of about 6 lb/hr produces 1 horsepower of usable mechanical power at the output of the engine. Metric units have come to be more commonly used, in which

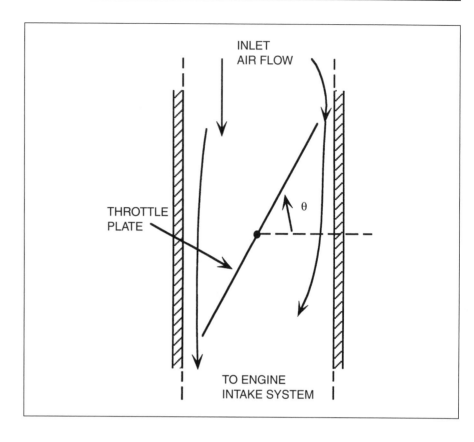

engine power is given in kilowatts (kw) and air mass is given in kilograms (kg). In mathematical terms we can write:

$$P_b = KM_A$$

where

P_b = power from the engine (hp or kw)
M_A = mass air flow rate (kg/hr) or (lb/hr)
K = constant relating power to air flow (kw/kg/hr) or (hp/lb/hr)

Of course, it is assumed that all parts of the engine, including ignition timing, are functioning correctly for this relationship to be valid.

We consider next an electronic engine control system that regulates fuel flow to the engine. An electronic engine control system is an assembly of electronic and electromechanical components that continuously varies the fuel and spark settings in order to satisfy government exhaust emission and fuel economy regulations. Figure 5.4 is a block diagram of a generalized electronic engine control system.

**Figure 5.4
Generic Electronic
Engine Control
System**

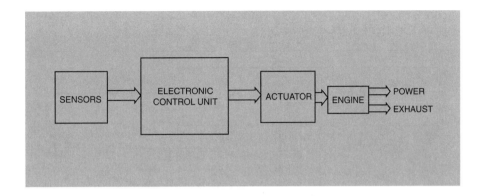

It will be explained later in this chapter that an automotive engine control has both open-loop and closed-loop operating modes (see Chapter 2). As explained in Chapter 2, a closed-loop control system requires measurements of certain output variables that tell the controller the state of the system being controlled, whereas an open-loop system does not. The electronic engine control system receives input electrical signals from the various sensors that measure the state of the engine. From these signals, the controller generates output electrical signals to the actuators that determine the engine calibration (i.e., correct fuel delivery and spark timing).

Examples of automotive engine control system sensors will be discussed in Chapter 6. As mentioned, the configuration and control for an automotive engine control system are determined in part by the set of sensors that is available to measure the variables. In many cases, the sensors available for automotive use involve compromises between performance and cost. In other cases, only indirect measurements of certain variables are feasible. From measurement of these variables, the desired variable is found by computation.

Overall engine functions that are subject to electronic engine controls are air/fuel ratio, spark control, and exhaust gas recirculation.

Figure 5.5 identifies the automotive functions that surround the engine. There is a fuel metering system to set the air–fuel mixture flowing into the engine through the intake manifold. Spark control determines when the air–fuel mixture is ignited after it is compressed in the cylinders of the engine. The power is delivered at the driveshaft, and the gases that result from combustion flow out of the exhaust system. In the exhaust system, there is a valve to control the amount of exhaust gas being recirculated back to the input, and a catalytic converter to further control emissions. This addition to the engine, as well as various sensors and actuators depicted in Figure 5.5, is explained later.

At one stage of development, the electronic engine control consisted of separate subsystems for fuel control, spark control, and exhaust gas recirculation. The ignition system in Figure 5.5 is shown as a separate control system, although engine control is evolving toward an integrated digital system (see Chapter 7).

Figure 5.5
Engine Functions and Control

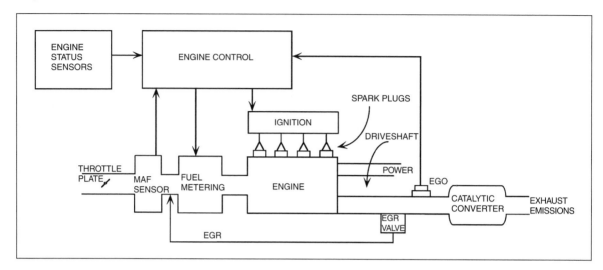

This chapter discusses the various electronic engine control functions separately and explains how each function is implemented by a separate control system. Chapter 7 shows how these separate control systems are being integrated into one system.

DEFINITION OF GENERAL TERMS

Before proceeding with the details of engine control systems, certain definitions of terms must be clarified—first some general terms and then some specific engine performance terms.

Parameters

Design parameters such as engine size, compression ratio, and so forth, are fixed; therefore, they are not subject to any engine operating control.

A *parameter* is a numerical value of some engine dimension that is fixed by design. Examples of engine design parameters include the piston diameter (*bore*), the distance the piston travels on one stroke (*stroke*), and the length of the crankshaft lever arm (*throw*). The bore and stroke determine the cylinder volume and the displacement. *Displacement* is the total volume of air that is displaced as the engine rotates through two complete revolutions. *Compression ratio* is the ratio of cylinder volume at BDC to the volume at TDC. Other parameters that engine designers must specify include combustion chamber shape, camshaft cam profile, intake and exhaust valve size, and valve timing. All of these design parameters are fixed and are not subject to control while the engine is operating.

**Figure 5.6
Major Controller
Inputs from Engine**

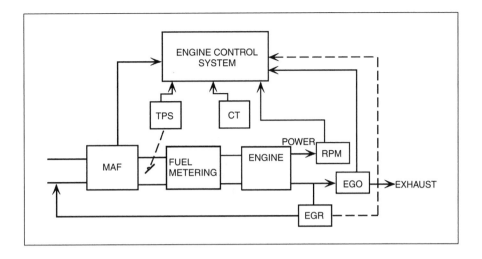

Variables

A *variable* is a quantity that changes or may be changed as the engine operates, typically under the control of the electronic control system. Some of the important engine variables are mass air flow, fuel flow rate, spark timing, power, intake manifold pressure, and many others that will be encountered in this chapter.

Inputs to Controllers

A variable is a quantity that can be changed as the engine operates.

Figure 5.6 identifies the major physical quantities that are sensed and provided to the electronic controller as inputs. They are as follows:

1. Throttle position sensor (TPS)
2. Mass air flow rate (MAF)
3. Engine temperature (coolant temperature) (CT)
4. Engine speed (RPM) and angular position
5. Exhaust gas recirculation (EGR) valve position
6. Exhaust gas oxygen (EGO) concentration

Outputs from Controllers

Figure 5.7 identifies the major physical quantities that are outputs from the controller. These outputs are

1. Fuel metering control
2. Ignition control
3. Ignition timing
4. Exhaust gas recirculation control

**Figure 5.7
Major Controller
Outputs to Engine**

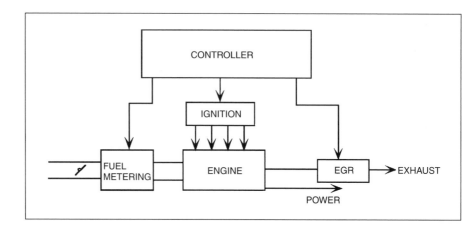

DEFINITION OF ENGINE PERFORMANCE TERMS

Several common terms are used to describe an engine's performance. Here are a few.

Power

Power is a measurement of an engine's ability to perform useful work. Brake power, which is measured with an engine dynamometer, is the actual power developed by the engine minus losses due to internal friction.

The most common performance rating that has been applied to automobiles is a power rating of the engine. It normally is given in kilowatts or, formerly, in horsepower (note: .746 kilowatt = 1 horsepower). *Power* is the rate at which the engine is doing useful work. It varies with engine speed and throttle angle. Power may be measured at the drive wheels or at the engine output shaft. It is more convenient and useful to the designer of an electronic engine control system to know the output power of only the engine than the power delivered to the wheels. This permits realistic comparisons of engine data as engine controls are varied. To make such measurements, an engine dynamometer is used. This dynamometer is similar to the one in Figure 5.1 except that the engine output shaft drives the dynamometer directly instead of coupling the output through wheels and rollers.

The power delivered by the engine to the dynamometer is called the *brake power* and is designated P_b. The brake power of an engine is always less than the total amount of power that is actually developed in the engine. This developed power is called the *indicated power* of the engine and is denoted P_i. The indicated power differs from the brake power by the loss of power in the engine due to friction between cylinders and pistons, and other friction losses. That is,

$$P_b = P_i - \text{friction and other losses}$$

BSFC

BSFC is a measurement of an engine's fuel economy. It is the ratio of fuel flow to the brake power output of the engine.

Fuel economy can be measured while the engine delivers power to the dynamometer. The engine is typically operated at a fixed RPM and a fixed brake power (fixed dynamometer load), and the fuel flow rate (in kg/hr or lb/hr) is measured. The fuel consumption is then given as the ratio of the fuel flow rate (r_f) to the brake power output (P_b). This fuel consumption is known as the *brake-specific fuel consumption*, or BSFC.

$$\text{BSFC} = \frac{r_f}{P_b}$$

The units for BSFC are lb/hr/horsepower. By improving the BSFC of the engine, the fuel economy of the vehicle in which it is installed is also improved. Electronic controls help to improve BSFC.

Torque

Torque is the twisting force of an engine's crankshaft.

Engine *torque* is the twisting action produced on the crankshaft by the cylinder pressure pushing on the piston during the power stroke. Torque is produced whenever a force is applied to a lever. The length of the lever (the lever arm) in the engine is determined by the throw of the crankshaft (the offset from the crankshaft centerline of the point where the force is applied). The torque is expressed as the product of this force and the length of the lever. The units of torque are N·m (newton meters) in the metric system or ft lb (foot-pounds) in the U.S. system. (One ft lb is the torque produced by one pound acting on a lever arm one foot long.) The torque of a typical engine varies with RPM.

Volumetric Efficiency

Other measurements of engine performance include volumetric, or "breathing," efficiency and thermal efficiency.

The variation in torque with RPM is strongly influenced by the *volumetric efficiency*, or "breathing efficiency." Volumetric efficiency actually describes how well the engine functions as an air pump, drawing air and fuel into the various cylinders. It depends on various engine design parameters such as piston size, piston stroke, and number of cylinders and is strongly influenced by camshaft design.

Thermal Efficiency

Thermal efficiency expresses the mechanical energy that is delivered to the vehicle relative to the energy content of the fuel. In the typical SI engine, 35% of the energy that is available in the fuel is lost as heat to the coolant and lubricating oil, 40% is lost as heat and unburned fuel in exhaust gases, and another 5% is lost in engine and drivetrain friction. This means that only about 20% is available to drive the vehicle and accessories. These percentages vary somewhat with operating conditions but are valid on the average.

Calibration

The definition of engine *calibration* is the setting of the air/fuel ratio and ignition timing for the engine. With the new electronic control systems, calibration is determined by the electronic engine control system.

ENGINE MAPPING

Engine mapping is a process by which measurements are made of important engine variables while the engine is operated throughout its speed and load ranges.

The development of any control system comes from knowledge of the plant, or system to be controlled. In the case of the automobile engine, this knowledge of the plant (the engine) comes primarily from a process called *engine mapping.*

For engine mapping, the engine is connected to a dynamometer and operated throughout its entire speed and load range. Measurements are made of the important engine variables while quantities, such as the air/fuel ratio and the spark control, are varied in a known and systematic manner. Such engine mapping is done in engine test cells that have engine dynamometers and complex instrumentation that collects data under computer control.

From this mapping, a mathematical model is developed that explains the influence of every measurable variable and parameter on engine performance. The control system designer must select a control configuration, control variables, and control strategy that will satisfy all performance requirements (including stability) as computed from this model and that are within the other design limits such as cost, quality, and reliability. To understand a typical engine control system, it is instructive to consider the influence of control variables on engine performance.

Effect of Air/Fuel Ratio on Performance

Figure 5.8 illustrates the variation in the performance variables of torque (T) and brake power (BSFC) as well as engine emissions with variations in the air/fuel ratio with fixed spark timing and a constant engine speed.

In this figure the exhaust gases are represented in brake-specific form. This is a standard way to characterize exhaust gases whose absolute emission levels are proportional to power. The definitions for the brake-specific emission rates are

$$BSHC = \text{brake-specific HC concentration}$$

$$= \frac{r_{HC}}{P_b}$$

$$BSCO = \text{brake-specific CO concentration}$$

$$= \frac{r_{CO}}{P_b}$$

$$BSNO_x = \text{brake-specific } NO_x \text{ concentration}$$

$$= \frac{r_{NO_x}}{P_b}$$

where

$$r_{HC} = \text{HC rate of flow}$$
$$r_{CO} = \text{CO rate of flow}$$
$$r_{NO_x} = NO_x \text{ rate of flow}$$

One specific air/fuel ratio is highly significant in electronic fuel control systems, namely, the *stoichiometric mixture*. The stoichiometric (i.e., chemically correct) mixture corresponds to an air and fuel combination such that if combustion were perfect all of the hydrogen and carbon in the fuel would be converted by the burning process to H_2O and CO_2. For gasoline the stoichiometric mixture ratio is $14.7 : 1$.

Stoichiometry is sufficiently important that the fuel and air mixture is often represented by a ratio called the *equivalence ratio*, which is given the specific designation λ (i.e., the Greek letter lambda). The equivalence ratio is defined as follows:

$$\lambda = \frac{(\text{air}/\text{fuel})}{(\text{air}/\text{fuel stoichiometry})}$$

A relatively low air/fuel ratio, below 14.7 (corresponding to $\lambda < 1$), is called a *rich* mixture; an air/fuel ratio above 14.7 (corresponding to $\lambda > 1$) is called a *lean* mixture. Emission control is strongly affected by air/fuel ratio, or by λ.

Note from Figure 5.8 that torque (T) reaches a maximum in the air/fuel ratio range of 12 to 14. The exact air/fuel ratio for which torque is maximum depends on the engine configuration, engine speed, and ignition timing.

> The air/fuel ratio has a significant effect on engine torque and emissions.

Also note that the CO and unburned hydrocarbons tend to decrease sharply with increasing air/fuel ratios, as one might expect because there is relatively more oxygen available for combustion with lean mixtures than with rich mixtures.

Unfortunately for the purposes of controlling exhaust emissions, the NO_x exhaust concentration increases with increasing air/fuel ratios. That is, there is no air/fuel ratio that simultaneously minimizes all regulated exhaust gases.

Effect of Spark Timing on Performance

> Spark timing also has a major effect on emissions and engine performance. Maximum engine torque occurs at MBT.

Spark advance is the time before top dead center (TDC) when the spark is initiated. It is usually expressed in number of degrees of crankshaft rotation relative to TDC. Figure 5.9 reveals the influence of spark timing on brake-specific exhaust emissions with constant speed and constant air/fuel ratio. Note that both NO_x and HC generally increase with increased advance of spark timing. BSFC and torque are also strongly influenced by timing. Figure 5.9

Figure 5.8
Typical Variation of Performance with a Variation in Air/Fuel Ratio

Most (but not all) values are optimized at or near Stoichiometry.

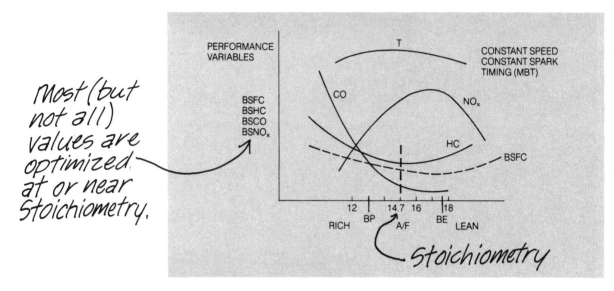

Stoichiometry

Figure 5.9
Typical Variation of Performance with Spark Timing

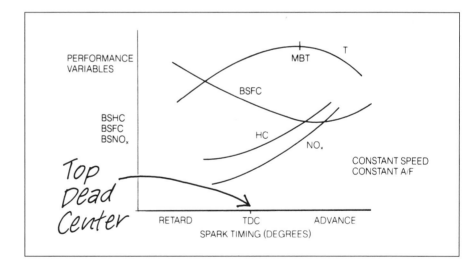

Top Dead Center

shows that maximum torque occurs at a particular advanced timing denoted MBT.

Operation at or near MBT is desirable since this spark timing tends to optimize performance. This optimal spark timing varies with RPM. As will be explained, engine control strategy involves regulating fuel delivery at a stoichiometric mixture and varying ignition timing for optimized performance. However, there is yet another variable to be controlled, which assists the engine control system in meeting exhaust gas emission regulations.

Effect of Exhaust Gas Recirculation on Performance

Exhaust gas recirculation greatly reduces nitrous oxide emissions.

Up to this point in the discussion, only the traditional calibration parameters of the engine (air/fuel ratio and spark timing) have been considered. However, by adding another control variable, the undesirable exhaust gas emission of NO_x can be significantly reduced while maintaining a relatively high level of torque. This new control variable, *exhaust gas recirculation* (EGR), consists of recirculating a precisely controlled amount of exhaust gas into the intake. Figure 5.5 shows that exhaust gas recirculation is a major subsystem of the overall control system. Its influence on emissions is shown in Figures 5.10 and 5.11 as a function of the percentage of exhaust gas in the intake. Figure 5.10 shows the dramatic reduction in NO_x emission when plotted against air/fuel ratio, and Figure 5.11 shows the effect on performance variables as the percentage of EGR is increased. Note that the emission rate of NO_x is most strongly influenced by EGR and decreases as the percentage of EGR increases. The HC emission rate increases with increasing EGR; however, for relatively low EGR percentages, the HC rate changes only slightly.

The mechanism by which EGR affects NO_x production is related to the peak combustion temperature. Roughly speaking, the NO_x generation rate increases with increasing peak combustion temperature if all other variables

**Figure 5.10
NO_x Emission as a
Function of EGR at
Various Air/Fuel
Ratios**

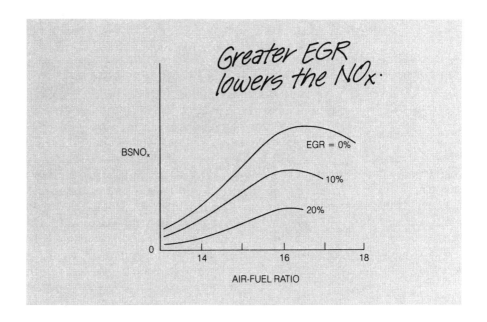

**Figure 5.11
Typical Variation of
Engine Performance
with EGR**

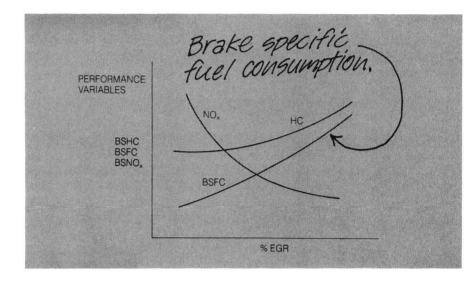

remain fixed. Increasing EGR tends to lower this temperature; therefore, it tends to lower NO_x generation.

CONTROL STRATEGY

It is the task of the electronic control system to set the calibration for each engine operating condition. There are many possible control strategies for setting the variables for any given engine, and each tends to have its own advantages and disadvantages. Moreover, each automobile manufacturer has a specific configuration that differs in certain details from competitive systems. However, this discussion is about a typical electronic control system that is highly representative of the systems for engines used by U.S. manufacturers. This typical system is one that has a catalytic converter in the exhaust system. Exhaust gases passed through this device are chemically altered in a way that helps meet EPA standards. Essentially, the catalytic converter reduces the concentration of undesirable exhaust gases coming out of the tailpipe relative to engine-out gases (the gases coming out of the exhaust manifold).

The use of catalytic converters to reduce emissions leaving the tailpipe allows engines to be calibrated for better performance and still meet emission regulations.

The EPA regulates only the exhaust gases that leave the tailpipe; therefore, if the catalytic converter reduces exhaust gas emission concentrations by 90%, the engine exhaust gas emissions at the exhaust manifold can be about 10 times higher than the EPA requirements. This has the significant benefit of allowing engine calibration to be set for better performance than would be permitted if exhaust emissions in the engine exhaust manifold had to satisfy EPA regulations. This is the type of system that is chosen for the typical electronic engine control system.

Several types of catalytic converters are available for use on an automobile. The desired functions of a catalytic converter include

**Figure 5.12
Oxidizing Catalytic
Converter**

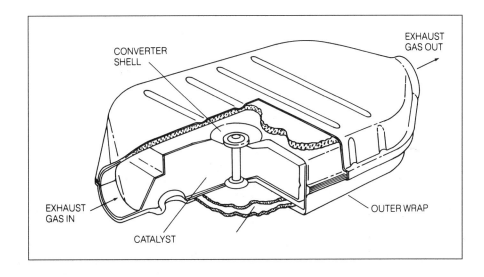

1. Oxidation of hydrocarbon emissions to carbon dioxide (CO_2) and water (H_2O)
2. Oxidation of CO to CO_2
3. Reduction of NO_x to nitrogen (N_2) and oxygen (O_2)

Oxidizing Catalytic Converter

The oxidizing catalytic converter increases the rate of oxidation of HC and CO to further reduce HC and CO emissions.

The oxidizing catalytic converter (Figure 5.12) has been one of the more significant devices for controlling exhaust emissions since the era of emission control began. The purpose of the oxidizing catalyst (OC) is to increase the rate of chemical reaction, which initially takes place in the cylinder as the compressed air–fuel mixture burns, toward an exhaust gas that has a complete oxidation of HC and CO to H_2O and CO_2.

The extra oxygen required for this oxidation is often supplied by adding air to the exhaust stream from an engine-driven air pump. This air, called *secondary air*, is normally introduced into the exhaust manifold.

The most significant measure of the performance of the OC is its conversion efficiency, n_c.

$$n_c = \frac{M_o}{M_i}$$

where

M_o is the mass flow rate of gas that has been oxidized leaving the converter

M_i is the mass air flow rate of gas into the converter

Figure 5.13
Oxidizing Catalyst Conversion Efficiency versus Temperature

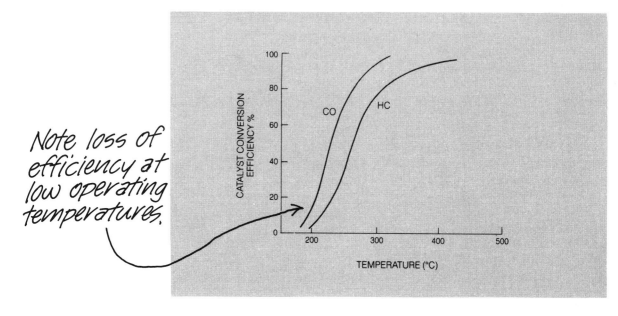

Note loss of efficiency at low operating temperatures.

The conversion efficiency of the OC depends on its temperature. Figure 5.13 shows the conversion efficiency of a typical OC for both HC and CO as functions of temperature. Above about 300°C, the efficiency approaches 98% to 99% for CO and more than 95% for HC.

The Three-Way Catalyst

The three-way catalyst uses a specific chemical design to reduce all three major emissions (HC, CO, and NO_x) by approximately 90%.

Another catalytic converter configuration that is extremely important for modern emission control systems is called the three-way catalyst (TWC). It uses a specific catalyst formulation containing platinum, palladium, and rhodium to reduce NO_x and oxidize HC and CO all at the same time. It is called three-way because it simultaneously reduces the concentration of all three major undesirable exhaust gases by about 90% if used optimally.

The conversion efficiency of the TWC for the three exhaust gases depends mostly on the air/fuel ratio. Unfortunately, the air/fuel ratio for which NO_x conversion efficiency is highest corresponds to a very low conversion efficiency for HC and CO and vice versa. However, as shown in Figure 5.14, there is a very narrow range of air/fuel ratio (called the window) in which an acceptable compromise exists between NO_x and HC/CO conversion efficiencies. The conversion efficiencies within this window are sufficiently high to meet the very stringent EPA requirements established so far.

**Figure 5.14
Conversion
Efficiency of a TWC**

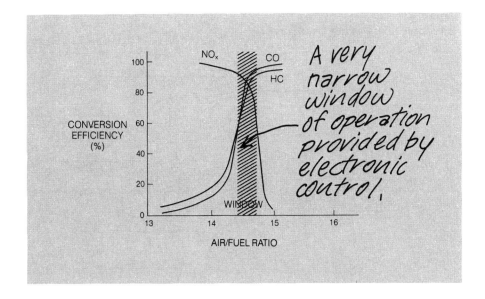

Note that this window is only about 0.1 air/fuel ratio wide (±0.05 air/fuel ratio) and is centered at stoichiometry. (Recall that stoichiometry is the air/fuel ratio that would result in complete oxidation of all carbon and hydrogen in the fuel if burning in the cylinder were perfect; for gasoline, stoichiometry corresponds to an air/fuel ratio of 14.7.) This ratio and the concept of stoichiometry is extremely important in an electronic fuel controller. In fact, the primary function of most modern electronic fuel control systems is to maintain average air/fuel ratio at stoichiometry. The operation of the three-way catalytic converter is adversely affected by lead. Thus, in automobiles using any catalyst, it is necessary to use lead-free fuel.

The TWC operates at peak efficiency when the air/fuel ratio is at or very near stoichiometry. An electronic fuel control system is required to maintain the required air/fuel ratio.

Controlling the average air/fuel ratio to the tolerances of the TWC window (for 100,000 miles) requires accurate measurement of mass air flow rate and precise fuel delivery and is the primary function of the electronic engine control system. A modern electronic fuel control system can meet these precise fuel requirements. In addition, it can maintain the necessary tolerances for government regulations for over 100,000 miles.

ELECTRONIC FUEL CONTROL SYSTEM

For an understanding of the configuration of an electronic fuel control system, refer to the block diagram of Figure 5.15. The primary function of this fuel control system is to accurately determine the mass air flow rate into the engine. Then the control system precisely regulates fuel delivery such that the ratio of the mass of air to the mass of fuel in each cylinder is as close as possible to stoichiometry (i.e., 14.7).

Figure 5.15
Electronic Fuel Control Configuration

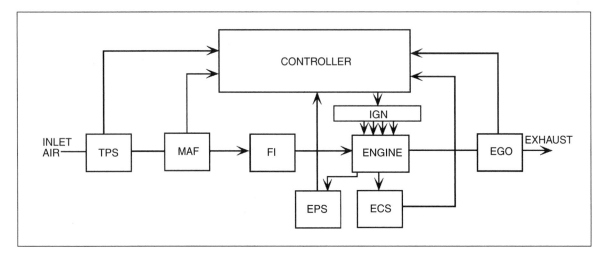

The components of this block diagram are as follows:

1. Throttle position sensor (TPS)
2. Mass air flow sensor (MAF)
3. Fuel injectors (FI)
4. Ignition systems (IGN)
5. Exhaust gas oxygen sensor (EGO)
6. Engine coolant sensor (ECS)
7. Engine position sensor (EPS)

The EPS has the capability of measuring crankshaft angular speed (RPM) as well as crankshaft angular position when it is used in conjunction with a stable and precise electronic clock (in the controller).

The signals from the various sensors enable the controller to determine the correct fuel flow in relation to the air flow to obtain the stoichiometric mixture. From this calculation the correct fuel delivery is regulated via fuel injectors. In addition, optimum ignition timing is determined and appropriate timing pulses are sent to the ignition control module (IGN).

The intake air passes through the individual pipes of the intake manifold to the various cylinders. The set of fuel injectors (one for each cylinder) is normally located near the intake valve (see Chapter 1). Each fuel injector is an electrically operated valve that is either fully open or fully closed. When the valve is closed, there is, of course, no fuel delivery. When the valve is open, fuel is delivered at a fixed rate as set by the fuel injector characteristics as well as fuel pressure. The amount of fuel delivered to each cylinder is determined by the length of time that the fuel injector valve is open. This time is, in turn, computed in the engine controller to achieve the desired air/fuel ratio. Typically, the fuel injector open timing is set to coincide with the time that air is flowing into the cylinder during the intake stroke (see Chapter 1).

There is an important property of the catalytic converter that allows for momentary (very short term) fluctuations of the air/fuel ratio outside the narrow window. As the exhaust gases flow through the catalytic converter they are actually in it for a short (but nonzero) amount of time, during which the conversions described above take place. Because of this time interval the conversion efficiency is unaffected by rapid fluctuations above and below stoichiometry (and outside the window) as long as the average air/fuel ratio over time remains at stoichiometry and provided the fluctuations are rapid enough. A practical fuel control system maintains the mixture at stoichiometry but has minor (relatively rapid) fluctuations about the average, as explained below.

The electronic fuel control system operates in two modes: open loop and closed loop. Recall the concepts for open-loop and closed-loop control as explained in Chapter 2. In the open-loop mode (also called feedforward), the mass air flow rate into the engine is measured. Then the fuel control system determines the quantity of fuel to be delivered to meet the required air/fuel ratio.

In the closed-loop control mode (also called feedback), a measurement of the controlled variable is provided to the controller (i.e., it is fed back) such that an error signal between the actual and desired values of the controlled variable is obtained. Then the controller generates an actuating signal that tends to reduce the error to zero.

In the case of fuel control, the desired variables to be measured are HC, CO, and NO_x concentrations. Unfortunately there is no cost-effective, practical sensor for such measurements that can be built into the car's exhaust system. On the other hand, there is a relatively inexpensive sensor that gives an indirect measurement of HC, CO, and NO_x concentrations. This sensor generates an output that depends on the concentration of residual oxygen in the exhaust after combustion. As will be explained in detail in Chapter 6, this sensor is called an *exhaust gas oxygen* (EGO) *sensor*. It will be shown that the EGO sensor output switches abruptly between two voltage levels depending on whether the input air/fuel ratio is richer than or leaner than stoichiometry. Such a sensor is appropriate for use in a limit-cycle type of closed-loop control (described in Chapter 2). Although the EGO sensor is a switching-type sensor, it provides sufficient information to the controller to maintain the average air/fuel ratio over time at stoichiometry, thereby meeting the mixture requirements for optimum performance of the three-way catalytic converter.

In a typical modern electronic fuel control system, the fuel delivery is partly open loop and partly closed loop. The open-loop portion of the fuel flow is determined by measurement of air flow. This portion sets the air/fuel ratio at approximately stoichiometry. A closed-loop portion is added to the fuel delivery to ensure that time-average air/fuel ratio is at stoichiometry (within the tolerances of the window).

There are exceptions to the stoichiometric mixture setting during certain engine operating conditions, including engine start, heavy acceleration, and deceleration. These conditions represent a very small fraction of the overall engine operating times and are discussed in Chapter 7, which explains the operation of a modern, practical digital electronic engine control system.

Engine Control Sequence

Referring to Figure 5.15, the step-by-step process of events in fuel control begins with engine start. During engine cranking the mixture is set rich by an amount depending on the engine temperature (measured via the engine coolant sensor), as explained in detail in Chapter 7. Generally speaking, the mixture is relatively rich for starting and operating a cold engine as compared with a warm engine. However, the discussion of this requirement is deferred to Chapter 7. Once the engine starts and until a specific set of conditions is satisfied, the engine control operates in the open-loop mode. In this mode the mass air flow is measured (via MAF sensor). The correct fuel amount is computed in the electronic controller as a function of engine temperature. The correct actuating signal is then computed and sent to the fuel metering actuator. In essentially all modern engines, fuel metering is accomplished by a set of fuel injectors (described in detail in Chapter 6).

After combustion the exhaust gases flow past the EGO sensor, through the TWC, and out the tailpipe. Once the EGO sensor has reached its operating temperature (typically a few seconds to about 2 min), the EGO sensor signal is read by the controller and the system begins closed-loop operation.

Open-Loop Control

Fuel control for an electronically controlled engine operates open loop any time the conditions are not met for closed-loop operation. Among many conditions (which are discussed in detail in Chapter 7) for closed-loop operations are some temperature requirements. After operating for a sufficiently long period after starting, a liquid-cooled automotive engine operates at a steady temperature.

However, an engine that is started cold initially operates in open-loop mode. This operating mode requires, at minimum, measurement of the mass air flow into the engine, and a measurement of RPM as well as measurement of coolant temperature. The mass air flow rate measurement in combination with RPM permits computation (by the engine controller) of the mass of air (M_a) drawn into each cylinder during intake. The correct fuel mass (M_f) that is injected with the intake air is computed by the electronic controller

$$M_f = r_{fa} M_a$$

where

r_{fa} = desired ratio of fuel to air

For a fully warmed-up engine, this ratio is 1/14.7 which is about .068. That is, one lb of fuel is injected for each 14.7 lb of air, making the air/fuel ratio 14.7 (i.e., stoichiometry). The desired fuel/air ratio varies with temperature in a known way such that the correct value can be found from the measurement of coolant temperature. For a very cold engine, the mixture ratio can go as low as about 2 (i.e., $r_{fa} \cong .5$).

Theoretically, if there were no changes to the engine, the sensors, or the fuel injector, an engine control system could operate open loop at all times. In practice, owing to variations in manufactured components, as well as to factors such as wear, the open-loop control would not be able to maintain the mixture at the desired air/fuel ratio. In order to maintain the very precise air/fuel mixture ratio required for emission control over the full life of the vehicle, the engine controller is operated in closed-loop mode for as much of the time as possible.

Closed-Loop Control

In the closed-loop mode of operation, the signals from the EGO sensor are used by the electronic controller to adjust the air/fuel ratio through the fuel metering actuator.

Referring to Figure 5.16, the control system in closed-loop mode operates as follows. For any given set of operating conditions, the fuel metering actuator provides fuel flow to produce an air/fuel ratio set by the controller output. This mixture is burned in the cylinder and the combustion products leave the engine through the exhaust pipe. The EGO sensor generates a feedback signal for the controller input that depends on the air/fuel ratio in the intake mixture. This signal tells the controller to adjust the fuel flow rate for the required air/fuel ratio, thus completing the loop.

One control scheme that has been used in practice results in the air/fuel ratio cycling around the desired set point of stoichiometry. Recall from Chapter 2 that this type of control is provided by a limit-cycle controller (e.g., a typical furnace controller). The important parameters for this type of control include the amplitude and frequency of excursion away from the desired stoichiometric set point. Fortunately, the three-way catalytic converter's characteristics are such that only the time-average air/fuel ratio determines its performance. The variation in air/fuel ratio during the limit-cycle operation is so rapid that it has no effect on engine performance or emissions, provided that the average air/fuel ratio remains at stoichiometry.

Exhaust Gas Oxygen Concentration

The EGO sensor is used to determine the air/fuel ratio.

The EGO sensor, which provides feedback, will be explained in Chapter 6. In essence, the EGO generates an output signal that depends on the amount of oxygen in the exhaust. This oxygen level, in turn, depends on the air/fuel

Figure 5.16
Simplified Typical Closed-Loop Fuel Control System

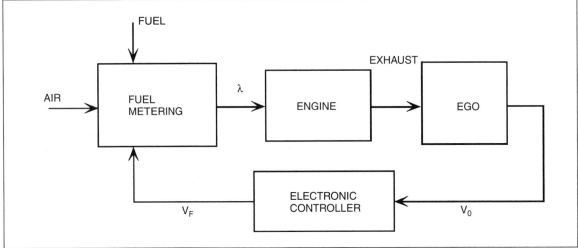

ratio entering the engine. The amount of oxygen is relatively low for rich mixtures and relatively high for lean mixtures. In terms of equivalence ratio (λ), recall that $\lambda = 1$ corresponds to stoichiometry, $\lambda > 1$ corresponds to a lean mixture with an air/fuel ratio greater than stoichiometry, and $\lambda < 1$ corresponds to a rich mixture with an air/fuel ratio less than stoichiometry. (The EGO sensor is sometimes called a lambda sensor.)

Fuel entering each cylinder having a relatively lean mixture (i.e., excess oxygen) results in a relatively high oxygen concentration in the exhaust after combustion. Correspondingly, intake fuel and air having a relatively rich mixture (i.e., low oxygen) results in relatively low oxygen concentration in the exhaust.

Lambda is used in the block diagram of Figure 5.16 to represent the equivalence ratio at the intake manifold. The exhaust gas oxygen concentration determines the EGO output voltage (V_o). The EGO output voltage abruptly switches between the lean and the rich levels as the air/fuel ratio crosses stoichiometry. The EGO sensor output voltage is at its higher of two levels for a rich mixture and at its lower level for a lean mixture.

In a closed-loop system, the time delay between sensing a deviation and performing an action to correct for the deviation must be compensated for in system design.

The operation of the control system of Figure 5.16 using EGO output voltage is complicated somewhat because of the delay from the time that λ changes at the input until V_o changes at the exhaust. This time delay, t_D, is in the range of 0.1 to 0.2 second, depending on engine speed. It is the time that it takes the output of the system to respond to a change at the input. The electrical signal from the EGO sensor voltage going into the controller produces a controller output of V_F, which energizes the fuel metering actuator.

Figure 5.17
Simplified Waveforms in a Closed-Loop Fuel Control System

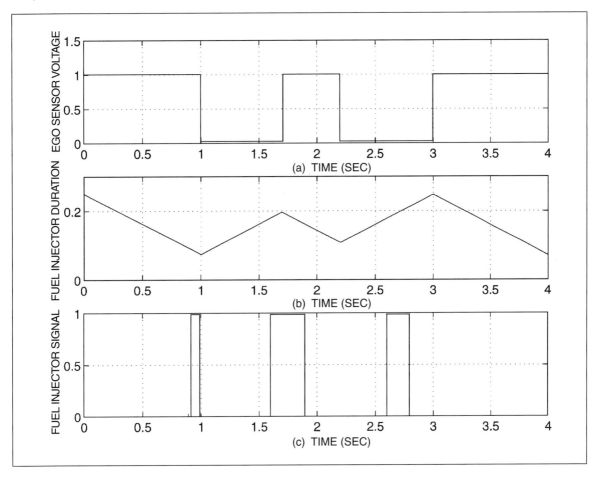

Closed-Loop Operation

Reduced to its essential features, the engine control system operates as a limit-cycle controller in which the air/fuel ratio cycles up and down about the set point of stoichiometry, as shown by the idealized waveforms in Figure 5.17. The air/fuel ratio is either increasing or decreasing; it is never constant. The increase or decrease is determined by the EGO sensor output voltage. Whenever the EGO output voltage level indicates a lean mixture, the controller causes the air/fuel ratio to decrease, that is, to change in the direction of a rich mixture. On the other hand, whenever the EGO sensor output voltage indicates a rich mixture, the controller changes the air/fuel ratio in the direction of a lean mixture.

The air/fuel ratio in a closed-loop system is always increasing or decreasing in the vicinity of stoichiometry. This is in response to the EGO sensor's output, which indicates a rich or lean fuel mixture.

The electronic fuel controller changes the mixture by changing the duration of the actuating signal to each fuel injector. Increasing this duration causes more fuel to be delivered, thereby causing the mixture to become richer. Correspondingly, decreasing this duration causes the mixture to become leaner. Figure 5.17b shows the fuel injector signal duration.

In Figure 5.17a the EGO sensor output voltage is at the higher of two levels over several time intervals, including 0 to 1 and 1.7 to 2.2. This high voltage indicates that the mixture is rich. The controller causes the pulse duration (Figure 5.17b) to decrease during this interval. At time 1 sec the EGO sensor voltage switches low, indicating a lean mixture. At this point the controller begins increasing the actuating time interval to tend toward a rich mixture. This increasing actuator interval continues until the EGO sensor switches high, causing the controller to decrease the fuel injector actuating interval. The process continues this way, cycling back and forth between rich and lean around stoichiometry.

During any one of the intervals shown in Figure 5.17, the fuel injectors may be activated several times. The engine controller continuously computes the desired fuel injector actuating interval (as explained later) and maintains the current value in memory. At the appropriate time in the intake cycle (see Chapter 1), the controller reads the value of the fuel injector duration and generates a pulse of the correct duration to activate the proper fuel injector.

Figure 5.17c illustrates the actuating signals for a single fuel injector. The pulses correspond to the times at which this fuel injector is activated. The duration of each pulse determines the quantity of fuel delivered during that activation interval. This fuel injector is switched on repeatedly at the desired time. The on duration is determined from the height of the desired actuator duration of Figure 5.17b. Note that the first pulse corresponds to a relatively low value. The second corresponds to a relatively high value, and the duration of the on time shown in Figure 5.17c is correspondingly longer. The last pulse shown happens to occur at an intermediate duration value and is depicted as being of duration between the other two. The pulses depicted in Figure 5.17c are somewhat exaggerated relative to an actual fuel control to illustrate the principle of this type of control system. It should be emphasized that the situation depicted in Figure 5.17 is highly idealized and simplified compared to an actual practical fuel control system.

One point that needs to be stressed at this juncture is that the air/fuel ratio deviates from stoichiometry. However, the catalytic converter will function as desired as long as the time-average air/fuel ratio is at stoichiometry. The controller continuously computes the average of the EGO sensor voltage. Ideally the air/fuel ratio should spend as much time rich of stoichiometry as it does lean of stoichiometry. In the simplest case, the average EGO sensor voltage should be halfway between the rich and the lean values:

$$\text{avg.}V_{\text{EGO}} = \frac{V_{\text{Rich}} + V_{\text{Lean}}}{2}$$

Whenever this condition is not met, the controller adapts its computation of pulse duration (from EGO sensor voltage) to achieve the desired average stoichiometric mixture. Chapter 7 explains this adaptive control in more detail.

Frequency and Deviation of the Fuel Controller

Recall from Chapter 2 that a limit cycle controls a system between two limits and that it has an oscillatory behavior; that is, the control variable oscillates about the set point or the desired value for the variable. The simplified fuel controller operates in a limit-cycle mode and, as shown in Figure 5.17, the air/fuel ratio oscillates about stoichiometry (i.e., average air/fuel ratio is 14.7). The two end limits are determined by the rich and lean voltage levels of the EGO sensor, by the controller, and by the characteristics of the fuel metering actuator. The time necessary for the EGO sensor to sense a change in fuel metering is known as the transport delay. As engine speed increases, the transport delay decreases.

The frequency of oscillation f_L of this limit-cycle control system is defined as the reciprocal of its period. The period of one complete cycle is denoted T_p, which is proportional to transport delay. Thus, the frequency of oscillation is

$$f_L = \frac{1}{T_p}$$

where f_L is the frequency of oscillation in hertz (cycles per second). This means that the shorter the transport delay, the higher the frequency of the limit cycle. The transport delay decreases as engine speed increases; therefore, the limit-cycle frequency increases as engine speed increases. This is depicted in Figure 5.18 for a typical engine.

Another important aspect of limit-cycle operation is the maximum deviation of air/fuel ratio from stoichiometry. It is important to keep this deviation small because the net TWC conversion efficiency is optimum for stoichiometry. The maximum deviation typically corresponds to an air/fuel ratio deviation of about ±1.0.

It is important to realize that the air/fuel ratio oscillates between a maximum value and a minimum value. There is, however, an average value for the air/fuel ratio that is intermediate between these extremes. Although the deviation of the air/fuel ratio during this limit-cycle operation is about ±1.0, the *average* air/fuel ratio is held to within ±0.05 of the desired value of 14.7.

Generally, the maximum deviation decreases with increasing engine speed because of the corresponding decrease in transport delay. The parameters

Although the air/fuel ratio is constantly swinging up and down, the average value of deviation is held within ±0.05 of the 14.7 : 1 ratio.

Figure 5.18
Typical Limit-Cycle
Frequency versus
RPM

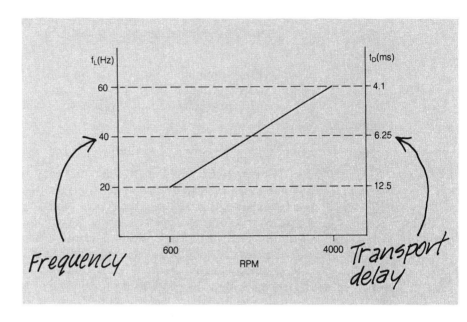

of the control system are adjusted such that at the worst case the deviation is within the required acceptable limits for the TWC used.

The preceding discussion applies only to a simplified idealized fuel control system. Chapter 7 explains the operation of practical electronic fuel control systems in which the main signal processing is done with digital techniques.

ANALYSIS OF INTAKE MANIFOLD PRESSURE

As explained earlier, fuel control is based on a measurement of mass air flow rate and on regulation of fuel flow to maintain a desired air/fuel ratio. Mass air flow measurement can be accomplished either directly or indirectly via computation based on measurement of other intake variables. For an understanding of this important measurement, it is helpful to consider the characteristics of the intake system.

The MAP sensor output voltage is proportional to the average pressure within the intake manifold.

Figure 5.19 is a very simplified sketch of an intake manifold. In this simplified sketch, the engine is viewed as an air pump drawing air into the intake manifold. Whenever the engine is not running, no air is being pumped and the intake MAP is at atmospheric pressure. This is the highest intake MAP for an unsupercharged engine. (A supercharged engine has an external air pump called a supercharger.) When the engine is running, the air flow is impeded by the partially closed throttle plate. This reduces the pressure in the intake manifold so it is lower than atmospheric pressure; therefore, a partial vacuum exists in the intake.

**Figure 5.19
Simplified Intake
System**

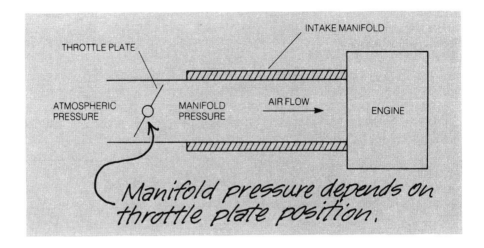

The manifold absolute pressure varies from near atmospheric pressure when the throttle plate is fully opened to near zero pressure when the throttle plate is closed.

If the engine were a perfect air pump and if the throttle plate were tightly closed, a perfect vacuum could be created in the intake manifold. A perfect vacuum corresponds to zero absolute pressure. However, the engine is not a perfect pump and some air always leaks past the throttle plate. (In fact, some air must get past a closed throttle or the engine cannot idle.) Therefore, the intake MAP fluctuates during the stroke of each cylinder and as pumping is switched from one cylinder to the next.

Each cylinder contributes to the pumping action every second crankshaft revolution. For an N-cylinder engine, the frequency f_p, in cycles per second, of the manifold pressure fluctuation for an engine running at a certain RPM is given by

$$f_p = \frac{N \times \text{RPM}}{120}$$

Figure 5.20 shows manifold pressure fluctuations as well as average MAP.

For a control system application, only average manifold pressure is required. The torque produced by an engine at a constant RPM is approximately proportional to the average value of MAP. The rapid fluctuations in instantaneous MAP are not of interest to the engine controller. Therefore, the manifold pressure measurement method should filter out the pressure fluctuations at frequency f_p and measure only the average pressure. One way to achieve this filtering is to connect the MAP sensor to the intake manifold through a very small diameter tube. The rapid fluctuations in pressure do not pass through this tube, but the average pressure does. The MAP sensor output voltage then corresponds only to the average manifold pressure.

**Figure 5.20
Intake Manifold
Pressure Fluctuations**

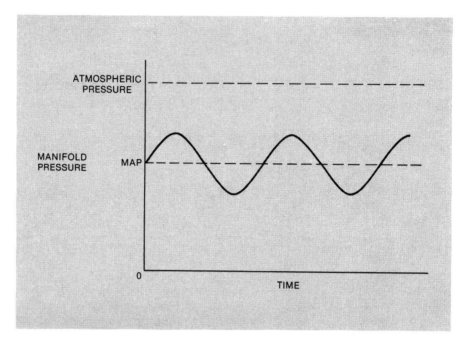

Measuring Air Mass

A critically important aspect of fuel control is the requirement to measure the mass of air that is drawn into the cylinder (i.e., the air *charge*). The amount of fuel delivered can then be calculated such as to maintain the desired air/fuel ratio. There is no practically feasible way of measuring the mass of air in the cylinder directly. However, the air charge can be determined from the mass flow rate of air into the engine intake since all of this air eventually is distributed to the cylinders (ideally uniformly).

There are two methods of determining the mass flow rate of air into the engine. One method uses a single sensor that directly measures mass air flow rate. The operation of this sensor is explained in Chapter 6. The other method uses a number of sensors that provide data from which mass flow rate can be computed. This method is known as the *speed-density method*.

Speed-Density Method

The concept for this method is based on the mass density of air as illustrated in Figure 5.21a. For a given volume of air (V) at a specific pressure (p) and temperature (T), the density of the air (d_a) is the ratio of the mass of air in that volume (M_a) divided by V:

$$d_a = \frac{M_a}{V}$$

**Figure 5.21
Volume Flow Rate
Calculation**

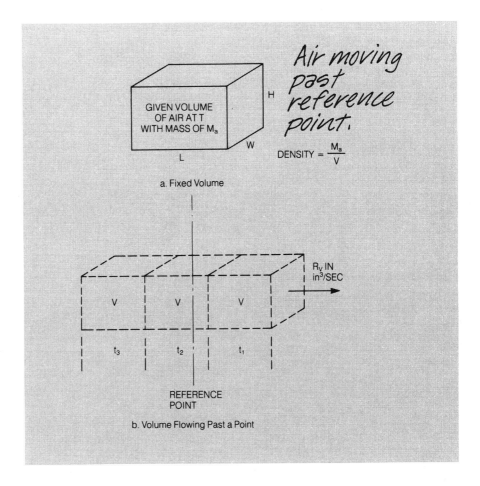

a. Fixed Volume

b. Volume Flowing Past a Point

Another way of looking at this is that the mass of air in the volume V is the product of its density and volume:

$$M_a = d_a V$$

This concept can be extended to moving air, as depicted in Figure 5.21b. Here air is assumed to be moving through a uniform tube (e.g., the intake pipe for an engine) past a reference point for a specific period of time. This is known as the volume flow rate. The mass flow rate is the product of the volume flow rate and the air density. The air density in the intake manifold can be computed from measurements of the intake manifold absolute pressure and the intake manifold air temperature (T_i).

In mathematical terms, if we define

R_m = mass flow rate of air flowing through the intake manifold
R_v = volume flow rate of air flowing through the intake manifold
d_a = air density in the intake manifold

then the following equation expresses the relationship between R_m, R_v, and d_a:

$$R_m = R_v d_a$$

The intake manifold air density is determined by the absolute pressure and temperature of the intake air. The intake manifold absolute pressure is determined by the ambient air pressure (i.e., the air outside the engine), the throttle position as set by the driver, the RPM, and by the shape and size of the intake manifold. The intake air temperature is determined by the ambient air temperature and by the pressure change from ambient air across the throttle.

The intake air density can be computed from the basic physics of air known as the perfect gas law. The density of any gas (including air) is directly proportional to pressure and inversely proportional to absolute temperature. (Absolute temperature is the temperature relative to absolute zero.) Using the Fahrenheit scale, absolute temperature is the temperature added to 459° in degrees Fahrenheit.

The intake air can be computed relative to a standard condition. Normally, the standard condition is sea level on a so-called standard day (SLSD). The SLSD conditions are denoted d_0, p_0, T_0, referring to density, absolute pressure, and absolute temperature. These parameters are constants for air for the entire planet and are known to great precision. In mathematical terms, the intake air density is given by

$$d_a = d_0 \times \left(\frac{p}{p_0} \right) \times \frac{T_0}{T_i}$$

That is, intake air density is found by multiplying standard density by the ratio of intake manifold pressure to standard pressure and by the ratio of standard temperature to intake manifold air temperature. Such a calculation is readily performed in a digital engine controller based on measurements of intake manifold absolute pressure (MAP) and intake air absolute temperature (IAT).

A relatively close estimate of R_v can be made using inexpensive sensors. As discussed previously, the engine acts like an air pump during intake. If it were a perfect pump, it would draw in a volume of air equal to its displacement for each of two complete crankshaft revolutions. Then, for this ideal engine, the volume flow rate would be

$$R_v = \left(\frac{\text{RPM}}{60} \right) \left(\frac{D}{2} \right) \text{ ideal volume flow rate}$$

where

  R_v is the volume flow rate
  D is the engine displacement
  RPM is the engine speed

For this ideal engine, with D known, R_v could be obtained simply by measuring RPM.

Unfortunately, the engine is not a perfect air pump. In fact, the actual volume flow rate for an engine having displacement D and running at speed RPM is given by

$$R_v = \left(\frac{\text{RPM}}{60}\right)\left(\frac{D}{2}\right)n_v$$

where n_v is the volumetric efficiency.

Volumetric Efficiency

Volumetric efficiency varies with MAP and engine speed. A table of values representing volumetric efficiency for given speeds and MAP values can be stored in memory as a lookup table.

The volumetric efficiency is a number between 0 and 1 that depends on intake manifold pressure (MAP) and RPM for all engine operating conditions. For any given engine, the value of n_v can be measured for any set of operating conditions. A table of values of n_v as a function of RPM and MAP can be prepared from these data. In a digital system, the table can be stored in memory as a lookup table. By knowing the displacement of the engine, measuring the RPM and MAP, and looking up the value of n_v for that RPM and MAP, the R_v can be computed using the previous equation.

Volumetric efficiency is determined by the intake manifold, the valve sizes, and locations, as well as the timing and profile of the cam lobe characteristics. The design of the cam lobe profile determines when the valves open and close and determines the maximum valve opening (lift). Any given cam profile is optimum only for a relatively narrow range of RPMs and throttle settings. Compromises are made between low, high, and midrange RPMs as well as part throttle versus open or closed throttle.

Ideally, it would be desirable to vary valve timing and lift continuously as the engine operates so as to optimize volumetric efficiency. One technology having promise for such variable valve timing (VVT) and lift would involve electromechanical or electrohydraulic valve actuation. However, at the time of the present writing, this technology appears to be somewhat in the future.

A technology that is suboptimal to fully variable valve timing and lift (which is in limited production today) is variable valve phasing. This technology involves separate camshafts for intake and exhaust valves. These two camshafts are driven via a mechanism that varies the relative timing for intake and exhaust. This mechanism (which is an electromechanical actuator) and its operation are explained in Chapter 6. There it is shown that the exhaust valve timing is varied relative to the intake valve timing. The control strategy for regulating VVT is explained in Chapter 7.

Recall from Chapter 1 that the exhaust valve is open during the exhaust stroke and that the intake valve is open during the intake stroke. Typically in automotive engines, the exhaust valve remains open during the initial portion of the intake valve-opening period. The crankshaft angle over which the two valves are both open (or partially open) is called overlap. Valve overlap permits exhaust action to assist the intake and improve volumetric efficiency. It also permits some exhaust gas to be mixed with intake gases such that the EGR system can be eliminated. In a variable cam phasing system, this overlap is minimum at idle and varies with operating conditions to optimize emissions and performance.

<u>Including EGR</u>

Exhaust gas recirculation also must be considered when calculating volume flow rate. The true volume flow rate of air is calculated by subtracting the volume flow rate of EGR from the total volume flow rate.

Calculating R_v is relatively easy for a computer, but another factor must be taken into account. Exhaust gas recirculation requires that a certain portion of the charge into the cylinders be exhaust gas. Because of this, a portion of the displacement D is exhaust gas; therefore, the volume flow rate of EGR must be known. A valve-positioning sensor in the EGR valve can be calibrated to provide the flow rate.

From this information, the true volume flow rate of air, R_a, can be determined by subtracting the volume flow rate of EGR (R_{EGR}) from R_v. The total cylinder air charge is thus given as follows:

$$R_a = R_v - R_{EGR}$$

The volume flow rate of EGR is known from the position of the EGR valve and from engine operating conditions, as explained in Chapter 7.

Substituting the equation for R_v, the volume flow rate of air is

$$R_a = \left[\left(\frac{\text{RPM}}{60}\right)\left(\frac{D}{2}\right)n_v\right] - R_{EGR}$$

Knowing R_a and the density d_a gives the mass flow rate of air R_m as follows:

$$R_m = R_a d_a$$

Knowing R_m, the stoichiometric mass flow rate for the fuel, R_{fm}, can be calculated as follows:

$$R_{fm} = \frac{R_m}{14.7}$$

It is the function of the fuel metering actuator to set the fuel mass flow rate at this desired value based on the value of R_a. The control system continuously calculates R_m from R_a and d_a at the temperature involved, and generates an output electrical signal to operate the fuel injectors to produce a stoichiometric mass fuel flow rate. For a practical engine control system, it completes such a measurement, computation, and control signal generation at least once for each cylinder firing.

ELECTRONIC IGNITION

The engine ignition system exists solely to provide an electric spark to ignite the mixture in the cylinder. As explained earlier in this chapter, the engine performance is strongly influenced by the spark timing relative to the engine position during the compression stroke (see also Chapter 1). The spark advance (relative to TDC) is determined in the electronic engine control based on a number of measurements made by sensors. As will be explained in Chapter 7, the optimum spark advance varies with intake manifold pressure, RPM, and temperature.

However, in order to generate a spark at the correct spark advance the electronic engine control must have a measurement of the engine position. Engine position is determined by a sensor coupled to the camshaft or the crankshaft, or a combination of each, depending on the configuration for the electronic ignition.

Recall from Chapter 1 that the voltage pulse to fire the spark plug in any given cylinder was routed from the coil to the relevant spark plug via a rotary switch called a distributor. In modern engines, the distributor has been replaced with multiple coils, with each coil dedicated to one (or sometimes two) cylinder(s).

Electronic ignition can be implemented as part of an integrated system or as a stand-alone ignition system. A block diagram for the latter system is shown in Figure 5.22. Based on measurements from the sensors for engine position, mass air flow or manifold pressure, and RPM, the electronic controller computes the correct spark advance for each cylinder. At the appropriate time the controller sends a trigger signal to the driver circuits, thereby initiating spark. Before the spark occurs, the driver circuit sends a relatively large current through the primary (P) of the coil. When the spark is to occur, a trigger pulse is sent to the driver circuit for the coil associated with the appropriate spark plug. This trigger causes the driver circuit to interrupt

**Figure 5.22
Electronic
Distributorless
Ignition System**

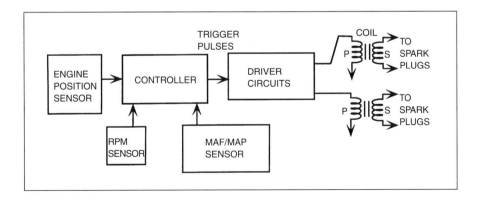

the current in the primary. A very high voltage is induced at this time in the secondary (S) of the coil. This high voltage is applied to the spark plugs, causing them to fire. In those cases for which a coil is associated with two cylinders, one of the two cylinders will be in this compression stroke. Combustion will occur in this cylinder, resulting in power delivery during its power stroke. The other cylinder will be in its exhaust stroke and the spark will have no effect. Most engines have an even number of cylinders and there will be a separate driver circuit and coil for each pair of cylinders.

An ignition system such as this is often called a *distributorless ignition system* (DIS) because the multiple coil packs and drivers are a modern replacement for the (now essentially obsolete) distributor (see Chapter 1).

Quiz for Chapter 5

1. What is the primary motivation for engine controls?
   a. consumer demand for precise controls
   b. the automotive industry's desire to innovate
   c. government regulations concerning emissions and fuel economy

2. What is the primary purpose of fuel control?
   a. to minimize fuel economy
   b. to eliminate exhaust emissions
   c. to optimize catalytic converter efficiency
   d. to maximize engine torque

3. What is the primary purpose of spark timing controls?
   a. to maximize fuel economy
   b. to minimize exhaust emissions
   c. to optimize catalytic converter efficiency
   d. to optimize some aspect of engine performance (e.g., torque)

4. What does exhaust gas recirculation do?
   a. improves fuel economy
   b. reduces NO_x emission
   c. increases engine torque
   d. provides air for the catalytic converter

5. What does secondary air do?
   a. dilutes the air/fuel ratio
   b. helps oxidize HC and CO in the exhaust manifold
   c. helps oxidize NO_x and CO in the catalytic converter
   d. helps reduce the production of NO_x

6. What is air/fuel ratio?
   a. the mass of air in a cylinder divided by the mass of fuel
   b. the volume of air in a cylinder divided by the volume of fuel
   c. the ratio of the mass of HC to mass of NO_x

7. What electronic device is used in engine controls?
   a. AM radio
   b. catalytic converter
   c. microcomputer

8. What air/fuel ratio is desired for a three-way catalytic converter?
   a. $12:1$
   b. $17:1$
   c. $14.7:1$
   d. none of the above

9. What is the desired operation of a catalytic converter on HC emissions?
   a. oxidation to H_2O and CO_2
   b. reduction to H and C
   c. reaction with NO_x
   d. none of the above

10. What is the desired operation of a catalytic converter on NO_x emissions?
- **a.** reaction with HC
- **b.** oxidation to N_2 and O_2
- **c.** reduction to N_2 and O_2
- **d.** none of the above

11. What is stoichiometry?
- **a.** a very lean air/fuel ratio
- **b.** a very rich air/fuel ratio
- **c.** an air/fuel ratio for which complete combustion is theoretically possible
- **d.** none of the above

12. How is CO emission affected by air/fuel ratio?
- **a.** it generally decreases with increasing air/fuel ratio
- **b.** it increases monotonically with air/fuel ratio
- **c.** it is unaffected by air/fuel ratio
- **d.** none of the above

13. What is MBT?
- **a.** mean before top-center
- **b.** miles per brake torque
- **c.** mean spark advance for best torque
- **d.** none of the above

14. What is the function of electronic fuel control in a vehicle having a three-way catalyst?
- **a.** to maximize brake-specific fuel consumption
- **b.** to maintain the average air/fuel ratio at stoichiometry
- **c.** to always keep the air/fuel ratio within ± 0.05 of stoichiometry
- **d.** to minimize NO_x emissions

15. What is the fuel flow rate for an electronic fuel control system for a vehicle having a three-way catalyst?
- **a.** $R_{fm} = R_m/14.7$
- **b.** $R_a/14.7$
- **c.** $R_v - R_{EGR}/14.7$
- **d.** none of the above

16. What engine quantities are measured to determine spark advance for an electronic ignition system?
- **a.** manifold pressure, RPM, and temperature
- **b.** coolant temperature and mass air flow
- **c.** manifold position and crankshaft position
- **d.** none of the above

17. In an electronic fuel control system, what causes the time delay between fuel metering and the EGO sensor response?
- **a.** dynamic response of the electronics
- **b.** transport time of the air and fuel through the engine
- **c.** limit-cycle theory
- **d.** none of the above

18. Brake power of an engine is
- **a.** the power required to decelerate the car
- **b.** an electronic system for stopping the car
- **c.** the difference between indicated power and power losses in the engine
- **d.** none of the above

19. What is engine calibration?
   a. adjustment of air/fuel ratio, spark timing, and EGR
   b. instrumentation parameter setting
   c. electronic control system parameters
   d. none of the above

Sensors and Actuators

The previous chapter introduced two critically important components found in any electronic control system: sensors and actuators. This chapter explains the operation of the sensors and actuators used throughout a modern car. Special emphasis is placed on sensors and actuators used for power train (i.e., engine and transmission) applications since these systems normally employ the largest number of such devices. However, this chapter will also discuss sensors found in other subsystems on modern cars.

In any control system, sensors provide measurements of important plant variables in a format suitable for the digital microcontroller. Similarly, actuators are electrically operated devices that regulate inputs to the plant that directly control its output. For example, as we shall see, fuel injectors are electrically driven actuators that regulate the flow of fuel into an engine for engine control applications.

Recall from Chapter 2 that fundamentally an electronic control system uses measurements of the plant variable being regulated for feedback control. The measured variable is compared with a desired value for the variable to produce an error signal. The electronic controller generates output electrical signals that regulate inputs to the plant in such a way as to reduce the error to zero.

As will be shown throughout the remainder of this book, automotive electronics have many examples of electronic control in virtually every subsystem. Modern automotive electronic control systems use microcontrollers based on microprocessors (as explained in Chapter 4) to implement almost all control functions. Each of these subsystems requires one or more sensors and actuators in order to operate.

AUTOMOTIVE CONTROL SYSTEM APPLICATIONS OF SENSORS AND ACTUATORS

In control system applications, sensors and actuators are in many cases the critical components for determining system performance. This is especially true for automotive control system applications. The availability of appropriate sensors and actuators dictates the design of the control system and the type of function it can perform.

Sensors and actuators play a critical role in determining automotive control system performance.

The sensors and actuators that are available to a control system designer are not always what the designer wants, because the ideal device may not be commercially available at acceptable costs. For this reason, often special signal processors or interface circuits are designed to adapt to an available sensor or actuator, or the control system is designed in a specific way to fit available

Figure 6.1
Typical Electronic Engine Control System

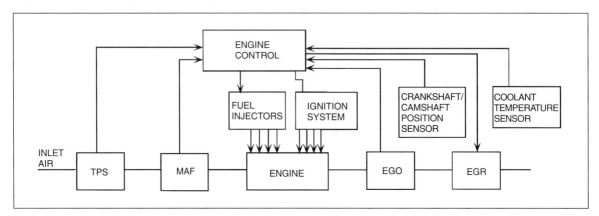

sensors or actuators. However, because of the large potential production run for automotive control systems, it is often worthwhile to develop a sensor for a particular application, even though it may take a long and expensive research project to do so.

Although there are many subsystems on automobiles that operate with sensors and actuators, we begin our discussion with a survey of the devices for power train control. To motivate the discussion of engine control sensors and actuators it is helpful to review the variables measured (sensors) and the controlled variables (actuators). Figure 6.1 is a representative block diagram of a typical electronic engine control system illustrating most of the relevant sensors used for engine control. The position of the throttle plate, sensed by the throttle position sensor (TPS), directly regulates the air flow into the engine, thereby controlling output power. A set of fuel injectors (one for each cylinder) delivers the correct amount of fuel to a corresponding cylinder during the intake stroke under control of the electronic engine controller. A fuel injector is, as will presently be shown, one of the important actuators used in automotive electronic application. The ignition control system fires each spark plug at the appropriate time under control of the electronic engine controller. The exhaust gas recirculation (EGR) is controlled by yet another output from the engine controller. All critical engine control functions are based on measurements made by various sensors connected to the engine in an appropriate way. Computations made within the engine controller based on these inputs yield output signals to the actuators. We consider inputs (sensors) to the control system first, then we will discuss the outputs (actuators).

Variables to Be Measured

The set of variables sensed for any given engine is specific to the associated engine control configuration. Space limitations for this book prohibit a complete survey of all engine control systems and relevant sensor and actuator selections for all car models. Nevertheless, it is possible to review a superset of possible sensors, which is done in this chapter, and to present representative examples of practical digital control configurations, which is done in the next chapter.

The superset of variables sensed in engine control includes the following:

1. Mass air flow (MAF) rate
2. Exhaust gas oxygen concentration (possibly heated)
3. Throttle plate angular position
4. Crankshaft angular position/RPM
5. Coolant temperature
6. Intake air temperature
7. Manifold absolute pressure (MAP)
8. Differential exhaust gas pressure
9. Vehicle speed
10. Transmission gear selector position

In addition to measurements of the above variables, engine control is also based on the status of the vehicle as monitored by a set of switches. These switches include the following:

1. Air conditioner clutch engaged
2. Brake on/off
3. Wide open throttle
4. Closed throttle

AIR FLOW RATE SENSOR

In Chapter 5 we showed that the correct operation of an electronically controlled engine operating with government-regulated exhaust emissions requires a measurement of the mass flow rate of air (R_m) into the engine. The majority of cars produced since the early 1990s use a relatively simple and inexpensive mass air flow rate (MAF) sensor. This is normally mounted as part of the air cleaner assembly, where it measures air flow into the intake manifold. It is a ruggedly packaged, single-unit sensor that includes solid-state electronic signal processing. In operation, the MAF sensor generates a continuous signal that varies nearly linearly with true mass air flow R_m.

The MAF sensor is a variation of a classic air flow sensor that was known as a hot wire anemometer and was used, for example, to measure wind velocity for weather forecasting. In the MAF, the hot-wire, or sensing, element is replaced by a hot-film structure mounted on a substrate. On the air inlet side is mounted a honeycomb flow straightener that "smooths" the air flow (causing nominally laminar air flow over the film element). At the lower portion of the structure is the signal processing circuitry.

The film element is electrically heated to a constant temperature above that of the inlet air. The latter air temperature is sensed using a solid-state temperature sensor (explained later in this chapter). The hot-film element is incorporated in a Wheatstone bridge circuit (Figure 6.2a). The power supply for the bridge circuit comes from an amplifier.

The Wheatstone bridge consists of three fixed resistors R_1, R_2, and R_3 and a hot-film element having resistance R_{HW}. With no air flow the resistors R_1, R_2, and R_3 are chosen such that voltage v_a and v_b are equal (i.e., the bridge is said to be balanced). As air flows across the hot film, heat is carried away from the film by the moving air. The amount of heat carried away varies in proportion to the mass flow rate of the air. The heat lost by the film to the air tends to cause the resistance of the film to vary, which unbalances the bridge circuit, thereby producing an input voltage to the amplifier. The output of the amplifier is connected to the bridge circuit and provides the power for this circuit. The amplified voltage changes the resistance in such a way as to maintain a fixed hot-film temperature relative to the inlet temperature.

The amplifier output voltage v_c varies with MAF and serves as a measure of R_m. Typically the conversion of MAF to voltage is slightly nonlinear, as indicated by the calibration curve depicted in Figure 6.2b. Fortunately, a modern digital engine controller can convert the analog bridge output voltage directly to mass air flow by simple computation. As will be shown in Chapter 7, in which digital engine control is discussed, it is advantageous to convert analog sensor voltages to a digital format within the solid-state electronics associated with the sensor. This conversion is convenient since it eliminates the need for an analog-to-digital converter, which can be relatively expensive (see Chapter 4).

One scheme for converting the analog output voltage to a digital signal uses a device that is known as a voltage-to-frequency (v/f) converter. This circuit is a variable-frequency oscillator whose frequency f is proportional to the input voltage (in this case, the amplifier output voltage).

The variable-frequency output voltage (v_f) is applied through an electronic gate, which is essentially an electrically operated switch. Control circuitry (also part of the sensor solid-state electronics) repeatedly closes the switch for a fixed interval t. Then it opens it for another fixed interval. During the first interval the variable-frequency signal from the v/f circuit is connected to the binary counter (BC) (see Chapter 3). The BC counts (in binary) at the instantaneous frequency of the v/f, which is proportional to the amplifier output voltage v_f, which in turn varies with mass air flow rate.

During each cycle of the electronic gate, the BC contains a binary number given by the product of the v/f frequency and the time interval. For example, if the mass air flow were such that the v/f frequency were 1,000 cycles/sec and the switch were closed for 0.1 sec, then the BC would contain

**Figure 6.2
Mass Air Flow Sensor**

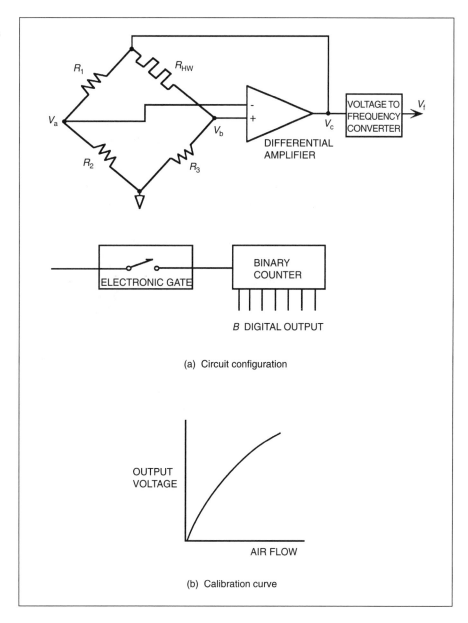

(a) Circuit configuration

(b) Calibration curve

the binary equivalent of decimal 100 (i.e., $1,000 \times 0.1 = 100$). If the mass air flow increased such that the v/f frequency were 1,500 cycles/sec, then the BC count would be the binary equivalent of 150. In mathematical terms, the BC count B is given by the binary equivalent of

$$B = ft$$

where

B = BC count
f = frequency of v/f
t = duration of closure of electronic gate

After the engine controller reads the count, the BC is reset to zero to be ready for the next sample. In actual operation, repeated measurements of frequency f are made under control of the digital engine control module (see Chapter 7).

This conversion of voltage to frequency is advantageous in digital engine control applications because the frequency is readily converted to digital format without requiring an analog-to-digital converter.

Indirect Measurement of Mass Air Flow

Recall that Chapter 5 presented an alternative to direct mass air flow measurement in the form of the so-called speed-density method. This method computes an estimate of mass air flow from measurements of manifold absolute pressure (MAP), RPM, and inlet air temperature. We consider first sensors for measuring manifold absolute pressure.

MAP Sensor Concepts

Several MAP sensor configurations have been used in automotive applications. The earliest sensors were derived from aerospace instrumentation concepts, but these proved more expensive than desirable for automotive applications and have been replaced with more cost-effective designs.

It is interesting to note that none of the MAP sensors in use measures manifold pressure directly, but instead measure the displacement of a diaphragm that is deflected by manifold pressure. The details of the diaphragm displacement and the measurement of this displacement vary from one configuration to another.

Strain Gauge MAP Sensor

One relatively inexpensive MAP sensor configuration is the silicon-diaphragm diffused strain gauge sensor shown in Figure 6.3. This sensor uses a silicon chip that is approximately 3 millimeters square. Along the outer edges, the chip is approximately 250 micrometers (1 micrometer = 1 millionth of a meter) thick, but the center area is only 25 micrometers thick and forms a diaphragm. The edge of the chip is sealed to a Pyrex plate under vacuum, thereby forming a vacuum chamber between the plate and the center area of the silicon chip.

**Figure 6.3
Typical Silicon-
Diaphragm Strain
Gauge MAP Sensor**

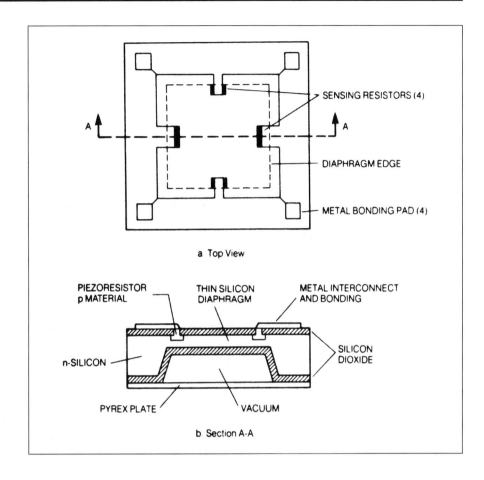

SENSING RESISTORS (4)

DIAPHRAGM EDGE

METAL BONDING PAD (4)

a Top View

PIEZORESISTOR
p MATERIAL

THIN SILICON
DIAPHRAGM

METAL INTERCONNECT
AND BONDING

n-SILICON

SILICON
DIOXIDE

PYREX PLATE

VACUUM

b Section A-A

In the strain gauge MAP sensor, manifold pressure applied to the diaphragm causes a resistance change within the semiconductor material that corresponds to the manifold pressure.

A set of sensing resistors is formed around the edge of this chamber, as indicated in Figure 6.3. The resistors are formed by diffusing a doping impurity into the silicon. External connections to these resistors are made through wires connected to the metal bonding pads. This entire assembly is placed in a sealed housing that is connected to the intake manifold by a small-diameter tube. Manifold pressure applied to the diaphragm causes it to deflect.

The resistance of the sensing resistors changes in proportion to the applied manifold pressure by a phenomenon that is known as *piezoresistivity*. Piezoresistivity occurs in certain semiconductors so that the actual resistivity (a property of the material) changes in proportion to the strain (fractional change in length). The strain induced in each resistor is proportional to the diaphragm deflection, which, in turn, is proportional to the pressure on the outside surface of the diaphragm. This pressure is the manifold pressure.

A pressure sensor having the configuration of Figure 6.3 is also used for measuring absolute atmospheric pressure. It will be shown in Chapter 7 that this absolute pressure can be used in engine control applications, as can the manifold pressure.

The resistors in the strain gauge MAP sensor are connected in a Wheatstone bridge circuit. Output voltage of the circuit varies as the resistance varies in response to manifold pressure variations.

An electrical signal that is proportional to the manifold pressure is obtained by connecting the resistors in a circuit called a Wheatstone bridge, as shown in the schematic of Figure 6.4a. Note the similarity in the Wheatstone bridge of Figure 6.4a with that employed in the MAF sensor of Figure 6.2. The voltage regulator holds a constant dc voltage across the bridge. The resistors diffused into the diaphragm are denoted R_1, R_2, R_3, and R_4 in Figure 6.4a. When there is no strain on the diaphragm, all four resistances are equal, the bridge is balanced, and the voltage between points A and B is zero. When manifold pressure changes, it causes these resistances to change in such a way that R_1 and R_3 increase by an amount that is proportional to pressure; at the same time, R_2 and R_4 decrease by an identical amount. This unbalances the bridge and a net difference voltage is present between points A and B. The differential amplifier generates an output voltage proportional to the difference between the two input voltages (which is, in turn, proportional to the pressure), as shown in Figure 6.4b.

ENGINE CRANKSHAFT ANGULAR POSITION SENSOR

Crankshaft angular position is an important variable in automotive control systems, particularly for controlling ignition timing and fuel injection timing.

Besides pressure, the position of shafts, valves, and levers must be sensed for automotive control systems. Measurements of the angular position or velocity of shafts are common in automotive electronics. It is highly desirable that these measurements be made without any mechanical contact with the rotating shaft. Such noncontacting measurements can be made in a variety of ways, but the commonest of these in automotive electronics use magnetic or optical phenomena as the physical basis. Magnetic means of such measurements are generally preferred in engine applications since they are unaffected by oil, dirt, or other contaminants.

The principles involved in measuring rotating shafts can be illustrated by one of the most significant applications for engine control: the measurement of crankshaft angular position or angular velocity (i.e., RPM). Imagine the engine as viewed from the rear, as shown in Figure 6.5. On the rear of the crankshaft is a large, heavy, circular steel disk called the *flywheel* that is connected to and rotates with the crankshaft. Let's mark a point on the flywheel, as shown in Figure 6.5, and draw a line through this point and the axis of rotation. Let's draw another line through the axis of rotation parallel to the horizontal center line of the engine as a reference line. The crankshaft angular position is the angle between the reference line and the mark on the flywheel.

Imagine that the flywheel is rotated so that the mark is directly on the reference line. This is an angular position of zero degrees. For our purposes, assume that this angular position corresponds to the No. 1 cylinder at TDC (top dead center). As the crankshaft rotates, this angle increases from zero to 360° in one revolution. However, one full engine cycle from intake through

**Figure 6.4
Circuit Diagram for
MAP Sensor Using
Strain Gauges**

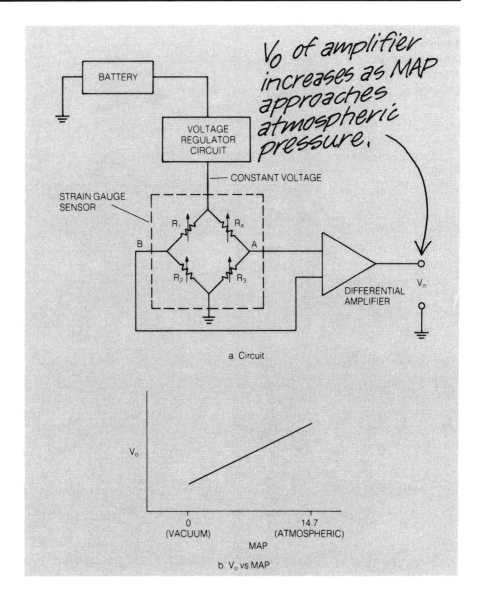

a. Circuit

b. V_o vs MAP

V_o of amplifier increases as MAP approaches atmospheric pressure.

exhaust requires two complete revolutions of the crankshaft. That is, one complete engine cycle corresponds to the crankshaft angular position going from zero to 720°. During each cycle, it is important to measure the crankshaft position with reference to TDC for each cylinder. This information is used by the electronic engine controller to set ignition timing and, in most cases, to set the fuel injector pulse timing.

**Figure 6.5
Engine Crankshaft
Angular Position
Measurement**

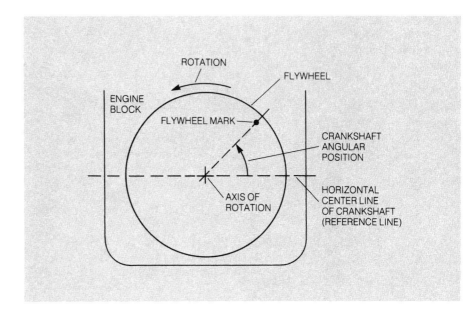

Crankshaft angular
position can be sensed
directly at the camshaft,
since the camshaft
rotates at exactly one-
half the speed of the
crankshaft.

In automobiles with electronic engine control systems, angular position
can be sensed on the crankshaft directly or on the camshaft. Recall that the
piston drives the crankshaft directly, while the valves and the distributor for
the spark ignition are driven from the camshaft. The camshaft is driven from
the crankshaft through a 1:2 reduction drivetrain, which can be gears, belt,
or chain. Therefore, the camshaft rotational speed is one-half that of the
crankshaft, so the camshaft angular position goes from zero to 360° for one
complete engine cycle. Either of these sensing locations can be used in
electronic control systems. Although the crankshaft location is potentially
superior for accuracy because of torsional and gear backlash errors in the
camshaft drivetrain, many production systems locate this sensor such that it
measures camshaft position. At the present time, there appears to be a trend
toward measuring crankshaft position directly rather than indirectly via
camshaft position. In fact, it is sufficient for engine control purposes to
measure crankshaft/camshaft position at a small number of fixed points. The
number of such measurements (or samples) is determined by the number of
cylinders.

It is desirable to measure engine angular position with a noncontacting
sensor to avoid mechanical wear and corresponding changes in accuracy of the
measurement. The two most common methods for noncontact coupling to a
rotating shaft employ magnetic fields or optics. Let's consider the concepts
used for magnetically coupled sensors first.

Magnetic Reluctance Position Sensor

In the magnetic reluctance position sensor, a coil wrapped around the magnet senses the changing intensity of the magnetic field as the tabs of a ferrous disk pass between the poles of the magnet.

One engine sensor configuration that measures crankshaft position directly (using magnetic phenomena) is illustrated in Figure 6.6. This sensor consists of a permanent magnet with a coil of wire wound around it. A steel disk that is mounted on the crankshaft (usually in front of the engine) has tabs that pass between the pole pieces of this magnet. In Figure 6.6, the steel disk has four protruding tabs, which is appropriate for an 8-cylinder engine. The passage of each tab can correspond to the TDC position of a cylinder on its power stroke, although other reference positions are also possible.

This sensor is of the magnetic reluctance type and is based on the concept of a magnetic circuit. A *magnetic circuit* is a closed path through a magnetic material (e.g., iron, cobalt, nickel, or synthetic magnetic material called ferrite). In the case of the sensor in Figure 6.6, the magnetic circuit is the closed path through the magnet material and across the gap between the pole pieces.

The magnetic field in a magnetic circuit is described by a pair of field quantities that can be compared to the voltage and current of an ordinary electric circuit. One of these quantities is called the *magnetic field intensity*. It exerts a force similar to the voltage of a battery. The response of the magnetic circuit to the magnetic field intensity is described by the second quantity, which is called *magnetic flux*. A line of constant magnetic flux is a closed path

Figure 6.6
Magnetic Reluctance Crankshaft Position Sensor

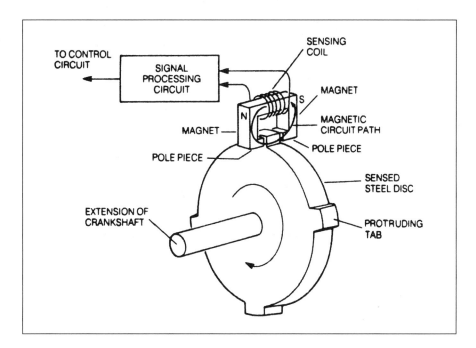

**Figure 6.7
Magnetic Circuit of
the Reluctance
Sensor**

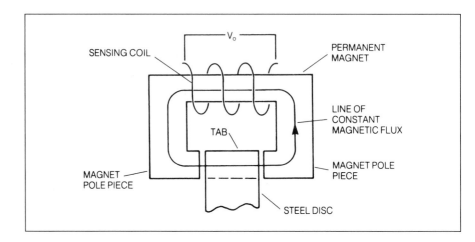

The voltage generated by the magnetic reluctance position sensor is determined by the strength of the magnetic flux. When a tab on the steel disk passes through the gap, the flow of the magnetic flux changes significantly.

through the magnetic material. The magnetic flux is similar to the current that flows when a resistor is connected across a battery to form a closed electrical circuit.

As we shall see, the voltage generated by the reluctance sensor is determined by the strength of this magnetic flux. The strength of the magnetic flux is, in turn, determined by the reluctance of the magnetic circuit. *Reluctance* is to a magnetic circuit what resistance is to an electrical circuit.

The path for the magnetic flux of the reluctance sensor is illustrated in Figure 6.7. The reluctance of a magnetic circuit is inversely proportional to the magnetic permeability of the material along the path. The magnetic permeability of steel is a few thousand times larger than air; therefore, the reluctance of steel is much lower than air. Note that when one of the tabs of the steel disk is located between the pole pieces of the magnet, a large part of the gap between the pole pieces is filled by the steel. Since the steel has a lower reluctance than air, the "flow" of magnetic flux increases to a relatively large value.

On the other hand, when a tab is not between the magnet pole pieces, the gap is filled by air only. This creates a high-reluctance circuit for which the magnetic flux is relatively small. Thus, the magnitude of the magnetic flux that "flows" through the magnetic circuit depends on the position of the tab, which, in turn, depends on the crankshaft angular position.

The magnetic flux is least when none of the tabs is near the magnet pole pieces. As a tab begins to pass through the gap, the magnetic flux increases. It reaches a maximum when the tab is exactly between the pole pieces, and then decreases as the tab passes out of the pole piece region. In most control systems, the position of maximum magnetic flux has a fixed relationship to TDC for one of the cylinders.

**Figure 6.8
Output Voltage
Waveform from the
Magnetic Reluctance
Crankshaft Position
Sensor Coil**

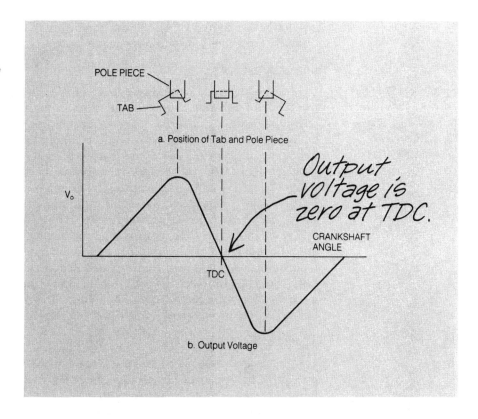

a. Position of Tab and Pole Piece

POLE PIECE

TAB

V_o

Output voltage is zero at TDC.

CRANKSHAFT ANGLE

TDC

b. Output Voltage

The voltage induced in the sensing coil varies with the rate of change of the magnetic flux. When the tab is centered between the poles of the magnet, the voltage is zero because the flux is not changing.

The *change in magnetic flux* induces a voltage, V_o, in the sensing coil that is proportional to the *rate of change* of the magnetic flux. Since the magnetic flux must be changing to induce a voltage in the sensing coil, its output voltage is zero whenever the engine is not running, regardless of the position of the crankshaft. This is a serious disadvantage for this type of sensor because the engine timing cannot be set statically.

As shown in Figure 6.8, the coil voltage, V_o, begins to increase from zero as a tab begins to pass between the pole pieces, reaches a maximum, then falls to zero when the tab is exactly between the pole pieces (see Figure 6.8a). (Note that although the value of magnetic flux is maximum at this point, the rate of change of magnetic flux is zero; therefore, the induced voltage in the sensing coil is zero.) Then it increases with the opposite polarity, reaches a maximum, and falls to zero as the tab passes out of the gap between the pole pieces. The coil voltage waveform shown in Figure 6.8b occurs each time one of the cylinders reaches TDC on its power stroke. It should be noted that if the disk is mounted on the crankshaft, then the number of tabs for this crankshaft position sensor always will be half the number of cylinders because it takes two crankshaft rotations for a complete engine cycle.

Engine Speed Sensor

Engine speed can be calculated in a number of ways. Digital circuits use counters and crankshaft sensors to calculate actual engine speed.

An engine speed sensor is needed to provide an input for the electronic controller for several functions. The position sensor discussed previously can be used to measure engine speed. The reluctance sensor is used in this case as an example; however, any of the other position sensor techniques could be used as well. Refer to Figure 6.6 and notice that the four tabs will pass through the sensing coil once for each crankshaft revolution. Therefore, if we count the pulses of voltage from the sensing coil in one minute and divide by four, we will know the engine speed in revolutions per minute (RPM).

This is easy to do with digital circuits. Precise timing circuits such as those used in digital watches can start a counter circuit that will count pulses until the timing circuit stops it. The counter can have the divide-by-four function included in it, or a separate divider circuit may be used. In many cases, the actual RPM sensor disk is mounted near the flywheel and has many more than four tabs; in such cases, the counter does not actually count for a full minute before the speed is calculated, but the results are the same.

Timing Sensor for Ignition and Fuel Delivery

In electronic engine control it is often desirable to measure the angular position of the engine relative to a specific point in the cycle. For such measurement it is normally necessary to measure the position of the camshaft. The measurement of engine position via crankshaft and camshaft position sensors (as well as its use in timing fuel delivery and ignition) is described in Chapter 7. Normally it is sufficient to measure camshaft position at a fixed point. Such a sample of camshaft position is readily achieved by a magnetic sensor similar to that described above for the crankshaft position measurement.

This sensor detects a reference point on the angular position of the camshaft that defines a beginning to a complete engine cycle (e.g., power stroke for all cylinders). Once this reference point has been detected, crankshaft position measurements (as described above) provide sufficient information for timing fuel injection pulses and ignition.

In one scheme a variable-reluctance sensor is located near a ferromagnetic disk on the camshaft. This disk has a notch cut (or it can have a protruding tab), as shown in Figure 6.9. The disk provides a low-reluctance path (yielding high magnetic flux) except when the notch aligns with the sensor axis. Whenever the notch aligns with the sensor axis, the reluctance of this magnetic path is increased because the permeability of air in the notch is very much lower than the permeability of the disk. This relatively high reluctance through the notch causes the magnetic flux to decrease and produces a change in sensor output voltage.

**Figure 6.9
Crankshaft Position
Sensor**

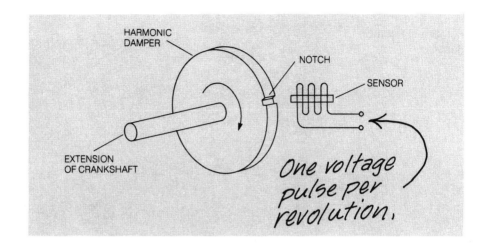

One voltage pulse per revolution.

The notched position sensor uses an effect opposite to that of the tab position sensor. As a notch in a rotating steel disk passes by a variable-reluctance sensor, the decrease in magnetic flux generates a voltage pulse in the sensor coil.

The Hall element is a thin slab of semiconductor material that is placed between the magnets so it can sense the magnetic flux variations as the tab passes. A constant current is passed through the semi-conductor in one direction, and a voltage is generated that varies with the strength of the magnetic flux.

As the camshaft rotates, the notch passes under the sensor once for every two crankshaft revolutions. The magnetic flux abruptly decreases, then increases as the notch passes the sensor. This generates a voltage pulse that can be used in electronic control systems for timing purposes.

Hall-Effect Position Sensor

As mentioned previously, one of the main disadvantages of the magnetic reluctance sensor is its lack of output when the engine isn't running. A crankshaft position sensor that avoids this problem is the Hall-effect position sensor. This sensor can be used to measure either camshaft position or crankshaft position.

A Hall-effect position sensor is shown in Figure 6.10. This sensor is similar to the reluctance sensor in that it employs a steel disk having protruding tabs and a magnet for coupling the disk to the sensing element. Another similarity is that the steel disk varies the reluctance of the magnetic path as the tabs pass between the magnet pole pieces.

The Hall Effect

The Hall element is a small, thin, flat slab of semiconductor material. When a current, I, is passed through this slab by means of an external circuit as shown in Figure 6.11a, a voltage is developed across the slab perpendicular to the direction of current flow and perpendicular to the direction of magnetic flux. This voltage is proportional to both the current and magnetic flux density that flows through the slab. This effect—the generation of a voltage that is dependent on a magnetic field—is called the *Hall effect*.

In Figure 6.11b, the current, I, is represented by electrons, e, which have negative charge, flowing from left to right. The magnetic flux flows along the

**Figure 6.10
Hall-Effect Position
Sensor**

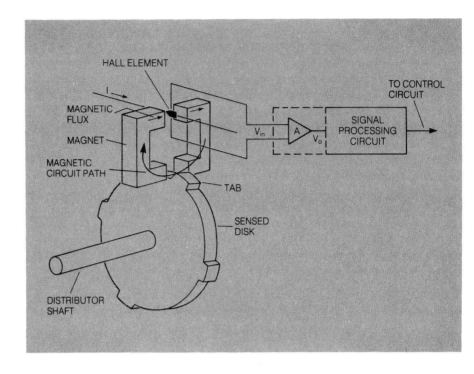

legs of the magnet as indicated and is generally perpendicular to the face of the semiconductor Hall element. Whenever an electron moves through a magnetic field, a force (called the *Lorentz force*) that is proportional to the electron velocity and the strength of the magnetic flux is exerted on the electron. The direction of this force is perpendicular to the direction in which the electron is moving. In Figure 6.11b, the Lorentz force direction is such that the electrons are deflected toward the lower sense electrode. Thus, this electrode is more negative than the upper electrode and a voltage exists between the electrodes, having the polarity shown in Figure 6.11b.

As the strength of the magnetic flux density increases, more of the electrons are deflected downward. If the current, I, is held constant, then the voltage, V_o, is proportional to the strength of the magnetic flux density, which, in turn, is determined by the position of the tabs. This voltage tends to be relatively weak so it is amplified, as shown in Figure 6.10.

<u>Output Waveform</u>

It was shown in the discussion of the reluctance crankshaft position sensor that the magnetic flux density for this configuration depends on the position of the tab. Recall that the magnetic flux is largest when one of the tabs

Figure 6.11
The Hall Effect

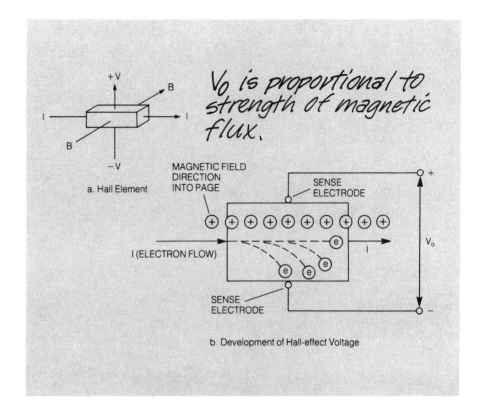

V_0 is proportional to strength of magnetic flux.

a. Hall Element

b. Development of Hall-effect Voltage

is positioned symmetrically between the magnet pole pieces and that this position normally corresponds closely to TDC of one of the cylinders.

Because the Hall-effect sensor produces the same output voltage waveform regardless of engine speed, the engine timing can be set when the engine is not running.

The voltage waveform V_o that is produced by the Hall element in the position sensor of Figure 6.10 is illustrated in Figure 6.12. Since V_o is proportional to the magnetic flux density, it reaches maximum when any of the tabs is symmetrically located between the magnet pole pieces (corresponding to TDC of a cylinder). If the disk is driven by the camshaft, then the disk must have as many tabs as the engine has cylinders. Therefore, the disk shown would be for a 4-cylinder engine. It is important to realize that voltage output versus crankshaft angle is independent of engine speed. Thus, this sensor can be used for setting the engine timing when the engine is not running (e.g., when it is being motored at the end of an assembly line).

Shielded-Field Sensor

Figure 6.13a shows another concept that uses the Hall-effect element in a way different from that just discussed. In this method, the Hall element is

**Figure 6.12
Waveform of Hall
Element Output
Voltage for Position
Sensor of Figure 6.10**

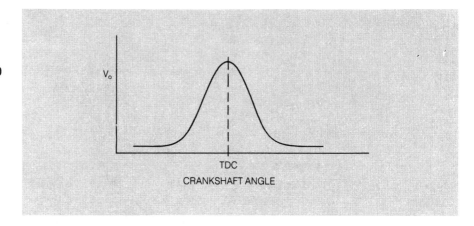

**Figure 6.13
Hall-Effect Position
Sensor That Shields
the Magnetic Circuit**

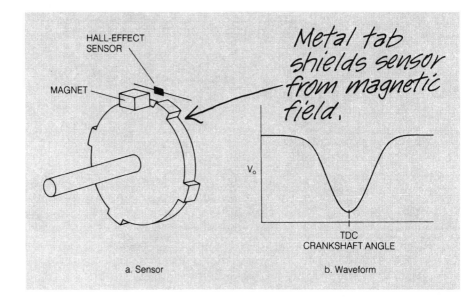

normally exposed to a magnetic field and produces an output voltage. When
one of the tabs passes between the magnet and the sensor element, the low
reluctance of the tab and disk provides a path for the magnetic flux that
bypasses the Hall-effect sensor element, and the sensor output drops to near
zero. Note in Figure 6.13b that the waveform is just the opposite of the one in
Figure 6.12.

Optical Crankshaft Position Sensor

In the optical crank-shaft position sensor, a disk coupled to the crankshaft has holes to pass light between the LED and the phototransistor. An output pulse is generated as each hole passes the LED.

In a sufficiently clean environment a shaft position can also be sensed using optical techniques. Figure 6.14 illustrates such a system. Again, as with the magnetic system, a disk is directly coupled to the crankshaft. This time, the disk has holes in it that correspond to the number of tabs on the disks of the magnetic systems. Mounted on each side of the disk are fiber-optic light pipes. The hole in the disk allows transmission of light through the light pipes from the light-emitting diode (LED) source to the phototransistor used as a light sensor. Light would not be transmitted from source to sensor when there is no hole because the solid disk blocks the light. As shown in Figure 6.14, the pulse of light is detected by the phototransistor and coupled to an amplifier to

**Figure 6.14
Optical Position Sensor**

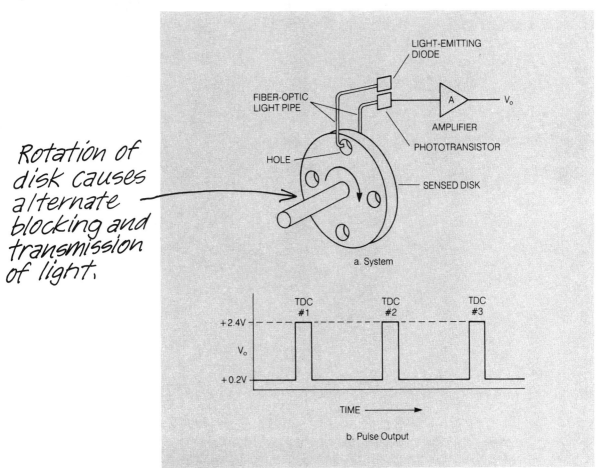

Rotation of disk causes alternate blocking and transmission of light.

obtain a satisfactory signal level. The output pulse level can very easily be standard transistor logic levels of +2.4 V for the high level and +0.8 V for the low level. Used as pulses, the signals provide time-referenced pulses that can be signal processed easily with digital integrated circuits.

One of the problems with optical sensors is that they must be protected from dirt and oil; otherwise, they will not work properly. They have the advantages that they can sense position without the engine running and that the pulse amplitude is constant with variation in speed.

THROTTLE ANGLE SENSOR

Still another variable that must be measured for electronic engine control is the throttle plate angular position. As explained in Chapter 1, the throttle plate is linked mechanically to the accelerator pedal. When the driver depresses the accelerator pedal, this linkage causes the throttle plate angle to increase, allowing more air to enter the engine and thereby increasing engine power.

Measurement of the instantaneous throttle angle is important for control purposes, as will be explained in Chapter 7. Most throttle angle sensors are essentially potentiometers. A *potentiometer* consists of a resistor with a movable contact, as illustrated in Figure 6.15.

**Figure 6.15
Throttle Angle
Sensor: A
Potentiometer**

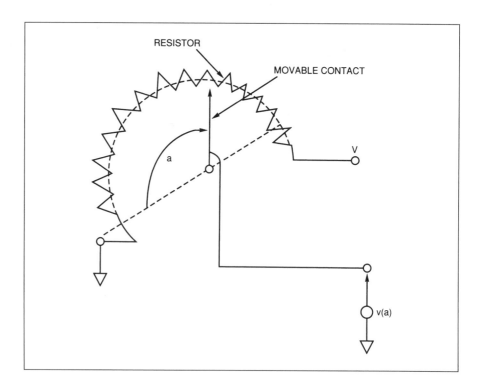

A section of resistance material is placed in an arc around the pivot axis for the movable contact. One end of the resistor is connected to ground, the other to a fixed voltage V (e.g., 5 volts). The voltage at the contact point of the movable contact is proportional to the angle (a) from the ground contact to the movable contact. Thus,

$$v(a) = ka$$

where $v(a)$ is the voltage at the contact point, k is a constant, and a is the angle of the contact point from the ground connection.

This potentiometer can be used to measure any angular rotation. In particular, it is well suited for measuring throttle angle. The only disadvantage to the potentiometer for automotive applications is its analog output. For digital engine control, the voltage $v(a)$ must be converted to digital format using an analog-to-digital converter.

TEMPERATURE SENSORS

Temperature is an important parameter throughout the automotive system. In operation of an electronic fuel control system it is vital to know the temperature of the coolant, the temperature of the inlet air, and the temperature of the exhaust gas oxygen sensor (a sensor to be discussed in the next section). Several sensor configurations are available for measuring these temperatures, but we can illustrate the basic operation of most of the temperature sensors by explaining the operation of a typical coolant sensor.

Typical Coolant Sensor

One kind of co-olant sensor uses a temperature-sensitive semiconductor called a *thermistor*. The sensor is typically connected as a varying resistance across a fixed reference voltage. As the temperature increases, the output voltage decreases.

A typical coolant sensor, shown in Figure 6.16, consists of a thermistor mounted in a housing that is designed to be inserted in the coolant stream. This housing is typically threaded with pipe threads that seal the assembly against coolant leakage.

A *thermistor* is made of semiconductor material whose resistance varies inversely with temperature. For example, at −40°C a typical coolant sensor has a resistance of 100,000 ohms. The resistance decreases to about 70,000 ohms at 130°C.

The sensor is typically connected in an electrical circuit like that shown in Figure 6.17, in which the coolant temperature sensor resistance is denoted R_T. This resistance is connected to a reference voltage through a fixed resistance R. The sensor output voltage, V_T, is given by the following equation:

$$V_T = V \frac{R_T}{R + R_T}$$

The sensor output voltage varies inversely with temperature; that is, the output voltage decreases as the temperature increases.

**Figure 6.16
Coolant Temperature
Sensor**

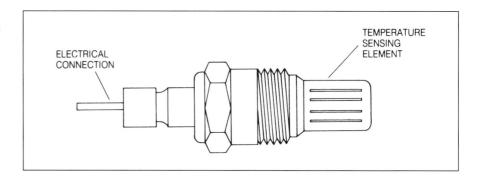

**Figure 6.17
Typical Coolant
Temperature Sensor
Circuit**

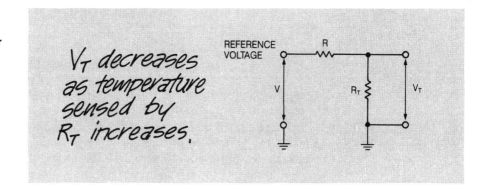

SENSORS FOR FEEDBACK CONTROL

The sensors that we have discussed to this point have been part of the open-loop (i.e., feedforward) control. We consider next sensors that are appropriate for feedback engine control. Recall from Chapter 5 that feedback control for fuel delivery is based on maintaining the air/fuel ratio at stoichiometry (i.e., 14.7 : 1). The primary sensor for fuel control is the exhaust gas oxygen sensor.

Exhaust Gas Oxygen Sensor

Recall from Chapter 5 that the amount of oxygen in the exhaust gas is used as an indirect measurement of the air/fuel ratio. As a result, one of the most significant automotive sensors in use today is the exhaust gas oxygen (EGO) sensor. This sensor is often called a *lambda sensor* from the Greek letter lambda (λ), which is commonly used to denote the equivalence ratio:

$$\lambda = \frac{(\text{air}/\text{fuel})}{(\text{air}/\text{fuel at stoichiometry})}$$

**Figure 6.18
Zirconium Dioxide
(ZrO₂) EGO Sensor**

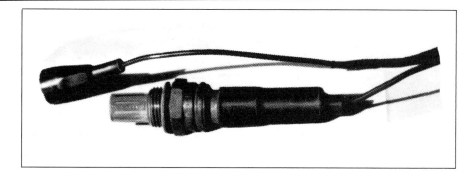

Whenever the air/fuel ratio is at stoichiometry, the value for λ is 1. When the air–fuel mixture is too lean, the condition is represented by lambda greater than one (denoted $\lambda > 1$). Conversely, when the air–fuel mixture is too rich, the condition is represented by an equivalence ratio of lambda less than one ($\lambda < 1$).

The two types of EGO sensors that have been used are based on the use of active oxides of two types of materials. One uses zirconium dioxide (ZrO_2) and the other uses titanium dioxide (TiO_2). The former is the most commonly used type today. Figure 6.18 is a photograph of a typical ZrO_2 EGO sensor and Figure 6.19 shows the physical structure. Figure 6.18 indicates that a voltage, V_o, is generated across the ZrO_2 material. This voltage depends on the exhaust gas oxygen concentration, which in turn depends on the engine air/fuel ratio.

The zirconium dioxide EGO sensor uses zirconium dioxide sandwiched between two platinum electrodes. One electrode is exposed to exhaust gas and the other is exposed to normal air for reference.

In essence, the EGO sensor consists of a thimble-shaped section of ZrO_2 with thin platinum electrodes on the inside and outside of the ZrO_2. The inside electrode is exposed to air, and the outside electrode is exposed to exhaust gas through a porous protective overcoat.

A simplified explanation of EGO sensor operation is based on the distribution of oxygen ions. An *ion* is an electrically charged atom. Oxygen ions have two excess electrons and each electron has a negative charge; thus, oxygen ions are negatively charged. The ZrO_2 has a tendency to attract the oxygen ions, which accumulate on the ZrO_2 surface just inside the platinum electrodes.

The platinum plate on the air reference side of the ZrO_2 is exposed to a much higher concentration of oxygen ions than the exhaust gas side. The air reference side becomes electrically more negative than the exhaust gas side; therefore, an electric field exists across the ZrO_2 material and a voltage, V_o, results. The polarity of this voltage is positive on the exhaust gas side and negative on the air reference side of the ZrO_2. The magnitude of this voltage depends on the concentration of oxygen in the exhaust gas and on the sensor temperature.

**Figure 6.19
EGO Mounting and
Structure**

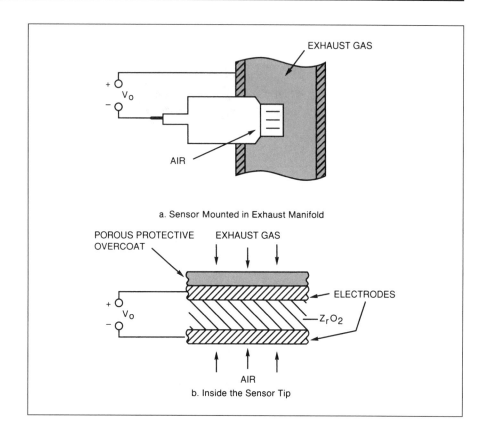

a. Sensor Mounted in Exhaust Manifold

b. Inside the Sensor Tip

Because the exhaust contains fewer oxygen ions than air, the "air" electrode becomes negative with respect to the "exhaust" electrode.

The quantity of oxygen in the exhaust gas is represented by the oxygen partial pressure. Basically, this partial pressure is that proportion of the total exhaust gas pressure (nearly at atmospheric pressure) that is due to the quantity of oxygen. The exhaust gas oxygen partial pressure for a rich mixture varies over the range of 10^{-16} to 10^{-32} of atmospheric pressure. The oxygen partial pressure for a lean mixture is roughly 10^{-2} atmosphere. Consequently, for a rich mixture there is a relatively low oxygen concentration in the exhaust and a higher EGO sensor output. Correspondingly, for a lean mixture the exhaust gas oxygen concentration is relatively high (meaning that the difference between exhaust gas and atmospheric oxygen concentrations is lower), resulting in a relatively low EGO sensor output voltage. For a fully warmed EGO sensor the output voltage is about 1 volt for a rich mixture and about 0.1 volt for a lean mixture.

Desirable EGO Characteristics

An *ideal* EGO sensor would have an abrupt, rapid, and significant change in output voltage as the mixture passes through stoichiometry. The output voltage would not change as exhaust gas temperature changes.

The EGO sensor characteristics that are desirable for the type of limit-cycle fuel control system that was discussed in Chapter 5 are as follows:

1. Abrupt change in voltage at stoichiometry
2. Rapid switching of output voltage in response to exhaust gas oxygen changes
3. Large difference in sensor output voltage between rich and lean mixture conditions
4. Stable voltages with respect to exhaust temperature

Switching Characteristics

Hysteresis is the difference in the switching point of the output voltage with respect to stoichiometry as a mixture passes from lean to rich, as contrasted to a mixture that passes from rich to lean.

The switching time for the EGO sensor also must be considered in control applications. An ideal characteristic for a limit-cycle controller is shown in Figure 6.20. The actual characteristics of a new EGO sensor are shown in Figure 6.21. These data were obtained by slowly varying air/fuel ratios across stoichiometry. The arrow pointing down indicates the change in V_o as the air/fuel ratio was varied from rich to lean. The up arrow indicates the change in V_o as the air/fuel ratio was varied from lean to rich. Note that the sensor output doesn't change at exactly the same point for increasing air/fuel ratio as for decreasing air/fuel ratio. This phenomenon is called *hysteresis*.

Temperature affects switching times and output voltage. Switching times at two temperatures are shown in Figure 6.22. Note that the time per division

**Figure 6.20
Ideal EGO Switching
Characteristics**

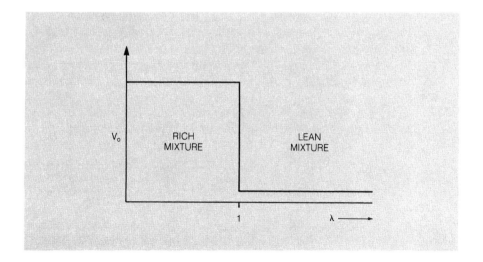

**Figure 6.21
Typical EGO Sensor
Characteristics**

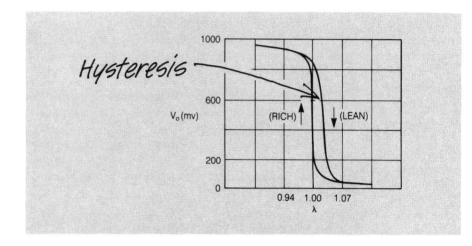

**Figure 6.22
Typical Voltage
Switching
Characteristics of
EGO Sensor**

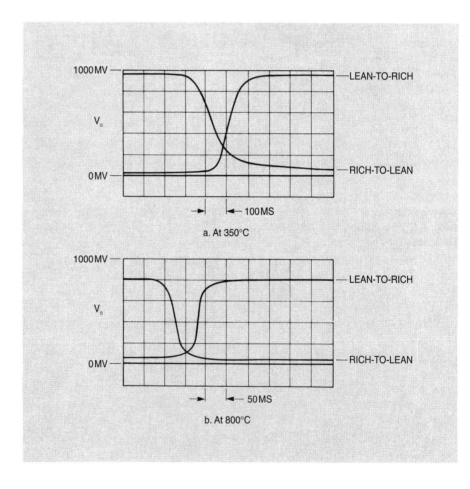

Figure 6.23
Typical Influence of Mixture and Temperature on EGO Output Voltage

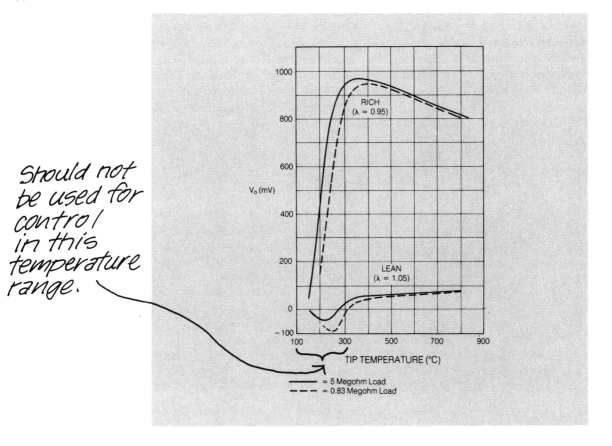

Should not be used for control in this temperature range.

is twice as much for the display at 350°C as at 800°C. This means that the switching times are roughly 0.1 second at 350°C, whereas at 800°C they are about 0.05 second. This is a 2 : 1 change in switching times due to changing temperature.

The temperature dependence of the EGO sensor output voltage is very important. The graph in Figure 6.23 shows the temperature dependence of an EGO sensor output voltage for lean and rich mixtures and for two different load resistances—5 megohms (5 million ohms) and 0.83 megohm. The EGO sensor output voltage for a rich mixture is in the range of about 0.80 to 1.0 volt for an exhaust temperature range of 350°C to 800°C. For a lean mixture, this voltage is roughly in the range of 0.05 to 0.07 volt for the same temperature range.

EGO sensors are not used for control when exhaust gas temperature falls below 300°C because the voltage difference between rich and lean conditions is minimal in this range.

Under certain conditions, the fuel control using an EGO sensor will be operated in open-loop mode and for other conditions it will be operated in closed-loop mode (as will be explained in Chapter 7). The EGO sensor should not be used for control at temperatures below about 300°C because the difference between rich and lean voltages decreases rapidly with temperature in this region. This important property of the sensor is partly responsible for the requirement to operate the fuel control system in the open-loop mode at low exhaust temperature. Closed-loop operation with the EGO output voltage used as the error input cannot begin until the EGO sensor temperature exceeds about 300°C.

Heated EGO Sensors

The increasingly stringent exhaust emission requirements for automobiles in the 1990s have forced automakers to shorten the time from engine start to the point at which the EGO sensor is at operating temperature. This requirement has led to the development of the heated exhaust gas oxygen (HEGO) sensor. This sensor is electrically heated from start-up until it yields an output signal of sufficient magnitude to be useful in closed-loop control.

The HEGO sensor includes a section of resistance material. Electrical power from the car battery is applied at start-up, which quickly warms the sensor to usable temperatures. This heating potentially shortens the time interval until closed-loop operation is possible, thereby minimizing the time during warm-up that the air/fuel ratio deviates from stoichiometry and correspondingly reduces undesirable exhaust gas emissions.

Knock Sensors

Another sensor having applications in closed-loop engine control is the so-called knock sensor. As explained in Chapter 7, this sensor is employed in closed-loop ignition timing to prevent undesirable knock. Although a more detailed explanation of knock is given in Chapter 7, for the purposes of this chapter it can be described generally as a rapid rise in cylinder pressure during combustion. It does not occur normally, but only under special conditions. It occurs most commonly with high manifold pressure and excessive spark advance. It is important to detect knock and avoid excessive knock; otherwise, there may be damage to the engine.

Some engine knock sensors use rods within a magnetic field to detect the presence of knock. Other use vibration-sensitive crystals or semiconductors.

One way of controlling knocking is to sense when knocking begins and then retard the ignition until the knocking stops. A key to the control loop for this method is a knock sensor. A knock sensor using magnetostrictive techniques is shown in Figure 6.24. *Magnetostriction* is a phenomenon whereby the magnetic properties of a material depend on stress (due to an applied force). When sensing knock, the magnetostrictive rods, which are in a magnetic field, change the flux field in the coil due to knock-induced forces. This change in flux produces a voltage change in the coil. This voltage is used

**Figure 6.24
Knock Sensor**

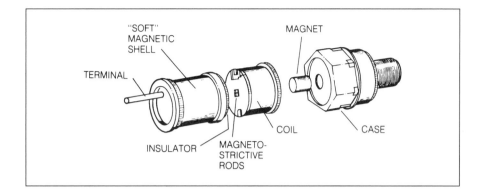

to sense excessive knock (see Chapter 7). Other sensors use piezoelectric crystals or the piezoresistance of a doped silicon semiconductor. Whichever type of sensor is used, it forms a closed-loop system that retards the ignition to reduce the knock detected at the cylinders. Systems using knock sensors are explained in Chapter 7. The problem of detecting knock is complicated by the presence of other vibrations and noises in the engine.

AUTOMOTIVE ENGINE CONTROL ACTUATORS

In addition to the set of sensors, electronic engine control is critically dependent on a set of actuators to control air/fuel ratio, ignition, and EGR. Each of these devices will be discussed separately.

In general, an actuator is a device that receives an electrical input (e.g., from the engine controller) and produces a mechanical or thermal (or other) output. Examples of actuators include various types of electric motors, solenoids, and piezoelectric force generators. In automotive electronic systems the solenoid is the most commonly used device because it is relatively simple and inexpensive.

The solenoid is used in applications ranging from precise fuel control to mundane applications such as electric door locks. A solenoid is in essence a powerful electromagnet having a configuration generally similar to that illustrated in Figure 6.25. The solenoid consists of a fixed steel (i.e., ferromagnetic) frame with a movable steel element. A spring holds the movable element in position such that there is a gap between the end of the movable element and the opening in the frame. A coil is wound around the steel frame, forming a powerful electromagnet.

When a current passes through the coil, a magnetic field is created that tends to pull the movable element toward the steel frame. When the magnetic field, which is proportional to the current, is sufficient to overcome the force at the spring holding the movable element, then it begins to move toward the frame. As this element moves, the size of the gap is reduced, causing an

**Figure 6.25
Schematic Drawing of
a Solenoid**

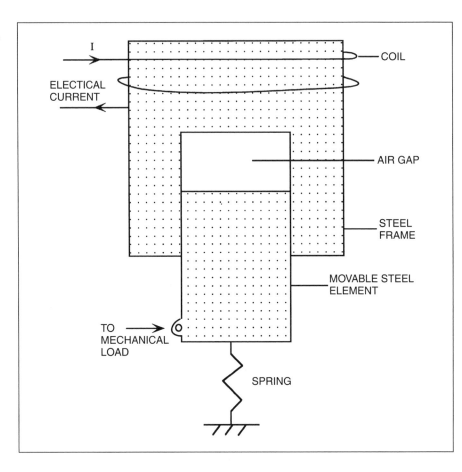

increase in the strength of the magnetic field. This increase causes the movable element to accelerate toward the frame until it reaches the stop.

This abrupt motion of the movable element is essentially in the form of a mechanical switching action such that the solenoid tends to be either in its rest position (as held by the spring) or against the mechanical stop. The movable element is typically connected to a mechanism that is correspondingly moved by the snap action of this element. Applications of solenoids in automotive electronics include fuel injectors and EGR valves.

Fuel Injection

A fuel injector is (in essence) a solenoid-operated valve. The valve opens or closes to permit or block fuel flow to the engine. The valve is attached to the movable element of the solenoid and is switched by the solenoid activation (Figure 6.25).

**Figure 6.26
Schematic Drawing of
Fuel Injector**

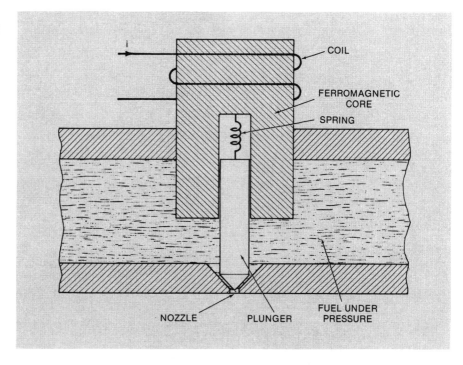

In a fuel injector with no current flowing, the solenoid movable element is held down against the stop, covering the aperture or nozzle. Fuel is thereby blocked from flowing from the pressurized fuel chamber into the aperture. When current flows through the solenoid coil, the movable element is switched upward, the aperture is exposed, and fuel (under pressure) sprays through this aperture.

The fuel flow rate through the nozzle is constant for a given regulated fuel pressure and nozzle geometry; therefore, the quantity of fuel injected into the air stream is proportional to the time the valve is open. The control current that operates the fuel injector is pulsed on and off to deliver precise quantities of fuel.

Fuel Injector Signal

Consider an idealized fuel injector as shown in Figure 6.26, in which the injector is open when the applied voltage is on and is closed when the applied voltage is off. In this idealization, the control voltage operating the fuel injector is a binary pulse train (i.e., either on or off). For a pulse train signal, the ratio of on time t to the period of the pulse T (on time plus off time) is called the *duty cycle*. This is shown in Figure 6.27. The fuel injector is energized for time

Figure 6.27
Pulse Mode Fuel Control Signal to Fuel Injector

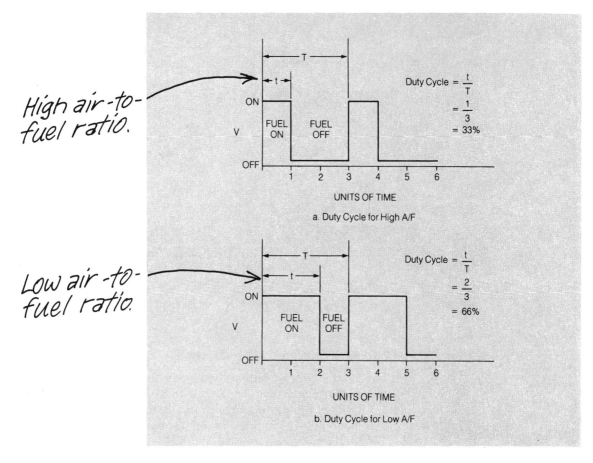

High air-to-fuel ratio.

Low air-to-fuel ratio.

a. Duty Cycle for High A/F

b. Duty Cycle for Low A/F

t to allow fuel to spray from the nozzle into the air stream going to the intake manifold. The injector is deenergized for the remainder of the period. Therefore, a low duty cycle, as seen in Figure 6.27a, is used for a high air/fuel ratio (lean mixture), and a high duty cycle (Figure 6.27b) is used for a low air/fuel ratio (rich mixture).

Exhaust Gas Recirculation Actuator

In Chapter 5 it was explained that exhaust gas recirculation (EGR) is utilized to reduce NO_x emissions. The amount of EGR is regulated by the engine controller, as explained in Chapter 7. When the correct amount of EGR has been determined by the controller based on measurements from the

Figure 6.28
EGR Actuator Control

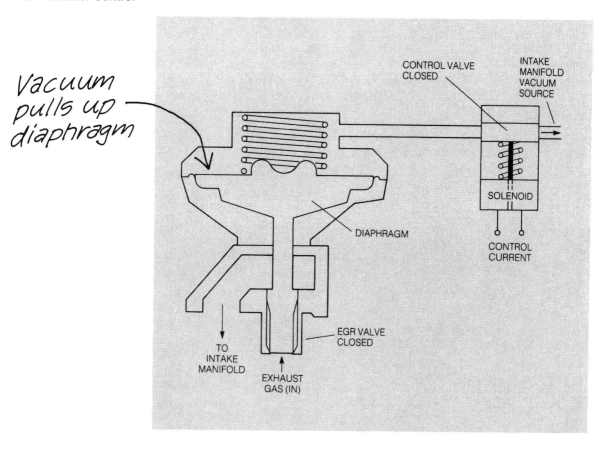

Vacuum pulls up diaphragm

CONTROL VALVE CLOSED

INTAKE MANIFOLD VACUUM SOURCE

SOLENOID

CONTROL CURRENT

DIAPHRAGM

TO INTAKE MANIFOLD

EXHAUST GAS (IN)

EGR VALVE CLOSED

various engine control sensors, the controller sends an electrical signal to the EGR actuator. Typically, this actuator is a variable-position valve that regulates the EGR as a function of intake manifold pressure and exhaust gas pressure.

Although there are many EGR configurations, only one representative example will be discussed to explain the basic operation of this type of actuator. The example EGR actuator is shown schematically in Figure 6.28. This actuator is a vacuum-operated diaphragm valve with a spring that holds the valve closed if no vacuum is applied. The vacuum that operates the diaphragm is supplied by the intake manifold and is controlled by a solenoid-operated valve. This solenoid valve is controlled by the output of the control system.

One kind of EGR actuator consists of a vacuum-operated valve with the vacuum supply controlled by a solenoid. When the EGR valve is open, exhaust gas flows into the intake manifold.

This solenoid operates essentially the same as that explained in the discussion on fuel injectors. Whenever the solenoid is energized (i.e., by current supplied by the control system flowing through the coil), the EGR valve is opened by the applied vacuum.

The amount of valve opening is determined by the average pressure on the vacuum side of the diaphragm. This pressure is regulated by pulsing the solenoid with a variable-duty-cycle electrical control current. The duty cycle (see discussion on fuel injectors) of this pulsing current controls the average pressure in the chamber that affects the diaphragm deflection, thereby regulating the amount of EGR.

Ignition System

The equivalent of an actuator for the ignition system on an engine is the combination of the spark plug, the ignition coil, and driver electronic circuits. This is the subsystem that receives the electrical signal from the engine controller and delivers as its output the spark that ignites the mixture during the end of the compression stroke (see Chapter 1).

Figure 6.29 is a block diagram schematic drawing illustrating this subsystem. The primary circuit of the coil (depicted as the left portion P of the coil in Figure 6.29) is connected to the battery and through a power transistor to ground. For convenience, the collector, emitter, and base are denoted c, e, and b, respectively (see Chapter 3). The coil secondary S is connected to one or more spark plugs, as explained in Chapter 7.

The electronic controller supplies base current to the power transistor, rendering it fully conductive (i.e., in saturation). When it is conducting, the transistor acts essentially like a closed switch. A relatively large current (denoted I_p) flows through the primary windings of the coil (P), creating a relatively large magnetic field that is linked to the secondary coil. At the appropriate time for ignition the controller switches off the base current, causing the transistor to be nonconducting. At this instant the primary current drops to zero very quickly, causing the magnetic field strength to drop rapidly also.

**Figure 6.29
Electronic Ignition
Subsystem**

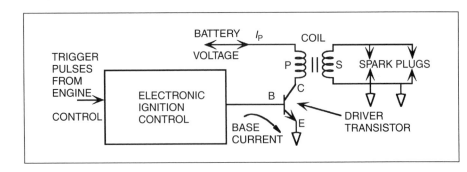

The very rapid drop in the magnetic field (linked to the secondary S) generates a very high voltage (30,000 to 50,000 volts), which, in turn, creates the spark across the spark plug electrodes, igniting the mixture and, finally, initiating the power stroke for the engine. It should be noted that the coil secondary is connected to a pair of spark plugs in Figure 6.29. Firing a pair of spark plugs on two separate cylinders has become commonplace today (see Chapters 1 and 7).

VARIABLE VALVE TIMING (VVT)

In the discussion of the four-stroke IC engine presented in Chapter 1, it was explained that the intake and exhaust valves were opened by a mechanism that is driven from the camshaft. It was explained that the intake valve is opened only during the intake stroke and closed otherwise. Similarly, the exhaust valve is opened only during the exhaust stroke. The exact time during the engine cycle at which these valves open and close is determined by the profile of the camshaft lobes.

The engine performance (including power output and exhaust emissions) is determined by the timing of these openings and closings relative to top dead center (TDC) and bottom dead center (BDC) as well as by the amount of opening (valve lift). It has long been known that optimal cam timing and lift vary with engine operating conditions (i.e., load and RPM). The design of a cam profile has been a compromise that yields acceptable performance over the entire engine operating envelope.

A long-sought goal for the four-stroke IC engine has been the ability to continuously vary cam timing and lift to achieve optimum performance at all operating conditions. Recently, General Motors has begun production of an engine that comes close to achieving this optimum goal. An inline six-cylinder engine having dual camshafts (one for intake and one for exhaust), four valves/cylinder incorporates a mechanism capable of varying exhaust valve timing relative to intake valve timing. GM calls this method variable valve phasing. In this system, the intake valve timing is fixed, but the exhaust valve timing can be advanced or retarded relative to the intake timing. By delaying the exhaust valve relative to intake, the exhaust valve remains open during a portion of the cycle in which the intake valve is open. This portion of the cycle (usually measured in crankshaft angular rotation) is called valve overlap.

In the production system, the valve overlap is minimum at idle. At other operating conditions, the amount of overlap is electronically regulated to optimize performance (including exhaust emissions).

The mechanism for exhaust valve phasing is depicted in Figure 6.30. Figure 6.30a is a front view of the engine. Both camshafts are driven via sprocket gears that are, in turn, driven by a sprocket gear mounted at the end of the crankshaft. These sprocket gears are coupled via a chain.

The exhaust cam sprocket includes a housing within which is a helical spline gear that engages an inner gear connected rigidly to this sprocket gear.

Figure 6.30 Mechanism for Exhaust Valve Phasing; (a) Front View, (b) Cutaway View, and (c) Exploded View

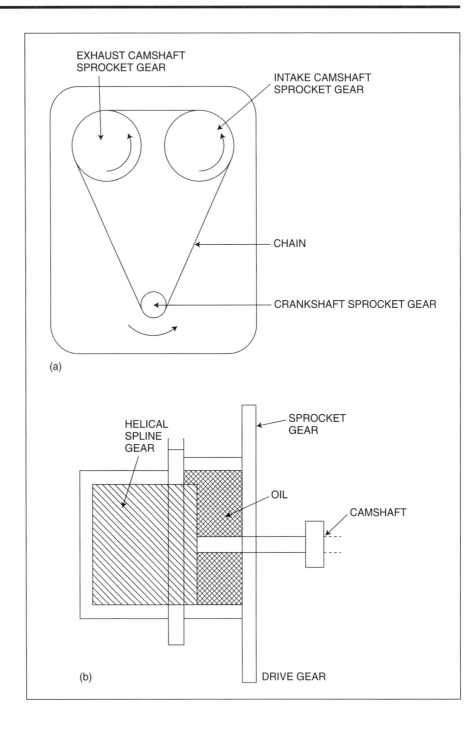

**Figure 6.30
Continued**

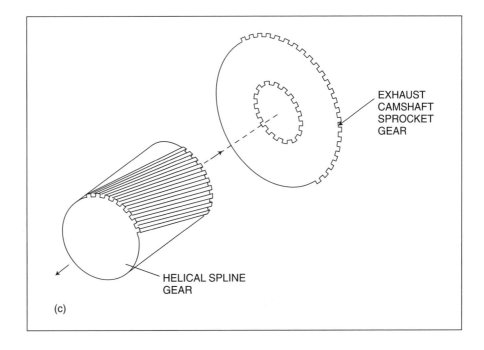

EXHAUST
CAMSHAFT
SPROCKET
GEAR

HELICAL SPLINE
GEAR

(c)

Figure 6.30b shows a cutaway view of the camshaft phasing mechanism assembly. Figure 6.30c shows an exploded view of the helical gear and the camshaft sprocket gear. The exhaust camshaft is connected to the helical spline and rotates with it relative to the sprocket as the helical gear moves axially. This conversion of axial displacement to relative rotary motion is responsible for advancing and retarding the exhaust camshaft relative to the exhaust camshaft sprocket.

The helical gear is moved axially by engine lubricating oil acting on one of its ends acting against a spring. Oil under pressure is supplied to a sealed chamber, one end of which is the helical gear (acting as a piston). The axial displacement of the helical gear is regulated by a solenoid-activated control valve that is itself regulated by the engine electronic control system. The operation of this control system is explained in Chapter 7. By regulating the axial displacement of the helical gear, the engine control system controls the relative phasing of the exhaust and intake camshafts.

ELECTRIC MOTORS FOR HYBRID/ELECTRIC VEHICLES

The development of the hybrid vehicle that combines an IC engine and an electric motor for propulsion was described briefly in Chapter 1. As of the time of this writing, this is a relatively new vehicle type, and only a few hybrid cars have been sold in the United States. At least one car model utilizes a relatively new type of electric motor known as a brushless DC motor. A

**Figure 6.31
Brushless DC Motor**

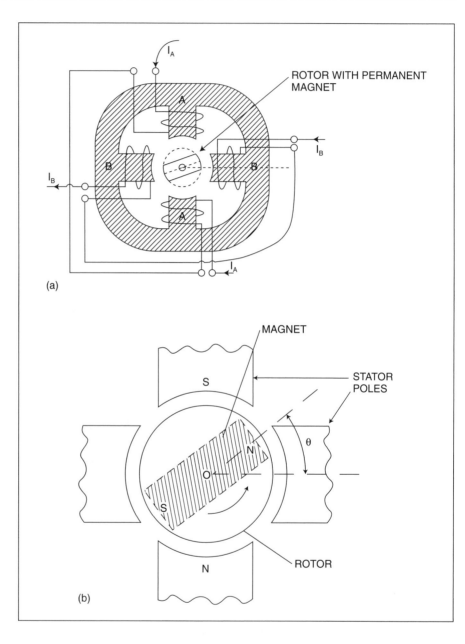

(a)

(b)

brushless DC motor is not a DC motor at all in that the excitation for the stator is AC. However, it derives its name from physical and performance similarity to a shunt-connected DC motor with a constant field current. This type of motor incorporates a permanent magnet in the rotor and electromagnet poles in the stator as depicted in Figure 6.31.

**Figure 6.31
Continued**

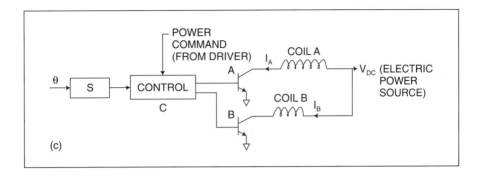

(c)

The stator poles are excited in opposite pairs by currents I_a and I_b. These currents are alternately switched on and off from a DC source at a frequency that matches the speed of rotation. The switching is done electronically with a system that includes an angular position sensor attached to the rotor. This switching is done so that the magnetic field produced by the stator electromagnets always applies a torque on the rotor in the direction of its rotation.

A simplified block diagram of the motor control system for the motor of Figure 6.31a,b is shown in Figure 6.31c. A sensor S measures the angular position θ of the rotor relative to the axes of the magnetic poles of the stator. A controller determines the time for switching currents I_a and I_b on as well as the duration. The switching times are determined such that a torque is applied to the rotor in the direction of rotation.

At the appropriate time, transistor A is switched on, and electric power from the on-board DC source (e.g., battery pack) is supplied to the poles A of the motor. The duration of this current is regulated by controller C to produce the desired power (as commanded by the driver). After rotating approximately 90°, current I_b is switched on by activating transistor B via a signal sent by controller C.

The frequency at which the currents to the stator coils are switched is always synchronous with the speed of rotation. This speed is determined by the mechanical load on the motor and the power commanded by the driver. The driver command, in turn, comes from a position sensor connected to the accelerator pedal. As the accelerator pedal is depressed, the controller responds by increasing the duration of the current pulse supplied to each stator coil. The power delivered by the motor is proportional to the fraction of each cycle that the current is on (i.e., the so-called duty cycle).

With the background in sensors and actuators from this chapter, it is now possible to discuss the various automotive control systems.

Quiz for Chapter 6

1. What does a sensor do?
  a. It selects transmission gear ratio.
  b. It measures some variable.
  c. It is an output device.
  d. It sends signals to the driver.

2. What does an actuator do?
  a. It is an input device for an engine control system.
  b. It provides a mathematical model for an engine.
  c. It causes an action to be performed in response to an electrical signal.
  d. It indicates the results of a measurement.

3. What is a MAP sensor?
  a. a sensor that measures manifold absolute pressure
  b. a vacation route planning scheme
  c. a measurement of fluctuations in manifold air
  d. an acronym for mean atmospheric pressure

4. What is an EGO sensor?
  a. a measure of the self-centeredness of the driver
  b. a device for measuring the oxygen concentration in the exhaust of an engine
  c. a spark advance mechanism
  d. a measure of crankshaft acceleration

5. The crankshaft angular position sensor measures
  a. the angle between the connecting rods and the crankshaft
  b. the angle between a line drawn through the crankshaft axis and a mark on the flywheel and a reference line
  c. the pitch angle of the crankshaft
  d. the oil pressure angle

6. The Hall effect is
  a. the resonance of a long, narrow corridor
  b. the flow of air through the intake manifold
  c. zero crossing error in camshaft position measurements
  d. a phenomenon occurring in semiconductor materials in which a voltage is generated that is proportional to the strength of a magnetic field

7. A mass air flow sensor measures
  a. the density of atmospheric air
  b. the composition of air
  c. the rate at which air is flowing into an engine measured in terms of its mass
  d. the flow of exhaust out of the engine

8. A thermistor is
   a. a semiconductor temperature sensor
   b. a device for regulating engine temperature
   c. a temperature control system for the passenger
   d. a new type of transistor

9. Piezoresistivity is
   a. a property of certain semiconductors in which resistivity varies with strain
   b. a resistance property of insulators
   c. metal bonding pads
   d. an Italian resistor

10. Reluctance is
    a. the reciprocal of permeability
    b. a property of a magnetic circuit that is analogous to resistance in an electrical circuit
    c. a line of constant magnetic flux
    d. none of the above

11. An optical crankshaft position sensor
    a. senses crankshaft angular position
    b. operates by alternately passing or stopping a beam of light from a source to an optical detector
    c. operates in a pulsed mode
    d. all of the above

12. The resistance of a thermistor
    a. varies inversely with temperature
    b. varies directly with temperature
    c. is always 100,000 ohms
    d. none of the above

13. Duty cycle in a fuel injector actuator refers to the ratio of
    a. fuel on time to fuel off time
    b. fuel off time to fuel on time
    c. fuel on time to fuel on time plus fuel off time
    d. none of the above

14. An EGO sensor is
    a. a perfectly linear sensor
    b. a sensor having two different output levels depending on air/fuel ratio
    c. unaffected by exhaust oxygen levels
    d. unaffected by temperature

15. A potentiometer is
    a. a variable-capacitance circuit component
    b. sometimes used to sense air flow
    c. usable in a throttle angle sensor
    d. all of the above

Digital Engine Control Systems

INTRODUCTION

Traditionally, the term *powertrain* has been thought to include the engine, transmission, differential, and drive axle/wheel assemblies. With the advent of electronic controls, the powertrain also includes the electronic control system (in whatever configuration it has). In addition to engine control functions for emissions regulation, fuel economy, and performance, electronic controls are also used in the automatic transmission to select shifting as a function of operating conditions. Moreover, certain vehicles employ electronically controlled clutches in the differential (transaxle) for traction control.

These electronic controls for these major powertrain components can either be separate (i.e., one for each component) or an integrated system regulating the powertrain as a unit.

This latter integrated control system has the benefit of obtaining optimal vehicle performance within the constraints of exhaust emission and fuel economy regulations. Each of the control systems is discussed separately beginning with electronic engine control. Then a brief discussion of integrated powertrain follows. This chapter concludes with a discussion of hybrid vehicle control systems in which propulsive power comes from an IC engine or an electric motor, or a combination of both. The proper balance of power between these two sources is a very complex function of operating conditions and governmental regulations.

DIGITAL ENGINE CONTROL

Chapter 5 discussed some of the fundamental issues involved in electronic engine control. This chapter explores some practical digital control systems. There is, of course, considerable variation in the configuration and control concept from one manufacturer to another. However, this chapter describes representative control systems that are not necessarily based on the system of any given manufacturer, thereby giving the reader an understanding of the configuration and operating principles of a generic representative system. As such, the systems in this discussion are a compilation of the features used by several manufacturers.

In Chapter 5, engine control was discussed with respect to continuous-time representation. In fact, most modern engine control systems, such as discussed in this chapter, are digital. A typical engine control system incorporates a microprocessor and is essentially a special-purpose computer (or microcontroller).

Electronic engine control has evolved from a relatively rudimentary fuel control system employing discrete analog components to the highly precise fuel and ignition control through 32-bit (sometimes more) microprocessor-based integrated digital electronic power train control. The motivation for development of the more sophisticated digital control systems has been the increasingly stringent exhaust emission and fuel economy regulations. It has proven to be cost effective to implement the power train controller as a multimode computer-based system to satisfy these requirements.

A multimode controller operates in one of many possible modes, and, among other tasks, changes the various calibration parameters as operating conditions change in order to optimize performance. To implement multimode control in analog electronics it would be necessary to change hardware parameters (for example, via switching systems) to accommodate various operating conditions. In a computer-based controller, however, the control law and system parameters are changed via program (i.e., software) control. The hardware remains fixed but the software are reconfigured in accordance with operating conditions as determined by sensor measurements and switch inputs to the controller.

This chapter will explain how the microcontroller under program control is responsible for generating the electrical signals that operate the fuel injectors and trigger the ignition pulses. This chapter also discusses secondary functions (including management of secondary air that must be provided to the catalytic converter EGR regulation and evaporative emission control) that have not been discussed in detail before.

DIGITAL ENGINE CONTROL FEATURES

Recall from Chapter 5 that the primary purpose of the electronic engine control system is to regulate the mixture (i.e., air–fuel), the ignition timing, and EGR. Virtually all major manufacturers of cars sold in the United States (both foreign and domestic) use the three-way catalyst for meeting exhaust emission constraints. For such cars, the air/fuel ratio is held as closely as possible to the stoichiometric value of about 14.7 for as much of the time as possible. Ignition timing and EGR are controlled separately to optimize performance and fuel economy.

Figure 7.1 illustrates the primary components of an electronic engine control system. In this figure, the engine control system is a microcontroller, typically implemented with a specially designed microprocessor and operating under program control. Typically, the controller incorporates hardware multiply and ROM (see Chapter 4). The hardware multiply greatly speeds up the multiplication operation required at several stages of engine control relative

Figure 7.1
Components of an Electronically Controlled Engine

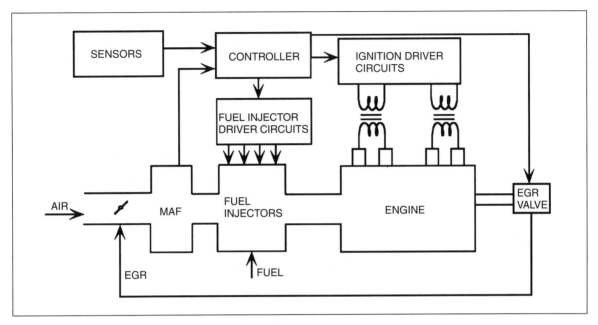

to software multiplication routines, which are generally cumbersome and slow. The associated ROM contains the program for each mode as well as calibration parameters and lookup tables. The earliest such systems incorporated 8-bit microprocessors, although the trend is toward implementation with 32-bit microprocessors. The microcontroller under program control generates output electrical signals to operate the fuel injectors so as to maintain the desired mixture and ignition to optimize performance. The correct mixture is obtained by regulating the quantity of fuel delivered into each cylinder during the intake stroke in accordance with the air mass, as explained in Chapter 5.

In determining the correct fuel flow, the controller obtains a measurement or estimate of the mass air flow rate into the cylinder. As explained in Chapter 5, the measurement is obtained using a mass air flow sensor (MAF). Alternatively, the mass air flow rate is estimated (calculated) using the speed-density method, also explained in Chapter 5. This estimate can be found from measurement of the intake manifold absolute pressure (MAP), the RPM, and the inlet air temperature.

Using this measurement or estimate, the quantity of fuel to be delivered is determined by the controller in accordance with the instantaneous control mode. The quantity of fuel delivered by the fuel injector is determined by the operation of the fuel injector. As explained in Chapter 6, a fuel injector is essentially a solenoid-operated valve. Fuel that is supplied to each injector from the fuel pump is supplied to each fuel injector at a regulated fuel pressure. When the injector valve is opened, fuel flows at a rate R_f (in gal/sec) that is determined by the (constant) regulated pressure and by the geometry of the fuel injector valve. The quantity of fuel F delivered to any cylinder is proportional to the time T that this valve is opened:

$$F = R_f T$$

The engine control system, then, determines the correct quantity of fuel to be delivered to each cylinder (for a given operating condition) via measurement of mass air flow rate. The controller then generates an electrical signal that opens the fuel injector valve for the appropriate time interval T to deliver this desired fuel quantity to the cylinder such that a stoichiometric air/fuel ratio is maintained.

The controller also determines the correct time for fuel delivery to correspond to the intake stroke for the relevant cylinder. This timing is determined by measurements of crankshaft and camshaft position using sensors such as those described in Chapter 6.

CONTROL MODES FOR FUEL CONTROL

The engine control system is responsible for controlling fuel and ignition for all possible engine operating conditions. However, there are a number of distinct categories of engine operation, each of which corresponds to a separate and distinct operating mode for the engine control system. The differences between these operating modes are sufficiently great that different software is used for each. The control system must determine the operating mode from the existing sensor data and call the particular corresponding software routine.

Engines have different modes of operation as the operating conditions change. Seven different modes of operation commonly affect fuel control.

For a typical engine there are seven different engine operating modes that affect fuel control: engine crank, engine warm-up, open-loop control, closed-loop control, hard acceleration, deceleration, and idle. The program for mode control logic determines the engine operating mode from sensor data and timers.

In the earliest versions of electronic fuel control systems, the fuel metering actuator typically consisted of one or two fuel injectors mounted near the throttle plate so as to deliver fuel into the throttle body. These throttle body fuel injectors (TBFI) were in effect an electromechanical replacement for the carburetor. Requirements for the TBFI were such that they only had to deliver fuel at the correct average flow rate for any given mass air flow. Mixing of the fuel and air, as well as distribution to the individual cylinders, took place in the intake manifold system.

The more stringent exhaust emissions regulations of the late 1980s and the 1990s have demanded more precise fuel delivery than can normally be achieved by TBFI. These regulations and the need for improved performance have led to timed sequential port fuel injection (TSPFI). In such a system there is a fuel injector for each cylinder that is mounted so as to spray fuel directly into the intake of the associated cylinder. Fuel delivery is timed to occur during the intake stroke for that cylinder.

The digital engine control system requires sensors for measuring the engine variables and parameters discussed in Chapter 5. Referring to F igure 7.1, the set of sensors may include, for example, mass air flow (MAF), exhaust gas oxygen concentration (EGO), and crankshaft angular position (CPS), as well as RPM, camshaft position (possibly a single reference point for each engine cycle), coolant temperature (CT), throttle plate angular position (TPS), intake air temperature, and exhaust pressure ratio (EPR) for EGR control.

In the example configuration of Figure 7.1, fuel delivery is assumed to be TSPFI (i.e., via individual fuel injectors located so as to spray fuel directly into the intake port and timed to coincide with the intake stroke). Air flow measurement is via an MAF sensor. In addition to MAF, sensors are available for the measurement of exhaust gas oxygen (EGO) concentration, RPM, inlet air and coolant temperatures, throttle position, crankshaft (and possibly camshaft) position, and exhaust differential pressure (for EGR calculation). Some engine controllers involve vehicle speed sensors and various switches to identify brake on/off and the transmission gear, depending on the particular control strategy employed.

When the ignition key is switched on initially, the mode control logic automatically selects an engine start control scheme that provides the low air/fuel ratio required for starting the engine. Once the engine RPM rises above the cranking value, the controller identifies the "engine started" mode and passes control to the program for the engine warm-up mode. This operating mode keeps the air/fuel ratio low to prevent engine stall during cool weather until the engine coolant temperature rises above some minimum value. The instantaneous air/fuel is a function of coolant temperature. The particular value for the minimum coolant temperature is specific to any given engine and, in particular, to the fuel metering system. (Alternatively, the low air/fuel ratio may be maintained for a fixed time interval following start, depending on start-up engine temperature.)

When the coolant temperature rises sufficiently, the mode control logic directs the system to operate in the open-loop control mode until the EGO sensor warms up enough to provide accurate readings. This condition is detected by monitoring the EGO sensor's output for voltage readings above a certain minimum rich air/fuel mixture voltage set point. When the sensor has indicated rich at least once and after the engine has been in open loop for a specific time, the control mode selection logic selects the closed-loop mode for the system. (Note: other criteria may also be used.) The engine remains in the closed-loop mode until either the EGO sensor cools and fails to read a rich mixture for a certain length of time or a hard acceleration or deceleration

During engine crank and engine warm-up modes, the controller holds the air/fuel ratio to a purposely low value (a rich fuel mixture).

After warm-up, the controller switches to open-loop control until accurate readings can be obtained from the EGO sensor. The controller then changes to, and remains in, closed-loop mode under ordinary driving conditions.

During conditions of hard acceleration or deceleration, the controller adjusts the air/fuel ratio as needed. During idle periods, the controller adjusts engine speed to reduce engine roughness and stalling.

occurs. If the sensor cools, the control mode logic selects the open-loop mode again.

During hard acceleration or heavy engine load, the control mode selection logic chooses a scheme that provides a rich air/fuel mixture for the duration of the acceleration or heavy load. This scheme provides maximum torque but relatively poor emissions control and poor fuel economy regulation as compared with a stoichiometric air/fuel ratio. After the need for enrichment has passed, control is returned to either open-loop or closed-loop mode, depending on the control mode logic selection conditions that exist at that time.

During periods of deceleration, the air/fuel ratio is increased to reduce emissions of HC and CO due to unburned excess fuel. When idle conditions are present, control mode logic passes system control to the idle speed control mode. In this mode, the engine speed is controlled to reduce engine roughness and stalling that might occur because the idle load has changed due to air conditioner compressor operation, alternator operation, or gearshift positioning from park/neutral to drive, although stoichiometric mixture is used if the engine is warm.

In modern engine control systems, the controller is a special-purpose digital computer built around a microprocessor. A block diagram of a typical modern digital engine control system is depicted in Figure 7.2. The controller also includes ROM containing the main program (of several thousand lines of code) as well as RAM for temporary storage of data during computation. The sensor signals are connected to the controller via an input/output (I/O) subsystem. Similarly, the I/O subsystem provides the output signals to drive the fuel injectors (shown as the fuel metering block of Figure 7.2) as well as to trigger pulses to the ignition system (described later in this chapter). In addition, this solid-state control system includes hardware for sampling and analog-to-digital conversion such that all sensor measurements are in a format suitable for reading by the microprocessor. (*Note:* See Chapter 4 for a detailed discussion of these components.)

The sensors that measure various engine variables for control are as follows:

MAF	Mass air flow sensor
CT	Engine temperature as represented by coolant temperature
HEGO	(One or two) heated exhaust gas oxygen sensor(s)
POS/RPM	Crankshaft angular position and RPM sensor cycle Camshaft position sensor for determining start of each engine cycle
TPS	Throttle position sensor

Figure 7.2
Digital Engine Control System Diagram

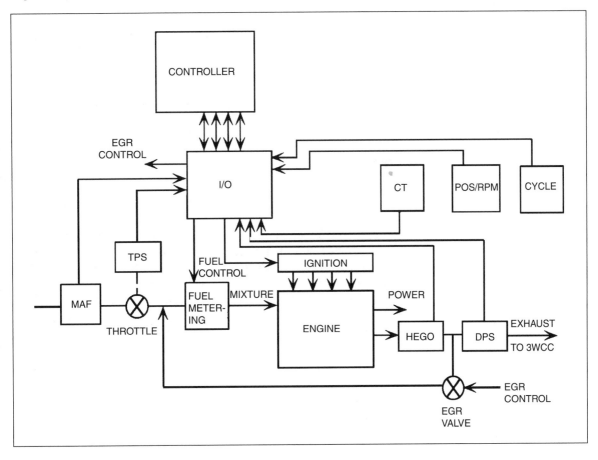

DPS	Differential pressure sensor (exhaust to intake) for EGR control

The control system selects an operating mode based on the instantaneous operating condition as determined from the sensor measurements. Within any given operating mode the desired air/fuel ratio $(A/F)_d$ is selected. The controller then determines the quantity of fuel to be injected into each cylinder during each engine cycle. This quantity of fuel depends on the particular engine operating condition as well as the controller mode of operation, as will presently be explained.

**Figure 7.3
Illustration of Lookup
Table for Desired
Air/Fuel Ratio**

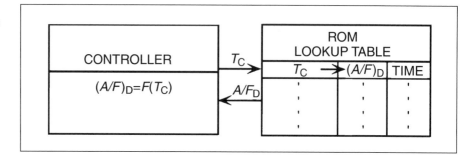

Engine Crank

During engine crank, the controller compares the value from the coolant temperature sensor with values stored in a lookup table to determine the correct air/fuel ratio at that temperature.

While the engine is being cranked, the fuel control system must provide an intake air/fuel ratio of anywhere from $2:1$ to $12:1$, depending on engine temperature. The correct air/fuel ratio (i.e., $[A/F]_d$) is selected from a ROM lookup table as a function of coolant temperature. Low temperatures affect the ability of the fuel metering system to atomize or mix the incoming air and fuel. At low temperatures, the fuel tends to form into large droplets in the air, which do not burn as efficiently as tiny droplets. The larger fuel droplets tend to increase the apparent air/fuel ratio, because the amount of usable fuel (on the surface of the droplets) in the air is reduced; therefore, the fuel metering system must provide a decreased air/fuel ratio to provide the engine with a more combustible air/fuel mixture. During engine crank the primary issue is to achieve engine start as rapidly as possible. Once the engine is started the controller switches to an engine warm-up mode.

Engine Warm-Up

The controller selects a warm-up time from a lookup table based on the temperature of the coolant. During engine warm-up the air/fuel ratio is still rich, but it is changed by the controller as the coolant temperature increases.

While the engine is warming up, an enriched air/fuel ratio is still needed to keep it running smoothly, but the required air/fuel ratio changes as the temperature increases. Therefore, the fuel control system stays in the open-loop mode, but the air/fuel ratio commands continue to be altered due to the temperature changes. The emphasis in this control mode is on rapid and smooth engine warm-up. Fuel economy and emission control are still a secondary concern.

A diagram illustrating the lookup table selection of desired air/fuel ratios is shown in Figure 7.3. Essentially, the measured coolant temperature (CT) is converted to an address for the lookup table. This address is supplied to the ROM table via the system address bus (A/B). The data stored at this address in the ROM are the desired air/fuel ratio $(A/F)_d$ for that temperature. These data are sent to the controller via the system data bus (D/B).

There is always the possibility of a coolant temperature failure. Such a failure could result in excessively rich or lean mixtures, which can seriously degrade the performance of both the engine and the three-way catalytic converter (3wcc). One scheme that can circumvent a temperature sensor failure involves having a time function to limit the duration of the engine warm-up mode. The nominal time to warm the engine from cold soak at various temperatures is known. The controller is configured to switch from engine warm-up mode to an open-loop (warmed-up engine) mode after a sufficient time by means of an internal timer.

It is worthwhile at this point to explain how the quantity of fuel to be injected is determined. This method is implemented in essentially all operating modes and is described here as a generic method, even though each engine control scheme may vary somewhat from the following. The quantity of fuel to be injected during the intake stroke of any given cylinder (which we call F) is determined by the mass of air (A) drawn into that cylinder (i.e., the air charge) during that intake stroke. That quantity of fuel is given by the air charge divided by the desired air/fuel ratio:

$$F = \frac{A}{(A/F)_d}$$

The quantity of air drawn into the cylinder, A, is computed from the mass air flow rate and the RPM. The mass air flow rate (MAF) will be given in kg/sec. If the engine speed in revolutions/minute is RPM, then the number of revolutions/second (which we call r) is

$$r = \frac{\text{RPM}}{60}$$

Then, the mass air flow is distributed approximately uniformly to half the cylinders during each revolution. If the number of cylinders is N then the air charge (mass) in each cylinder during one revolution is

$$A = \frac{\text{MAF}}{r(N/2)}$$

In this case, the mass of fuel delivered to each cylinder is

$$F = \frac{\text{MAF}}{r(N/2)(A/F)_d}$$

This computation is carried out by the controller continuously so that the fuel quantity can be varied quickly to accommodate rapid changes in engine operating condition. The fuel injector pulse duration T corresponding to this fuel quantity is computed using the known fuel injector delivery rate R_f:

$$T = \frac{F}{R_f}$$

This pulse width is known as the *base pulse width*. The actual pulse width used is modified from this according to the mode of operation at any time, as will presently be explained.

Open-Loop Control

After engine warm-up, open-loop control is used. The most popular method uses the mass density equation to calculate the amount of air entering the intake manifold.

For a warmed-up engine, the controller will operate in an open loop if the closed-loop mode is not available for any reason. For example, the engine may be warmed sufficiently but the EGO sensor may not provide a usable signal. In any event, as soon as possible it is important to have a stoichiometric mixture to minimize exhaust emissions. The base pulse width T_b is computed as described above, except that the desired air/fuel ratio $(A/F)_d$ is 14.7 (stoichiometry):

$$T_b = \frac{MAF}{r(N/2)(14.7)R_f} \qquad \text{base pulse width}$$

Corrections of the base pulse width occur whenever anything affects the accuracy of the fuel delivery. For example, low battery voltage might affect the pressure in the fuel rail that delivers fuel to the fuel injectors. Corrections to the base pulse width are then made using the actual battery voltage.

As explained in Chapter 5, an alternate method of computing mass air flow rate is the speed-density method. Although the speed-density method has essentially been replaced by direct mass air flow measurements, there will continue to be a number of cars employing this method for years to come, so it is arguably worthwhile to include a brief discussion in this chapter. This method, which is illustrated in Figure 7.4, is based on measurements of manifold absolute pressure (MAP), RPM, and intake air temperature T_i. The air density d_a is computed from MAP and T_i, and the volume flow rate R_v of combined air and EGR is computed from RPM and volumetric efficiency, the latter being a function of MAP and RPM. The volume rate for air is found by subtracting the EGR volume flow rate from the combined air and EGR. Finally, the mass air flow rate is computed as the product of the volume flow rate for air and the intake air density. Given the complexity of the speed-density method it is easy to see why automobile manufacturers would choose the direct mass air flow measurement once a cost-effective mass air flow sensor became available.

The speed-density method can be implemented either by computation in the engine control computer or via lookup tables. Figure 7.5 is an illustration of the lookup table implementation. In this figure, three variables need to be determined: volumetric efficiency (n_v), intake density (d_a), and EGR volume flow rate (R_E). The volumetric efficiency is read from ROM with an address determined from RPM and MAP measurements. The intake air density is read from another section of ROM with an address determined from MAP and T_i measurements. The EGR volume flow rate is read from still another section of

Figure 7.4
Engine Control System Using the Speed-Density Method

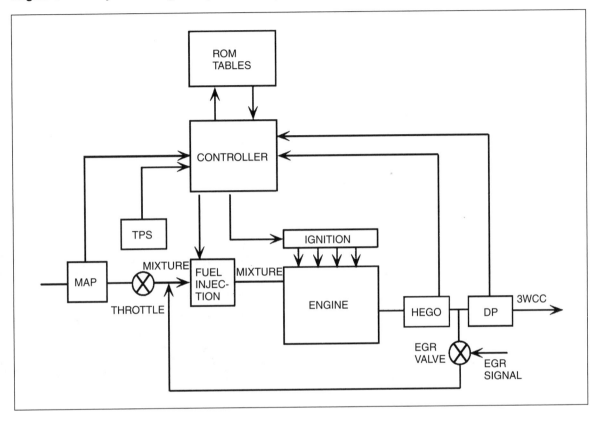

ROM with an address determined from differential pressure (DP) and EGR valve position. These variables are combined to yield the mass air flow rate:

$$\text{MAF} = d_a\left[\left(\frac{\text{RPM}}{60}\right)\left(\frac{D}{2}\right)n_v - R_E\right]$$

where D is the engine displacement.

Closed-Loop Control

Perhaps the most important adjustment to the fuel injector pulse duration comes when the control is in the closed-loop mode. In the open-loop mode the accuracy of the fuel delivery is dependent on the accuracy of the measurements of the important variables. However, any physical system is susceptible to changes with either operating conditions (e.g., temperature) or with time (aging or wear of components).

Figure 7.5
Lookup Table Determination of d_a, R_E, and n_v

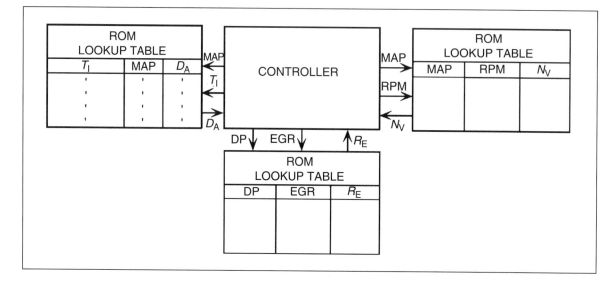

In any closed-loop control system a measurement of the output variables is compared with the desired value for those variables. In the case of fuel control, the variables being regulated are exhaust gas concentrations of HC, CO, and NO$_x$, as explained in Chapter 5. Although direct measurement of these exhaust gases is not feasible in production automobiles, it is sufficient for fuel control purposes to measure the exhaust gas oxygen concentration. Recall from Chapter 5 that these regulated gases can be optimally controlled with a stoichiometric mixture. Recall further from Chapter 6 that the EGO sensor is, in essence, a switching sensor that changes output voltage abruptly as the input mixture crosses the stoichiometric mixture of 14.7.

The closed-loop mode can only be activated when the EGO (or HEGO) sensor is sufficiently warmed. Recall from Chapter 6 that the output voltage of the sensor is high (approximately 1 volt) when the exhaust oxygen concentration is low (i.e., for a rich mixture relative to stoichiometry). The EGO sensor voltage is low (approximately 0.1 volt) whenever the exhaust oxygen concentration is high (i.e., for a mixture that is lean relative to stoichiometry).

The time-average EGO sensor output voltage provides the feedback signal for fuel control in the closed-loop mode. The instantaneous EGO sensor voltage fluctuates rapidly from high to low values, but the average value is a good indication of the mixture.

As explained earlier, fuel delivery is regulated by the engine control system by controlling the pulse duration (T) for each fuel injector. The engine controller continuously adjusts the pulse duration for varying operating conditions and for operating parameters. A representative algorithm for fuel injector pulse duration for a given injector during the nth computation cycle, $T(n)$, is given by

$$T(n) = T_b(n) \times [1 + C_L(n)]$$

where

> $T_b(n)$ is the base pulse width as determined from measurements of mass air flow rate and the desired air/fuel ratio
>
> $C_L(n)$ is the closed-loop correction factor

For open-loop operation, $C_L(n)$ equals 0; for closed-loop operation, C_L is given by

$$C_L(n) = \alpha I(n) + \beta P(n)$$

where

> $I(n)$ is the integral part of the closed-loop correction
>
> $P(n)$ is the proportional part of the closed-loop correction
>
> α and β are constants

These latter variables are determined from the output of the exhaust gas oxygen (EGO) sensor as described in Chapter 6.

Whenever the EGO sensor indicates a rich mixture (i.e., EGO sensor voltage is high), then the integral term is reduced by the controller for the next cycle,

$$I(n+1) = I(n) - 1$$

for a rich mixture.

Whenever the EGO sensor indicates a lean mixture (i.e., low output voltage), the controller increments $I(n)$ for the next cycle,

$$I(n+1) = I(n) + 1$$

for a lean mixture. The integral part of C_L continues to increase or decrease in a limit-cycle operation, as explained in Chapter 5 for continuous-time operation.

The computation of the closed-loop correction factor continues at a rate determined within the controller. This rate is normally high enough to permit rapid adjustment of the fuel injector pulse width during rapid throttle changes at high engine speed. The period between successive computations is the computation cycle described above.

In addition to the integral component of the closed-loop correction to pulse duration is the proportional term. This term, $P(n)$, is proportional to the deviation of the average EGO sensor signal from its mid-range value (corresponding to stoichiometry). The combined terms change with

Figure 7.6
Closed-Loop Correction Factor

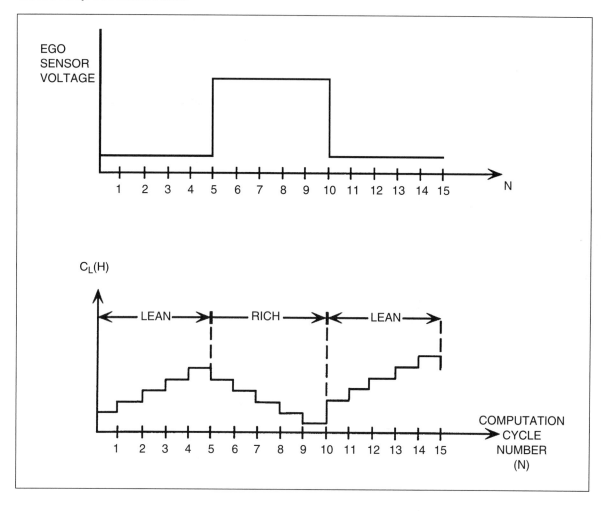

computation cycle as depicted in Figure 7.6. In this figure the regions of lean and rich (relative to stoichiometry) are depicted. During relatively lean periods the closed-loop correction term increases for each computation cycle, whereas during relatively rich intervals this term decreases.

Once the computation of the closed-loop correction factor is completed, the value is stored in a specific memory location (RAM) in the controller. At the appropriate time for fuel injector activation (during the intake stroke), the instantaneous closed-loop correction factor is read from its location in RAM and an actual pulse of the corrected duration is generated by the engine control.

Acceleration Enrichment

The mixture is enriched to maximize torque during very heavy load (for example, a wide open throttle).

During periods of heavy engine load such as during hard acceleration, fuel control is adjusted to provide an enriched air/fuel ratio to maximize engine torque and neglect fuel economy and emissions. This condition of enrichment is permitted within the regulations of the EPA as it is only a temporary condition. It is well recognized that hard acceleration is occasionally required for maneuvering in certain situations and is, in fact, related at times to safety.

The computer detects this condition by reading the throttle angle sensor voltage. High throttle angle corresponds to heavy engine load and is an indication that heavy acceleration is called for by the driver. In some vehicles a switch is provided to detect wide open throttle. The fuel system controller responds by increasing the pulse duration of the fuel injector signal for the duration of the heavy load. This enrichment enables the engine to operate with a torque greater than that allowed when emissions and fuel economy are controlled. Enrichment of the air/fuel ratio to about 12:1 is sometimes used.

Deceleration Leaning

Fuel flow is reduced during deceleration with closed throttle.

During periods of light engine load and high RPM such as during coasting or hard deceleration, the engine operates with a very lean air/fuel ratio to reduce excess emissions of HC and CO. Deceleration is indicated by a sudden decrease in throttle angle or by closure of a switch when the throttle is closed (depending on the particular vehicle configuration). When these conditions are detected by the control computer, it computes a decrease in the pulse duration of the fuel injector signal. The fuel may even be turned off completely for very heavy deceleration.

Idle Speed Control

When the throttle angle reaches its closed position and engine RPM falls below a preset value, the controller switches to idle speed control. A stepping motor opens a valve, allowing a limited amount of air to bypass the closed throttle plate.

Idle speed control is used by some manufacturers to prevent engine stall during idle. The goal is to allow the engine to idle at as low an RPM as possible, yet keep the engine from running rough and stalling when power-consuming accessories, such as air conditioning compressors and alternators, turn on.

The control mode selection logic switches to idle speed control when the throttle angle reaches its zero (completely closed) position and engine RPM falls below a minimum value, and when the vehicle is stationary. Idle speed is controlled by using an electronically controlled throttle bypass valve (Figure 7.7a) that allows air to flow around the throttle plate and produces the same effect as if the throttle had been slightly opened.

There are various schemes for operating a valve to introduce bypass air for idle control. One relatively common method for controlling the idle speed bypass air uses a special type of motor called a *stepper motor*. A stepper motor moves in fixed angular increments when activated by pulses on its two sets of windings (i.e., open or close). Such a motor can be operated in either direction

Figure 7.7a
Idle Air Control

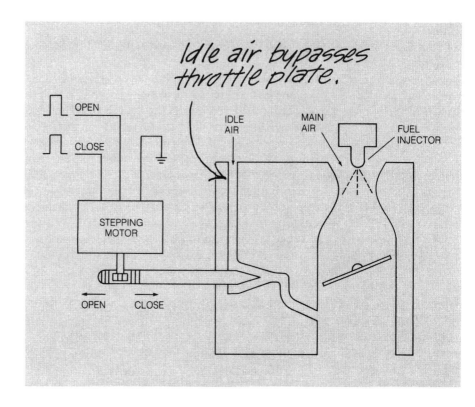

by supplying pulses in the proper phase to the windings. This is advantageous for idle speed control since the controller can very precisely position the idle bypass valve by sending the proper number of pulses of the correct phasing.

The engine control computer can know precisely the position of the valve in a number of ways. In one way the computer can send sufficient pulses to completely close the valve when the ignition is first switched on. Then it can send open pulses (phased to open the valve) to a specified (known) position.

A block diagram of a simplified idle speed control system is shown in Figure 7.7b. Idle speed is detected by the RPM sensor, and the speed is adjusted to maintain a constant idle RPM. The computer receives digital on/off status inputs from several power-consuming devices attached to the engine, such as the air conditioner clutch switch, park-neutral switch, and the battery charge indicator. These inputs indicate the load that is applied to the engine during idle.

When the engine is not idling, the idle speed control valve may be completely closed so that the throttle plate has total control of intake air. During periods of deceleration leaning, the idle speed valve may be opened to provide extra air to increase the air/fuel ratio in order to reduce HC emissions.

Figure 7.7b
Idle Air Control

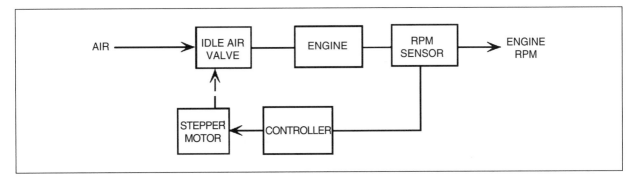

EGR CONTROL

A second electronic engine control subsystem is the control of exhaust gas that is recirculated back to the intake manifold. Under normal operating conditions, engine cylinder temperatures can reach more than 3,000°F. The higher the temperature, the more chance the exhaust will have NO_x emissions. As explained in Chapter 5, a small amount of exhaust gas is introduced into the cylinder to replace normal intake air. This results in lower combustion temperatures, which reduces NO_x emissions.

The engine controller also must determine when the EGR valve should be opened or closed.

The control mode selection logic determines when EGR is turned off or on. EGR is turned off during cranking, cold engine temperature (engine warm-up), idling, acceleration, or other conditions demanding high torque.

Since exhaust gas recirculation was first introduced as a concept for reducing NO_x exhaust emissions, its implementation has gone through considerable change. There are in fact many schemes and configurations for EGR realization. We discuss here one method of EGR implementation that incorporates enough features to be representative of all schemes in use today and in the near future.

Fundamental to all EGR schemes is a passageway or port connecting the exhaust and intake manifolds. A valve is positioned along this passageway whose position regulates EGR from zero to some maximum value. Typically, the valve is operated by a diaphragm connected to a variable vacuum source, as explained in Chapter 6. The controller operates a solenoid in a periodic variable-duty-cycle mode. The average level of vacuum on the diaphragm (see Chapter 6) varies with the duty cycle. By varying this duty cycle, the control system has proportional control over the EGR valve opening and thereby over the amount of EGR.

In many EGR control systems the controller monitors the differential pressure between the exhaust and intake manifold via a differential pressure

**Figure 7.8a
EGR Control**

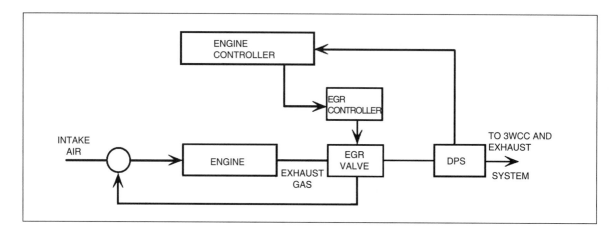

sensor (DPS). With the signal from this sensor the controller can calculate the valve opening for the desired EGR level. The amount of EGR required is a predetermined function of the load on the engine (i.e., power produced).

A simplified block diagram for an EGR control system is depicted in Figure 7.8a. In this figure the EGR valve is operated by a solenoid-regulated vacuum actuator (coming from the intake). An explanation of this proportional actuator is given in Chapter 6. The engine controller determines the required amount of EGR based on the engine operating condition and the signal from the differential pressure sensor (DPS) between intake and exhaust manifolds. The controller then commands the correct EGR valve position to achieve the desired amount of EGR.

VARIABLE VALVE TIMING CONTROL

Chapter 5 introduced the concept and relative benefits of variable valve timing for improved volumetric efficiency. There it was explained that performance improvement and emissions reductions could be achieved if the opening and closing times (and ideally the valve lift) of both intake and exhaust valves could be controlled as a function of operating conditions. In Chapter 6, a mechanism was discussed for varying camshaft phasing that is in production in certain vehicles that is used for varying exhaust camshaft phasing. This system improves volumetric efficiency by varying valve overlap from exhaust closing to intake opening. In addition to improving volumetric efficiency, this variable valve phasing can achieve desired EGR fraction.

The amount of valve overlap is directly related to the relative exhaust-intake camshaft phasing. Generally, minimal overlap is desired at idle. The

**Figure 7.8b
Closed-Loop Control
System**

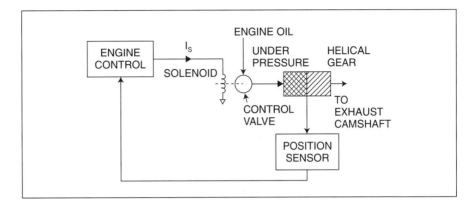

desired optimal amount of overlap is determined during engine development as a function of RPM and load (e.g., by engine mapping).

The desired exhaust camshaft phasing is stored in memory (ROM) in the engine control system as a function of RPM and load. Then during engine operation the correct camshaft phasing can be found via table look up and interpolation (see Chapter 4), based on measurements of RPM and load. The RPM measurement is achieved using a noncontacting angular speed sensor (see Chapter 5). Load is measured either using a manifold absolute pressure (MAP) sensor directly or it is computed from mass air flow as well as RPM (see Chapter 5).

Once the desired camshaft phasing has been determined, the engine control system sends an appropriate electrical control signal to a solenoid operated valve. In Chapter 5 it was shown that camshaft phasing is regulated by the axial position of a helical spline gear. This axial position is determined by the pressure of (engine) oil action on one face of the helical spline gear acting against a spring. This oil pressure is regulated by the solenoid-operated valve.

Control of camshaft phasing can be either open loop or closed loop. In the open-loop case, the correct camshaft phasing depends on the relationship between axial position of the helical spline gear and the oil pressure/return spring relationship.

Since this cam closed phasing system is in fact a position control system, loop control of exhaust camshaft operation requires a measurement of camshaft phase relative to intake. This phase measurement can be accomplished by measuring axial displacement of the helical gear because there is a unique mechanical relationship between this axial displacement and exhaust camshaft phasing. Figure 7.8b depicts a block diagram of a representative camshaft phasing control system.

The control system shown in Figure 7.8b presumes a closed-loop control system. This VVT control system could also be an open-loop control system in which no position sensor would be required.

For the hypothetical control system of Figure 6.31, the engine control system calculates desired camshaft angular displacement (as a function of load and RPM) and compares that with actual angular displacement. The difference between these represents an error signal from which solenoid current I_s is determined. The solenoid regulates oil supplied to the chamber that moves the helical gear. This gear moves until actual exhaust camshaft phasing matches the desired value, thereby optimizing engine performance.

ELECTRONIC IGNITION CONTROL

As we have seen in Chapter 1, an engine must be provided with fuel and air in correct proportions and the means to ignite this mixture in the form of an electric spark. Before the development of electronic ignition the traditional ignition system included spark plugs, a distributor, and a high-voltage ignition coil (see Chapter 1). The distributor would sequentially connect the coil output high voltage to the correct spark plug. In addition, it would cause the coil to generate the spark by interrupting the primary current (ignition points) in the desired coil, thereby generating the required spark. The time of occurrence of this spark (i.e., the ignition timing) in relation of the piston to TDC influences the torque generated.

In most present-day electronically controlled engines the distributor has been replaced by multiple coils. Each coil supplies the spark to either one or two cylinders. In such a system the controller selects the appropriate coil and delivers a trigger pulse to ignition control circuitry at the correct time for each cylinder. (*Note:* In some cases the coil is on the spark plug as an integral unit.)

Figure 7.9a illustrates such a system for an example 4-cylinder engine. In this example a pair of coils provides the spark for firing two cylinders for each coil. Cylinder pairs are selected such that one cylinder is on its compression stroke while the other is on exhaust. The cylinder on compression is the cylinder to be fired (at a time somewhat before it reaches TDC). The other cylinder is on exhaust.

The coil fires the spark plugs for these two cylinders simultaneously. For the former cylinder, the mixture is ignited and combustion begins for the power stroke that follows. For the other cylinder (on exhaust stroke), the combustion has already taken place and the spark has no effect.

Although the mixture for modern emission-regulated engines is constrained by emissions regulations, the spark timing can be varied in order to achieve optimum performance within the mixture constraint. For example, the ignition timing can be chosen to produce the best possible engine torque for any given operating condition. This optimum ignition timing is known for any given engine configuration from studies of engine performance as measured on an engine dynamometer.

Figure 7.9a is a schematic of a representative electronic ignition system. In this example configuration the spark advance value is computed in the main

Figure 7.9a
Distributorless Ignition System

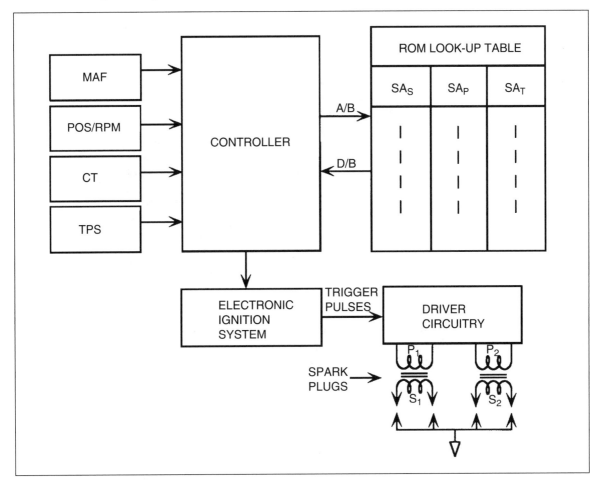

Ignition timing can be adjusted to maximize engine performance within emission constraints. The engine control system calculates spark advance from several variables, including MAP and RPM.

engine control (i.e., the controller that regulates fuel). This system receives data from the various sensors (as described above with respect to fuel control) and determines the correct spark advance for the instantaneous operating condition.

The variables that influence the optimum spark timing at any operating condition include RPM, manifold pressure (or mass air flow), barometric pressure, and coolant temperature. The correct ignition timing for each value of these variables is stored in a ROM lookup table. For example, the variation of spark advance (SA) with RPM for a representative engine is shown in Figure 7.9b. The engine control system obtains readings from the various

**Figure 7.9b
Spark Advance
versus RPM**

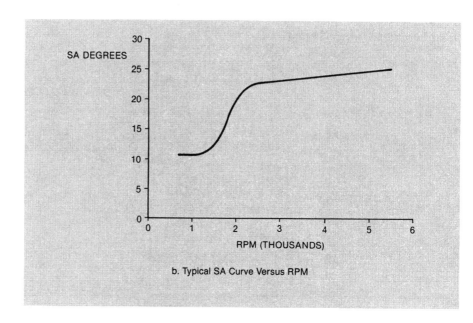

b. Typical SA Curve Versus RPM

sensors and generates an address to the lookup table (ROM). After reading the data from the lookup tables, the control system computes the correct spark advance. An output signal is generated at the appropriate time to activate the spark.

In the configuration depicted in Figure 7.9a, the electronic ignition is implemented in a stand-alone ignition module. This solid-state module receives the correct spark advance data and generates electrical signals that operate the coil driver circuitry. These signals are produced in response to timing inputs coming from crankshaft and camshaft signals (POS/RPM).

The coil driver circuits generate the primary current in windings P_1 and P_2 of the coil packs depicted in Figure 7.9a. These primary currents build up during the so-called *dwell period* before the spark is to occur. At the correct time the driver circuits interrupt the primary currents via a solid-state switch. This interruption of the primary current causes the magnetic field in the coil pack to drop rapidly, inducing a very high voltage (20,000–40,000 volts) that causes a spark. In the example depicted in Figure 7.9a, a pair of coil packs, each firing two spark plugs, is shown. Such a configuration would be appropriate for a 4-cylinder engine. Normally there would be one coil pack for each pair of cylinders.

The ignition system described above is known as a *distributorless ignition system* (DIS) since it uses no distributor (see Chapter 1). There are a number of older car models on the road that utilize a distributor. However, the electronic ignition system is the same as that shown in Figure 7.9a, up to the coil packs. In distributor-equipped engines there is only one coil, and its secondary is connected to the rotary switch (or distributor) as described in Chapter 1.

In a typical electronic ignition control system, the total spark advance, SA (in degrees before TDC), is made up of several components that are added together:

$$SA = SA_S + SA_P + SA_T$$

The first component, SA_S, is the basic spark advance, which is a tabulated function of RPM and MAP. The control system reads RPM and MAP, and calculates the address in ROM of the SA_S that corresponds to these values. Typically, the advance of RPM from idle to about 1200 RPM is relatively slow. Then, from about 1200 to about 2300 RPM the increase in RPM is relatively quick. Beyond 2300 RPM, the increase in RPM is again relatively slow. Each engine configuration has its own spark advance characteristic, which is normally a compromise between a number of conflicting factors (the details of which are beyond the scope of this book).

The second component, SA_P, is the contribution to spark advance due to manifold pressure. This value is obtained from ROM lookup tables. Generally speaking, the SA is reduced as pressure increases.

The final component, SA_T, is the contribution to spark advance due to temperature. Temperature effects on spark advance are relatively complex, including such effects as cold cranking, cold start, warm-up, and fully warmed-up conditions and are beyond the scope of this book.

Closed-Loop Ignition Timing

The ignition system described in the foregoing is an open-loop system. The major disadvantage of open-loop control is that it cannot automatically compensate for mechanical changes in the system. Closed-loop control of ignition timing is desirable from the standpoint of improving engine performance and maintaining that performance in spite of system changes.

For best performance, spark is advanced until excessive knock occurs.

One scheme for closed-loop ignition timing is based on the improvement in performance that is achieved by advancing the ignition timing relative to TDC. For a given RPM and manifold pressure, the variation in torque with spark advance is as depicted in Figure 7.10. One can see that advancing the spark relative to TDC increases the torque until a point is reached at which best torque is produced. This spark advance is known as *mean best torque*, or MBT.

When the spark is advanced too far, an abnormal combustion phenomenon occurs that is known as *knocking*. Although the details of what causes knocking are beyond the scope of this book, it is generally a result of a portion of the air–fuel mixture autoigniting, as opposed to being normally

**Figure 7.10
Torque versus SA for
Typical Engine**

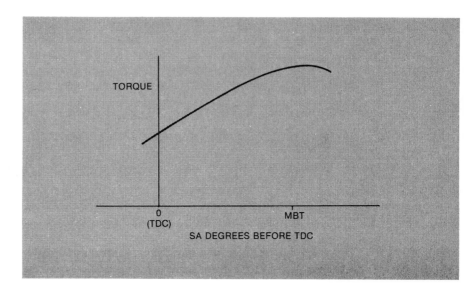

ignited by the advancing flame front that occurs in normal combustion following spark ignition. Roughly speaking, the amplitude of knock is proportional to the fraction of the total air and fuel mixture that autoignites. It is characterized by an abnormally rapid rise in cylinder pressure during combustion, followed by very rapid oscillations in cylinder pressure. The frequency of these oscillations is specific to a given engine configuration and is typically in the range of a few kilohertz. Figure 7.11 is a graph of a typical cylinder pressure versus time under knocking conditions. A relatively low level of knock is arguably beneficial to performance, although excessive knock is unquestionably damaging to the engine and must be avoided.

One control strategy for spark advance under closed-loop control is to advance the spark timing until the knock level becomes unacceptable. At this point, the control system reduces the spark advance (retarded spark) until acceptable levels of knock are achieved. Of course, a spark advance control scheme based on limiting the levels of knocking requires a knock sensor such as that explained in Chapter 6. This sensor responds to the acoustical energy in the spectrum of the rapid cylinder pressure oscillations, as shown in Figure 7.11.

Figure 7.12 is a diagram of the instrumentation for measuring knock intensity. Output voltage V_E of the knock sensor is proportional to the acoustical energy in the engine block at the sensor mounting point. This voltage is sent to a narrow bandpass filter that is tuned to the knock frequency. The filter output voltage V_F is proportional to the amplitude of the knock oscillations, and is thus a "knock signal." The envelope voltage of these

**Figure 7.11
Cylinder Pressure
(Knocking Condition)**

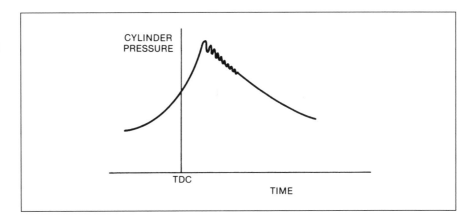

oscillations, V_d, is obtained with a detector circuit. This voltage is sent to the controller, where it is compared with a level corresponding to the knock intensity threshold. Whenever the knock level is less than the threshold, the spark is advanced. Whenever it exceeds the threshold, the spark is retarded.

Following the detector in the circuit of Figure 7.12 is an electronic gate that examines the knock sensor output at the time for which the knock amplitude is largest (i.e., shortly after TDC). The gate is, in essence, an electronic switch that is normally open, but is closed for a short interval (from 0 to T) following TDC. It is during this interval that the knock signal is largest in relationship to engine noise. The probability of successfully detecting the knock signal is greatest during this interval. Similarly, the possibility of mistaking engine noise for true knock signal is smallest during this interval.

The final stage in the knock-measuring instrumentation is integration with respect to time; this can be accomplished using an operational amplifier. For example, the circuit of Figure 7.13 could be used to integrate the gate output. The electronic gate actually controls switches S_1 and S_2. The output voltage V_K at the end of the gate interval T is given by:

$$V_K = -(1/RC)\int_0^T V_d(t)dt$$

This voltage increases sharply (negative), reaching a maximum amplitude at the end of the gate interval, as shown in Figure 7.13, provided that knock occurs. However, if there is no knock, V_K remains near zero.

The acoustical knock signal is compared with a threshold level corresponding to unacceptable knock.

The level of knock intensity is indicated by voltage $V_K(T)$ at the end of the gate interval. The spark control system compares this voltage with a threshold voltage (using an analog comparator) to determine whether knock has or has not occurred (Figure 7.14). The comparator output voltage is binary valued, depending on the relative amplitude of $V_K(T)$ and the threshold voltage. Whenever $V_K(T)$ is less than the threshold voltage, the comparator

**Figure 7.12
Instrumentation and
Waveforms for
Closed-Loop Ignition
Control**

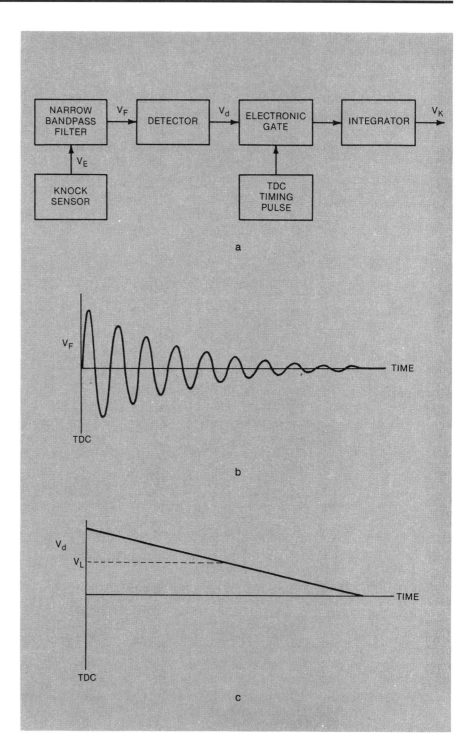

**Figure 7.13
Example Integrator
Circuit Diagram**

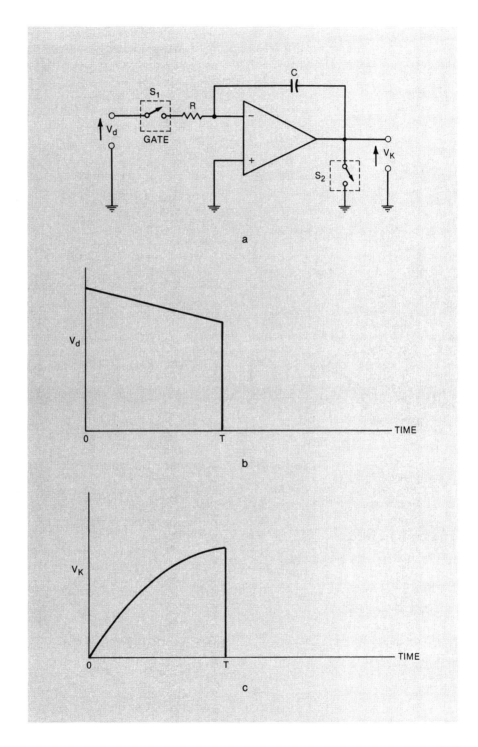

**Figure 7.14
Knock Level Detector
Circuit**

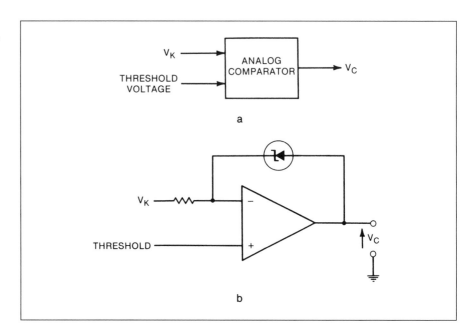

output is low, indicating no knock. Whenever $V_K(T)$ is greater than the threshold value, the comparator output is high, indicating knock.

Although this scheme for knock detection has shown a constant threshold, there are some production applications that have a variable threshold. The threshold in such cases increases with RPM because the competing noises in the engine increase with RPM.

Spark Advance Correction Scheme

Whenever knock is excessive, a closed-loop spark advance system causes spark to retard.

Although the details of spark advance control vary from manufacturer to manufacturer, there are generally two classes of correction that are used: fast correction and slow correction. In the fast correction scheme, the spark advance is decreased for the next engine cycle by a fixed amount (typically from 5° to 10°) whenever knock is detected. Then the spark advance is advanced in one-degree increments every 5 to 20 crankshaft revolutions.

The fast correction ensures that minimum time is spent under heavy knocking conditions. Further, this scheme compensates for hysteresis (i.e., for one degree of spark advance to cause knocking, more than one degree must be removed to eliminate knocking). The fast correction scheme is depicted in Figure 7.15.

In the slow correction scheme (Figure 7.16), spark advance is decreased by one (or more) degree each time knock is detected, until no knocking is detected. The spark advance proceeds in one-degree increments after many engine cycles.

**Figure 7.15
Fast Correction Spark
Advance**

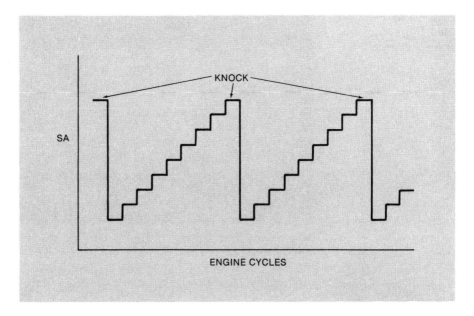

The slow correction scheme is more of an adaptive closed-loop control than is the fast correction scheme. It is primarily employed to compensate for relatively slow changes in engine condition or fuel quality (i.e., octane rating).

INTEGRATED ENGINE CONTROL SYSTEM

Each control subsystem for fuel control, spark control, and EGR has been discussed separately. However, a fully integrated electronic engine control system can include these subsystems and provide additional functions. (Usually the flexibility of the digital control system allows such expansion quite easily because the computer program can be changed to accomplish the expanded functions.) Several of these additional functions are discussed in the following.

Secondary Air Management

Secondary air management is used to improve performance of the catalytic converter. During engine warm-up, secondary air is routed to the exhaust manifold to speed warm-up of the converter.

Secondary air management is used to improve the performance of the catalytic converter by providing extra (oxygen-rich) air to either the converter itself or to the exhaust manifold. The catalyst temperature must be above about 200°C to efficiently oxidize HC and CO and reduce NO_x. During engine warm-up when the catalytic converter is cold, HC and CO are oxidized in the exhaust manifold by routing secondary air to the manifold. This creates extra heat to speed warm-up of the converter and EGO sensor, enabling the fuel controller to go to the closed-loop mode more quickly.

Figure 7.16
Slow Correction
Spark Advance

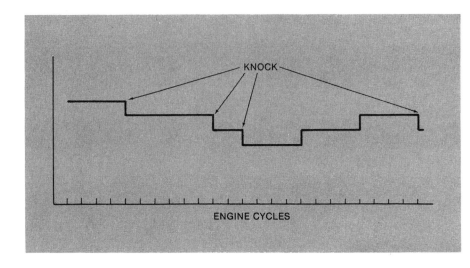

The converter can be damaged if too much heat is applied to it. This can occur if large amounts of HC and CO are oxidized in the manifold during periods of heavy loads, which call for fuel enrichment, or during severe deceleration. In such cases, the secondary air is directed to the air cleaner, where it has no effect on exhaust temperatures.

After warm-up, the main use of secondary air is to provide an oxygen-rich atmosphere in the second chamber of the three-way catalyst, dual-chamber converter system. In a dual-chamber converter, the first chamber contains rhodium, palladium, and platinum to reduce NO_x and to oxidize HC and CO. The second chamber contains only platinum and palladium. The extra oxygen from the secondary air improves the converter's ability to oxidize HC and CO in the second converter chamber.

> The computer controls secondary air by using two solenoid-operated valves that route air to the air cleaner, exhaust manifold, or directly to the converter.

The computer program for the control mode selection logic can be modified to include the conditions for controlling secondary air. The computer controls secondary air by using two solenoid valves similar to the EGR valve. One valve switches air flow to the air cleaner or to the exhaust system. The other valve switches air flow to the exhaust manifold or to the converter. The air routing is based on engine coolant temperature and air/fuel ratio. The control system diagram for secondary air is shown in Figure 7.17.

Evaporative Emissions Canister Purge

During engine-off conditions, the fuel stored in the fuel system tends to evaporate into the atmosphere. To reduce these HC emissions, the fuel tank is sealed and evaporative gases are collected by a charcoal filter in a canister. The collected fuel is released into the intake through a solenoid valve controlled by the computer. This is done during closed-loop operation to reduce fuel calculation complications in the open-loop mode.

Figure 7.17
Secondary Air Control System

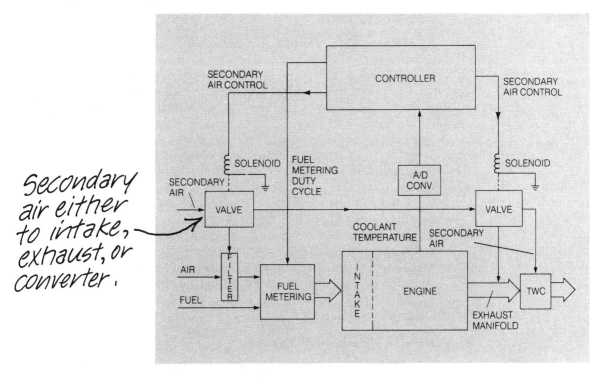

Secondary air either to intake, exhaust, or converter.

Automatic System Adjustment

A digital control system can actually "learn" from previous performances.

Another important feature of microcomputer engine control systems is their ability to be programmed to adapt to parameter changes. Many control systems use this feature to enable the computer to modify lookup table values for computing open-loop air/fuel ratios. While the computer is in the closed-loop mode, the computer checks its open-loop calculated air/fuel ratios and compares them with the closed-loop average limit-cycle values. If they match closely, the open-loop lookup tables are unchanged. If the difference is large, the system controller corrects the lookup tables so that the open-loop values more closely match the closed-loop values. This updated open-loop lookup table is stored in separate memory (RAM), which is always powered directly by a car battery so that the new values are not lost while the ignition key is turned off. The next time the engine is started, the new lookup table values will be used in the open-loop mode and will provide more accurate control of the air/fuel ratio. This feature is very important because it allows the system controller to adjust to long-term changes in engine and fuel system conditions. This feature can be applied in individual subsystem control systems or in the fully integrated control system. If not available initially, it may be added to the system by modifying its control program.

System Diagnosis

Another important feature of microcomputer engine control systems is their ability to diagnose failures in their control systems and alert the operator. Sensor and actuator failures or misadjustments can be easily detected by the computer. For instance, the computer will detect a malfunctioning MAF sensor if the sensor's output goes above or below certain specified limits, or fails to change for long periods of time. A prime example is the automatic adjustment system just discussed. If the open-loop calculations consistently come up wrong, the engine control computer may determine that one of the many sensors used in the open-loop calculations has failed.

Abnormal responses from sensors or actuators can be detected by microcomputer engine control systems.

If the computer detects the loss of a primary control sensor or actuator, it may choose to operate in a different mode until the problem is repaired. The operator is notified of a failure by an indicator on the instrument panel (e.g., check engine). Because of the flexibility of the microcomputer engine control system, additional diagnostic programs might be added to accommodate different engine models that contain more or fewer sensors. Keeping the system totally integrated gives the microcomputer controller access to more sensor inputs so they can be checked. Chapter 10 discusses system diagnosis more fully.

SUMMARY OF CONTROL MODES

Now that a typical electronic engine control system has been discussed, let's summarize what happens in an integrated system operating in the various modes.

Engine Crank (Start)

The following list is a summary of the engine operations in the engine crank (starting) mode. Here, the primary control concern is reliable engine start.

1. Engine RPM at cranking speed.
2. Engine coolant at low temperature.
3. Air/fuel ratio low.
4. Spark retarded.
5. EGR off.
6. Secondary air to exhaust manifold.
7. Fuel economy not closely controlled.
8. Emissions not closely controlled.

Engine Warm-Up

While the engine is warming up, the engine temperature is rising to its normal operating value. Here, the primary control concern is rapid and smooth engine warm-up. A summary of the engine operations during this period follows:

1. Engine RPM above cranking speed at command of driver.
2. Engine coolant temperature rises to minimum threshold.
3. Air/fuel ratio low.
4. Spark timing set by controller.
5. EGR off.
6. Secondary air to exhaust manifold.
7. Fuel economy not closely controlled.
8. Emissions not closely controlled.

Open-Loop Control

The following list summarizes the engine operations when the engine is being controlled with an open-loop system. This is before the EGO sensor has reached the correct temperature for closed-loop operation. Fuel economy and emissions are closely controlled.

1. Engine RPM at command of driver.
2. Engine temperature above warm-up threshold.
3. Air/fuel ratio controlled by an open-loop system to 14.7.
4. EGO sensor temperature less than minimum threshold.
5. Spark timing set by controller.
6. EGR controlled.
7. Secondary air to catalytic converter.
8. Fuel economy controlled.
9. Emissions controlled.

Closed-Loop Control

For the closest control of emissions and fuel economy under various driving conditions, the electronic engine control system is in a closed loop. Fuel economy and emissions are controlled very tightly. The following is a summary of the engine operations during this period:

1. Engine RPM at command of driver.
2. Engine temperature in normal range (above warm-up threshold).
3. Average air/fuel ratio controlled to 14.7, ±0.05.
4. EGO sensor's temperature above minimum threshold detected by a sensor output voltage indicating a rich mixture of air and fuel for a minimum amount of time.
5. System returns to open loop if EGO sensor cools below minimum threshold or fails to indicate rich mixture for given length of time.
6. EGR controlled.
7. Secondary air to catalytic converter.

8. Fuel economy tightly controlled.
9. Emissions tightly controlled.

Hard Acceleration

When the engine must be accelerated quickly or if the engine is under heavy load, it is in a special mode. Now, the engine controller is primarily concerned with providing maximum performance. Here is a summary of the operations under these conditions:

1. Driver asking for sharp increase in RPM or in engine power, demanding maximum torque.
2. Engine temperature in normal range.
3. Air/fuel ratio rich mixture.
4. EGO not in loop.
5. EGR off.
6. Secondary air to intake.
7. Relatively poor fuel economy.
8. Relatively poor emissions control.

Deceleration and Idle

Slowing down, stopping, and idling are combined in another special mode. The engine controller is primarily concerned with reducing excess emissions during deceleration, and keeping idle fuel consumption at a minimum. This engine operation is summarized in the following list.

1. RPM decreasing rapidly due to driver command or else held constant at idle.
2. Engine temperature in normal range.
3. Air/fuel ratio lean mixture.
4. Special mode in deceleration to reduce emissions.
5. Special mode in idle to keep RPM constant at idle as load varies due to air conditioner, automatic transmission engagement, etc.
6. EGR on.
7. Secondary air to intake.
8. Good fuel economy during deceleration.
9. Poor fuel economy during idle, but fuel consumption kept to minimum possible.

IMPROVEMENTS IN ELECTRONIC ENGINE CONTROL

Although major improvements have been made in electronic engine control, the fuel strategy continues to maintain stoichiometry.

The digital engine control system in this chapter has been made possible by a rapid evolution of the state of technology. Some of this technology has been briefly mentioned in this chapter. It is worthwhile to review some of the technological improvements that have occurred in digital engine control in greater detail to fully appreciate the capabilities of modern digital engine control.

Integrated Engine Control System

One of the developments that has occurred since the introduction of digital engine control technology is the integration of the various functions into a single control unit. Whereas the earlier systems in many cases had separate control systems for fuel and ignition control, the trend is toward integrated control. This trend has been made possible, in part, by improvements in digital hardware and in computational algorithms and software. For example, one of the hardware improvements that has been achieved is the operation of the microprocessor (MPU) at higher clock frequencies. This higher frequency results in a reduction of the time for any given MPU computation, thereby permitting greater computational capability. This increased computational capability has made it possible, in turn, to have more precise control of fuel delivery during rapid transient engine operation.

Except for long steady cruise while driving on certain rural roads or freeways, the automobile engine is operated under changing load and RPM conditions. The limitations in the computational capability of early engine control systems restricted the ability of the controller to continuously maintain the air/fuel ratio at stoichiometry under such changing operating conditions. The newer, more capable digital engine control systems are more precise than the earlier versions at maintaining stoichiometry and therefore operate more of the time within the optimum window for the three-way catalytic converter.

Moreover, since the control of fuel and ignition requires, in some cases, data from the same sensor set, it is advantageous to have a single integrated system for fuel and ignition timing control. The newer engine controllers have the capability to maintain stoichiometry and simultaneously optimize ignition timing.

Oxygen Sensor Improvements

Improvements have also been made in the exhaust gas oxygen sensor, which remains today as the primary sensor for closed-loop operation in cars equipped with the three-way catalyst. As we have seen, the signal from the oxygen sensor is not useful for closed-loop control until the sensor has reached a temperature of about 300°C. Typically, the temperature of the sensor is too low during the starting and engine warm-up phase, but it can also be too low during relatively long periods of deceleration. It is desirable to return to closed-loop operation in as short a time as possible. Thus the oxygen sensor must reach its minimum operating temperature in the shortest possible time.

An improved exhaust gas oxygen sensor has been developed that incorporates an electric heating element inside the sensor, as shown in Figure 7.18. This EGO sensor is known as the heated exhaust gas oxygen, or HEGO, sensor. The heat current is automatically switched on and off depending on the engine operating condition. The operating regions in which heating is applied are determined by the engine control system as derived from engine RPM and

**Figure 7.18
Heated Exhaust Gas
Oxygen Sensor**

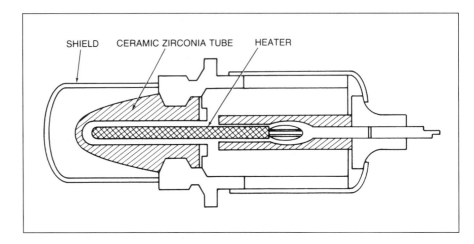

MAP sensors. The heating element is made from resistive material and derives heat from the power dissipated in the associated resistance. The HEGO sensor is packaged in such a way that this heat is largely maintained within the sensor housing, thereby leading to a relatively rapid temperature rise.

Normally, the heating element need only be turned on for cold-start operations. Shortly after engine start the exhaust gas has sufficient heat to maintain the EGO sensor at a suitable temperature.

Fuel Injection Timing

Earlier in this chapter, the fuel control methods and algorithms were explained for a sequential multipoint fuel injection system. In such a fuel control system, it was shown that a separate fuel injector is provided for each cylinder. The fuel injector for each cylinder is typically mounted in the intake manifold such that fuel is sprayed directly into the intake port of the corresponding cylinder during the intake stroke.

During the intake stroke, the intake valve is opened and the piston is moving down from top dead center (TDC). Figure 7.19 illustrates the timing for the fuel injectors for a 4-cylinder engine. It can be seen that in two complete engine revolutions (as indicated by the No. 1 cylinder position), all four injectors have been switched on for a time $T(n)$. This pulse duration results in delivery of the desired quantity of fuel for the nth engine cycle. This system provides for highly uniform fueling of all the cylinders and is superior in performance to either carburetors or throttle body fuel injectors.

Automatic Transmission Control

The vast majority of cars and light trucks sold in the United States are equipped with automatic transmissions. The majority of these transmissions are controlled electronically. The configuration of an automatic transmission

**Figure 7.19
Injector Timing for
4-Cylinder Engine**

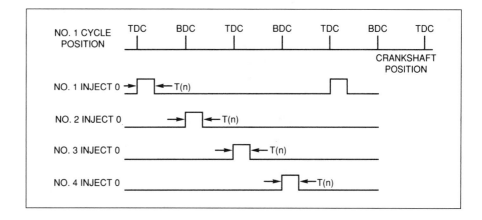

was explained in Chapter 1 where it was shown that it consists of a torque converter and a sequence of planetary gear sets. Control of an automatic transmission consists of selecting the appropriate gear ratio from input shaft to output shaft as a function of operating condition. The operating condition in this case includes load, engine RPM, and vehicle speed (or equivalently RPM of the drive shaft). The gear ratio for the transmission is set by activating clutches on the components of the various planetary gear systems as explained in Chapter 1.

The relevant clutches are activated by the pressure of transmission fluid acting on piston-like mechanisms. The pressure is switched on at the appropriate clutch via solenoid-activated valves that are supplied with automatic transmission fluid under pressure.

The gear ratio for the planetary gear sets is uniquely determined by the combination of clutches that are activated. The electronic transmission controller determines the desired gear ratio from measurements of engine load and RPM as well as transmission output shaft RPM. These RPM measurements are made using noncontacting angular speed sensors (usually magnetic in nature) as explained in Chapter 6. Engine load can be measured directly from manifold absolute pressure (MAP) or from mass air flow (MAF) (see Chapter 6) and from a somewhat complicated algorithm relating these measurements to desired gear ratio. Once this desired gear ratio is determined, the set of clutches to be activated is uniquely determined, and control signals are sent to the appropriate clutches.

Normally, the highest gear ratio (i.e., ratio of input shaft speed to output shaft speed) is desired when the vehicle is at low speed such as in accelerating from a stop. As vehicle speed increases from a stop, a switching level will be reached at which the next lowest gear ratio is selected. This switching (gear-changing) threshold is an increasing function of load (i.e., MAP).

At times (particularly under steady vehicle speed conditions), the driver demands increasing engine power (e.g., for heavy acceleration). In this case, the controller shifts to a higher gear ratio, resulting in higher acceleration than would be possible in the previous gear setting. The functional relationship between gear ratio and operating condition is often termed the "shift schedule."

Torque Converter Lock-up Control

Automatic transmissions use a hydraulic or fluid coupling to transmit engine power to the wheels. Because of slip, the fluid coupling is less efficient than the nonslip coupling of a pressure-plate manual clutch used with a manual transmission. Thus, fuel economy is usually lower with an automatic transmission than with a standard transmission. This problem has been partially remedied by placing a clutch functionally similar to a standard pressure-plate clutch inside the torque converter of the automatic transmission and engaging it during periods of steady cruise. This enables the automatic transmission to provide fuel economy near that of a manual transmission and still retain the automatic shifting convenience.

Here is a good example of the ease of adding a function to the electronic engine control system. The torque converter locking clutch (TCC) is activated by a lock-up solenoid controlled by the engine control system computer. The computer determines when a period of steady cruise exists from throttle position and vehicle speed changes. It pulls in the locking clutch and keeps it engaged until it senses conditions that call for disengagement.

Traction Control

In Chapter 1, it was explained that the transmission output shaft is coupled to the drive axles via the differential. The differential is a necessary component of the drivetrain because the left and right drive wheels turn at different speeds whenever the car moves along a curve (e.g., turning a corner). Unfortunately, wherever there is a large difference between the tire/road friction from left to right, the differential will tend to spin the low friction wheel. An extreme example of this occurs whenever one drive wheel is on ice and the other is on dry road. In this case, the tire on the ice side will spin and the wheel on the dry side will not. Typically, the vehicle will not move in such circumstances.

Certain cars are equipped with so-called traction control devices that can overcome this disadvantage of the differential. Such cars have differentials that incorporate solenoid-activated clutches that can "lock" the differential, permitting power to be delivered to both drive wheels. It is only desirable to activate these clutches in certain conditions and to disable them during normal driving, permitting the differential to perform its intended task.

A traction control system incorporates sensors for measuring wheel speed and a controller that determines the wheel slip condition based on these relative speeds. Wherever a wheel spin condition is detected, the controller sends electrical signals to the solenoids, thereby activating the clutches to eliminate the wheel slip.

Hybrid Vehicle Powertrain Control

The concept of a hybrid vehicle, in which propulsive power comes from an IC engine and an electric motor, was introduced in Chapter 1. As explained in Chapter 1, the hybrid vehicle combines the low (ideally zero) emissions of an electric vehicle with the range and performance capabilities of IC engine-powered cars. However, optimization of emissions performance and/or fuel economy is a complex control problem.

There are numerous issues and considerations involved in hybrid vehicle powertrain control, including the efficiencies of the IC engine and electric motor as a function of operating condition; the size of the vehicle and the power capacity of the IC engine and electric motor; the storage capacity and state of charge of the battery pack; accessory load characteristics of the vehicle; and finally the driving characteristics. With respect to this latter issue, it would be possible to optimize vehicle emissions and performance if the exact route, including vehicle speed, acceleration, deceleration, road inclination, and wind characteristics, could be programmed into the control memory before any trip were to begin. It is highly impractical to do such pre-programming. However, by monitoring instantaneous vehicle operation, it is possible to achieve good, though suboptimal, vehicle performance and emissions.

Depending on operating conditions, the controller can command pure electric vehicle operation, pure IC engine operation, or a combination. Whenever the IC engine is operating, the controller should attempt to keep it at its peak efficiency.

Certain special operating conditions should be noted. For example, the IC engine is stopped wherever the vehicle is stopped. Clearly, such stoppage benefits vehicle fuel economy and improves air quality when the vehicle is driven in dense traffic with long stoppages such as those that occur while driving in large urban areas.

There are two major types of hybrid electric vehicles depending on the mechanism for coupling the IC engine (ICE) and the electric motor (EM). Figure 7.20 is a schematic representation of one hybrid vehicle configuration known as a series hybrid vehicle (SHV). In this SHV, the ICE drives a generator and has no direct mechanical connection to the drive axles. The vehicle is propelled by the electric motor, which receives its input electrical power from a high-voltage bus. This bus, in turn, receives its power either from the engine-driven generator (for ICE propulsion) or from the battery pack (for EM propulsion), or from a combination of the two.

In this figure, mechanical power is denoted MP and electrical power EP. The mechanical connection from the EM to the transaxle (T/A) provides propulsive power to the drive wheels (DW).

**Figure 7.20
Series Hybrid Vehicle
Representation**

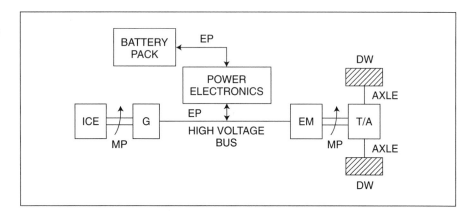

Figure 7.21 is a schematic of a hybrid vehicle type known as a parallel hybrid. The parallel hybrid of Figure 7.21a can operate with ICE alone by engaging both solenoid-operated clutches on either side of the EM but with no electrical power supplied to the EM. In this case, the MP supplied by the ICE directly drives the T/A, and the EM rotor spins essentially without any mechanical drag. This hybrid vehicle can also operate with the EM supplying propulsive power by switching off the ICE, disengaging clutch C_1, engaging clutch C_2, and providing electrical power to the EM from the high-voltage bus (HVB). Of course, if both ICE and EM are to produce propulsive power, then both clutches are engaged. Not shown in Figure 7.21 is a separate controller for the brushless DC motor (see Chapter 6). Also not shown in this figure but discussed later in this section is the powertrain controller that optimizes performance and emissions for the overall vehicle and engages/disengages clutches as required.

The HV of Figure 7.21b operates similarly to that of Figure 7.21a except that mechanical power from ICE and EM are combined in a mechanism denoted coupler. For the system of Figure 7.21b pure ICE propulsion involves engaging clutch C_1, disengaging clutch C_2, and providing no electrical power to the EM. Alternatively, pure EM propulsion involves disengaging clutch C_1, switching off the ICE, engaging clutch C_2, and providing electrical power to the EM via the high-voltage bus (HVB). Simultaneous ICE and EM propulsion involves running the ICE, providing electrical power to the EM, and engaging both clutches.

For either series or parallel hybrid vehicle, dynamic braking is possible during vehicle deceleration, with the EM acting as a generator. The EM/generator supplies power to the high-voltage bus which is converted to the low-voltage bus (LVB) voltage level by the power electronics subsystem. In this deceleration circumstance the energy that began as vehicle kinetic energy is recovered with the motor acting as a generator and is stored in the battery pack. This storage of energy occurs as an increase in the state of charge (SOC)

**Figure 7.21
Parallel Hybrid
Schematic**

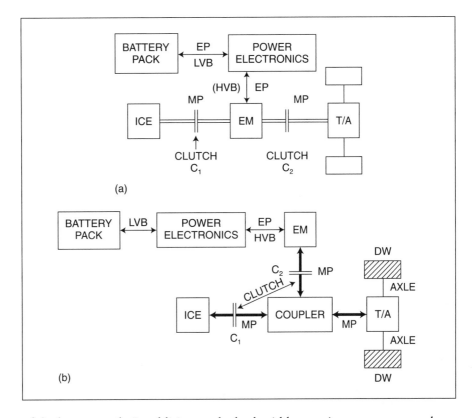

of the battery pack. In addition to the lead acid battery in common use today, there are new energy storage means including nickel-metal-hydride (NiMH) and even special capacitors called ultra-caps (see Chapter 11). Each of these electrical energy storage technologies has advantages and disadvantages for hybrid vehicle application.

The battery pack has a maximum SOC that is fixed by its capacity. Dynamic braking is available as an energy recovery strategy as long as SOC is below its maximum value. Nevertheless, dynamic braking is an important part of hybrid vehicle fuel efficiency. It is the only way some of the energy supplied by the ICE and/or EM can be recovered instead of being dissipated in the vehicle brakes.

The storage of the energy recovered during dynamic braking requires that the corresponding electrical energy be direct current and at a voltage compatible with the battery pack. The trend in the worldwide automotive industry is toward a 42-volt battery pack consisting, for example, of three 12-volt (rated) batteries connected in series. The 42-volt system receives this nominal rating since a fully charged (so-called 12-volt) storage battery as well as the LVB voltage is approximately 14 volts. Thus, the 42-volt terminology is a suitable way to represent this type of battery pack.

**Figure 7.22
Transformer Structure
and Conversion of
Voltages**

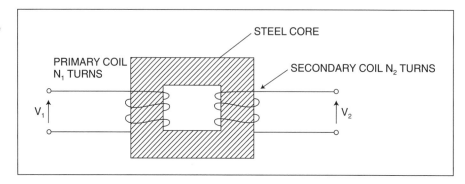

**Figure 7.23
DC to DC Converter**

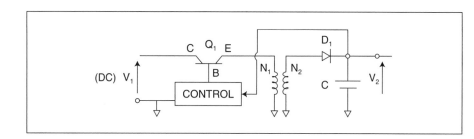

On the other hand, efficient EM operation is achieved for a much higher voltage level than the 42-volt LVB voltage. The desired HVB voltage for supplying the EM is something on the order of 250 volts.

Conversion of electrical power from one voltage level V_1 to a second V_2 is straightforward using a transformer as long as this power is alternating current. Figure 7.22 schematically illustrates transformer structure and the conversion of voltages from one level to another.

A transformer consists of a core of magnetically permeable material (usually a steel alloy) around which a pair of closely wrapped coils are formed. One coil (termed the primary) consists of N_1 turns and the other (termed the secondary) consists of N_2 turns.

Assuming (arbitrarily) that AC electrical power comes from a source (e.g., an AC generator) at peak voltage V_1, then the power flowing from the transformer secondary to a load will be at a peak voltage V_2 where

$$V_2 = (N_2/N_1)V_1$$

The validity of this simple model for a transformer depends on many factors, but for an introduction to transformer operating theory it is sufficient.

Conversion of DC electrical power from one voltage to another can be accomplished using a transformer only if the DC power is converted to AC power. Figure 7.23 is a greatly simplified schematic of a DC to DC converter

DIGITAL ENGINE CONTROL SYSTEMS

in which a transistor is used to convert an input DC signal to AC that is sent to a transformer for conversion to a different voltage.

The control electronics supplies a pulsating signal to the base B of transistor Q_1, alternately switching it on and off. When Q_1 is on (i.e., conducting), voltage V_1 is applied to the transformer primary (i.e., N_1). When Q_1 is off (i.e., nonconducting), transformer primary voltage is zero. In this case, the pulsating AC voltage that is alternately V_1 and 0 applied to the primary results in an AC voltage in the secondary that is essentially N_2/N_1 times the primary voltage. This secondary voltage is converted to DC by rectification using diode D_1 and filtering via capacitor C (see Chapter 3). The secondary voltage is fed back to the control electronics, which varies the relative ON and OFF times to maintain V_2 at the desired level.

A variation of the circuit of Figure 7.23 appears in the power electronics module for conversion between the LVB and the HVB. Of course, the specific details of the relevant power electronics depend on the hybrid vehicle manufacturer.

Powertrain control for a hybrid vehicle is achieved using a multimode digital control system. It is somewhat more complicated than the digital engine control system discussed earlier in this chapter in that it must control an IC engine as well as an EM motor. In addition, it must achieve the balance between ICE and EM power, and it must engage or disengage the solenoid-operated clutches (if present).

The inputs to this controller come from sensors that measure:

- Power demand from driver (accelerator pedal)
- State of charge of battery pack
- Vehicle speed
- ICE RPM and load
- EM voltage and current

The system outputs include control signals to:

- ICE throttle position
- EM motor control inputs
- Clutch engage/disengage
- Switch ICE ignition on/off

In this vehicle, there is no direct mechanical link from the accelerator pedal to the throttle. Rather, the throttle position (as measured by a sensor) is set by the control system via an electrical signal sent to an actuator (motor) that moves the throttle in a system called drive-by-wire.

The control system itself is a digital controller using the inputs and outputs listed above and has the capability of controlling the hybrid powertrain in many different modes. These modes include starting from a standing stop, steady cruise, regenerative braking, recharging battery pack, and many others that are specific to a particular vehicle configuration.

In almost all circumstances, it is desirable for the IC engine to be off at all vehicle stops. Clearly, it is a waste of fuel and an unnecessary contribution to exhaust emissions for an IC engine to run in a stopped vehicle. Exceptions to this rule involve cold weather operations in which it is desirable or even necessary to have some limited engine operations with a stopped vehicle. In addition, a low-battery SOC might call for ICE operation at certain vehicle stops.

When starting from a standing start, normally the EM propulsion is used to accelerate the car to desired speed, assuming the battery has sufficient charge. If charge is low, then the controller can engage the clutch to the ICE such that the EM can begin acceleration and at the same time crank the ICE to start it. Then, depending on the time that the vehicle is in motion, the ICE can provide propulsive power and/or battery charge power. Should the vehicle go to a steady cruise for engine operation near its optimum, then the control strategy normally is to switch off the electric power to the EM and power the vehicle solely with the ICE. In other cruise conditions, the controller can balance power between ICE and EM in a way that maximizes total fuel economy (subject to emission constraints).

For urban driving with frequent stops, the control strategy favors EM operation as long as SOC is sufficient. In this operating mode regenerative braking (in which energy is absorbed by vehicle deceleration), the recovered energy appears as increased SOC.

The various operating modes and control strategies for an HV depend on many factors, including vehicle weight; relative size and power capacity of ICE/EM; and exhaust emissions and fuel economy of the ICE (as installed in the particular vehicle). It is beyond the scope of this book to attempt to cover all possible operating modes for all HV configurations. However, the above discussion has provided background within which specific HV configurations' operating modes and control strategies can be understood.

Quiz for Chapter 7

1. A typical fuel control system may include the following components:
   a. MAF sensor
   b fuel injector
   c. EGO sensor
   d. all of the above

2. A fuel control system
   a. has many operating modes
   b. is never operated in open-loop mode
   c. does not control air/fuel ratio during warm-up
   d. none of the above

3. During hard deceleration the engine requires
   a. very rich mixture
   b. very lean mixture
   c. stoichiometric mixture
   d. none of the above

4. Electronic control system for ignition can perform
   a. timing for maximum torque
   b. correct timing calculation with respect to RPM
   c. correct timing calculation with respect to MAP
   d. all of the above

5. The controller discussed in this chapter is what type of controller?
   a. analog
   b. digital
   c. both analog and digital

6. A low air/fuel ratio is what type of fuel mixture?
   a. lean
   b. rich
   c. poor
   d. fat

7. Open- and closed-loop fuel control systems control air/fuel ratio near which of the following?
   a. rich
   b. lean
   c. stoichiometry
   d. rich and lean

8. Acceleration enrichment is used for what purpose?
   a. reduce fuel consumption
   b. reduce exhaust emissions
   c. provide maximum torque
   d. provide minimum fuel economy

9. Idle speed control is used for what reason?
   a. maximum idle speed
   b. minimum idle fuel consumption
   c. deceleration leaning
   d. maintaining desired idle speeds

10. Under closed-loop ignition timing control, spark advance is limited by
   a. the distributor rotation
   b. knock
   c. MBT
   d. coolant temperature

11. The secondary air management system is used
    a. to control EGR
    b. to avoid knock
    c. with low-octane fuels
    d. to improve performance of the catalytic converter

12. When knock is detected in a closed-loop ignition system, spark timing is
    a. initially advanced then retarded slowly
    b. always advanced to BDC
    c. retarded then advanced
    d. none of the above

13. Secondary functions of a digital engine control system may include
    a. evaporative emissions canister purge
    b. torque converter lockup
    c. secondary air management
    d. all of the above

14. In a distributorless electronic ignition control system
    a. the distributor is not required
    b. spark plugs are not needed
    c. the coil is not needed
    d. none of the above

Vehicle Motion Control

INTRODUCTION

Electronic controls can automate some driver functions that were previously performed manually.

The term *vehicle motion* refers to its translation along and rotation about all three axes (i.e., longitudinal, lateral, and vertical). By the term *longitudinal axis*, we mean the axis that is parallel to the ground (vehicle at rest) along the length of the car. The lateral axis is orthogonal to the longitudinal axis and is also parallel to the ground (vehicle at rest). The vertical axis is orthogonal to both the longitudinal and lateral axes.

Rotations of the vehicle around these three axes correspond to angular displacement of the car body in roll, yaw, and pitch. *Roll* refers to angular displacement about the longitudinal axis; *yaw* refers to angular displacement about the vertical axis; and *pitch* refers to angular displacement about the lateral axis.

Electronic controls have been recently developed with the capability to regulate the motion along and about all three axes. Individual car models employ various selected combinations of these controls. This chapter discusses motion control electronics beginning with control of motion along the longitudinal axis in the form of a cruise control system.

The forces that influence vehicle motion along the longitudinal axis include the powertrain (including, in selected models, traction control), the brakes, the aerodynamic drag, and tire-rolling resistance, as well as the influence of gravity when the car is moving on a road with a nonzero inclination (or grade). In a traditional cruise control system, the tractive force due to the powertrain is balanced against the total drag forces to maintain a constant speed. In an advanced cruise control system, brakes are also automatically applied as required to maintain speed when going down a hill of sufficiently steep grade.

TYPICAL CRUISE CONTROL SYSTEM

A cruise control is a closed-loop system that uses feedback of vehicle speed to adjust throttle position.

Automotive cruise control is an excellent example of the type of electronic feedback control system that was discussed in general terms in Chapter 2. Recall that the components of a control system include the plant, or system being controlled, and a sensor for measuring the plant variable being regulated. It also includes an electronic control system that receives inputs in the form of the desired value of the regulated variable and the measured value of that variable from the sensor. The control system generates an error signal constituting the difference between the desired and actual values of this variable. It then generates an output from this error signal that drives an electromechanical actuator. The actuator controls the input to the plant in such a way that the regulated plant variable is moved toward the desired value.

In the case of a cruise control, the variable being regulated is the vehicle speed. The driver manually sets the car speed at the desired value via the accelerator pedal. Upon reaching the desired speed the driver activates a momentary contact switch that sets that speed as the command input to the control system. From that point on, the cruise control system maintains the desired speed automatically by operating the throttle via a throttle actuator.

Under normal driving circumstances, the total drag forces acting on the vehicle are such that a net positive traction force (from the powertrain) is required to maintain a constant vehicle speed. However, when the car is on a downward sloping road of sufficient grade, constant vehicle speed requires a negative tractive force that the powertrain can't deliver. In this case, the car will accelerate unless brakes are applied. For our initial discussion, we assume this latter condition does not occur and that no braking is required.

The plant being controlled consists of the powertrain (i.e., engine and drivetrain), which drives the vehicle through the drive axles and wheels. As described above, the load on this plant includes friction and aerodynamic drag as well as a portion of the vehicle weight when the car is going up and down hills.

The configuration for a typical automotive cruise control is shown in Figure 8.1. The momentary contact (pushbutton) switch that sets the command speed is denoted S_1 in Figure 8.1. Also shown in this figure is a disable switch that completely disengages the cruise control system from the power supply such that throttle control reverts back to the accelerator pedal. This switch is denoted S_2 in Figure 8.1 and is a safety feature. In an actual cruise control system the disable function can be activated in a variety of ways, including the master power switch for the cruise control system, and a brake pedal–activated switch that disables the cruise control any time that the brake pedal is moved from its rest position. The throttle actuator opens and closes the throttle in response to the error between the desired and actual speed. Whenever the actual speed is less than the desired speed the throttle opening is increased by the actuator, which increases vehicle speed until the error is zero, at which point the throttle opening remains fixed until either a disturbance occurs or the driver calls for a new desired speed.

A block diagram of a cruise control system is shown in Figure 8.2. In the cruise control depicted in this figure, a proportional integral (PI) control strategy has been assumed. However, there are many cruise control systems still on the road today with proportional (P) controllers. Nevertheless, the PI controller is representative of good design for such a control system since it can reduce speed errors due to disturbances (such as hills) to zero (as explained in Chapter 2). In this strategy an error e is formed by subtracting (electronically) the actual speed V_a from the desired speed V_d:

Figure 8.1
Cruise Control Configuration

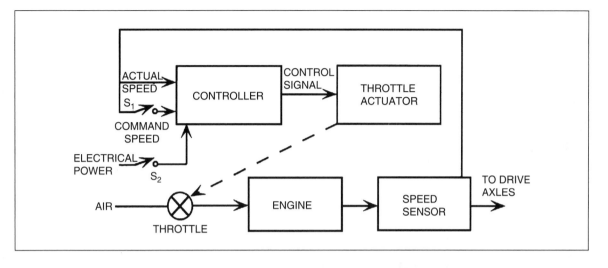

$$e = V_d - V_a$$

The controller then electronically generates the actuator signal by combining a term proportional to the error ($K_p e$) and a term proportional to the integral of the error:

$$K_I \int edt$$

The actuator signal u is a combination of these two terms:

$$u = K_p e + K_I \int edt$$

The throttle opening is proportional to the value of this actuator signal.

Operation of the system can be understood by first considering the operation of a proportional controller (that is, imagine that the integral term is not present for the sake of this preliminary discussion). We assume that the driver has reached the desired speed (say, 60 mph) and activated the speed set switch. If the car is traveling on a level road at the desired speed, then the error is zero and the throttle remains at a fixed position.

If the car were then to enter a long hill with a steady positive slope (i.e., a hill going up) while the throttle is set at the cruise position for level road, the engine will produce less power than required to maintain that speed on the hill. The hill represents a disturbance to the cruise control system. The vehicle speed will decrease, thereby introducing an error to the control system. This error, in turn, results in an increase in the signal to the actuator, causing an

**Figure 8.2
Cruise Control Block
Diagram**

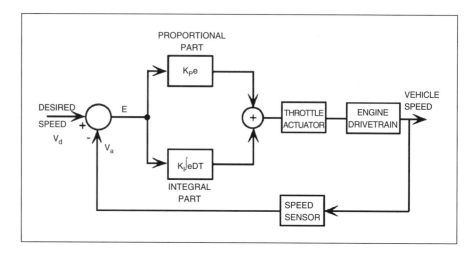

increase in engine power. This increased power results in an increase in speed. However, in a proportional control system the speed error is not reduced to zero since a nonzero error is required so that the engine will produce enough power to balance the increased load of the disturbance (i.e., the hill).

The speed response to the disturbance is shown in Figure 8.3a. When the disturbance occurs, the speed drops off and the control system reacts immediately to increase power. However, a certain amount of time is required for the car to accelerate toward the desired speed. As time progresses, the speed reaches a steady value that is less than the desired speed, thereby accounting for the steady error (e_s) depicted in Figure 8.3a (i.e., the final speed is less than the starting 60 mph).

If we now consider a PI control system, we will see that the steady error when integrated produces an ever-increasing output from the integrator. This increasing output causes the actuator to increase further, with a resulting speed increase. In this case the actuator output will increase until the error is reduced to zero. The response of the cruise control with PI control is shown in Figure 8.3b.

The response characteristics of a PI controller depend strongly on the choice of the gain parameters K_P and K_I. It is possible to select values for these parameters to increase the speed of the system response to disturbance. If the speed increases too rapidly, however, overshoot will occur and the actual speed will oscillate around the desired speed. The amplitude of oscillations decreases by an amount determined by a parameter called the *damping ratio*. The damping ratio that produces the fastest response without overshoot is called *critical damping*. A damping ratio less than critically damped is said to be *underdamped*, and one greater than critically damped is said to be *overdamped*.

Speed Response Curves

When a new speed is requested, the time required for the vehicle to reach that speed is affected by the control system's damping coefficient.

The curves of Figure 8.3c show the response of a cruise control system with a PI control strategy to a sudden disturbance. These curves are all for the same car cruising initially at 60 mph along a level road and encountering an upsloping hill. The only difference in the response of these curves is the controller gain parameters.

Consider, first, the curve that initially drops to about 30 mph and then increases, overshooting the desired speed and oscillating above and below the desired speed until it eventually decays to the desired 60 mph. This curve has a relatively low damping ratio as determined by the controller parameters K_P and K_I and takes more time to come to the final steady value.

Next, consider the curve that drops initially to about 40 mph, then increases with a small overshoot and decays to the desired speed. The numerical value for this damping ratio (see Chapter 2) is about 0.7, whereas the first curve had a damping ratio of about 0.4. Finally, consider the solid curve of Figure 8.3c. This curve corresponds to critical damping. This situation involves the most rapid response of the car to a disturbance, with no overshoot.

The importance of these performance curves is that they demonstrate how the performance of a cruise control system is affected by the controller gains. These gains are simply parameters that are contained in the control system. They determine the relationship between the error, the integral of the error, and the actuator control signal.

Usually a control system designer attempts to balance the proportional and integral control gains so that the system is optimally damped. However, because of system characteristics, in many cases it is impossible, impractical, or inefficient to achieve the optimal time response and therefore another response is chosen. The control system should make the engine drive force react quickly and accurately to the command speed, but should not overtax the engine in the process. Therefore, the system designer chooses the control electronics that provide the following system qualities:

1. Quick response
2. Relative stability
3. Small steady-state error
4. Optimization of the control effort required

Digital Cruise Control

The explanation of the operation of cruise control thus far has been based on a continuous-time formulation of the problem. This formulation correctly describes the concept for cruise control regardless of whether the implementation is by analog or digital electronics. Cruise control is now mostly implemented digitally using a microprocessor-based computer. For such a system, proportional and integral control computations are performed numerically in the computer. A block diagram for a typical digital cruise

Figure 8.3
Cruise Control Speed Performance

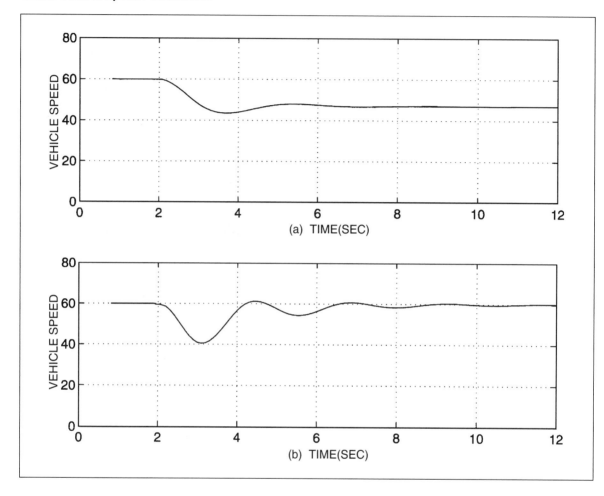

control is shown in Figure 8.4. The vehicle speed sensor (described later in this chapter) is digital. When the car reaches the desired speed, S_d, the driver activates the speed set switch. At this time, the output of the vehicle speed sensor is transferred to a storage register.

    The computer continuously reads the actual vehicle speed, S_a, and generates an error, e_n, at the sample time, t_n (n is an integer). $e_n = S_d - S_a$ at time t_n. A control signal, d, is computed that has the following form:

$$d_n = K_P e_n + K_I \sum_{m=1}^{M} e_{n-m}$$

Figure 8.3
Continued

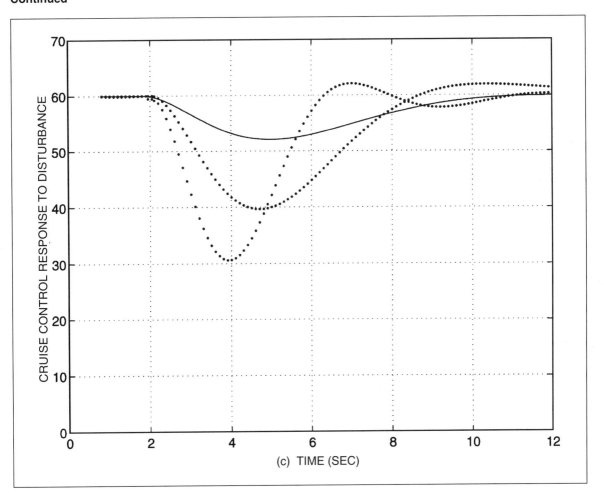

(c) TIME (SEC)

(*Note:* The symbol Σ in this equation means to add the *M* previously calculated errors to the present error.) This sum, which is computed in the cruise control computer, is then multiplied by the integral gain K_I and added to the most recent error multiplied by the proportional gain K_P to form the control signal.

This control signal is actually the duty cycle of a square wave (V_c) that is applied to the throttle actuator (as explained later). The throttle opening increases or decreases as *d* increases or decreases due to the action of the throttle actuator.

**Figure 8.4
Digital Cruise Control
System**

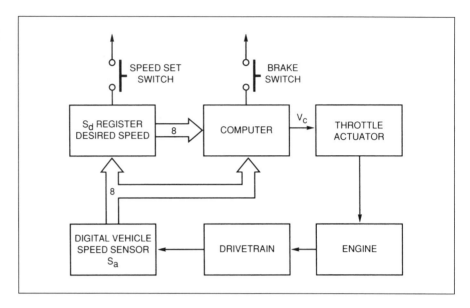

The operation of the cruise control system can be further understood by examining the vehicle speed sensor and the actuator in detail. Figure 8.5a is a sketch of a sensor suitable for vehicle speed measurement.

In a typical vehicle speed measurement system, the vehicle speed information is mechanically coupled to the speed sensor by a flexible cable coming from the driveshaft, which rotates at an angular speed proportional to vehicle speed. A speed sensor driven by this cable generates a pulsed electrical signal (Figure 8.5b) that is processed by the computer to obtain a digital measurement of speed.

A speed sensor can be implemented magnetically or optically. The magnetic speed sensor was discussed in Chapter 6, so we hypothesize an optical sensor for the purposes of this discussion. For the hypothetical optical sensor, a flexible cable drives a slotted disk that rotates between a light source and a light detector. The placement of the source, disk, and detector is such that the slotted disk interrupts or passes the light from source to detector, depending on whether a slot is in the line of sight from source to detector. The light detector produces an output voltage whenever a pulse of light from the light source passes through a slot to the detector. The number of pulses generated per second is proportional to the number of slots in the disk and the vehicle speed:

$$f = NSK$$

where

Figure 8.5a
Digital Speed Sensor

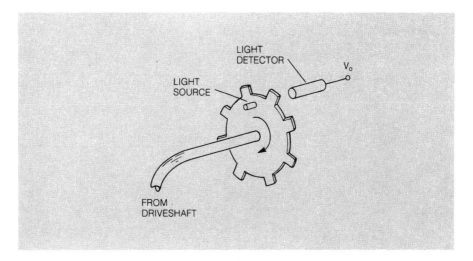

Figure 8.5b
Digital Speed Sensor

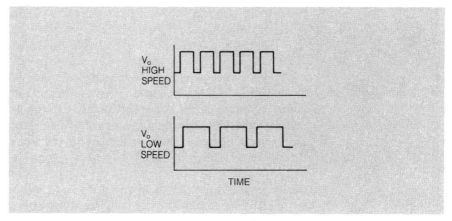

f is the frequency in pulses per second
N is the number of slots in the sensor disk
S is the vehicle speed
K is the proportionality constant that accounts for differential gear ratio and wheel size

It should be noted that either a magnetic or an optical speed sensor generates a pulse train such as described here.

The output pulses are passed through a sample gate to a digital counter (Figure 8.6). The gate is an electronic switch that either passes the pulses to the counter or does not pass them depending on whether the switch is closed or open. The time interval during which the gate is closed is precisely controlled by the computer. The digital counter counts the number of pulses from the

**Figure 8.6
Digital Speed
Measurement System**

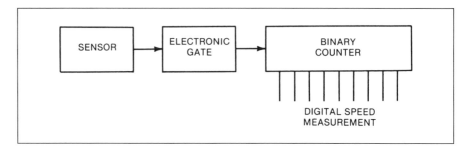

light detector during time t that the gate is open. The number of pulses P that is counted by the digital counter is given by:

$$P = tNSK$$

That is, the number P is proportional to vehicle speed S. The electrical signal in the binary counter is in a digital format that is suitable for reading by the cruise control computer.

Throttle Actuator

The throttle actuator is an electromechanical device that, in response to an electrical input from the controller, moves the throttle through some appropriate mechanical linkage. Two relatively common throttle actuators operate either from manifold vacuum or with a stepper motor. The stepper motor implementation operates similarly to the idle speed control actuator described in Chapter 7. The throttle opening is either increased or decreased by the stepper motor in response to the sequences of pulses sent to the two windings depending on the relative phase of the two sets of pulses.

The throttle actuator that is operated by manifold vacuum through a solenoid valve is similar to that used for the EGR valve described in Chapter 7 and further explained later in this chapter. During cruise control operation the throttle position is set automatically by the throttle actuator in response to the actuator signal generated in the control system. This type of manifold-vacuum-operated actuator is illustrated in Figure 8.7.

Throttle actuators use manifold vacuum to pull a piston that is mechanically linked to the throttle. The amount of vacuum provided is controlled by a solenoid valve that is turned on and off rapidly.

A pneumatic piston arrangement is driven from the intake manifold vacuum. The piston-connecting rod assembly is attached to the throttle lever. There is also a spring attached to the lever. If there is no force applied by the piston, the spring pulls the throttle closed. When an actuator input signal energizes the electromagnet in the control solenoid, the pressure control valve is pulled down and changes the actuator cylinder pressure by providing a path to manifold pressure. Manifold pressure is lower than atmospheric pressure, so the actuator cylinder pressure quickly drops, causing the piston to pull against the throttle lever to open the throttle.

Figure 8.7
Vacuum-Operated
Throttle Actuator

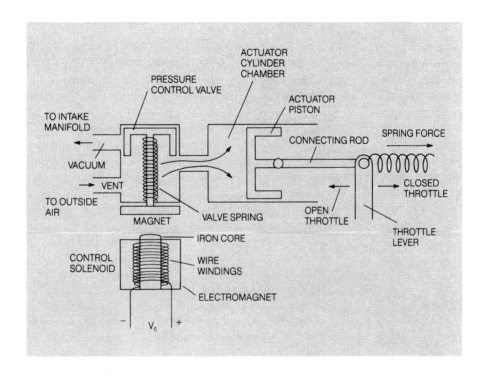

A switching, duty-cycle type of signal is applied to the solenoid coil. By varying the duty cycle, the amount of vacuum, and hence the corresponding throttle angle, is varied.

The force exerted by the piston is varied by changing the average pressure in the cylinder chamber. This is done by rapidly switching the pressure control valve between the outside air port, which provides atmospheric pressure, and the manifold pressure port, the pressure of which is lower than atmospheric pressure. In one implementation of a throttle actuator, the actuator control signal V_c is a variable-duty-cycle type of signal like that discussed for the fuel injector actuator. A high V_c signal energizes the electromagnet; a low V_c signal deenergizes the electromagnet. Switching back and forth between the two pressure sources causes the average pressure in the chamber to be somewhere between the low manifold pressure and outside atmospheric pressure. This average pressure and, consequently, the piston force are proportional to the duty cycle of the valve control signal V_c. The duty cycle is in turn proportional to the control signal d (explained above) that is computed from the sampled error signal e_n.

This type of duty-cycle-controlled throttle actuator is ideally suited for use in digital control systems. If used in an analog control system, the analog control signal must first be converted to a duty-cycle control signal. The same frequency response considerations apply to the throttle actuator as to the speed sensor. In fact, with both in the closed-loop control system, each contributes to the total system phase shift and gain.

CRUISE CONTROL ELECTRONICS

In an analog cruise control system, an error amplifier compares actual speed and desired (command) speed. The error signal output is fed to a proportional amplifier and an integral amplifier. The resultant outputs are combined by a summing amplifier.

Cruise control can be implemented electronically in various ways, including with a microcontroller with special-purpose digital electronics or with analog electronics. It can also be implemented (in proportional control strategy alone) with an electromechanical speed governor.

The physical configuration for a digital, microprocessor-based cruise control is depicted in Figure 8.8. A system such as is depicted in Figure 8.8 is often called a *microcontroller* since it is implemented with a microprocessor operating under program control. The actual program that causes the various calculations to be performed is stored in read-only memory (ROM). Typically, the ROM also stores parameters that are critical to the correct calculations. Normally a relatively small-capacity RAM memory is provided to store the command speed and to store any temporary calculation results. Input from the speed sensor and output to the throttle actuator are handled by the I/O interface (normally an integrated circuit that is a companion to the microprocessor). The output from the controller (i.e., the control signal) is sent via the I/O (on one of its output ports) to so-called driver electronics. The latter electronics receives this control signal and generates a signal of the correct format and power level to operate the actuator (as explained below).

A microprocessor-based cruise control system performs all of the required control law computations digitally under program control. For example, a PI control strategy is implemented as explained above, with a proportional term and an integral term that is formed by a summation. In performing this task the controller continuously receives samples of the speed error e_n and where n is a counting index ($n = 1, 2, 3, 4, \ldots$). This sampling occurs at a sufficiently high rate to be able to adjust the control signal to the actuator in time to compensate for changes in operating condition or to disturbances. At each sample the controller reads the most recent error. As explained earlier, that error is multiplied by a constant K_P that is called the proportional gain, yielding the proportional term in the control law. It also computes the sum of a number of previous error samples (the exact sum is chosen by the control system designer in accordance with the desired steady-state error). Then this sum is multiplied by a constant K_I and added to the proportional term, yielding the control signal.

The control signal at this point is simply a number that is stored in a memory location in the digital controller. The use of this number by the electronic circuitry that drives the throttle actuator to regulate vehicle speed depends on the configuration of the particular control system and on the actuator used by that system.

Stepper Motor-Based Actuator

For example, in the case of a stepper motor actuator, the actuator driver electronics reads this number and then generates a sequence of pulses to the

Figure 8.8
Digital Cruise Control Configuration

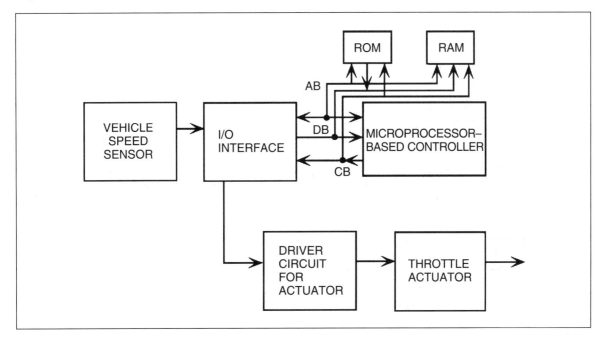

pair of windings on the stepper motor (with the correct relative phasing) to cause the stepper motor to either advance or retard the throttle setting as required to bring the error toward zero.

An illustrative example of driver circuitry for a stepper motor actuator is shown in Figure 8.9. The basic idea for this circuitry is to continuously drive the stepper motor to advance or retard the throttle in accordance with the control signal that is stored in memory. Just as the controller periodically updates the actuator control signal, the stepper motor driver electronics continually adjusts the throttle by an amount determined by the actuator signal.

This signal is, in effect, a signed number (i.e., a positive or negative numerical value). A sign bit indicates the direction of the throttle movement (advance or retard). The numerical value determines the amount of advance or retard.

The magnitude of the actuator signal (in binary format) is loaded into a parallel load serial down-count binary counter. The direction of movement is in the form of the sign bit (SB of Figure 8.9). The stepper motor is activated by a pair of quadrature phase signals (i.e., signals that are a quarter of a cycle out of phase) coming from a pair of oscillators. To advance the throttle, phase

Figure 8.9
Stepper Motor Actuator for Cruise Control

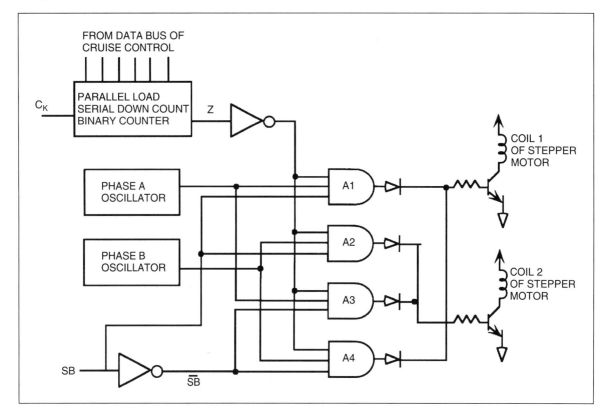

A signal is applied to coil 1 and phase B to coil 2. To retard the throttle these phases are each switched to the opposite coil. The amount of movement in either direction is determined by the number of cycles of A and B, one step for each cycle.

The number of cycles of these two phases is controlled by a logical signal (Z in Figure 8.9). This logical signal is switched high, enabling a pair of AND gates (from the set A1, A2, A3, A4). The length of time that it is switched high determines the number of cycles and corresponds to the number of steps of the motor.

The logical variable Z corresponds to the contents of the binary counter being zero. As long as Z is not zero, a pair of AND gates (A1 and A3, or A2 and A4) is enabled, permitting phase A and phase B signals to be sent to the stepper motor. The pair of gates enabled is determined by the sign bit. When the sign bit is high, A1 and A3 are enabled and the stepper motor advances the throttle as long as Z is not zero. Similarly, when the sign bit is low, A2 and A4 are enabled and the stepper motor retards the throttle.

To control the number of steps, the controller loads a binary value into the binary counter. With the contents not zero the appropriate pair of AND gates is enabled. When loaded with data, the binary counter counts down at the frequency of a clock (C_K in Figure 8.9). When the countdown reaches zero, the gates are disabled and the stepper motor stops moving.

The time required to count down to zero is determined by the numerical value loaded into the binary counter. By loading signed binary numbers into the binary counter, the cruise controller regulates the amount and direction of movement of the stepper motor and thereby the corresponding movement of the throttle.

Vacuum-Operated Actuator

The driver electronics for a cruise control based on a vacuum-operated system generates a variable-duty-cycle signal as described in Chapter 6. In this type of system, the duty cycle at any time is proportional to the control signal. For example, if at any given instant a large positive error exists between the command and actual signal then a relatively large control signal will be generated. This control signal will cause the driver electronics to produce a large duty-cycle signal to operate the solenoid so that most of the time the actuator cylinder chamber is nearly at manifold vacuum level. Consequently, the piston will move against the restoring spring and cause the throttle opening to increase. As a result, the engine will produce more power and will accelerate the vehicle until its speed matches the command speed.

It should be emphasized that, regardless of the actuator type used, a microprocessor-based cruise control system will:

1. Read the command speed.
2. Measure actual vehicle speed.
3. Compute an error (error = command − actual).
4. Compute a control signal using P, PI, or PID control law.
5. Send the control signal to the driver electronics.
6. Cause driver electronics to send a signal to the throttle actuator such that the error will be reduced.

An example of electronics for a cruise control system that is basically analog is shown in Figure 8.10. Notice that the system uses four operational amplifiers (op amps) as described in Chapter 3 and that each op amp is used for a specific purpose. Op amp 1 is used as an error amplifier. The output of op amp 1 is proportional to the difference between the command speed and the actual speed. The error signal is then used as an input to op amps 2 and 3. Op amp 2 is a proportional amplifier with a gain of $K_P = -R_2/R_1$. Notice that R_1 is variable so that the proportional amplifier gain can be adjusted. Op amp 3 is

**Figure 8.10a
Cruise Control
Electronics (Analog)**

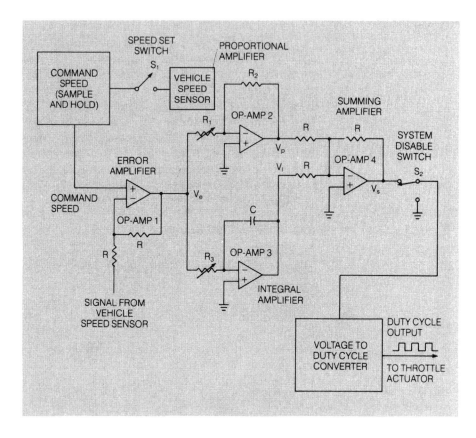

an integrator with a gain of $K_I = -1/R_3C$. Resistor R_3 is variable to permit adjustment of the gain. The op amp causes a current to flow into capacitor C that is equal to the current flowing into R_3. The voltage across R_3 is the error amplifier output voltage, V_e. The current in R_3 is found from Ohm's law to be

$$I = \frac{V_e}{R_3}$$

which is identical to the current flowing into the capacitor. If the error signal V_e is constant, the current I will be constant and the voltage across the capacitor will steadily change at a rate proportional to the current flow. That is, the capacitor voltage is proportional to the integral of the error signal:

$$V_I = -\frac{1}{R_3C}\int V_e dt$$

The output of the integral amplifier, V_I, increases or decreases with time depending on whether V_e is above or below zero volts. The voltage V_I is steady or unchanging only when the error is exactly zero; this is why the integral gain

Figure 8.10b
Typical Sample-and-Hold Circuit

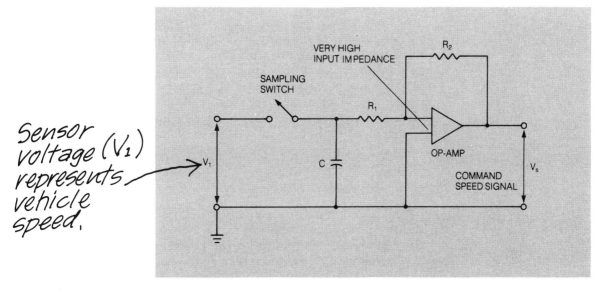

Sensor voltage (V₁) represents vehicle speed.

block in the diagram in Figure 8.10a can reduce the system steady-state error to zero. Even a small error (e.g., due to a disturbance) causes V_I to change to correct for the error.

The outputs of the proportional and integral amplifiers are added using a summing amplifier, op amp 4. The summing amplifier adds voltages V_P and V_I and inverts the resulting sum. The inversion is necessary because both the proportional and integral amplifiers invert their input signals while providing amplification. Inverting the sum restores the correct sense, or polarity, to the control signal.

Because the output of the summing amplifier is an analog signal, it must be converted into a duty-cycle signal to pulse the throttle actuator.

The summing amplifier op amp produces an analog voltage, V_s, that must be converted to a duty-cycle signal before it can drive the throttle actuator. A voltage-to-duty-cycle converter is used whose output directly drives the throttle actuator solenoid.

Two switches, S_1 and S_2, are shown in Figure 8.10a. Switch S_1 is operated by the driver to set the desired speed. It signals the sample-and-hold electronics (Figure 8.10b) to sample the present vehicle speed and hold that value. Voltage V_I, representing the vehicle speed at which the driver wishes to set the cruise controller, is sampled and it charges capacitor C. A very high input impedance amplifier detects the voltage on the capacitor without causing the charge on the capacitor to "leak" off. The output from this amplifier is a voltage, V_s, proportional to the command speed that is sent to the error amplifier.

Switch S_2 (Figure 8.10a) is used to disable the speed controller by interrupting the control signal to the throttle actuator. Switch S_2 disables the system whenever the ignition is turned off, the controller is turned off, or the brake pedal is pressed. The controller is switched on when the driver presses the speed set switch S_1.

For safety reasons, the brake turnoff is often performed in two ways. As just mentioned, pressing the brake pedal turns off or disables the electronic control. In certain cruise control configurations that use a vacuum-operated throttle actuator, the brake pedal also mechanically opens a separate valve that is located in a hose connected to the throttle actuator cylinder. When the valve is opened by depression of the brake pedal, it allows outside air to flow into the throttle actuator cylinder so that the throttle plate instantly snaps closed. The valve is shut off whenever the brake pedal is in its inactive position. This ensures a fast and complete shutdown of the speed control system whenever the driver presses the brake pedal.

Advanced Cruise Control

The cruise control system previously described is adequate for maintaining constant speed, provided that any required deceleration can be achieved by a throttle reduction (i.e., reduced engine power). The engine has limited braking capability with a closed throttle, and this braking in combination with aerodynamic drag and tire-rolling resistance may not provide sufficient deceleration to maintain the set speed. For example, a car entering a long, relatively steep downgrade may accelerate due to gravity even with the throttle closed.

For this driving condition, vehicle speed can be maintained only by application of the brakes. For cars equipped with a conventional cruise control system, the driver has to apply braking to hold speed.

An advanced cruise control (ACC) system has a means of automatic brake application whenever deceleration with throttle input alone is inadequate. A somewhat simplified block diagram of an ACC is shown in Figure 8.11 emphasizing the automatic braking portion.

This system consists of a conventional brake system with master cylinder wheel cylinders, vacuum boost (power brakes), and various brake lines. Figure 8.11 shows only a single-wheel cylinder, although there are four in actual practice. In addition, proportioning valves are present to regulate the front/rear brake force ratio.

In normal driving, the system functions like a conventional brake system. As the driver applies braking force through the brake pedal to the master cylinder, brake fluid (under pressure) flows out of port and through a brake line to the junction of check valves CV_1 and CV_2. Check valve CV_2 blocks brake fluid, whereas CV_1 permits flow through a pump assembly P and then through the apply valve (which is open) to the wheel cylinder(s), thereby applying brakes.

In cruise control mode, the ACC controller regulates the throttle (as explained above for a conventional cruise control) as well as the brake system

**Figure 8.11
ACC Emphasizing the
Automatic Braking
Portion**

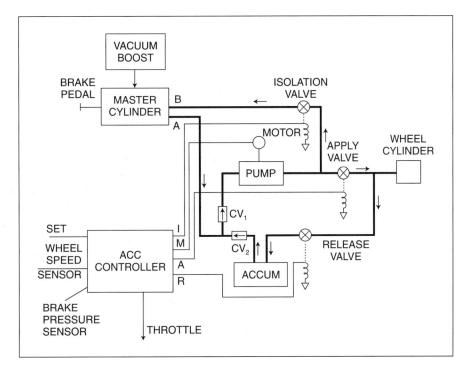

via electrical output signals and in response to inputs, including the vehicle speed sensor and set cruise speed switch. The ACC system functions as described above until the maximum available deceleration with closed throttle is inadequate. Whenever there is greater deceleration than this maximum valve, the ACC applies brakes automatically. In this automatic brake mode, an electrical signal is sent from the M (i.e., motor) output, causing the pump to send more brake fluid (under pressure) through the apply valve (maintained open) to the wheel cylinder. At the same time, the release valve remains closed such that brakes are applied.

The braking pressure can be regulated by varying the isolation valve, thereby bleeding some brake fluid back to the master cylinder. By activating isolation valves separately to the four wheels, brake proportioning can be achieved. Brake release can be accomplished by sending signals from the ACC to close the apply valve and open the release valve.

Another potential future application for automatic braking involves separate brake pressure applied individually to all four wheels. This independent brake application can be employed for improved handling when both braking and steering are active (e.g., braking on curves).

A further application of the ACC involves maintaining a constant headway (separation) behind another vehicle on the road. A discussion of this application is deferred to the final chapter.

ANTILOCK BRAKING SYSTEM

One of the most readily accepted applications of electronics in auto-mobiles has been the antilock brake system (ABS). ABS is a safety-related feature that assists the driver in deceleration of the vehicle in poor or marginal braking conditions (e.g., wet or icy roads). In such conditions, panic braking by the driver (in non-ABS-equipped cars) results in reduced braking effec-tiveness and, typically, loss of directional control due to the tendency of the wheels to lock.

In ABS-equipped cars, the wheel is prevented from locking by a mechanism that automatically regulates braking force to an optimum for any given low-friction condition. The physical configuration for an ABS is shown in Figure 8.12. In addition to the normal brake components, including brake pedal, master cylinder, vacuum boost, wheel cylinders, calipers/disks, and brake lines, this system has a set of angular speed sensors at each wheel, an electronic control module, and a hydraulic brake pressure modulator (regulator).

In order to understand the ABS operation, it is first necessary to under-stand the physical mechanism of wheel lock and vehicle skid that can occur during braking. Figure 8.13 illustrates the forces applied to the wheel by the road during braking.

The car is traveling at a speed U and the wheels are rotating at an angular speed w where

$$w = \frac{\pi \text{RPM}}{30}$$

**Figure 8.12
Antilock Braking
System**

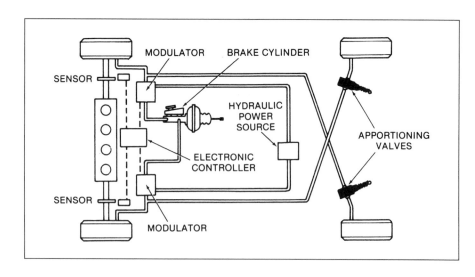

**Figure 8.13
Forces During
Braking**

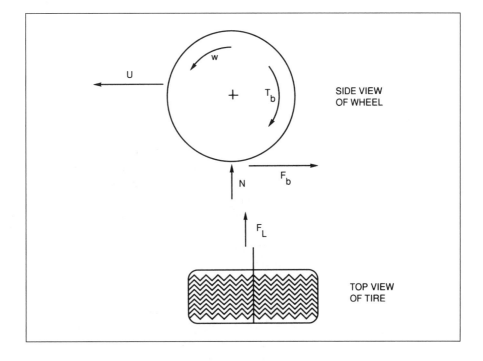

SIDE VIEW
OF WHEEL

TOP VIEW
OF TIRE

and where RPM is the wheel revolutions per minute. When the wheel is rolling (no applied brakes),

$$U = Rw$$

where R is the tire radius. When the brake pedal is depressed, the calipers are forced by hydraulic pressure against the disk, as explained in Chapter 1. This force acts as a torque T_b in opposition to the wheel rotation. The actual force that decelerates the car is shown as F_b in Figure 8.13. The lateral force that maintains directional control of the car is shown as F_L in Figure 8.13.

The wheel angular speed begins to decrease, causing a difference between the vehicle speed U and the tire speed over the road (i.e., wR). In effect, the tire slips relative to the road surface. The amount of slip (S) determines the braking force and lateral force. The slip, as a percentage of car speed, is given by

$$S = \frac{U - wR}{U} \times 100\%$$

Note: A rolling tire has slip $S = 0$, and a fully locked tire has $S = 100\%$.

The braking and lateral forces are proportional to the normal force (from the weight of the car) acting on the tire/road interface (N in Figure 8.13) and the friction coefficients for braking force (F_b) and lateral force (F_L):

$$F_b = N\mu_b$$
$$F_L = N\mu_L$$

where

μ_b is the braking friction coefficient
μ_L is the lateral friction coefficient

These coefficients depend markedly on slip, as shown in Figure 8.14. The solid curves are for a dry road and the dashed curves for a wet or icy road. As brake pedal force is increased from zero, slip increases from zero. For increasing slip, μ_b increases to $S = S_o$. Further increase in slip actually decreases μ_b, thereby reducing braking effectiveness.

On the other hand, μ_L decreases steadily with increasing S such that for fully locked wheels the lateral force has its lowest value. For wet or icy roads, μ_L at $S = 100\%$ is so low that the lateral force is insufficient to maintain directional control of the vehicle. However, directional control can often be maintained even in poor braking conditions if slip is optimally controlled. This is essentially the function of the ABS, which performs an operation equivalent to pumping the brakes (as done by experienced drivers before the development of ABS). In ABS-equipped cars under marginal or poor braking conditions, the driver simply applies a steady brake force and the system adjusts tire slip to optimum value automatically.

In a typical ABS configuration, control over slip is effected by controlling the brake line pressure under electronic control. The configuration for ABS is

Figure 8.14
Braking Coefficients versus Tire Slip (Solid curves for dry road, dashed curves for wet or icy road)

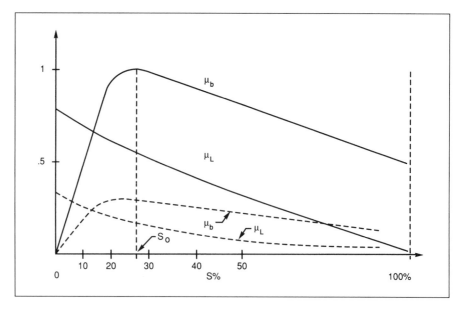

shown in Figure 8.12. This ABS regulates or modulates brake pressure to maintain slip as near to optimum as possible (e.g., at S_o in Figure 8.14). The operation of this ABS is based on estimating the torque T_w applied to the wheel at the road surface by the braking force F_b:

$$T_w = RF_b$$

In opposition to this torque is the braking torque T_b applied to the disk by the calipers in response to brake pressure P:

$$T_b = k_b P$$

where k_b is a constant for the given brakes.

The difference between these two torques acts to decelerate the wheel. In accordance with basic Newtonian mechanics, the wheel torque T_w is related to braking torque and wheel deceleration by the following equation:

$$T_w = T_b + I_w \dot{w}$$

where I_w is the wheel moment of inertia and $\dot{w}$ is the wheel deceleration (*dw/dt*, that is, the rate of change of wheel speed).

During heavy braking under marginal conditions, sufficient braking force is applied to cause wheel lock-up (in the absence of ABS control). We assume such heavy braking for the following discussion of the ABS. As brake pressure is applied, T_b increases and w decreases, causing slip to increase. The wheel torque is proportional to μ_b, which reaches a peak at slip S_o. Consequently, the wheel torque reaches a maximum value (assuming sufficient brake force is applied) at this level of slip.

Figure 8.15 is a sketch of wheel torque versus slip illustrating the peak T_w. After the peak wheel torque is sensed electronically, the electronic control system commands that brake pressure be reduced (via the brake pressure modulator). This point is indicated in Figure 8.15 as the limit point of slip for the ABS. As the brake pressure is reduced, slip is reduced and the wheel torque again passes through a maximum.

The wheel torque reaches a value below the peak on the low slip side and at this point brake pressure is again increased. The system will continue to cycle, maintaining slip near the optimal value as long as the brakes are applied and the braking conditions lead to wheel lock-up.

The mechanism for modulating brake pressure is illustrated in Figure 8.16. The numbers in Figure 8.16a refer to the following:

1. Applied master cylinder pressure
2. Bypass brake fluid
3. Normally open solenoid valve
4. EMB braking action

**Figure 8.15
Wheel Torque versus
Slip**

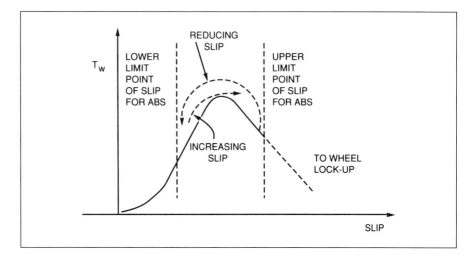

**Figure 8.16
Brake Pressure
Modulating
Mechanism**

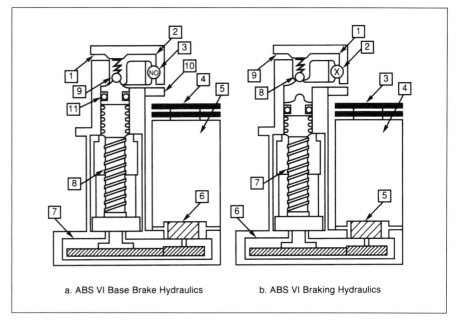

a. ABS VI Base Brake Hydraulics   b. ABS VI Braking Hydraulics

5. DC motor pack
6. ESB braking
7. Gear assembly
8. Ball screw
9. Check valve unseated
10. Outlet to brake cylinders
11. Piston

The numbers in Figure 8.16b refer to the following:

1. Trapped bypass brake fluid
2. Solenoid valve activated
3. EMB action released
4. DC motor pack
5. ESB braking action released
6. Gear assembly
7. Ball screw
8. Check valve seated
9. Applied master cylinder pressure

Under normal braking, brake pressure from the master cylinder passes without reduction through the passageways associated with check valve 9 and solenoid valve 3 in Figure 8.16a.

Whenever the wheel slip limit is reached, the solenoid valve is closed and the piston (11) retracts, closing the check valve. This action effectively isolates the brake cylinders from the master cylinder, and brake line pressure is controlled by the position of piston 11. This piston retracts, lowering the brake pressure sufficiently so that slip falls below S_o. At this point, the control system detects low T_w and the piston moves up, thereby increasing brake line pressure. The ABS system will continue to cycle until the vehicle has stopped, the braking conditions are normal, or the driver removes the brake pressure from the master cylinder.

In the latter case, the operation of the brake pressure modulator restores normal braking function. For example, should the driver release the brake pedal, then the pressure at the inlet (1) is reduced. At this point, the check valve (9) opens and brake line pressure is also removed. The solenoid valve opens and the piston returns to its normal position (fully up) such that the check valve is held open.

Figure 8.17 illustrates the braking during an ABS action. In this illustration, the vehicle is initially traveling at 55 mph and the brakes are applied as indicated by the rising brake pressure. The wheel speed begins to drop until the slip limit is reached. At this point, the ABS reduces brake pressure and the wheel speed increases. With the high applied brake pressure, the wheels again tend toward lock-up and ABS reduces brake pressure. The cycle continues until the vehicle is stopped.

It should be noted that by maintaining slip near S_o, the maximum deceleration is achieved for a given set of conditions. Some reduction in lateral force occurs from its maximum value by maintaining slip near S_o. However, in most cases the lateral force is large enough to maintain directional control.

In some antilock brake systems, the slip oscillations are shifted below S_o, sacrificing some braking effectiveness to enhance directional control. This can be accomplished by adjusting the upper and lower slip limits.

Figure 8.17
ABS Braking Action

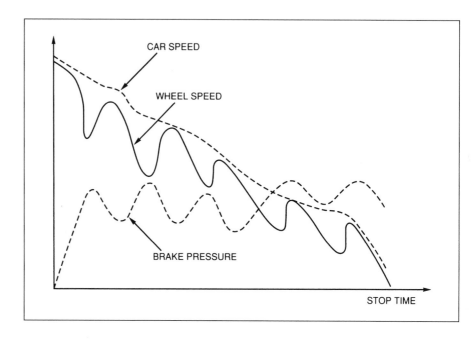

Tire-Slip Controller

Another benefit of the ABS is that the brake pressure modulator can be used for tire-slip control. Tire slip is effective in moving the car forward just as it is in braking. Under normal driving circumstances, the slip that was defined previously for braking is negative. That is, the tire is actually moving at a speed that is greater than for a purely rolling tire. In fact, the traction force is proportional to slip.

For wet or icy roads, the friction coefficient can become very low and excessive slip can develop. In extreme cases, one of the driving wheels may be on ice or in snow while the other is on a dry (or drier) surface. Because of the action of the differential (see Chapter 1), the low-friction tire will spin and relatively little torque will be applied to the dry-wheel side. In such circumstances, it may be difficult for the driver to move the car even though one wheel is on a relatively good friction surface.

The difficulty can be overcome by applying a braking force to the free spinning wheel. In this case, the differential action is such that torque is applied to the relatively dry wheel surface and the car can be moved. In the example ABS, such braking force can be applied to the free spinning wheel by the hydraulic brake pressure modulator (assuming a separate modulator for each drive wheel). Control of this modulator is based on measurements of the speed of the two drive wheels. Of course, the ABS already incorporates wheel speed measurements, as discussed previously.

The ABS electronics have the capability to perform comparisons of these two wheel speeds and to determine that braking is required of one drive wheel to prevent wheel spin.

Antilock braking can also be achieved with electrohydraulic brakes. An electrohydraulic brake system was described in the section of this chapter devoted to advanced cruise control (ACC).

Recall that for ACC a motor-driven pump supplied brake fluid through a solenoid-operated apply valve to the wheel cylinder. In the case of ABS, the driver supplies the pressurized brake fluid instead of the motor-driven pump. For ACC application of the brakes, the apply and isolation valves independently regulate the braking to each of the four wheels.

For ABS applications, the braking pressure is regulated by alternately opening and closing the apply and release valves. These valves are operated by output signals from the ABS controller in accordance with an algorithm applied to wheel speed measurements as described above, which attempts to maintain slip near a value corresponding to the maximum friction coefficient.

ELECTRONIC SUSPENSION SYSTEM

In Chapter 1, we described automotive suspension systems as consisting of springs, shock absorbers, and various linkages to connect the wheel assembly to the car frame. The purpose of the suspension system is to isolate the car body motion as much as possible from wheel motion due to rough road input. In Chapters 1 and 2, it was shown that the performance of the suspension system is strongly influenced by the damping parameter of the shock absorber.

The two primary subjective performance measures are ride and handling. *Ride* refers to the motion of the car body in response to road bumps or irregularities. *Handling* refers to how well the car body responds to dynamic vehicle motion such as cornering or hard braking.

Generally speaking, ride is improved by lowering the shock absorber damping, whereas handling is improved by increasing this damping. In traditional suspension design, the damping parameter is fixed and is chosen to achieve a compromise between ride and handling (i.e., an intermediate value for shock absorber damping is chosen).

In electronically controlled suspension systems, this damping can be varied depending on driving conditions and road roughness characteristics. That is, the suspension system adapts to inputs to maintain the best possible ride subject to handling constraints that are associated with safety.

There are two major classes of electronic suspension control systems: active and semiactive. The semiactive suspension system is purely dissipative (i.e., power is absorbed by the shock absorber under control of a microcontroller). In this system, the shock absorber damping is regulated to absorb the power of the wheel motion in accordance with the driving conditions.

In an active suspension system, power is added to the suspension system via a hydraulic or pneumatic power source. At the time of the writing of this book, commercial suspension systems are primarily semiactive. The active suspension system is just beginning to appear in production vehicles. In this chapter, we explain the semiactive system first, then the active one.

The primary purpose of the semiactive suspension system is to provide a good ride for as much of the time as possible without sacrificing handling. Good ride is achieved if the car's body is isolated as much as possible from the road. A semiactive suspension controls the shock absorber damping to achieve the best possible ride.

In addition to providing isolation of the sprung mass (i.e., car body and contents), the suspension system has another major function. It must also dynamically maintain the tire normal force as the unsprung mass (wheel assembly) travels up and down due to road roughness. Recall from the discussion of antilock braking that cornering forces depend on normal tire force. Of course in the long-term time average, the normal forces will total the vehicle weight plus any inertial forces due to acceleration, deceleration, or cornering.

However, as the car travels over the road, the unsprung mass moves up and down in response to road input. This motion causes a variation in normal force, with a corresponding variation in potential cornering or braking forces. For example, while driving on a rough curved road, there is a potential loss of steering or braking effectiveness if the suspension system doesn't have good damping characteristics.

Figure 8.18 illustrates typical tire normal force variation as a function of frequency of excitation for a fixed-amplitude, variable-frequency sinusoidal excitation (see Chapter 2 for a discussion of sinusoidal frequency response). The solid curve is the response for a relatively low-damping-coefficient shock absorber and the dashed curve is the response for a relatively high damping coefficient.

In Figure 8.18, the ordinate is the ratio of amplitude of force variation to the average normal load (i.e., due to weight). There are two relative peaks in this response. The lower peak is approximately 1 to 2 Hz and is generally associated with spring/sprung mass oscillation. The second peak, which is in the general region of 12 to 15 Hz, is resonance of the spring/unsprung mass combination.

Generally speaking, for any given fixed suspension system, ride and handling cannot both be optimized simultaneously, as explained in Chapter 1. A car with a good ride is one in which the sprung mass motion/acceleration due to rough road input is minimized. In particular, the sprung mass motion in the frequency region from about 2 to 8 Hz is most important for good subjective ride. Good ride is achieved for relatively low damping (low D in Figure 8.18).

Figure 8.18
Tire Force Variation

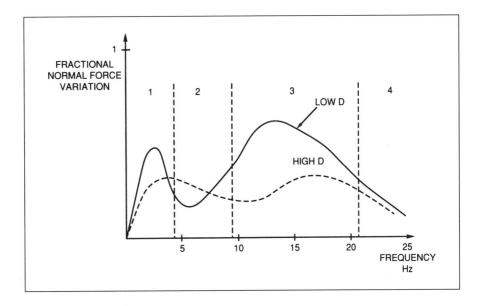

For low damping, the unsprung mass moves relatively freely due to road input while the sprung mass motion remains relatively low. Note from Figure 8.18 that this low damping results in relatively high variation in normal force, particularly near the two peak frequencies. That is, low damping results in relatively poor handling characteristics.

With respect to the four frequency regions of Figure 8.18, the following generally desired suspension damping characteristics can be identified.

Region	Frequency (Hz)	Damping
1: Sprung mass mode	1–2	High
2: Intermediate ride	2–8	Low
3: Unsprung mass resonance	8–20	High
4: Harshness	>20	Low

Another major input to the vehicle that affects handling is steering input that causes maneuvers parallel to the road surface (e.g., cornering). Whenever the car is executing such maneuvers, there is a lateral acceleration. This acceleration acting through the center of gravity causes the vehicle to roll in a direction opposite to the maneuver.

Car handling generally improves if the amount of roll for any given maneuver is reduced. The rolling rate for a given car and maneuver is improved if spring rate and shock absorber damping are increased. Although the semiactive control system regulates only the damping, handling is improved by increasing this damping as lateral acceleration increases.

Lateral acceleration A_L is proportional to vehicle speed and input steering angle:

$$A_L = kVq_s$$

where

V is the speed of the car

q_s is the steering angle

In Chapter 2, we discussed the dynamics of a spring/mass/damping system, identifying resonant frequency and critical damping D_c:

$$D_c = 2\sqrt{KM}$$

For good ride, the damping should be as low as possible. However, from practical design considerations, the minimum damping is generally in the region of $0.1 < D/D_c < 0.2$. For optimum handling, the damping is in the region of $0.6 < D/D_c < 0.8$.

Technology has been developed permitting the damping characteristics of shock absorber/strut assembly to be varied electrically, which in turn permits the ride/handling characteristics to be varied while the car is in motion. Under normal steady-cruise conditions, damping is electrically set low, yielding a good ride. However, under dynamic maneuvering conditions (e.g., cornering), the damping is set high to yield good handling. Generally speaking, high damping reduces vehicle roll in response to cornering or turning maneuvers, and it tends to maintain tire force on the road for increased cornering forces. Variable damping suspension systems can improve safety, particularly for vehicles with a relatively high center of gravity (e.g., SUVs).

As described in Chapter 1, the damping of a suspension system is determined by the viscosity of the fluid in the shock absorber/strut and by the size of the aperture through which the fluid flows as the wheel moves relative to the car body.

The earliest active or semiactive suspension systems employed variable aperture. One scheme for achieving variable damping is to switch between two aperture sizes using a solenoid. Another scheme varies aperture size continuously with a motor-driven mechanism.

Although there are many potential control strategies for regulating shock absorber damping, we consider first switched damping as in our example. In such a system, the shock absorber damping is switched to the higher value whenever lateral acceleration exceeds a predetermined threshold. Figure 8.19 illustrates such a system in which the threshold for switching to firm damping (i.e., higher damping) is 0.35 g.

The variation in shock absorber damping is achieved by varying the aperture in the oil passage through the piston (see Chapter 1 for discussion of shock absorber configuration). In practical semiactive suspension systems, there are two means used to vary this aperture size—a solenoid-operated

**Figure 8.19
Switching Threshold
versus Speed and
Steering Inputs**

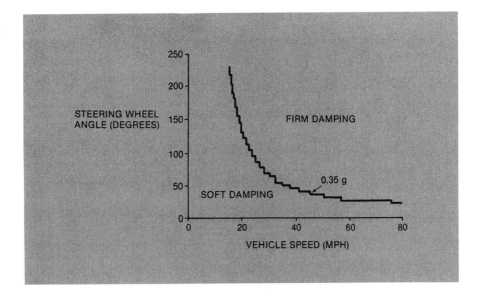

bypass valve and a motor-driven variable-orifice valve (Figure 8.20). Figure 8.21 is an illustration of the force/relative velocity characteristics of a shock absorber having a solenoid-switched aperture.

Variable Damping Via Variable Strut Fluid Viscosity

Variable suspension damping is also achieved with a fixed aperture and variable fluid viscosity. The fluid for such a system consists of a synthetic hydrocarbon with suspended iron particles and is called a magneto-rheological fluid (MR). An electromagnet is positioned such that a magnetic field is created whose strength is proportional to current through the coil. This magnetic field passes through the MR fluid. In the absence of the magnetic field, the iron particles are randomly distributed and the MR fluid has relatively low viscosity corresponding to low damping. As the magnetic field is increased from zero, the iron particles begin to align with the field, and the viscosity increases in proportion to the strength of the field (which is proportional to the current through the electromagnet coil). That is, the damping of the associated shock absorber/strut varies continuously with the electromagnet coil current.

Variable Spring Rate

Chapter 2 showed that the frequency response characteristics of a suspension system are influenced by the springs as well as the shock absorber damping. Conventional steel springs (i.e., coil or leaf) have a fixed spring rate (i.e., force-deflection characteristics). The vehicle height above the ground is

**Figure 8.20
Adjustable Shock
Absorber**

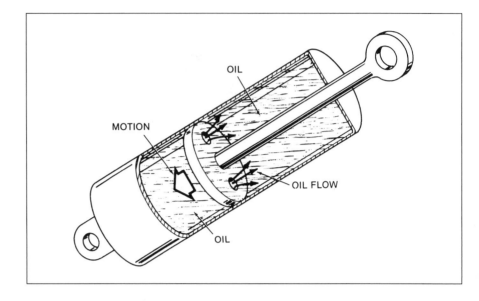

**Figure 8.21
Force versus Relative
Velocity of a
Solenoid-Switched
Aperture Shock
Absorber**

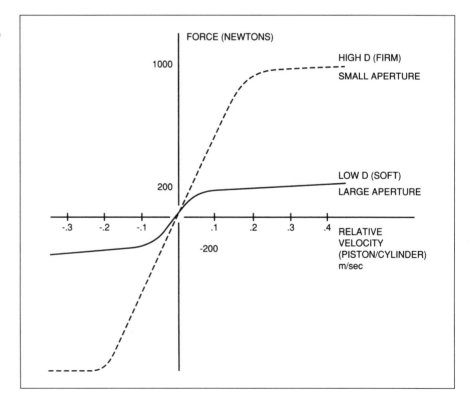

determined by vehicle weight, which in turn depends on loading (i.e., passengers, cargo, fuel). Some vehicles, having electronically controlled suspension, are also equipped with pneumatic springs as a replacement for steel springs. A pneumatic spring consists of a rubber bladder mounted in an assembly and filled with air under pressure. This mechanism is commonly called an air suspension system. The spring rate for such pneumatic springs is proportional to the pressure in the bladder. A motor-driven pump is provided that varies the pressure in the bladder, yielding a variable spring rate suspension. In conjunction with a suitable control system, the pneumatic springs can automatically adjust the vehicle height to accommodate various vehicle loadings.

Electronic Suspension Control System

The control system for a typical electronic suspension system is depicted in the block diagram of Figure 8.22. The control system configuration in Figure 8.22 is generic and not necessarily representative of the system for any production car. This system includes sensors for measuring vehicle speed;

**Figure 8.22
Electronic
Suspension System**

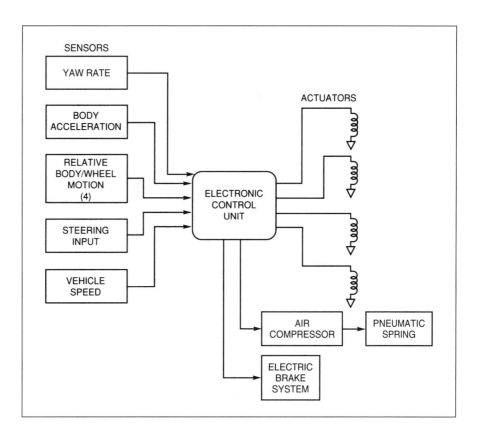

steering input (i.e., angular deflection of steered wheels); relative displacement of the wheel assembly and car body/chassis; lateral acceleration; and yaw rate. The outputs are electrical signals to the shock absorber/strut actuators and to the motor/compressor that pressurizes the pneumatic springs (if applicable). The actuators can be solenoid-operated (switched) orifices or motor-driven variable orifices or electromagnets for RH fluid-type variable viscosity struts.

The control system typically is in the form of a microcontroller or microprocessor-based digital controller. The inputs from each sensor are sampled, converted to digital format, and stored in memory. The body acceleration measurement can be used to evaluate ride quality. The controller does this by computing a weighted average of the spectrum of the acceleration. The relative body/wheel motion can be used to estimate tire normal force, and damping is then adjusted to try to optimize this normal force.

The yaw rate sensor provides data which in relationship to vehicle speed and steering input measurements can be used to evaluate cornering performance. In certain vehicles, these measurements combine in an algorithm that is used to activate the electrohydraulic brakes.

Under program control in accordance with the control strategy, the electronic control system generates output electrical signals to the various actuators. The variable damping actuators vary either the oil passage orifice or the RH fluid viscosity independently at each wheel to obtain the desired damping for that wheel.

There are many possible control strategies and many of these are actually used in production vehicles. For the purposes of this book, it is perhaps most beneficial to present a representative control strategy that typifies features of a number of actual production systems.

The important inputs to the vehicle suspension control system come from road roughness induced forces and inertial forces (due, for example, to cornering or maneuvering), steering inputs, and vehicle speed. In our hypothetical simplified control strategy these inputs are considered separately. When driving along a nominally straight road with small steering inputs, the road input is dominant. In this case, the control is based on the spectral content (frequency region) of the relative motion. The controller (under program control) calculates the spectrum of the relative velocity of the sprung and unsprung mass at each wheel (from the corresponding sensor's data). Whenever the weighted amplitude of the spectrum near the peak frequencies exceeds a threshold, damping is increased, yielding a firmer ride and improved handling. Otherwise, damping is kept low (soft suspension).

If in addition the vehicle is equipped with an accelerometer (usually located in the car body near the center of gravity) and with motor-driven variable-aperture shock absorbers, then an additional control strategy is possible. In this latter control strategy, the shock absorber apertures are adjusted to minimize sprung mass acceleration in the 2 to 8 Hz frequency region, thereby providing optimum ride control. However, at all times, the damping is adjusted to control unsprung mass motion to maintain wheel normal force variation at acceptably low levels for safety reasons. Whenever a relatively large steering input is sensed (sometimes in conjunction with yaw rate measurement), such as during a cornering maneuver, then the control strategy switches to the smaller aperture, yielding a "stiffer" suspension and improved handling. In particular, the combination of cornering on a relatively rough road calls for damping that optimizes tire normal force, thereby maximizing cornering forces.

ELECTRONIC STEERING CONTROL

In Chapter 1, the steering system was explained. There it was shown that the steering effort required of the driver to overcome restoring torque generally decreases with vehicle speed and increases with steering angle. Traditionally, the steering effort required by the driver has been reduced by incorporating a hydraulic power steering system in the vehicle. Whenever there is a steering input from the driver, hydraulic pressure from an engine-driven pump is applied to a hydraulic cylinder that boosts the steering effort of the driver.

Typically, the effort available from the pump increases with engine speed (i.e., with vehicle speed), whereas the required effort decreases. It would be desirable to reduce steering boost as vehicle speed increases. Such a feature is incorporated into a power steering system featuring electronic controls. An electronically controlled power steering system adjusts steering boost adaptively to driving conditions. Using electronic control of power steering, the available boost is reduced by controlling a pressure relief valve on the power steering pump.

An alternative power steering scheme utilizes a special electric motor to provide the boost required instead of the hydraulic boost. Electric boost power steering has several advantages over traditional hydraulic power steering. Electronic control of electric boost systems is straightforward and can be accomplished without any energy conversion from electrical power to mechanical actuation. Moreover, electronic control offers very sophisticated adaptive control in which the system can adapt to the driving environment.

An example of an electronically controlled steering system that has had commercial production is for four-wheel steering systems (4WS). In the 4WS-equipped vehicles, the front wheels are directly linked mechanically to the steering wheel, as in traditional vehicles. There is a power steering boost for the front wheels as in a standard two-wheel steering system. The rear wheels are steered under the control of a microcontroller via an actuator. Figure 8.23 is an illustration of the 4WS configuration.

In this illustration, the front wheels are steered to a steering angle δ_f by the driver's steering wheel input. A sensor (S) measures the steering angle and another sensor (U) gives the vehicle speed. The microcontroller (C) determines

Figure 8.23
4WS Configuration

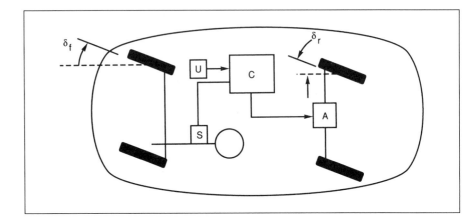

Figure 8.24
Lane Change
Maneuver

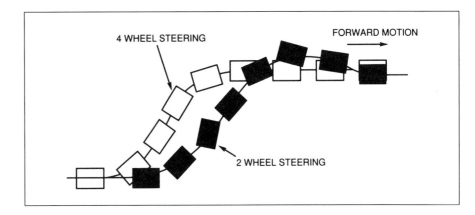

the desired rear steering angle δ_r under program control as a function of speed and front steering angle.

The details of the control strategy are proprietary and not available for this book. However, it is within the scope of this book to describe a representative example control strategy as follows.

For speeds below 10 mph, the rear steering angle is in the opposite direction to the front steering angle. This control strategy has the effect of decreasing the car's turning radius by as much as 30% from the value it has for front wheel steering only. Consequently, the maneuvering ability of the car at low speeds is enhanced (e.g., for parking).

At intermediate speeds (e.g., 11 mph < U < 30 mph), the steering might be front wheel only. At higher speeds (including highway cruise), the front and rear wheels are steered in the same direction. At least one automaker has an interesting strategy for higher speeds (e.g., at highway cruise speed). In this strategy, the rear wheels turn in the opposite direction to the front wheels for a very short period (on the order of one second) and then turn in the same direction as the front wheels. This strategy has a beneficial effect on maneuvers such as lane changes on the highway. Figure 8.24 illustrates the lane change for front wheel steering and for this latter 4WS strategy, in which the same front steering angle was used. Notice that the 4WS strategy yields a lane change in a shorter distance and avoids the overshoot common in a standard-steering vehicle.

Turning the wheels in the same direction at cruising speeds has another benefit for a vehicle towing a trailer. When front and rear wheels turn in the same direction, the angle between the car and trailer axes is less than it is for front wheel steering only. The reduction in this angle means that the lateral force applied to the rear wheels by the trailer in curves is less than that for front wheel only steering. This lateral force reduction improves the stability of the car or truck/trailer combination relative to front steering only.

Quiz for Chapter 8

1. A typical cruise control system senses the difference between
   a. vehicle speed and tire speed
   b. set speed and actual vehicle speed
   c. engine angular speed and wheel speed
   d. none of the above

2. A cruise control system controls vehicle speed using
   a. a feedback carburetor
   b. a distributorless ignition system
   c. a throttle actuator
   d. an MAF sensor

3. One of the major drawbacks to a proportional controller is
   a. steady-state error
   b. integral of the error
   c. gain error
   d. all of the above

4. A critically damped system has a response to a step input that
   a. has overshoot
   b. rises smoothly to the final value with no overshoot
   c. can only be achieved with a proportional control system
   d. is the slowest of all possible responses

5. A digital cruise control system
   a. operates on samples of the error signal
   b. computes a control signal numerically
   c. obtains a digital measurement of vehicle speed
   d. all of the above

6. In the example digital cruise control system of this chapter, the vehicle speed sensor
   a. counts pulses of light at a frequency that is proportional to vehicle speed
   b. generates an analog signal
   c. measures crankshaft rotation speed directly
   d. none of the above

7. One advantage of a digital motion control system is
   a. the ability to work with analog signals
   b. the stability of operation with respect to environmental extremes
   c. the exclusive ability to generate integrals of the error signal
   d. all of the above

8. A practical tire-slip controller is based on measurement of
   a. wheel speed
   b. vehicle speed
   c. both of the above
   d. neither of the above

9. An ideal antilock braking system measures skid by
   a. measuring the difference between wheel speed and vehicle speed
   b. differentiating vehicle speed with respect to time
   c. measuring crankshaft angular speed
   d. none of the above

10. The example digital ride control system of this chapter incorporates
   a. a special electrically adjustable shock absorber
   b. a measurement of steering angle
   c. a measurement of vehicle speed and brake line pressure
   d. all of the above

Automotive Instrumentation and Telematics

This chapter describes electronic instrumentation and the relatively new field of telematics. By the term *instrumentation*, we mean the equipment and devices that measure engine and other vehicle variables and parameters and display their status to the driver. By the term *telematics*, we refer to communication of all forms within the vehicle as well as communication to and from the vehicle. Communication within the vehicle takes the form of digital data links between various electronic subsystems. Communication to and from the vehicle spans all communication from voice and digital data via cell or satellite phone systems to digital data sent from land or satellite. Internet connections to an on-board PC (or the like) are included in those categories listed above. This chapter begins with a discussion of electronic instrumentation and concludes with telematics.

From about the late 1920s until the late 1950s, the standard automotive instrumentation included the speedometer, oil pressure gauge, coolant temperature gauge, battery charging rate gauge, and fuel quantity gauge. Strictly speaking, only the latter two are electrical instruments. In fact, this electrical instrumentation was generally regarded as a minor part of the automotive electrical system. By the late 1950s, however, the gauges for oil pressure, coolant temperature, and battery charging rate were replaced by warning lights that were turned on only if specified limits were exceeded. This was done primarily to reduce vehicle cost and because of the presumption that many people did not necessarily regularly monitor these instruments.

Automotive instrumentation was not really electronic until the 1970s. At that time, the availability of relatively low-cost solid-state electronics brought about a major change in automotive instrumentation; the use of low-cost electronics has increased with each new model year. This chapter presents a general overview of typical automotive electronic instrumentation.

In addition to providing measurements for display, modern automotive instrumentation performs limited diagnosis of problems with various subsystems. Whenever a problem is detected, a warning indicator alerts the driver of a problem and indicates the appropriate subsystem. For example, whenever self-diagnosis of the engine control system detects a problem, such as a loss of signal from a sensor, a lamp illuminates the "Check Engine" message on the instrument panel. Such warning messages alert the driver to seek repairs from authorized technicians who have the expertise and special equipment to perform necessary maintenance.

Low-cost solid-state electronics, including microprocessors, display devices, and some sensors, have brought about major changes in automotive instrumentation.

MODERN AUTOMOTIVE INSTRUMENTATION

The evolution of instrumentation in automobiles has been influenced by electronic technological advances in much the same way as the engine control system, which has already been discussed. Of particular importance has been the advent of the microprocessor, solid-state display devices, and solid-state sensors. In order to put these developments into perspective, recall the general block diagram for instrumentation (first given in Chapter 2), which is repeated here as Figure 9.1.

In electronic instrumentation, a sensor is required to convert any nonelectrical signal to an equivalent voltage or current. Electronic signal processing is then performed on the sensor output to produce an electrical signal that is capable of driving the display device. The display device is read by the vehicle driver. If a quantity to be measured is already in electrical form (e.g., the battery charging current) this signal can be used directly and no sensor is required.

In some modern automotive instrumentation, a microcomputer (or related digital subsystem) performs all of the signal processing operations for several measurements. The primary motivation for computer-based instrumentation is the great flexibility offered in the design of the instrument panel. A block diagram for such an instrumentation system is shown in Figure 9.2.

All measurements from the various sensors and switches are processed in a special-purpose digital computer. The processed signals are routed to the appropriate display or warning message. It is common practice in modern automotive instrumentation to integrate the display or warning in a single module that may include both solid-state alphanumeric display, lamps for illuminating specific messages, and traditional electromechanical indicators. For convenience, this display will be termed the *instrument panel* (IP).

The inputs to the instrumentation computer include sensors (or switches) for measuring (or sensing) various vehicle variables as well as diagnostic inputs from the other critical electronic subsystems. The vehicle status sensors may include any of the following:

**Figure 9.1
General
Instrumentation Block
Diagram**

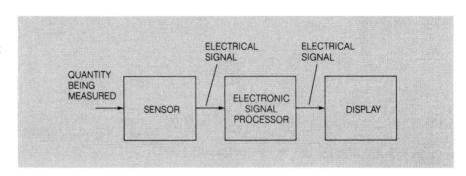

1. Fuel quantity
2. Fuel pump pressure
3. Fuel flow rate
4. Vehicle speed
5. Oil pressure
6. Oil quantity
7. Coolant temperature
8. Outside ambient temperature
9. Windshield washer fluid quantity
10. Brake fluid quantity

In addition to these variables, the input may include switches for detecting open doors and trunk, as well as IP selection switches for multifunction displays that permit the driver to select from various display modes or measurement units. For example, the driver may be able to select vehicle speed in miles per hour (mph) or kilometers per hour (kph).

An important function of modern instrumentation systems is to receive diagnostic information from certain subsystems and to display appropriate warning messages to the driver. The powertrain control system, for example, continuously performs self-diagnosis operations (see Chapter 10). If a problem has been detected, a fault code is set indicating the nature and location of the fault. This code is transmitted to the instrumentation system via a powertrain digital data line (PDDL in Figure 9.2). This code is interpreted in the instrumentation computer and a "Check Engine" warning message is

Figure 9.2
Computer-Based Instrumentation System

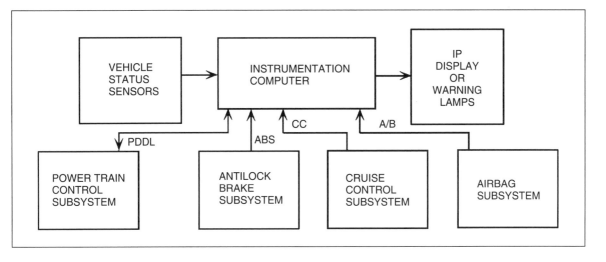

displayed. Similar diagnostic data are sent to the instrumentation system from each of the subsystems for which driver warning messages are deemed necessary (e.g., ABS, airbag, cruise control). The way in which a fault is detected is explained in greater detail in Chapter 10.

INPUT AND OUTPUT SIGNAL CONVERSION

Most sensors provide an analog output, whereas computers require digital inputs. A/D converters convert analog signals to digital codes appropriate for signal processing by the computer.

It should be emphasized that any single input can be either digital switched or analog, depending on the technology used for the sensor. A typical instrumentation computer is an integrated subsystem that is designed to accept all of these input formats. A typical system is designed with a separate input from each sensor or switch. An example of an analog input is the fuel quantity sensor, which is normally a potentiometer attached to a float, as described in detail later in this chapter. The measurement of vehicle speed given in Chapter 8 is an example of a measurement that is already in digital format.

The analog inputs must all be converted to digital format using an analog to digital (A/D) converter as explained in Chapter 4 and illustrated in Figure 9.3. The digital inputs are, of course, already in the desired format. The conversion process requires an amount of time that depends primarily on the A/D converter. After the conversion is complete, the digital output generated by the A/D converter is the closest possible approximation to the equivalent analog voltage, using an M-bit binary number (where M is chosen by the designer and is normally between 8 and 32). The A/D converter then signals

**Figure 9.3
Analog-to-Digital
Conversion**

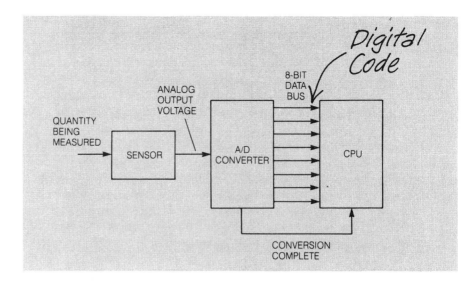

the computer by changing the logic state on a separate lead (labeled "conversion complete" in Figure 9.3) that is connected to the computer. (Recall the use of interrupts for this purpose, as discussed in Chapter 4.) The output voltage of each analog sensor for which the computer performs signal processing must be converted in this way. Once the conversion is complete, the digital output is transferred into a register in the computer. If the output is to drive a digital display, this output can be used directly. However, if an analog display is used, the binary number must be converted to the appropriate analog signal by using a digital-to-analog (D/A) converter (see Chapter 4).

When an analog output signal is required to drive an analog display, a D/A converter is used. The D/A converter generates a voltage that is proportional to the binary number that the computer sends to the converter.

Figure 9.4 illustrates a typical D/A converter used to transform digital computer output to an analog signal. The eight digital output leads ($M = 8$ in this example) transfer the results of the signal processing to a D/A converter. When the transfer is complete, the computer signals the D/A converter to start converting. The D/A output generates a voltage that is proportional to the binary number in the computer output. A low-pass filter (which could be as simple as a capacitor) is often connected across the D/A output to smooth the analog output between samples. The sampling of the sensor output, A/D conversion, digital signal processing, and D/A conversion all take place during the time slot allotted for the measurement of the variable in a sampling time sequence, to be discussed shortly.

**Figure 9.4
Digital-to-Analog
Conversion**

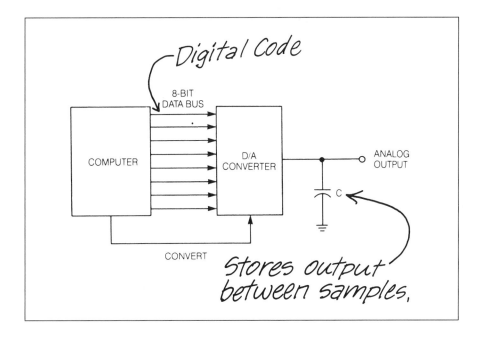

Multiplexing

The computer monitors each sensor individually and provides output signals to its display component before going on to another sensor.

Of course, the computer can only deal with the measurement of a single quantity at any one time. Therefore, the computer input must be connected to only one sensor at a time, and the computer output must be connected only to the corresponding display. The computer performs any necessary signal processing on a particular sensor signal and then generates an output signal to the appropriate display device.

In Figure 9.5 the various sensor outputs and display inputs are connected to a pair of multiposition rotary switches—one for the input and one for the output of the computer. The switches are functionally connected such that they rotate together. Whenever the input switch connects the computer input to the appropriate sensor for measuring some quantity, the output switch connects the computer output to the corresponding display or warning device. Thus, with the switches in a specific position, the automotive instrumentation system corresponds to the block diagram shown in Figure 9.1. At that instant of time, the entire system is devoted to measurement of the quantity corresponding to the given switch position.

**Figure 9.5
Input/Output
Switching Scheme for
Sampling**

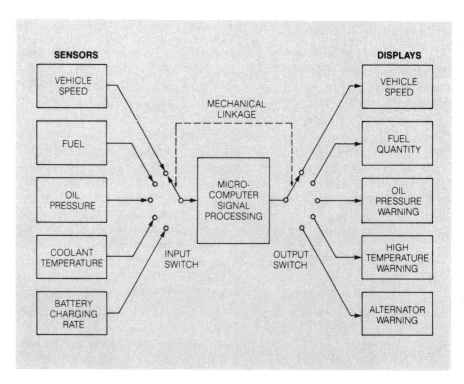

The switching of sensor and display inputs is performed with solid-state switches known as multiplexers; output switching is performed by demultiplexers.

Typically, the computer controls the input and output switching operation. However, instead of a mechanical switch as shown in Figure 9.5, the actual switching is done by means of a solid-state electronic switching device called a *multiplexer* (MUX) that selects one of several inputs for each output. Multiplexing can be done either with analog or digital signals. Figure 9.6 illustrates a digital MUX configuration. Here it is assumed that there are four inputs to the MUX (corresponding to data from four sensors). It is further presumed that the data are available in 8-bit digital format. Each of the multiplexers selects a single bit from each of the four inputs.

**Figure 9.6
Data Multiplexer**

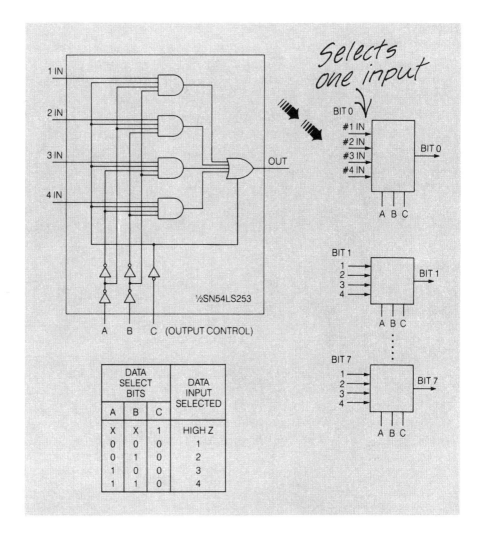

DATA SELECT BITS			DATA INPUT SELECTED
A	B	C	
X	X	1	HIGH Z
0	0	0	1
0	1	0	2
1	0	0	3
1	1	0	4

There must be eight such MUX circuits, each supplying one data bit. The output lines from each MUX are connected to a corresponding data bus line in the digital computer (see Chapter 4). Similarly, the output switching (which is often called demultiplexing, or DEMUX) is performed with a MUX connected in reverse, as shown in Figure 9.7. The MUX and DEMUX selection is controlled by the computer. Note that in Figures 9.6 and 9.7, each bit of the digital code is multiplexed and demultiplexed.

Figure 9.7
Data Demultiplexer

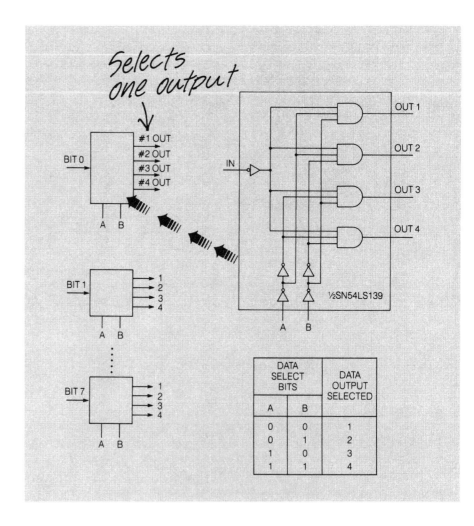

DATA SELECT BITS		DATA OUTPUT SELECTED
A	B	
0	0	1
0	1	2
1	0	3
1	1	4

SAMPLING

The measurement of any quantity takes place only when the input and output switches (MUX and DEMUX) functionally connect the corresponding sensor and display to the computer, respectively. There are several variables to be measured and displayed, but only one variable can be accommodated at any given instant. Once a quantity has been measured, the system must wait until the other variables have been measured before that particular variable is measured again. This process of measuring a quantity intermittently is called *sampling*, and the time between successive samples of the same quantity is called the *sample period*, as explained in Chapter 2.

One possible scheme for measuring several variables by this process is to sample each quantity sequentially, giving each measurement a fixed time slot, *t*, out of the total sample period, *T*, as illustrated in Figure 9.8. This method is satisfactory as long as the sample period is small compared with the time in which any quantity changes appreciably. Certain quantities, such as coolant temperature and fuel quantity, change very slowly with time. For such variables, a sample period of a few seconds or longer is often adequate.

On the other hand, variables such as vehicle speed, battery charge, and fuel consumption rate change relatively quickly and require a much shorter sample period, perhaps every second or every few tenths of a second. To accommodate the various rates of change of the automotive variables being measured, the sample period varies from one quantity to another. The most rapidly changing quantities are sampled with a very short sample period, whereas those that change slowly are sampled with a long sample period.

In addition to sample period, the time slot allotted for each quantity must be long enough to complete the measurement and any A/D or D/A

**Figure 9.8
Sequential Sampling**

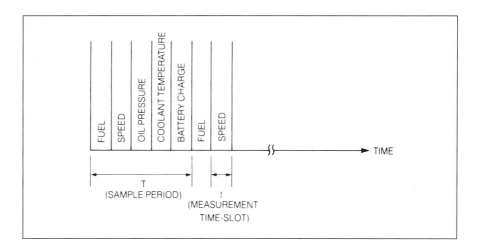

conversion required. The computer program is designed with all of these factors in mind so that adequate time slots and sample periods are allowed for each variable. The computer then simply follows the program schedule.

Advantages of Computer-Based Instrumentation

One of the big advantages of computer-based instrumentation is its great flexibility. To change from the instrumentation for one vehicle or one model to another requires only a change of computer program. This change can often be implemented by replacing one ROM (read-only memory) with another. Remember that the program is permanently stored in a ROM that is typically packaged in a single integrated circuit package (see Chapter 4).

Computer-based instrumentation is more accurate and, due to the computer's program, more easily changed than conventional instrumentation.

Another benefit of microcomputer-based electronic automotive instrumentation is its improved performance compared with conventional instrumentation. For example, the conventional fuel gauge system has errors that are associated with variations in the mechanical and geometrical characteristics of the tank, the sender unit, the instrument voltage regulator, and the indicator (galvanometer). The electronic instrumentation system eliminates the error that results from imperfect voltage regulation. Generally speaking, the electronic fuel quantity measurement maintains calibration over essentially the entire range of automotive electrical system conditions. Moreover, it significantly improves the display accuracy by replacing the electromechanical galvanometer display with an all-electronic digital display.

FUEL QUANTITY MEASUREMENT

Some fuel quantity sensors use a float within the fuel tank; the float is mechanically linked to a potentiometer that operates as a voltage divider.

During a measurement of fuel quantity, the MUX switch functionally connects the computer input to the fuel quantity sensor, as shown in Figure 9.9. This sensor output is converted to digital format and then sent to the computer for signal processing. (*Note:* In some automotive systems the analog sensor output is sent to the instrumentation subsystem, where the A/D conversion takes place.)

Several fuel quantity sensor configurations are available. Figure 9.10 illustrates the type of sensor to be described, which is a potentiometer connected via mechanical linkage to a float. Normally, the sensor is mounted so that the float remains laterally near the center of the tank for all fuel levels. A constant current passes through the sensor potentiometer, since it is connected directly across the regulated voltage source. The potentiometer is used as a voltage divider so that the voltage at the wiper arm is related to the float position, which is determined by fuel level.

The sensor output voltage is not directly proportional to fuel quantity in gallons because of the complex shape of the fuel tank. The computer memory contains the functional relationship between sensor voltage (in binary

**Figure 9.9
Fuel Quantity
Measurement**

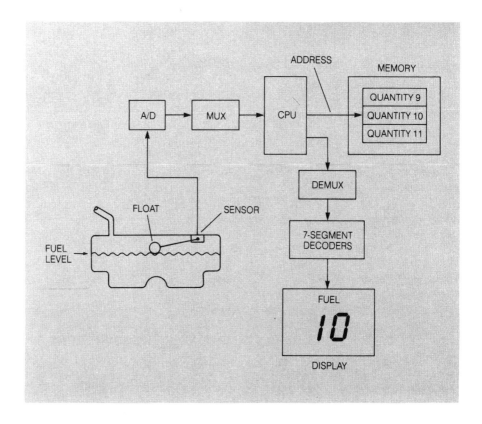

**Figure 9.10
Fuel Quantity Sensor**

*Voltage level
represents
fuel level.*

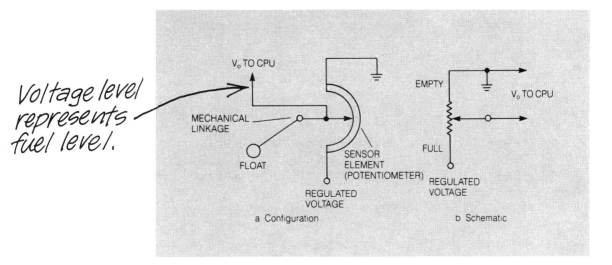

number equivalent) and fuel quantity for the particular fuel tank used on the vehicle.

The computer reads the binary number from the A/D converter that corresponds to sensor voltage and uses it to address a particular memory location. Another binary number corresponding to the actual fuel quantity in gallons for that sensor voltage is stored in that memory location. The computer then uses the number from memory to generate the appropriate display signal—either analog or digital, depending on display type—and sends that signal via DEMUX to the display.

Computer-based signal processing can also compensate for fuel slosh. As the car moves over the road, the fuel sloshes about and the float moves up and down around the average position that corresponds to the correct level for a stationary vehicle. The computer compensates for slosh by computing a running average. It does this by storing several samples over a few seconds and computing the arithmetic average of the sensor output. The oldest samples are continually discarded as new samples are obtained. The averaged output becomes the signal that drives the display. It should be noted that this is actually a form of digital filtering.

The computer compensates for fuel slosh by averaging float sensor readings over a period of time.

COOLANT TEMPERATURE MEASUREMENT

Another important automotive parameter that is measured by the instrumentation is the coolant temperature. The measurement of this quantity is different from that of fuel quantity because usually it is not important for the driver to know the actual temperature at all times. For safe operation of the engine, the driver only needs to know that the coolant temperature is less than a critical value. A block diagram of the measuring system is shown in Figure 9.11.

The coolant temperature sensor used in most cars is a solid-state sensor called a *thermistor*. Recall that this type of sensor was discussed in Chapter 6, where it was shown that the resistance of this sensor decreases with increasing temperature. Figure 9.12 shows the circuit connection and a sketch of a typical sensor output voltage versus temperature curve.

To measure coolant temperature, the sensor output from a thermistor is converted into a digital signal and compared to a maximum safe value stored in memory.

The sensor output voltage is sampled during the appropriate time slot and is converted to a binary number equivalent by the A/D converter. The computer compares this binary number to the one stored in memory that corresponds to the high temperature limit. If the coolant temperature exceeds the limit, an output signal is generated that activates the warning indicator. If the limit is not exceeded, the output signal is not generated and the warning message is not activated. A proportional display of actual temperature can be used if the memory contains a cross-reference table between sensor output voltage and the corresponding temperature, similar to that described for the fuel quantity table.

**Figure 9.11
Coolant Temperature
Measurement**

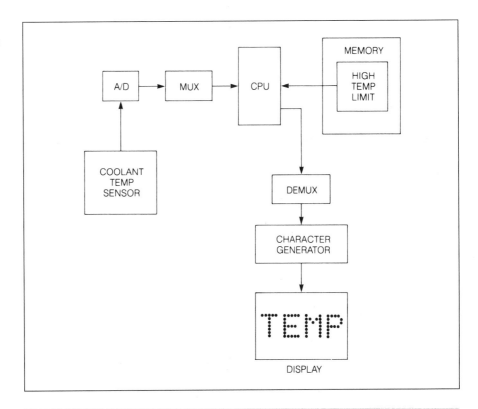

**Figure 9.12
Coolant Temperature
Sensor**

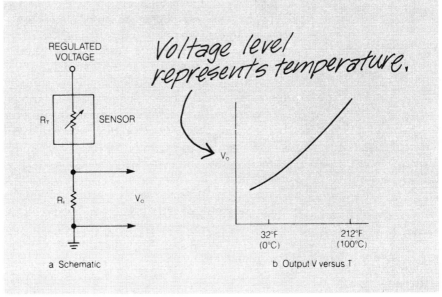

a Schematic

b Output V versus T

OIL PRESSURE MEASUREMENT

Oil pressure warning systems use a variable-resistance sensor as part of a voltage divider. This arrangement provides a varying voltage that corresponds to changes in oil pressure.

Engine oil pressure measurement is similar to coolant temperature measurement in that it uses a warning message display rather than an indicated numerical value. Whenever the oil pressure is outside allowable limits, a warning message is displayed to the driver. In the case of oil pressure, it is important for the driver to know whenever the oil pressure falls below a lower limit. It is also possible for the oil pressure to go above an allowable upper limit; however, many manufacturers do not include a high oil pressure warning in the instrumentation.

The simplest oil pressure warning system involves a spring-loaded switch connected to a diaphragm. The switch assembly is mounted in one of the oil passageways such that the diaphragm is exposed directly to the oil pressure. The force developed on the diaphragm by the oil pressure is sufficient to overcome the spring and to hold the switch open as long as the oil pressure exceeds the lower limit. Whenever the oil pressure falls below this limit the spring force is sufficient to close the switch. Switch closure is used to switch on the low oil pressure warning message lamp.

One of the deficiences of this simple switch-based oil pressure warning system is that it has a single fixed low oil pressure limit. In fact, the threshold oil pressure for safe operation varies with engine load. Whereas a relatively low oil pressure can protect bearing surfaces at low loads (e.g., at idle), a proportionately higher oil pressure threshold is required with increasing load (i.e., increasing horsepower and RPM).

An oil pressure instrument that operates with a load- or speed-dependent threshold requires an oil pressure sensor rather than a switch. Such an oil pressure warning system is illustrated in Figure 9.13. This system uses a variable-resistance oil pressure sensor such as seen in Figure 9.14. A voltage is developed across a fixed resistance connected in series with the sensor that is proportional to oil pressure. It should be noted that this assumed pressure sensor is hypothetical and used only for illustrative purposes.

During the measurement time slot, the oil pressure sensor voltage is sampled through the MUX switch and converted to a binary number in the A/D converter. The computer reads this binary number and compares it with the binary number in memory for the allowed oil pressure limits. The oil pressure limit is determined from load or crankshaft speed measurements that are already available in the engine control system. These measurement data can be sent to the instrument subsystem via the PDDL (see Figure 9.1). These measurements serve as the address for a ROM lookup table to find the oil pressure limit. If the oil pressure is below the allowed lower limit or above the allowed upper limit, an output signal is generated that activates the oil pressure warning light through the DEMUX.

It is also possible to use a proportional display of actual oil pressure if a cross-reference table, similar to the fuel quantity table, is used. A digital display

**Figure 9.13
Oil Pressure
Measurement**

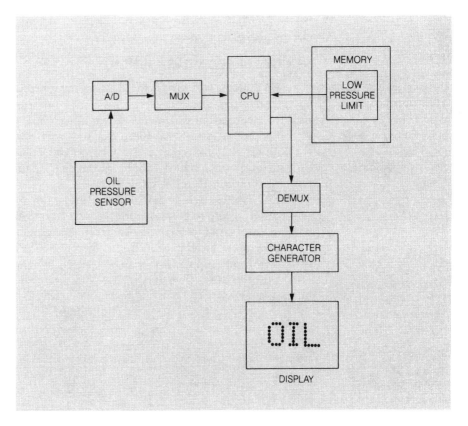

**Figure 9.14
Oil Pressure Sensor**

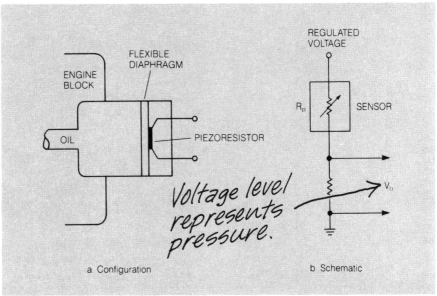

a. Configuration

b. Schematic

can be driven directly from the computer. An analog display, such as the electric gauge, requires a D/A converter.

VEHICLE SPEED MEASUREMENT

Digital measurement of vehicle speed is possible using a binary counter and a sensor having an output signal frequency that is proportional to speed.

An example of a digital speed sensor has already been described in Chapter 8 for a cruise control system. A sensor of this type is assumed to be used for car speed measurements. The output of this sensor is a binary number, P, that is proportional to car speed S. This binary number is contained in the output of a binary counter (see Chapter 8). A block diagram of the instrumentation for vehicle speed measurement that uses this digital speed sensor is shown in Figure 9.15.

The computer reads the number P in the binary counter, then resets the counter to zero to prepare it for the next count. After performing computations and filtering, the computer generates a signal for the display to indicate the vehicle speed. A digital display can be directly driven by the computer. Either mph or kph may be selected. If an analog display is used, a D/A converter must drive the display. Both mph and kph usually are calibrated on an analog scale.

**Figure 9.15
Vehicle Speed
Measurement**

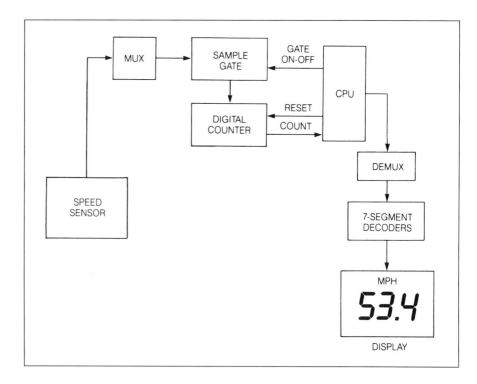

DISPLAY DEVICES

One of the most important components of any measuring instrument is the display device. In automotive instrumentation, the display device must present the results of the measurement to the driver in a form that is easy to read and understand. The speedometer, ammeter, and fuel quantity gauge were originally electromechanical devices. Then automotive manufacturers began using warning lamps instead of gauges to cut cost. A warning lamp can be considered as a type of electro-optical display.

Electromechanical and simple electro-optical displays are being replaced by sophisticated electronic displays that provide the driver with numeric or alphabetic information.

Recent developments in solid-state technology in the field called opto-electronics have led to sophisticated electro-optical display devices that are capable of indicating alphanumeric data. This means that both numeric and alphabetic information can be used to display the results of measurements of automotive variables or parameters. This capability allows messages in English or other languages to be given to the driver. The input for these devices is an electronic digital signal, which makes these devices compatible with computer-based instrumentation, whereas electromechanical displays require a D/A converter.

Automobile manufacturers have considered many different types of electronic displays for automotive instrumentation, but only four have been really practical: light-emitting diode (LED), liquid crystal (LCD), vacuum-fluorescent (VFD), and the cathode ray tube (CRT). It now appears that the VFD will be the predominant type of instrumentation for at least the near future. Each of these types is discussed briefly to explain their uses in automotive applications.

LED

LEDs are solid-state devices that emit light when current is passed through the diode. LEDs are difficult to view in bright sunlight.

The light-emitting diode is a semiconductor diode that is constructed in a manner and of a material so that light is emitted when an electrical current is passed through it. The semiconductor material most often used for an LED that emits red light is gallium arsenide phosphide. Light is emitted at the diode's PN junction when the positive carriers combine with the negative carriers at the junction (see Chapter 3 for a discussion of PN junctions). The diode is constructed so that the light generated at the junction can escape from the diode and be seen.

An LED display is normally made of small dots or rectangular segments arranged so that numbers and letters can be formed when selected dots or segments are turned on. The configuration for these segments is described in greater detail later in this chapter in the section on VFD. A single LED is not well suited for automotive display use because of its low brightness. Although it can be seen easily in darkness, it is difficult to impossible to see in bright sunlight. It also requires more electrical power than an LCD display; however, its power requirements are not great enough to be a problem for automotive use.

LCD

LCDs use a liquid that possesses the ability to rotate the polarization of polarized light. LCD displays have low power requirements.

The LCD display is commonly used in electronic digital watch displays because of its extremely low electrical power and relatively low voltage requirements. The heart of an LCD is a special liquid that is called a *twisted nematic liquid crystal*. This liquid has the capability of rotating the polarization of linearly polarized light. Linearly polarized light has all of the vibrations of the optical waves in the same direction. Light from the sun and from most artificial light sources is not polarized, and the waves vibrate randomly in many directions.

Nonpolarized light can be polarized by passing the light through a polarizing material. To illustrate, think of a picket fence with narrow gaps between the pickets. If a rope is passed between two of the pickets and its end is whipped up and down, the ripples in the rope will pass through the fence. The ripples represent light waves and the picket fence represents a polarizing material. If you whip the rope in any direction other than vertically, the ripples will not pass through.

Now visualize another picket fenced turned 90° so that the pickets are horizontal. Place this fence behind the vertical picket fence. This arrangement is called a cross-polarizer. If the rope is now whipped in any direction, no ripples will pass through both fences. Similarly, if a cross-polarizer is used for light, no light will pass through this structure.

The configuration of an LCD can be understood from the schematic drawings of Figure 9.16. The liquid crystal is sandwiched between a pair of glass plates that have transparent, electrically conductive coatings. The transparent conductor is deposited on the front glass plate in the form of the character, or segment of a character, that is to be displayed. Next, a layer of dielectric (insulating) material is coated on the glass plate to produce the desired alignment of the liquid crystal molecules. The polarization of the molecules is vertical at the front, and they gradually rotate through the liquid crystal structure until the molecules at the back are horizontally polarized. Thus, the molecules of the liquid crystal rotate 90° from the front plate to the back plate so that their polarization matches that of the front and back polarizers with no voltage applied.

When current is not being applied to an LCD display, light entering the crystal is polarized by the front polarizer, rotated, passed through the rear polarizer, and then reflected off the reflector.

The operation of the LCD in the absence of applied voltage can be understood with reference to Figure 9.17a. Ambient light enters through the front polarizer so that the light entering the front plate is vertically polarized. As it passes through the liquid crystal, the light polarization is changed by the orientation of the molecules. When the light reaches the back of the crystal, its polarization has been rotated 90° so that it is horizontally polarized. The light is reflected from the reflector at the rear. It passes back through the liquid crystal structure, the polarization again being rotated, and passes out of the front polarizer. Thus, a viewer sees reflected ambient light.

**Figure 9.16
Typical LCD
Construction**

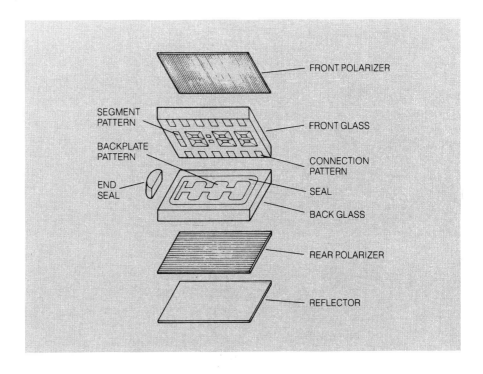

When a voltage is applied to a display segment, the crystal's molecules change and do not rotate the polarized light. Since the light cannot align with the rear polarizer, it is not reflected and the segment appears dark.

The effect of an applied voltage to the transmission of light through this device can be understood from Figure 9.17b. A voltage applied to any of the segments of the display causes the liquid crystal molecules under those segments only to be aligned in a straight line rather than twisted. In this case, the light that enters the liquid crystal in the vicinity of the segments passes through the crystal structure without the polarization being rotated. Since the light has been vertically polarized by the front vertical polarizing plate, the light is blocked by the horizontal polarizer so it cannot reach the reflector. Thus, light that enters the cell in the vicinity of energized segments is not returned to the front face. These segments will appear dark to the viewer, the surrounding area will be light, and the segments will be visible in the presence of ambient light.

The LCD is an excellent display device because of its low power requirement and relatively low cost. However, a big disadvantage of the LCD for automotive application is the need for an external light source for viewing in the dark. Its characteristic is just the opposite of the LED; that is, the LCD is readable in the daytime, but not at night. For night driving, the display must be illuminated by small lamps inside the display. Another disadvantage is that the display does not work well at the low temperatures that are encountered

Figure 9.17
Liquid Crystal Polarization

Only pass light in a specific direction.

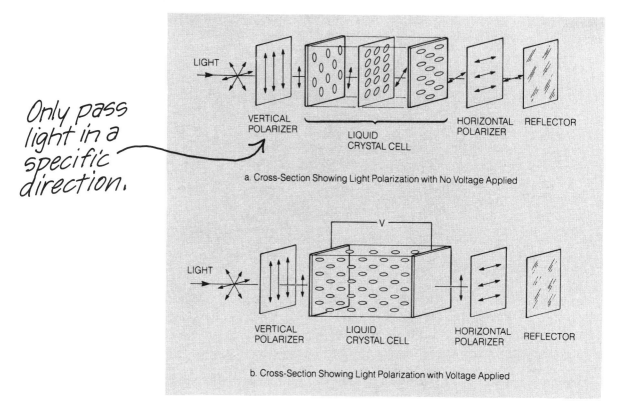

a. Cross-Section Showing Light Polarization with No Voltage Applied

b. Cross-Section Showing Light Polarization with Voltage Applied

during winter driving in some areas. These characteristics of the LCD have limited its use in automotive instrumentation.

Transmissive LCD

An LCD display can also function as an optical transmission device from a light source at the rear of the structure to the front face. A configuration such as this permits an LCD to display messages in low ambient light conditions (e.g., night time). In low ambient light conditions, a reflective LCD does not provide a visible display to the driver. The intensity of the back light is automatically adjusted to produce optimum illumination as a function of the signal from an ambient light-even sensor located inside the passenger compartment.

Some display manufacturers produce an LCD that combines reflective and transmissive structures in a so-called transflexive LCD structure. The combination of these two basic LCD types into using a package permits optimal readability to be achieved for automotive displays over the entire range of ambient light conditions from bright sunny days to the darkest night conditions.

Another evolution of LCD technology has permitted automotive displays to be available in multiple colors. The LCD configuration described above is a black and white display. A suitable color filter placed in front of the mirror in a reflective LCD or in front of the back light in a transmissive LCD yields a color display, with the color being determined by the optical filter.

Still another evolution in LCD technology is the development of a very large array of programmable multicolor display. Such displays are capable of presenting complex programmable alphanumeric messages to the driver and can also present graphical data or pictorial displays (e.g., electronic maps). Since the array structure LCD is functionally similar to the cathode ray tube, a detailed discussion of this array type is deferred to the section of this book devoted to CRT display.

VFD

VFDs use a phosphor (a material that emits light when bombarded by electrons). VFDs provide readability over a wide range of conditions.

The VFD display has been widely used in automotive instrumentation, although the multicolor LCD is becoming the preferred choice for this application. This device generates light in much the same way as a television picture tube does; that is, a material called phosphor emits light when it is bombarded by energetic electrons. The display uses a filament coated with material that generates free electrons when the filament is heated. The electrons are accelerated toward the anode by a relatively high voltage. When these high-speed electrons strike the phosphor on the anode, the phosphor emits light. A common VFD has a phosphor that emits a blue-green light that provides good readability in the wide range of ambient light conditions that are present in an automobile. However, other colors (e.g., red or yellow) are available by using other phosphors.

The numeric characters are formed by shaping the anode segments in the form of a standard seven-segment character. The basic structure of a typical VFD is depicted in Figure 9.18. The filament is a special type of resistance wire and is heated by passing an electrical current through it. The coating on the heated filament produces free electrons that are accelerated by the electric field produced by a voltage on the accelerating grid. This grid consists of a fine wire mesh that allows the electrons to pass through. The electrons pass through because they are attracted to the anode, which has a higher voltage than the grid. The high voltage is applied only to the anode of the segments needed to form the character to be displayed. The instrumentation computer selects the set of segments that are to emit light for any given message.

VFD brightness can be controlled by varying the voltage on the accelerator grid.

Since the ambient light in an automobile varies between sunlight and darkness, it is desirable to adjust the brightness of the display in accordance with the ambient light. The brightness is controlled by varying the voltage on the accelerating grid. The higher the voltage, the greater the energy of the

**Figure 9.18
Simplified Vacuum-
Fluorescent Display
Configuration**

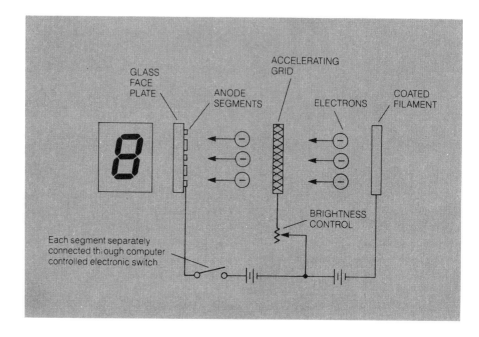

electrons striking the phosphor and the brighter the light. Figure 9.19 shows the brightness characteristics for a typical VFD device. A brightness of 200 fL (foot-lamberts) might be selected on a bright sunny day, whereas the brightness might be only 20 fL at night. The brightness can be set manually by the driver, or automatically. In the latter case, a photoresistor is used to vary the grid voltage in accordance with the amount of ambient light. A photoresistor is a device whose resistance varies in proportion to the amount of light striking it.

The VFD operates with relatively low power and operates over a wide temperature range. The most serious drawback for automotive application is its susceptibility to failure due to vibration and mechanical shock. However, this problem can be reduced by mounting the display on a shock-absorbing isolation mount.

CRT

The display devices that have been discussed to this point have one rather serious limitation. The characters that can be displayed are limited to those symbols that can be approximated by the segments that can be illuminated. Furthermore, illuminated warning messages such as "Check Engine" or "Oil Pressure" are *fixed* messages that are either displayed or not, depending on the engine conditions. The primary disadvantage of such ad hoc display devices is the limited flexibility of the displayed messages.

**Figure 9.19
Brightness Control
Range for
Vacuum-Fluorescent
Display**

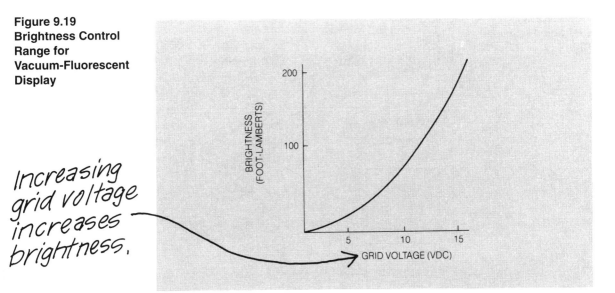

Increasing grid voltage increases brightness.

The cathode ray tube (CRT) is similar to a TV picture tube and was widely used in personal computers (monitor). The CTR and, more importantly, its solid-state equivalent have great potential for automotive display applications.

Arguably the display device with the greatest flexibility for presenting all types of data (including pictorial representations) is the cathode ray tube (CRT). The CRT is familiar to us all as the TV picture tube although it has also been used for personal computer monitors. Recently a solid state equivalent to the CRT has been developed that yields a flat panel display having all of the display capabilities of the CRT.

The CRT (or its solid-state equivalent) is being used increasingly for display purposes in the aerospace industry, where it is used to display aircraft attitude information (sometimes pictorially), aircraft engine or airframe parameters, navigational data, and warning messages. Clearly, the CRT-type display has great potential for automotive instrumentation display.

A technology that has the same flexibility of display as the CRT is the solid-state equivalent of a CRT. Such a display is sometimes called a *flat-panel display*. However, as it is functionally equivalent to the CRT and as the CRT is an existing, very mature technology, we first explain the CRT operation example. This solid-state equivalent of the CRT can be implemented in a number of technologies such as an LCD array.

Figure 9.20 is a sketch of a typical black and white CRT. It is an evacuated glass tube that has a nominally flat surface that is coated with a phosphorescent material. This surface is the surface or face on which the displayed messages appear. At the rear is a somewhat complex structure called

Figure 9.20a
CRT and Associated
Circuitry

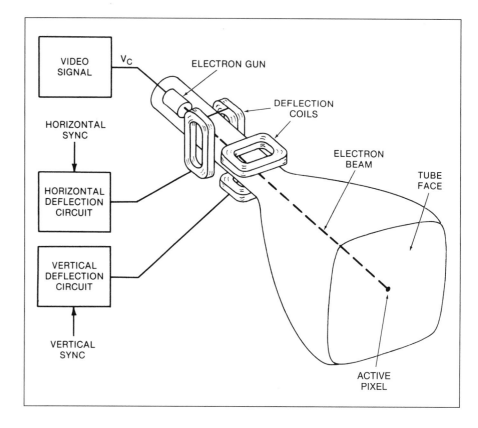

an *electron gun*. This device generates a stream of electrons that is accelerated toward the screen and brought to convergence at a spot on the screen. A system of coils in the form of electromagnets causes this convergence of electrons (or beam) and is referred to as the *magnetic focusing system*. The focused stream of electrons is called the *beam*.

The electron beam generates a spot of light at the point on the screen. The intensity of the light is proportional to the electron beam current. This current is controlled by the voltage (V_c), which is called the *video signal*, on an electrode that is located near the electron gun. A color CRT has three separate electron gun structures, with each focused on one of three dots at each picture location on the screen corresponding to red green blue (RGB).

A solid-state LCD display consists of an array of LCDs arranged in a matrix format as depicted in Figure 9.20b. In this structure, only one LCD is active at any time. The color and intensity of the active LCD is controlled by circuitry connected within the microstructure. The active LCD is selected via horizontal and vertical detection circuitry. In the solid-state CRT equivalent, each pixel has its own address.

**Figure 9.20b
Solid-State CRT**

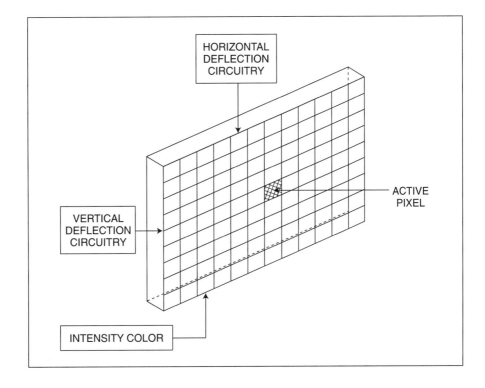

In the majority of applications (including TV), the CRT electron beam is scanned in a pattern known as a *raster* by means of specially located electromagnets (see Figure 9.20). The magnetic fields created by the scanning coils deflect the beam horizontally and vertically. The amount of deflection is proportional to the current flowing through the respective coils. The raster pattern traced by the beam is illustrated on the face of the CRT in Figure 9.21. The raster begins at the upper left of the screen and sweeps rapidly to the right. During this scan, the intensity of each electron gun varies in proportion to the brightness (of each color) to be illuminated at each picture element (known as a pixel). The next line in the raster begins at the left of the screen slightly below the previous line. The standard raster for U.S. television consists of 525 lines completed 30 times per second.

The scanning motion is done in synchronism with the source of information being displayed. At the end of each horizontal scan line, a synchronizing pulse (called *horizontal sync*) causes the beam to deflect rapidly to the left and then to begin scanning at a constant rate to the right. A similar synchronizing pulse is generated at a time when the beam is at the bottom of the CRT. This pulse (called *vertical sync*) causes the beam to deflect rapidly to the top of the CRT face and then to begin scanning downward at a uniform speed.

**Figure 9.21
Raster Pattern**

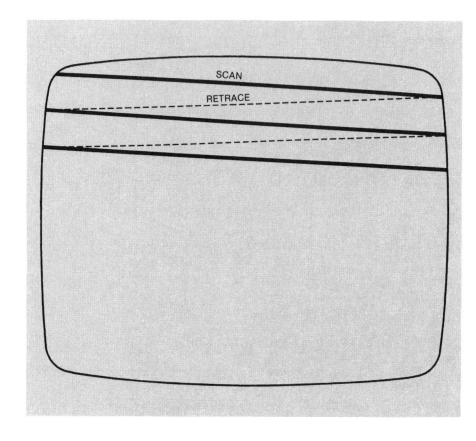

Scan Circuits

The raster scan for a CRT is accomplished by varying the current through the horizontal and vertical deflection coils (i.e., HDC and VDC). At the beginning of each horizontal line, the current through the HDC is such that the electron beam is at the left edge of the CRT face (as viewed from the front). Then this current increases with time such that the beam sweeps uniformly from left to right. At the time the beam is at the right edge, the current rapidly (ideally instantaneously) switches to the value corresponding to the left edge, and the scanning continues periodically. A graph of the beam horizontal position with respect to time resembles a sawtooth pattern and is called a sawtooth waveform. The frequency of this horizontal sweep signal (U.S. standard) is 15,750 Hz.

A similar sweep circuit causes the CRT beam to deflect verticall so that the entire screen is covered in $\frac{1}{30}$ sec. In actual fact, even number horizontal traces are scanned in $\frac{1}{60}$ sec and odd number lines in the next $\frac{1}{60}$ sec in a process called interlacing.

The horizontal and vertical signals can be generated using either analog or digital circuits, although modern CRT circuits are digital. One conceptually simple way to generate the horizontal and vertical sawtooth sweep waveforms uses a constant-frequency oscillator driving the trickle count input of a counter circuitry and digital-to-analog converter circuitry (see Chapter 3). Each cycle of the oscillator causes the counter to increment by one. In CRT systems, the counter output drives an A/D converter, creating an output signal having the required sawtooth waveform. The lowest count yields a current corresponding to the left edge of the CRT screen. The counter is automatically reset to this value once the electron beam position is at the right edge of the screen (controlled by horizontal synch pulses). Similar circuitry exists to drive vertical deflection.

Deflection of a solid-state (e.g., LCD) equivalent of the CRT is dependent on the wiring arrangement of the individual LCD elements. One scheme for achieving a solid-state raster scan display device is to construct an array of LCD elements as depicted in Figure 9.20b. These elements are interconnected with two grids of wires, one running vertically and one running horizontally. Each vertical wire is connected to all of the LCD elements in a given column. Each horizontal wire similarly interconnects all of the LCD elements in a given row.

A given LCD element (forming one pixel of the display) is activated by an electrical signal applied to the vertical wire associated with its column and the horizontal wire associated with its row. Scanning along a given row is achieved by sending an appropriate signal to the wire associated with that row and then sequentially sending a similar signal to the wire corresponding to a column.

Circuitry for raster scanning this type of LCD array can be implemented with a constant frequency oscillator and counter (similar to the CRT circuitry). However, instead of using an analog/digital converter, the solid-state scanning circuitry uses decoding logic that activates one of its many leads corresponding to the digital count in the counter. This latter circuitry has a separate output for each grid wire in the horizontal scan or vertical scan, respectively.

A typical solid-state raster scan display might have 240 rows and 480 columns of LCD elements. The horizontal decoding circuit has 480 separate outputs, each connected to a column grid wire. The horizontal counter has a maximum count of 480. Similarly, the vertical decoder has 240 output leads each connected to a row grid wire.

The intensity and/or color of the active LCD is controlled by a signal connected to that LCD. The appropriate signal is known as the video signal.

In a typical CRT or solid-state equivalent display device, the video voltage and sync pulses are generated in a special circuit called the *CRT controller*. A simplified block diagram for a system incorporating a CRT type display with the associated controller is depicted in Figure 9.22. The sensors and instrumentation computer, which are microprocessor (MPU) based, shown at the left of this illustration have the same function as the

In automotive instrumentation applications, a CRT display is driven by a special electronics system called the CRT controller.

**Figure 9.22
Automotive CRT
Instrumentation
System**

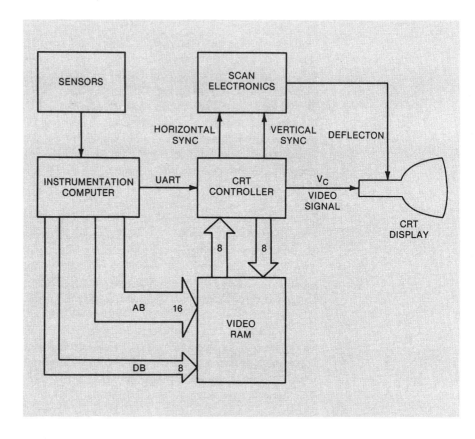

corresponding components of the system in Figure 9.2. The output of the instrumentation computer controls the CRT type display, working through the controller. The functional structure of the display is the same regardless of whether the display is a CRT or the solid-state equivalent.

In the example architecture of Figure 9.22, it is assumed that the instrumentation computer communicates with the CRT controller via data and address buses (DB and AB), and via a serial link along a line labeled UART (universal asynchronous receiver/transmitter). However, many other choices of data link are possible. The data that are sent over the DB are stored in a special memory called video RAM. This memory stores digital data that are to be displayed in alphanumeric or pictorial patterns on the CRT-type screen. The controller obtains data from the video RAM and converts them to the relevant video signal (V_c). At the same time, the controller generates the horizontal and vertical sync necessary to operate the raster scan in synchronism with the video signal.

The video controller in the example system (Figure 9.23) itself incorporates an MPU for controlling the CRT-type display. The data to be

**Figure 9.23
CRT-Type Controller
Configuration**

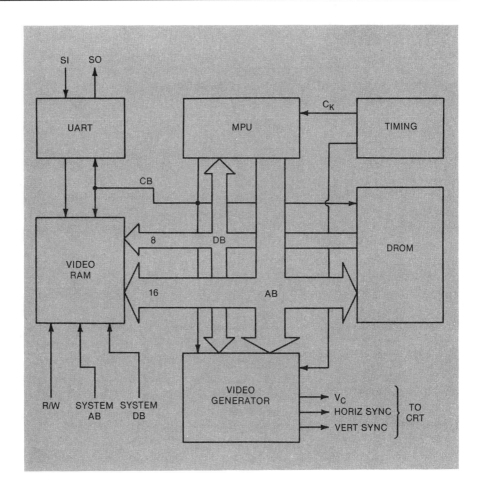

displayed are stored in the video RAM via the system buses under control of the instrumentation computer. The operation of the MPU is controlled by programs stored in a display ROM (DROM). This ROM might also store data that are required to generate particular characters. The various components of the display controller are internally connected by means of data and address buses similar to those used in the instrumentation computer.

The operation of the display controller is under control of the instrumentation computer. This computer transfers data that are to be displayed to the video RAM, and signals the CRT controller via the UART link. During the display time, the MPU operates under control of programs stored in the DROM. These programs cause the MPU to transfer data from the video RAM to the video generator in the correct sequence for display.

The details of the transfer of data to the video generator and the corresponding generation of video signals vary from system to system. In the

**Figure 9.24
Display of Characters
F and P**

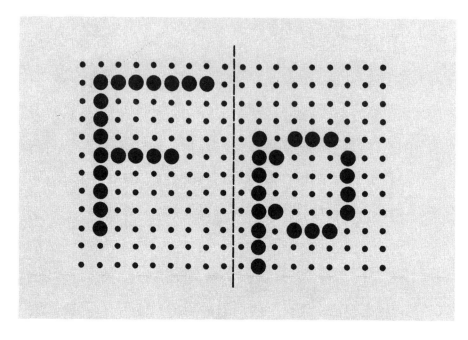

hypothetical system seen in Figure 9.22, the display is assumed to be an array of LCD elements arranged in 240 rows vertically by 480 columns horizontally. Here the display generates the characters F and P (see Figure 9.24). The dots are generated by switching on the active LCD element at the desired location. The LCD is switched by pulsing the video voltage at the time relative to the row and column of the active LCD at which a dot is to appear. The resolution of the display is one dot, which is often termed a picture element (i.e., a pixel).

A scheme for generating the suitable video signals for such a display is shown in a greatly simplified hypothetical example of a black and white solid-state display in the block diagram of Figure 9.25. During the horizontal retrace time when the raster scan position is moving rapidly from right to left, the MPU (under program control) determines which data pattern is to be displayed during the next scanning line. The MPU maintains an internal record of the current active line on the display by counting vertical sync pulses. The actual bit pattern associated with the character being displayed along the active line on the CRT is loaded into the shift register. In our hypothetical example, these data come in eight separated 8-bit bytes from video RAM. Then during the scanning of the active line, the bit pattern is shifted out one bit at a time by a pulse signal, H_{ck}, at a frequency that is 240 times that of the horizontal sync frequency.

Each bit location in the shift register corresponds to a pixel location on the display. A "1" stored at any shift register location corresponds to a bright

**Figure 9.25
Video Signal
Generation**

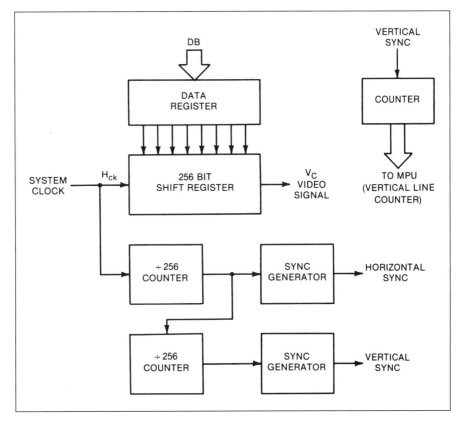

spot on the display. Thus, by placing a suitable pattern in the shift register for a particular line, it is possible to display complex alphanumeric or pictorial data on the display.

The enormous flexibility of the CRT type display offers the potential for a very sophisticated automotive instrumentation system. In addition to displaying the variables and parameters that have traditionally been available to the driver, the CRT type display can present engine data for diagnostic purposes (see Chapter 10), vehicle comfort control system parameters, and entertainment system variables. The data required for such displays can, for example, be transmitted via a high-speed digital data (HSDD) link between the various on-board electronics systems. This CRT-type display has sufficient flexibility and detailed resolution that graphical data or electronic maps can be shown to the driver (see discussion of navigation in Chapter 11).

There are several reasons for using the serial HSDD link for transmitting data between the various systems rather than tying the internal data buses together. For example, it is desirable to protect any given system from a failure in another. A defect affecting the data bus of the comfort system could adversely affect the engine control system. In addition, each internal data bus

**Figure 9.26
Integrated Vehicle
Electronic Systems**

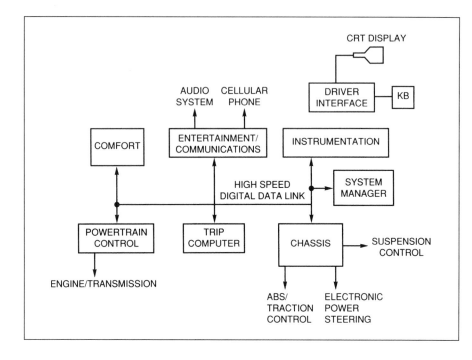

tends to be busy handling internal traffic. Moreover, the transfer of data to the instrumentation computer can take place at relatively low data rates (for the diagnostic application outlined here).

Figure 9.26 is a block diagram of an integrated vehicle instrumentation system in which all on-board electronic systems are coupled by an HSDD link. This system requires a keyboard (KB) or similar input device for operator control. The driver can, for example, select to display the entertainment system operation. This display mode permits the driver to select radio, tape, or CD, and to tune the radio to the desired station and set the volume. In vehicle diagnostic mode, the CRT can be configured to display the parameters required by the mechanic for performing a diagnosis of any on-board electronic system.

In Figure 9.26, several electronic systems are connected by the digital data link. Tying systems together this way has great potential performance benefits for the vehicle. Each automotive subsystem has its own primary variables, which are obtained through measurements via sensors. A primary variable in one subsystem might be a secondary variable in another system. It might not be cost-effective to provide a sensor for a secondary variable to achieve the best possible performance in a stand-alone subsystem. However, if measurement data can be shared via the digital data link, then the secondary measurement is potentially available for use in optimizing performance. Furthermore, redundant sensors for measuring primary variables can be eliminated by an integrated electronics system for the vehicle. For example, wheel speed measurements are primary variables for ABS systems and are also useful in electronic transmission control.

The various subsystems in Figure 9.26 have all been identified in other sections of this book and will not be discussed further here, except for the system manager. This subsystem is responsible for coordinating data transfer and regulating the use of the data bus so that no two systems are transmitting simultaneously.

Essentially, the digital data link provides a sophisticated communication system between various subsystems. Among the issues of importance for such a communication system are the protocol and message format. It is highly advantageous to have a standard protocol for all automobiles. The Society of Automotive Engineers (SAE) is working to develop a standard protocol for the high-speed digital data link. This link operates at a data rate of 1 megabit/sec and can be implemented with wire or optical fiber. Any of a number of bit-encoding schemes are useful for message formats, the details of which are unimportant for the present discussion.

Some form of network arbitration is required for determining priority of the use of the link whenever there is conflict between subsystems for its use. This feature is typically handled by the system manager.

The basic message structure is derived assuming that the majority of data on the link is regularly sent. This means that the content of each message is known (only the actual data varies).

CAN Network

Automotive electronic subsystems have become numerous and interdependent, requiring subsystem intercommunication. This need for digital communication between all on-board digital systems has led to the creation of a standard automotive communication network known as Control Area Network (CAN). Originally developed for passenger car applications, CAN is a form of local area network that permits data to be shared.

In the CAN concept, each electronic subsystem incorporates communication hardware and software, permitting it to function as a communication module referred to as a gateway. CAN is based on the so-called broadcast communication mechanism in which communication is achieved by the sending gateway (i.e., subsystem) transmitting messages over the network (e.g., wire interconnect). Each message has a specific format (protocol) that includes a message identifier. The identifier defines the content of the message, its priority, and is unique within the network. In addition to the data and identifier, each message includes error-checking bits as well as beginning and end of file.

The CAN communication system has great flexibility, permitting new subsystems to be added to an existing system without modification, provided the new additions are all receivers. Each gateway (subsystem) can be upgraded with new hardware and software at any time with equipment that was not available at the time the car left the manufacturing plant or even when it left the dealer. Essentially, the CAN concept with its open standards frees the development of new telematics applications from the somewhat lengthy development cycle of a typical automobile model. Furthermore, it offers the potential for the aftermarket addition of new subsystems.

THE GLASS COCKPIT

The development of a cost-effective solid-state equivalent of the CRT can have enormous application in automotive instrumentation. It can yield a completely reconfigurable display system similar to the multifunction display used in some modern transport aircraft. Such displays are termed a *glass cockpit* in aircraft parlance. It is also known as an electronic flight information system (EFIS).

A single CRT acting as a display for a digital instrumentation system has the capability of displaying any of several choices of data readout, including

1. Navigation data
2. Subsystem status parameters
3. Attitude (artificial horizon)
4. Air data (airspeed, altitude, etc.)

It can also be used for diagnosis of problems with various aircraft subsystems. In this case it can present a pictorial diagram of any aircraft subsystem (hydraulic system or electrical system) so that the flight crew doesn't have to resort to hunting through a manual for the aircraft to diagnose a problem with a subsystem.

One of the benefits of an automotive glass cockpit is its great flexibility. Any message in any format can be displayed. In fact, the format can be chosen by the driver via a set of switches or by a keypad arrangement. The driver selects a particular display format from a number of choices and the display will be reconfigured to his choice by software, that is, by the program stored in the instrumentation computer. A likely default choice would include a standard display having speed and fuel quantity and the capability of displaying warning messages to the driver.

Another benefit of the EFIS-type display is the capability of displaying diagnostic information to a service technician. The service technicians can select a display mode that presents fault codes from any vehicle subsystem whenever the car is taken for repairs or during routine maintenance operations.

Of particular importance is the capability of digital instrumentation to identify intermittent faults. The instrumentation computer can store fault codes with a time stamp that gives the time of occurrence to indicate to a service technician that a particular component or subsystem is experiencing intermittent failures. Such failures are extremely difficult to diagnose because they are often not present when the car is brought in for service. In this mode of operation the instrumentation computer along with its software-reconfigurable display is serving a role somewhat analogous to a flight data recorder on an aircraft.

TRIP INFORMATION COMPUTER

The trip information computer analyzes fuel flow, vehicle speed, and fuel tank quantities, and then calculates information such as miles to empty, average fuel economy, and estimated arrival time.

One of the most popular electronic instruments for automobiles is the trip information system. This system has a number of interesting functions and can display many useful pieces of information, including the following:

1. Present fuel economy
2. Average fuel economy
3. Average speed
4. Present vehicle location (relative to total trip distance)
5. Total elapsed trip time
6. Fuel remaining
7. Miles to empty fuel tank
8. Estimated time of arrival
9. Time of day
10. Engine RPM
11. Engine temperature
12. Average fuel cost per mile

Additional functions can be performed, which no doubt will be part of future developments. However, we will discuss a representative system having features that are common to most available systems.

A block diagram of this system is shown in Figure 9.27. Not shown in the block diagram are MUX, DEMUX, and A/D converter components, which are normally part of a computer-based instrument. This system can be implemented as a set of special functions of the main automotive instrumentation system, or it can be a stand-alone system employing its own computer.

The vehicle inputs to this system come from the three sensors that measure the following variables:

1. Quantity of fuel remaining in the tank
2. Instantaneous fuel flow rate
3. Vehicle speed

Other inputs that are obtained by the computer from other parts of the control system are

1. Odometer mileage
2. Time (from clock in the computer)

The driver enters inputs to the system through the keyboard. At the beginning of a trip, the driver initializes the system and enters the total trip

**Figure 9.27
Trip Information
System**

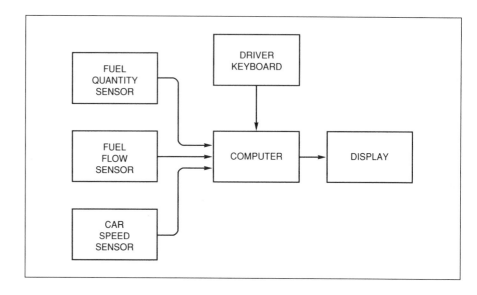

distance and fuel cost. At any time during the trip, the driver can use the keyboard to ask for information to be displayed.

The system computes a particular trip parameter from the input data. For example, instantaneous fuel economy in miles per gallon (MPG) can be found by computing

$$\text{MPG} = S/F$$

where

S is the speed in miles per hour
F is the fuel consumption rate in gallons per hour

As operating conditions change, the values provided by a trip information computer may also change.

Of course, this computation varies markedly as operating conditions vary. At a steady cruising speed along a level highway with a constant wind, fuel economy is constant. If the driver then depresses the accelerator (e.g., to pass traffic), the fuel consumption rate temporarily increases faster than speed, and MPG is reduced for that time. Various averages can be computed such that instant fuel economy, short-term average fuel economy, or long-term average fuel economy can be displayed.

Another important trip parameter that this system can display is the miles to empty fuel tank, D. This can be found by calculating

$$D = \text{MPG} \cdot Q$$

where Q is the quantity of fuel remaining in gallons. Since D depends on MPG, it also changes as operating conditions change (e.g., during heavy acceleration). In such cases, the calculation of miles to empty based on the above simple equation is grossly incorrect. However, this calculation gives a correct estimate of the miles to empty for steady cruise along a highway in which operating conditions are constant.

Still another pair of parameters that can be calculated and displayed by this system are distance to destination, D_d, and estimated time of arrival, ETA. These can be found by computing

$$D_d = D_T - D_P$$
$$ETA = T_1 + (D_d/S)$$

where

D_T is the trip distance (entered by the driver)
D_P is the present position (in miles traveled since start)
S is the present vehicle speed
T_1 is the start time

The computer can calculate the present position D_P by subtracting the start mileage, D_1 (obtained from the odometer reading when the trip computer was initialized by the driver), from the present odometer mileage.

The average fuel cost per mile C can be found by calculating

$$C = (D_P/MPG) \cdot \text{fuel cost per gallon}$$

There are many other useful and interesting operations that can be performed by the variety of available systems. Actually, the number of such functions that can be performed is limited primarily by cost and by the availability of sensors to measure the required variables.

TELEMATICS

Communications to and from an automobile has become routine as a result of both cell phone and satellite technology. In addition, the technology is evolving for area broadcast of road condition information on radio station subcarriers. Technology is also evolving that will permit Internet connections via cell phones, making the car in effect on Internet node. Automobile Internet connectivity opens a limitless range of services for the driver, from on-line navigation help to on-line diagnostic and/or road service for mechanical problems.

One of the major issues in telematics is how to present the information and services that are potentially available to the driver without distracting from the driving tasks. Of course, the various services can be made available to passengers without necessarily distracting the driver. For example, video monitors in rear seats can provide entertainment, game playing on any standard computer Internet terminal via on-board DVD, or wireless connection, be it cell phone or satellite links.

On the other hand, the use of any subsystem that provides information such as is described above is potentially distracting to the driver. The simple act of dialing a standard cell phone requires the use of at least one hand and at least a momentary look at the cell phone. Some state legislatures are passing laws prohibiting the driver's use of a standard cell phone while driving.

The driver's distraction through cell phone use is somewhat alleviated by voice-activated cell phone dialing in which the cell phone user verbally gives the phone number, speaking each digit separately. Included within the cell phone is a very sophisticated algorithm for recognizing speech. Speech recognition software identifies spoken words or numbers based on patterns in the waveform at the output of a microphone into which the user speaks. There are two major categories of speech recognition software: speaker dependent and speaker independent.

Speaker-dependent software recognizes the speech of a specific individual who must work with the system. The user is prompted to say a specific digit a number of times until the software can reliably identify the waveform patterns associated with that particular speaker. By this process, the system is "trained" to the individual user. It may not be capable of recognizing other users to whose speech it has been trained.

Speaker-independent voice recognition software can recognize spoken digits regardless of the user. It is generally more sophisticated than speaker-dependent speech recognition.

The cell phone connection can also be used to provide online navigation or other services by contacting a service with operators trained to provide this type of service. Alternatively, the cell phone can be used to provide an internet connection to an on-line navigation service that transmits data to the car for display on an electronic map.

The telematics technology is presently in its infancy and is certain to grow spectacularly in capability and flexibility, providing the motorist with virtually limitless services. Telematics functionality is probably limited more by imagination than by technology.

AUTOMOTIVE DIAGNOSTICS

The instrumentation computer can also be used as a diagnostic aid during vehicle manufacturing, operation, or repair.

In certain automobile models, the instrumentation computer can perform the important function of diagnosis of the electronic engine control system. This diagnosis takes place at several different levels. One level is used during manufacturing to test the system, and another level is used by mechanics or interested car owners to diagnose engine control system problems. Some levels operate continuously and others are available only on request from an external device that is connected to the car data link for diagnostic purposes by a technician. This application is explained in the next chapter.

In the continuous monitor mode, the diagnosis takes place under computer control. The computer activates connections to the vehicle sensors and looks for an open- or short-circuited sensor. If such a condition is detected, a failure warning message is given to the driver on the alphanumeric display or by turning on a labeled warning light. A detailed discussion of automotive diagnosis appears in Chapter 10.

Quiz for Chapter 9

1. What is the primary purpose of automotive instrumentation?
   a. to indicate to the driver the value of certain critical variables and parameters
   b. to extend engine life
   c. to control engine operation
   d. entertainment of passengers

2. What are the three functional components of electronic instrumentation?
   a. sensor, MAP, display
   b. sensor, signal processing, error amplifier
   c. display, sensor, signal processing
   d. none of the above

3. What is the function of a multiplexer in computer-based instrumentation?
   a. it measures several variables simultaneously
   b. it converts sensor analog signals to digital format
   c. it sequentially switches a set of sensor outputs to the instrumentation computer input

4. What is sampling?
   a. a signal processing algorithm
   b. a selective display method
   c. a method of measuring a continuously varying quantity at discrete time instants
   d. the rate of change of battery voltage

5. What is an A/D converter?
   a. a device that changes a continuously varying quantity to a digital format
   b. an 8-bit binary counter
   c. an analog-to-decimal converter
   d. a fluid coupling in the transmission

6. What type of sensor is commonly used for fuel quantity measurement?
   a. a thermistor
   b. a strain gauge
   c. a potentiometer whose movable arm is connected to a float
   d. a piezoelectric sensor

7. How is coolant temperature measured?
   a. with a mercury bulb thermometer
   b. with a strain gauge
   c. with a thermistor as a sensor
   d. none of the above

8. A digital vehicle speed sensor incorporates
   a. a variable-frequency pulse generator and digital counter
   b. a variable resistor
   c. a variable capacitance
   d. none of the above

9. What sensor input variables are used in a typical trip computer system?
   a. manifold pressure and engine speed
   b. RPM, barometric pressure, and fuel quantity remaining
   c. MPG and fuel consumption
   d. car speed, fuel flow rate, fuel quantity remaining in tank

10. A CRT display device uses
    a. a cathode ray tube scanned in a raster pattern
    b. a vacuum-fluorescent tube
    c. an incandescent light source
    d. none of the above

11. In the digital video signal generator used with a CRT display
    a. each bit in the shift register corresponds to a pixel location
    b. each pixel on the screen corresponds to a specific video voltage level
    c. scanning of the CRT by the electron beam is from right to left and from bottom to top
    d. all of the above are true

12. The term MUX refers to
    a. an electronic switch that selects one of a set of inputs per an input code
    b. a digital output device
    c. a time slot
    d. none of the above

13. A D/A converter
    a. is a disk access device
    b. converts the digital output of an instrumentation computer to analog form
    c. stores analog data
    d. enters digital data in a computer

14. LED refers to
    a. level-equalizing detector
    b. light-emitting diode
    c. liquid crystal display
    d. none of the above

15. An LCD display uses
    a. a nematic liquid
    b. an incandescent lamp
    c. large electrical power
    d. a picket fence

16. Light is produced in a VFD by
    a. ionic bombardment of a filament
    b. ambient temperature
    c. bombardment of a phosphor by energetic electrons
    d. chemical action

17. Fuel economy is calculated in a trip computer by:
    a. $S \cdot F$
    b. F/S
    c. S/F
    d. none of the above

Diagnostics

From the earliest days of the commercial sale of the automobile, it has been obvious that maintenance is required to keep automobiles operating properly. Of course, automobile dealerships have provided this service for years, as have independent repair shops and service stations. But until the early 1970s, a great deal of the routine maintenance and repair was done by car owners themselves, using inexpensive tools and equipment. However, the Clean Air Act affected not only the emissions produced by automobiles but also the complexity of the engine control systems and, as a result, the complexity of automobile maintenance and repair. Car owners can no longer, as a matter of course, do their own maintenance and repairs on certain automotive subsystems (particularly the engine). In fact, the traditional shop manual used for years by technicians for repairing cars is rapidly becoming obsolete and is being replaced by electronic technician aids.

The development of electronic engine control has increased the complexity of diagnosis and maintenance.

As will be shown later in this chapter, the trend in automotive maintenance is for the automobile manufacturer to distribute all required documentation, including parts lists (with figures) as well as repair procedures in electronic format via a dedicated communication link (e.g., via satellite) or via CD supplied to the mechanic. The repair information is then available to the technician at the repair site by use of a PC-like workstation.

On-board digital systems can also store diagnostic information wherever a failure or partial failure occurs in a component or subsystem. The relevant information can then be stored in a memory (e.g., RAM) that retains the information even if the car ignition is switched off. Then, when the car is delivered to a repair station (e.g., at the dealer), the technician can retrieve the diagnostic information electronically.

The change from traditional fluidic/pneumatic engine controls to microprocessor-based electronic engine controls was a direct result of the need to control automobile emissions, and has been chronicled throughout this book. However, little has been said thus far about the diagnostic problems involved in electronically controlled engines. This type of diagnostics requires a fundamentally different approach than that for traditionally controlled engines because it requires more sophisticated equipment than was required for diagnostics in pre-emission-control automobiles. In fact, the best diagnostic methods use special-purpose computers that are themselves microprocessor based. However, before launching into a discussion of electronic control system diagnostics, there are two nonmicroprocessor diagnostic instruments that are still used in garages and repair shops (particularly for older-model cars) that should be discussed: the timing light and the engine analyzer.

TIMING LIGHT

The timing light (Figure 10.1) is used to measure and set ignition timing. It is a special stroboscopic light source that generates very short duration light pulses, the timing of which coincides with ignition pulses. The timing of these pulses is obtained from a special probe connected to a spark-plug wire. Figure 10.2 is a block diagram of a typical timing light.

The probe generates a very short duration voltage pulse each time the spark plug fires. The pulse is amplified and then operates a trigger electrode on a flash lamp that is a gas discharge tube. When triggered, a current pulse flows through the flash lamp, generating a short burst of light.

In timing the ignition, the light from the flash lamp is directed at the pulley on the front end of the crankshaft. Adjacent to the pulley is a pointer, such as seen in Figure 10.3. On the pulley are several marks. The relationship between the pointer and these marks corresponds to specific crankshaft angular positions relative to top dead center (TDC). The relationship of the pointer and crankshaft pulley marks at the time of ignition can be seen by viewing the pulley using the light from the flash lamp. When the ignition timing is correct, the pointer will align with the correct pulley mark.

Figure 10.1
Typical Engine Timing Light

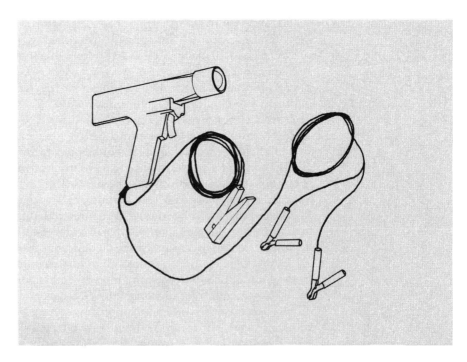

**Figure 10.2
Timing Light Block
Diagram**

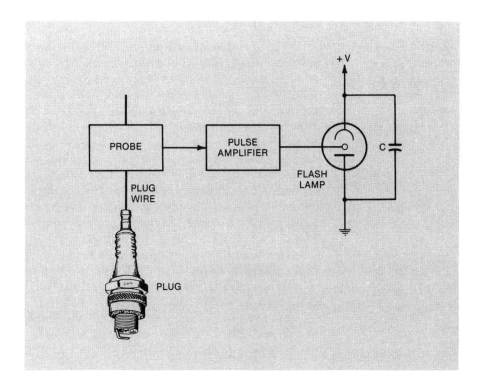

**Figure 10.3
Timing Marks**

ENGINE ANALYZER

The engine analyzer is an instrument that has existed for many years and continues to be used in garages for several tuneup tasks. It provides, for example, a means for optimally setting the gap for ignition points (in cars that still have them, of course) by measuring the so-called dwell. *Dwell* is essentially the fractional duration that the ignition points are closed. However, an engine analyzer's role in diagnosing cars that have digital engine control systems is markedly different than its role in the diagnosis of cars that have analog or mechanical control systems. For example, ignition points have virtually been eliminated in digitally controlled cars. Nevertheless, the concept of dwell is still applicable, only today it represents the amount of time current flows through the coil primary circuit before this circuit is interrupted (see Chapter 7). In addition, in certain cases ignition timing can be measured by measuring the relative strength (peak voltage) of ignition pulses. Although the engine analyzer continues to be a useful instrument, it is not adequate for diagnosing problems in electronically controlled systems.

While it is true that both the timing light and the engine analyzer will continue to be used because there are many cars still on the roads whose engines are controlled either by analog or mechanical systems, it is probable that the use of these two diagnostic instruments will be phased out within a few years.

ELECTRONIC CONTROL SYSTEM DIAGNOSTICS

Each microprocessor-based electronic subsystem has the capability of performing some limited self-diagnosis. A subsystem can, for example, detect a loss of signal from a sensor or detect an open circuit in an actuator circuit as well as other failures. As long as the subsystem computer is still functioning it can store fault codes for detected failures. Such diagnosis within a given subsystem is known as *on-board diagnosis*.

However, a higher level of diagnosis than the on-board diagnosis is typically done with an external computer-based system that is available in a service shop. Data stored in memory in an on-board subsystem are useful for completing diagnosis of any problem with the associated subsystem. Such diagnosis is known as *off-board diagnosis* and is usually conducted with a special-purpose computer.

In order for fault code data to be available to the off-board diagnosis computer, a communication link is required between the off-board equipment and the particular subsystem on board the vehicle. Such a communication system is typically in the form of a serial digital data link. A serial data link transmits digital data in a binary time sequence along a pair of wires (one of which is normally ground). Before discussing the details of on-board and off-board diagnosis, it is perhaps worthwhile to briefly discuss automotive digital communications.

Intermodule communications within an automobile itself and between each on-board subsystem and an off-board system are analogous to communications between computers. That is, they take the form of a local area network (LAN).

There are several important issues involved in any LAN, including the communication protocol, the bit rate, access to the network, and synchronization between the various subsystems. In a LAN, each subsystem connected to the serial data link is called a *node*. Normally one of the nodes serves as a *master* that has the capability of controlling access to the network. The other nodes are called *slaves* and respond to software-controlled commands issued by the master.

One of the possible problems that can occur in a LAN is the simultaneous transmission of messages by two separate nodes (called *collision*). Resolution of potential collisions is controlled by the master using a software capability known as *arbitration*.

An example of an automotive digital data system is the Controller Area Network (CAN) that was developed by the Robert Bosch Company in Germany and was described briefly in Chapter 9. CAN is a serial asynchronous communication protocol that connects electronic control modules' sensors and actuators in automobiles. Among its many functions and services is a digital data link.

CAN is an asynchronous system in that each node synchronizes to others' messages on the first bit leading edge of a message and on subsequent bit leading edges throughout the remainder of the message. The ability of any node to synchronize to another node is determined by the maximum differences in oscillator frequencies (see Chapter 4 for an explanation of microprocessor clocks). Other issues and critical periods include the duration of a bit, message duration and composition, and cooperative use of the network between master and slave, known as *handshaking*.

It is beyond the scope of this book to give a detailed account of CAN-type data communication. Rather, we wish to identify the use of data communication in automotive electronics and point out some critical issues.

One important application for digital communication in automobiles is the serial digital data link from the powertrain controller to an off-board diagnostic system. This data communications link has the capability of transmitting fault codes that have been stored in memory to the external device (among other uses). This off-board system can range in complexity from a computer-based diagnostic workstation (explained later in this chapter) to a simple portable scanner used to simply read and display fault codes in sequence as they are retrieved over the data link from the powertrain controller. Using these fault codes and following a fault tree diagnosis procedure, the service technician can normally diagnose powertrain control system problems. We consider next on-board and off-board diagnosis in detail, using specific examples.

On-Board Diagnostics

Existing microprocessor-
based engine control
systems incorporate
some self-diagnosis.

Limited diagnostic capability is provided in any modern microprocessor-based electronic control system. These diagnostic functions are performed by the microprocessor under the control of stored programs, and are performed only when the microprocessor is not fully committed to performing normal control calculations. While it is beyond the scope of this book to review the actual software involved in such diagnostic operations, the diagnostic procedures that are followed and explanations of on-board diagnostic functions can be reviewed.

During the normal operation of the car, there are intermittent periods during which various electrical and electronic components are tested. Whenever a fault is detected, the data are stored in memory using a specific fault code. At the same time, the controller generates or activates a warning lamp (or similar display) on the instrument panel, indicating that service is required.

The on-board diagnostic functions have one major limitation—they cannot detect intermittent failures reliably. For the system to detect and isolate a failure, the failure must be nonreversible. In most on-board diagnostics, the electronic control module stores trouble codes that are automatically cleared by the microprocessor after a set number of engine cycles have occurred without a fault reappearing.

The on-board diagnostic capabilities can be manually activated by causing the engine controller to enter a diagnostic mode. The method for accomplishing this task varies from car to car. For example, in certain older-model fuel-injected Cadillac cars, the diagnostic mode is entered by first switching on the ignition, then simultaneously depressing the Off and Warmer buttons on the climate control system.

A two-digit fault code is assigned to each failure.

The use of on-board diagnostics can easily be illustrated by outlining typical procedures and using the Cadillac system as an example system. Although display of the fault codes varies from car to car, in each case the codes must be readable as a numeric code. A typical method involves flashing the "Check Engine" light. The mechanic enters the display mode and then counts the number of times that this light is flashed, in two-digit groups. For example, a fault code 24 would be given by 2 flashes then 4 flashes. After a short time interval the next code would similarly be flashed in two-digit sequence. At one time Cadillac used the environment controller to display a two-digit code.

Figure 10.4 is a drawing of a Cadillac environmental system displaying code 88. This particular code is used to check that all display segments are working correctly and is the first display shown when the diagnostic mode is entered.

After verifying that all display segments are working, the fault codes for all component failures are displayed in sequence, beginning with the lowest and proceeding to the highest. The mechanic notes the fault codes that are

Figure 10.4
Fault Code Display

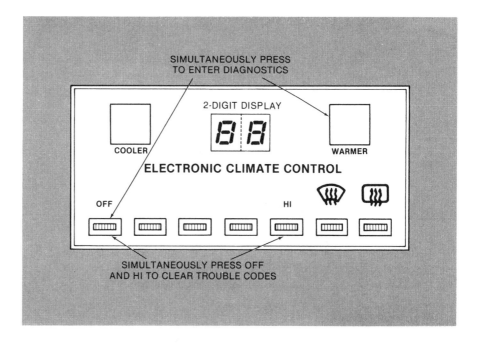

displayed and, using a reference manual, identifies the failed components. Table 10.1 is a summary of the Cadillac fault codes, which we present here simply as an example of two-digit fault code assignment. After all fault codes have been displayed, the number 70 appears on the climate control head, and the engine control system awaits further action by the mechanic.

Typically, the "Check Engine" light on the instrument panel is illuminated whenever any fault occurs. For codes 12 through 38 and 51 in Table 10.1, this warning light goes out automatically if the malfunction clears. However, the control module stores the code associated with the detected failure until the diagnostic system is manually cleared, or until 20 engine cycles occur with no malfunction. For codes 44 and 45, the "Check Engine" light will not go out until cleared from memory by the mechanic. For codes 60 through 68, there is no activation of the "Check Engine" light.

Whenever a defect occurs (as indicated by a fault code), the mechanic must follow a specific procedure to isolate the particular problem. These procedures are outlined for the mechanic as a sequence of steps to be followed. An example procedure will be illustrated here by following the steps necessary to respond to the specific fault code 13, which indicates that the oxygen (O_2 or EGO) sensor is not ready. Recall from the discussion in Chapter 6 that the O_2 sensor switches between approximately 0 and 1 volt as the mixture switches between the extreme conditions of lean and rich. Recall also that this voltage swing requires that the O_2 sensor must be at a temperature above 200°C. Fault

**Table 10.1
Summary of
Fault Codes**

Circuit Affected	Two-Digit Fault Code
No distributor signal	12
EGO sensor not ready	13
Coolant sensor circuit (short)	14
Coolant sensor (open)	15
Generator voltage out of range	16
Crank signal (short)	17
Crank signal (open)	18
Fuel pump circuit (short)	19
Fuel pump circuit (open)	20
Throttle position sensor circuit (short)	21
Throttle position sensor (open)	22
Ignition/Bypass	23
Engine speed sensor	24
Throttle switch (short)	26
Throttle switch (open)	27
Idle speed control	30
MAP sensor circuit (short)	31
MAP sensor circuit (open)	32
MAP/Baro sensor correlation	33
MAP signal too high	34
Baro sensor circuit (short)	35
Baro sensor circuit (open)	36
Manifold air temp (short)	37
Manifold air temp (open)	38
Lean exhaust signal	44
Rich exhaust signal	45
PROM error indicator	51
Transmission not in dive	60
"Set" and "resume" circuits engaged simultaneously	61
Car speed exceeds maximum limit	62

**Table 10.1
(Continued)**

Circuit Affected	Two-Digit Fault Code
Car and set speed tolerance exceeded	63
Car acceleration exceeds maximum limit	64
System ready for further tests	70
Cruise control bake circuit test	71
Throttle switch circuit test	72
Drive (ADL) circuit test	73
Reverse circuit test	74
Cruise on/off circuit test	75
"Set/Coast" circuit test	76
"Resume/Acceleration" circuit test	77
"Instant/Average" circuit test	78
"Reset" circuit test	79
Air conditioner clutch circuit test	80
Display check	88
System ready to display engine data	90
All diagnostics complete	00

code 13 means that the O_2 sensor will not swing above or below its cold voltage of approximately 0.5 volt, and that the electronic control system will not go into closed-loop operation (see Chapters 5 and 7).

Possible causes for fault code 13 include the following:

- O_2 sensor is not functioning correctly.
- Defective connections or leads.
- The control unit is not processing the O_2 sensor signal.

Further investigation is required to attempt to isolate the specific problem.

To check the operation of the O_2 sensor, the average value of its output voltage is measured using the electronic engine control system (the procedure for which is explained later in this chapter). The desired voltage is displayed on the climate control head in multiples of 0.01 volt. That is to say, "00" corresponds to 0 volts and "99" corresponds to 0.99 volt, and so forth.

**Figure 10.5
DFI Oxygen Sensor
Circuit**

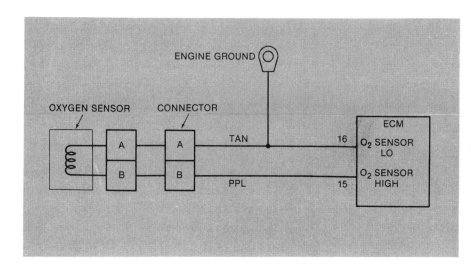

Using this voltage, the mechanic follows a procedure outlined in Figures 10.5, 10.6, and 10.7. If the voltage is less than 0.37 volt or greater than 0.57 volt, the mechanic is asked to investigate the wiring harness for defects.

If the O_2 sensor voltage is between 0.37 volt and 0.57 volt, tests are performed to determine whether the O_2 sensor or the control unit is faulty. The mechanic must jumper the O_2 sensor leads together at the input to the control unit, simulating a sensor short circuit, and must read the sensor voltage value using the climate control display. If this voltage is less than 0.05 volt, the control unit is functioning correctly and the O_2 sensor must be investigated for defects. If the indicated sensor voltage is greater than 0.05 volt, the control unit is faulty and should be replaced.

When diagnosing a problem, the mechanic might wish to clear a fault code from the electronic control memory. A good reason to do this, for example, would be to test whether a failure is "hard" or intermittent. To clear trouble codes (with the system in diagnostic mode), the mechanic simultaneously pushes the Off and Hi buttons on the climate control head until "00" is displayed. After all fault codes are cleared, code 70 will appear.

On-board diagnosis also examines the status of several switches.

Code 70 represents a decision point in the diagnostic procedure. At this point, the mechanic has several choices, including:

- Perform switch tests
- Display engine data
- Perform output cycling tests
- Perform cylinder select tests
- Exit from diagnostic mode

**Figure 10.6
DFI Code 13: Oxygen
Sensor Not Ready**

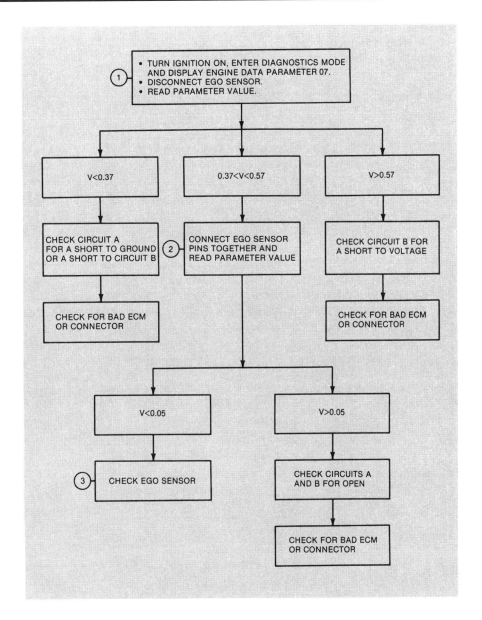

Each of the above procedures provides an important diagnostic capability to the mechanic.

The switch tests involve fault codes 71 to 80 and provide checks on the switches indicated in Figure 10.8. To begin the switch tests, the mechanic must depress and release the brake pedal. If there is no brake switch failure, then the

**Figure 10.7
DFI Chart No. 14:
Oxygen Sensor Test**

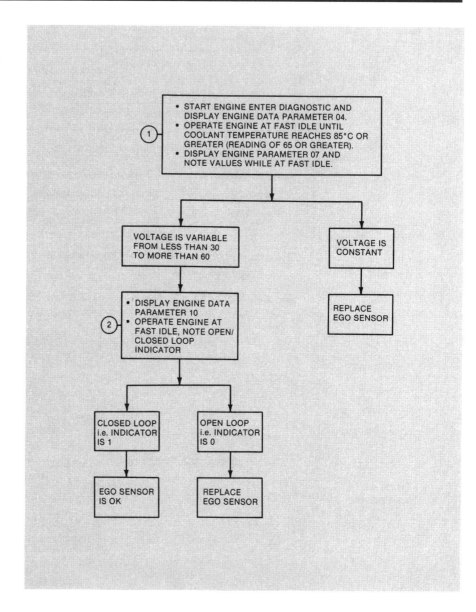

code advances to 71. If the display doesn't advance, then the control unit is not processing the brake switch signal and further diagnosis is required. For such a failure, the mechanic locates the specific chart (such as seen in Figures 10.9 and 10.10) for diagnosis of the particular switch failure and follows the procedure outlined. The detailed tests performed by the mechanic are continuity checks that are performed with a test light.

**Figure 10.8
Switch Test Series**

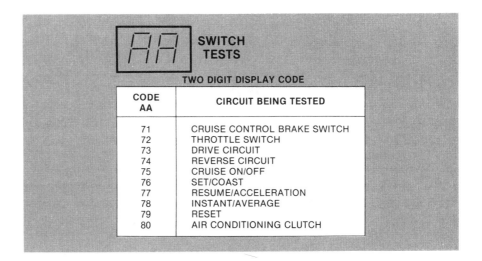

TWO DIGIT DISPLAY CODE

CODE AA	CIRCUIT BEING TESTED
71	CRUISE CONTROL BRAKE SWITCH
72	THROTTLE SWITCH
73	DRIVE CIRCUIT
74	REVERSE CIRCUIT
75	CRUISE ON/OFF
76	SET/COAST
77	RESUME/ACCELERATION
78	INSTANT/AVERAGE
79	RESET
80	AIR CONDITIONING CLUTCH

Similar procedures are followed for each switch test in the sequence. This procedure sequence is as follows:

1. With code 71 displayed, depress and release brake pedal. For normal operation, the display advances.

2. With 72 displayed, depress the throttle from idle position to wide open position. The control unit tests the throttle switch, and advances the display to 73 for normal operation.

3. With 73 displayed, the transmission selector is moved to drive and then neutral. This operation tests the drive switch, and the display advances to 74 for normal operation.

4. With 74 displayed, the transmission selector is moved to reverse and then to park. This tests the reverse switch operation, and the display advances to 75 for normal operation.

5. With 75 displayed, the cruise control is switched from off to on and back to off, testing the cruise control switch. For normal operation, the display advances to 76.

6. With code 76 displayed and the cruise control instrument panel switch on, depress and release the set/coast button. If the button (switch) is operating normally, the display advances to 77.

7. With 77 displayed and with the cruise control instrument on, depress and release the resume/acceleration switch. If the switch is operating normally, the display advances to 78.

8. With 78 displayed, depress and release the instant/average button on the MPG panel. If the button is working normally, the code advances to 79.

9. With 79 displayed, depress and release the reset button on the mph panel. If the reset button is working normally, the code will advance to 80.

**Figure 10.9
DFI Cruise Control
Brake Circuit**

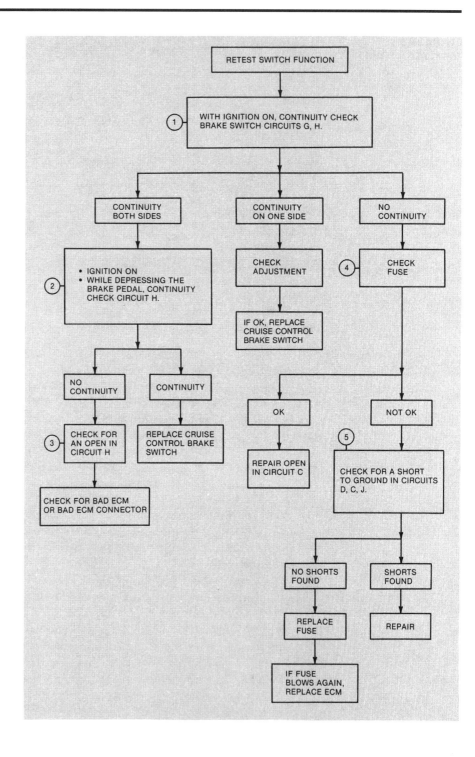

Figure 10.10
DFI Code 71: Cruise Control Brake Circuit

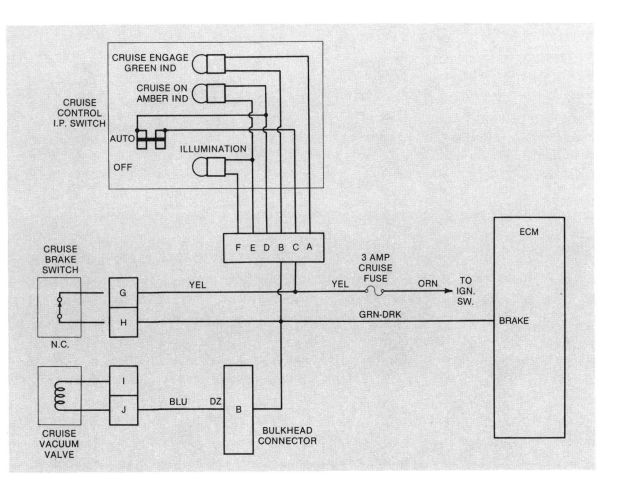

10. With 80 displayed, depress and release the rear defogger button on the climate control head. If the defogger switch is working normally, the code advances to 70, thereby completing the switch tests.

**Figure 10.11
Engine Data Display**

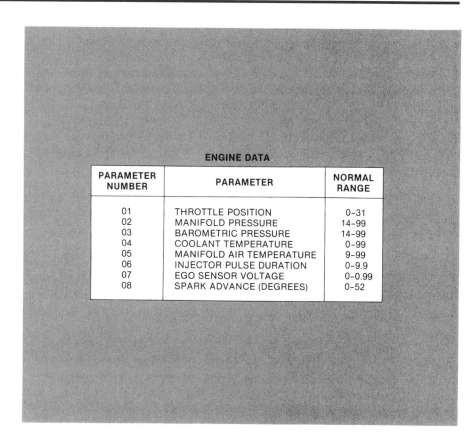

With code 70 displayed, the engine data can be displayed in sequence by switching the cruise control instrument panel off. The code should then advance to 90. To further advance the display, the mechanic must depress the instant/average button on the MPG panel (to return to the previously displayed parameter, the mechanic must depress the reset button on the MPG panel). To exit the engine parameter display mode, the mechanic simultaneously depresses the Off and Hi buttons on the climate control head. After the last parameter has been displayed, the code advances to 95.

Figure 10.11 shows the parameter values in sequence. Parameter 01 is the angular deflection of the throttle in degrees from idle position. Parameter 02 is the manifold absolute pressure in kilopascals (kPa). The range for this

**Table 10.2
Temperature
Conversion Table**

CODE	°F
0	−40
8	−12
12	1
16	15
21	32
25	46
30	64
35	81
40	98
45	115
50	133
52	140
54	147
56	153
58	160
60	167
62	174
64	181
66	188
68	195
70	202
72	209
73	212
75	219

parameter is 14 to 99, with 14 representing about the maximum manifold vacuum. Parameter 03 is the absolute atmospheric pressure in kPa. Normal atmospheric pressure is roughly 90 to 100 kPa at sea level. Parameter 04 is the coolant temperature. The conversion from this code to an actual temperature is given in Table 10.2. Parameter 05 is the manifold air temperature, which uses the same conversion as parameter 04.

Parameter 06 is the duration of the fuel injector pulse in msec. In reading this number, the mechanic assumes a decimal point between the two digits (i.e., 16 is read as 1.6 msec). Refer to Chapters 5, 6, and 7 for an explanation of the injector pulse widths and the influence of these pulse widths on fuel mixture.

Measurements of average O_2 sensor voltage are useful for diagnosis of this sensor.

Parameter 07 is the average value for the O_2 sensor output voltage. Reference was made earlier in this chapter to the diagnostic use of this parameter. Recall that the O_2 sensor switches between about 0 and 1 volt as the mixture oscillates between lean and rich. The displayed value is the time average for this voltage, which varies with the duty cycle of the mixture. A decimal point should be assumed at the left of the two digits (i.e., 52 is read as 0.52 volt).

Parameter 08 is the spark advance in degrees before TDC. This value should agree with that obtained using a timing light or engine analyzer. Parameter 09 is the number of ignition cycles that have occurred since a trouble code was set in memory. If 20 such cycles have occurred without a fault, this counter is set to zero and all trouble codes are cleared.

Parameter 10 is a logical (binary) variable that indicates whether the engine control system is operating in open or closed loop. A value of 1 corresponds to closed loop, which means that data from the O_2 sensor are fed back to the controller to be used in setting injector pulse duration. Zero for this variable indicates open-loop operation, as explained in Chapters 6 and 7. Parameter 11 is the battery voltage minus 10. A decimal point is assumed between the digits. Thus, 2.3 is read as 12.3 volts.

After completion of parameter data values, the climate control display will advance to 95. The remaining codes are specific to certain Cadillac models and are not germane to the present discussion.

In addition to manually reading the fault codes as described for earlier model cars, these codes are read automatically in later model cars by a special-purpose digital system. For example, there is a portable device (often called a scanner) that connects to a digital data bus within the car that has been designed to work with the scanner. The scanner has access to address and data buses of the subsystem containing the memory in which the relevant fault codes are stored. The scanner then sends addresses to the memory locations where the fault codes are stored and retrieves any fault code in each memory location associated with fault code storage. The scanner also includes a display device where it displays the fault code. Some diagnostic systems include storing the clock time of the occurrence of the fault. Such a system is useful for diagnosing intermittent faults (i.e., those that come and go randomly and are challenging for the technician to find).

Once the mechanic has read all of the fault codes, he or she proceeds with the diagnosis and repair using the shop manual (for older cars) in the same manner as explained for the Cadillac example, or the electronic version as presented on the screen of a shop workstation or "technicians terminal." For each fault code there is a procedure to be followed that attempts to isolate the specific components that have failed (similar to that described before for the older Cadillac example). Obviously, the process of diagnosing a problem can be lengthy and can involve many steps. However, without the aid of the on-board diagnostic capability of the electronic control system, such diagnosis would take much more time and might, in certain cases, be nearly impossible (e.g., for intermittent faults).

On-board diagnosis has also been mandated by government regulation, particularly if a vehicle failure could damage emission control systems. The California Air Resources Board (CARB), which has been at the forefront of automotive emission control regulations, has proposed a new, relatively severe requirement for on-board diagnosis that is known as OBDII (on-board diagnosis II). This requirement is intended to ensure that the emission control system is functioning as intended.

Automotive emission control systems, which have been discussed in Chapters 5 and 7, consist of fuel and ignition control, the three-way catalytic converter, EGR, secondary air injection, and evaporative emission. The OBDII regulations require real-time monitoring of the health of the emission control system components. For example, the performance of the catalytic converter must be monitored using a temperature sensor for measuring converter temperature and a pair of EGO sensors (one before and one after the converter).

Another requirement for OBDII is a misfire detection system. It is known that under misfiring conditions (failure of the mixture to ignite), exhaust emissions increase. In severe cases, the catalytic converter itself can be irreversibly damaged.

The only cost-effective means of meeting OBDII requirements involves electronic instrumentation. For example, one possible means of detecting misfire is based on measurements of the crankshaft instantaneous speed. That speed fluctuates about the average RPM in response to each cylinder firing event. Misfire can be detected in most cases by monitoring the crankshaft speed fluctuations using some relatively sophisticated electronic signal processing.

Off-Board Diagnosis

An alternative to the on-board diagnostics is available in the form of a service bay diagnostic system. This system uses a computer that has a greater diagnostic capability than the vehicle-based system because its computer is typically much larger and has only a single task to perform—that of diagnosing problems in engine control systems.

Special-purpose digital computers are coming into use in service bay diagnosis systems.

An example of an early service bay diagnostic system is General Motors' CAMS (Computerized Automotive Maintenance System). Although the system discussed here is essentially obsolete, it is at least representative of this

**Figure 10.12
Engine Data Display**

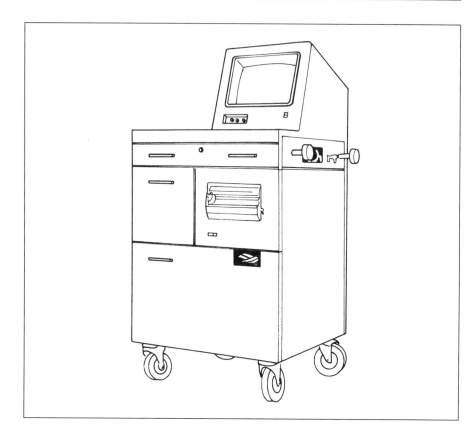

level of diagnosis. The GM-CAMS used an IBM PC/AT computer that had considerable computational capability for its time. Its memory included 640K of RAM, 1.2 million bytes on a 5.75-inch diskette drive and 20 million bytes on a fixed disk drive. This system was capable of detecting, analyzing, and isolating faults in late-model GM vehicles that are equipped with a digital engine control system. This system, commonly called the *technicians' terminal,* has a modem equivalent that operates in essentially the same way as the CAMS.

The technicians' terminal is mounted on a rugged portable cart (Figure 10.12) suitable for use in the garage. It connects to the vehicle through the assembly line data link (ALDL). The data required to perform diagnostics are obtained by the terminal through this link. The terminal has a color CRT monitor (similar to that of a typical home computer) that displays the data and procedures. It has a touch-sensitive screen for technician input to the system. The terminal features a keyboard for data entry, printer for hard copy output, and modem for a telephone link to a network that collects and routes GM-CAMS information.

The GM system also features a mainframe computer system at the General Motors Information Center (GMIC) that contains a master database that includes the most recent information relating to repair of applicable GM cars. This information, as well as computer software updates, is relayed throughout the network. Mechanics can also obtain diagnostic assistance by calling the GM-CAMS Customer Support Center.

When using the GM-CAMS, the mechanic enters the vehicle identification number (VIN) via the terminal. The computer responds by displaying a menu in which several choices are presented. To select a particular choice the technician touches the portion of the display associated with that choice. Next, the computer displays an additional menu of further choices; this continues until the mechanic has located the desired choice.

The service bay diagnostic system can be readily updated with new service bulletins.

Among the many capabilities of the technicians' terminal is its ability to store and display the diagnostic charts that appear in the shop manual. Whenever a fault is located, the appropriate chart(s) are automatically displayed for the mechanic. This capability greatly increases the efficiency of the diagnostic process. In addition, the GM-CAMS computer can store all of the data that are associated with the diagnostic procedures for several vehicles and then locate and display, virtually instantaneously, each specific procedure as required. Furthermore, updates and the most recent service bulletins are brought into the mechanics' terminal over the phone network so that mechanics lose no time trying to find the most recent data and procedures for diagnosing vehicular electronic systems.

The technology for the technicians' terminal has continued to evolve from the GM-CAMS system to the present-day system by incorporating all new digital technology. Of course, the computational capability and memory capacity of evolving systems have taken advantage of the latest improvements in computer and digital communication technology. Newer and faster microprocessors are incorporated as they become available. Memory capacity is many orders of magnitude greater than that available in GM-CAMS or similar systems. Repair procedures and illustrated parts lists are downloaded via a dedicated satellite link to the technicians' terminal as needed for any given repair, completely replacing the printed versions that were used in the past. This electronic version of the shop manual has greatly simplified the task of updating repair procedures and other maintenance/diagnostic data and information with respect to any model changes or any other changes that occur during the production run of a given car model.

In addition to storing and displaying shop manual data and procedures, a computer-based garage diagnostic system can automate the diagnostic process itself. In achieving this objective, the technicians' terminal has the capability to incorporate what is commonly called an *expert system.*

EXPERT SYSTEMS

An *expert system* is a form of artificial intelligence that has great potential for automotive diagnosis.

Although it is beyond the scope of the present book to explain expert systems, it is perhaps worthwhile to introduce some of the major concepts involved in this rapidly developing technology. An expert system is a computer program that employs human knowledge to solve problems normally requiring human expertise. The theory of expert systems is part of the general area of computer science known as artificial intelligence (AI). The major benefit of expert system technology is the consistent, uniform, and efficient application of the decision criteria or problem-solving strategies.

The diagnosis of electronic engine control systems by an expert system proceeds by following a set of rules that embody steps similar to the diagnostic charts in the shop manual. The diagnostic system receives data from the electronic control system (e.g., via the ALDL connector in the GM-CAMS) or through keyboard entry by the mechanic. The system processes these data logically under program control in accordance with the set of internally stored rules. The end result of the computer-aided diagnosis is an assessment of the problem and recommended repair procedures. The use of an expert system for diagnosis can significantly improve the efficiency of the diagnostic process and can thereby reduce maintenance time and costs.

An expert system takes information from experts and converts this to a set of logical rules.

The development of an expert system requires a computer specialist who is known in AI parlance as a *knowledge engineer*. The knowledge engineer must acquire the requisite knowledge and expertise for the expert system by interviewing the recognized experts in the field. In the case of automotive electronic engine control systems the experts include the design engineers as well as the test engineers, mechanics, and technicians involved in the development of the control system. In addition, expertise is developed by the mechanics who routinely repair the system in the field. The expertise of this latter group can be incorporated as evolutionary improvements in the expert system. The various stages of knowledge acquisition (obtained from the experts) are outlined in Figure 10.13. It can be seen from this illustration that several iterations are required to complete the knowledge acquisition. Thus, the process of interviewing experts is a continuing process.

Not to be overlooked in the development of an expert system is the personal relationship between the experts and the knowledge engineer. The experts must be fully willing to cooperate and to explain their expertise to the knowledge engineer if a successful expert system is to be developed. The personalities of the knowledge engineer and experts can become a factor in the development of an expert system.

Figure 10.14 represents the environment in which an expert system evolves. Of course, a digital computer of sufficient capacity is required for the development work. A summary of expert system development tools that are applicable for a mainframe computer is presented in Table 10.3.

**Figure 10.13
Stages of Knowledge
Acquisition**

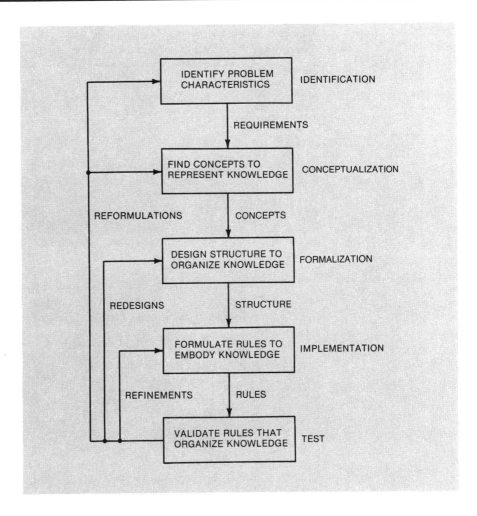

**Figure 10.14
Environment of an
Expert System**

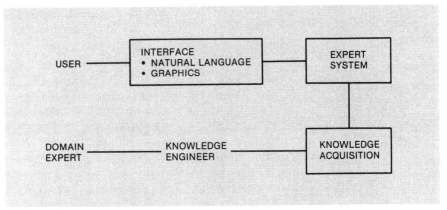

**Table 10.3
Expert System
Developing Tools for
Mainframes**

Name	Company	Machine
Ops5	Carnegie Mellon University	VAX
S.1	Teknowledge	VAX
		Xerox 1198
Loops	Xerox 1108	
Kee	Intelligenetics	Xerox 1198
Art	Inference	Symbolics

It is common practice to think of an expert system as having two major portions. The portion of the expert system in which the logical operations are performed is known as the *inference engine.* The various relationships and basic knowledge are known as the *knowledge base.*

The general diagnostic field to which an expert system is applicable is one in which the procedures used by the recognized experts can be expressed in a set of rules or logical relationships. The automotive diagnosis area is clearly such a field. The diagnostic charts that outline repair procedures (as outlined earlier in this chapter) represent good examples of such rules.

To clarify some of the ideas embodied in an expert system, consider the following example of the diagnosis of an automotive repair problem. This particular problem involves failure of the car engine to start. It is presumed in this example that the range of defects is very limited. Although this example is not very practical, it does illustrate some of the principles involved in an expert system.

A typical expert system formulates expertise in IF-THEN rules.

The fundamental concept underlying this example is the idea of condition-action pairs that are in the form of IF-THEN rules. These rules embody knowledge that is presumed to have come from human experts (e.g., experienced mechanics or automotive engineers).

The expert system of this example consists of three components:

1. A rule base of IF-THEN rules
2. A database of facts
3. A controlling mechanism

Each rule of the rule base is of the form of "if condition A is true, then action B should be taken or performed." The IF portion contains conditions that must be satisfied if the rule is to be applicable. The THEN portion states the action to be performed whenever the rule is activated (fired).

The database contains all of the facts and information that are known to be true about the problem being diagnosed. The rules from the rule base are compared with the knowledge base to ascertain which are the applicable rules. When a rule is fired, its actions normally modify the facts within the database.

The controlling mechanism of this expert system determines which actions are to be taken and when they are to be performed. The operation follows four basic steps:

1. Compare the rules to the database to determine which rules have the IF portion satisfied and can be executed. This group is known as the *conflict set* in AI parlance. A conflict set is a type of set, as in set theory.
2. If the conflict set contains more than one rule, resolve the conflict by selecting the highest priority rule. If there are no rules in the conflict set, stop the procedure.
3. Execute the selected rule by performing the actions specified in the THEN portion, and then modify the database as required.
4. Return to step 1 and repeat the process until there are no rules in the conflict set.

In the present simplified example, it is presumed that the rule base for diagnosing a problem starting a car is as given in Figure 10.15. Rules R2 through R7 draw conclusions about the suspected problem, and rule R1 identifies problem areas that should be investigated. It is implicitly assumed that the actions specified in the THEN portion include "add this fact to the database." In addition, some of the specified actions have an associated fractional number. These values represent the confidence of the expert who is responsible for the rule that the given action is true for the specified condition.

Further suppose that the facts known to be true are as shown in Figure 10.16. The controlling mechanism follows step 1 and discovers that only R1 is in the conflict set. This rule is executed, deriving these additional facts in performing steps 2 and 3:

- Suspect there is no spark
- Suspect too much fuel is reaching the engine

At step 4, the system returns to step 1 and learns that the conflict set includes R1, R4, and R6. Since R1 has been executed, it is dropped from the conflict set. In this simplified example, assume that the conflict is resolved by selecting the lowest-numbered rule (i.e., R4 in this case). Rule R4 yields the additional facts after completing steps 2 and 3 that there is a break in the fuel line (0.65). The value 0.65 refers to the confidence level of this conclusion.

The procedure is repeated with the resulting conflict set R6. After executing R6, the system returns to step 1, and finding no applicable rules, it stops. The final fact set is shown in Figure 10.17. Note that this diagnostic procedure has found two potential diagnoses: a break in the fuel line (confidence level 0.65), and mixture too rich (confidence level 0.70).

**Figure 10.15
Simple Automobile
Diagnostic Rule Base**

R1: IF starter turns engine but it fails to start
    THEN suspect no fuel reaches engine OR
         suspect there is no spark OR
         suspect too much fuel is reaching engine

R2: IF suspect no fuel reaches engine AND
       gas gauge works AND
       gas gauge is on empty
    THEN gas tank is empty (0.95)

R3: IF suspect no fuel reaches engine AND
       gas gauge is not on empty AND
       temperature is less than 32 degrees Fahrenheit
    THEN fuel line is frozen (0.75)

R4: IF suspect no fuel reaches engine AND
       can smell gas
    THEN break in fuel line (0.65)

R5: IF suspect no fuel reaches engine AND
       gas gauge is not on empty AND
       do not smell gas
    THEN water in gas tank (0.5) OR
         gas gauge broken (0.6)

R6: IF suspect too much fuel is reaching engine AND
       can smell gas
    THEN mixture is too rich (0.7)

R7: IF suspect there is no spark AND
       gas gauge not on empty AND
       (weather is damp OR weather is rainy)
    THEN spark plug wires are wet (0.6)

**Figure 10.16
Starting Database of
Known Facts**

gas gauge works
starter turns engine but it fails to start
gas gauge is not on empty
can smell gas

The previous example is intended merely to illustrate the application of artificial intelligence to automotive diagnosis and repair.

To perform diagnosis on a specific car using an expert system, the mechanic identifies all of the relevant features to the mechanic's terminal including, of course, the engine type. After connecting the data link from the electronic control system to the terminal, the diagnosis can begin. The terminal can ask the mechanic to perform specific tasks that are required to

**Figure 10.17
Final Resulting
Database of Known
Facts**

gas gauge works
starter turns engine but it fails to start
gas gauge is not on empty
can smell gas
suspect no fuel reaching engine
suspect there is no spark
suspect too much fuel is reaching engine
break in fuel line (0.65)
mixture too rich (0.7)

The mechanic uses
the expert system
interactively in
diagnosing problems.

complete the diagnosis, including, for example, starting or stopping the engine.

The expert system is an interactive program and, as such, has many interesting features. For example, when the expert system requests that the mechanic perform some specific task, the mechanic can ask the expert system why he or she should do this, or why the system asked the question. The expert system then explains the motivation for the task, much the way a human expert would do if he or she were guiding the mechanic. An expert system is frequently formulated on rules of thumb that have been acquired through years of experience by human experts. It often benefits the mechanic in his or her task to have requests for tasks explained in terms of both these rules and the experience base that has led to the development of the expert system.

The general science of expert systems is so broad that it cannot be covered in this book. The interested reader can contact any good engineering library for further material in this exciting area. In addition, the Society of Automotive Engineers has many publications covering the application of expert systems to automotive diagnosis.

From time to time, automotive maintenance problems will occur that are outside the scope of the expertise incorporated in the expert system. In these cases, an automotive diagnostic system needs to be supplemented by direct contact of the mechanic with human experts. Automobile manufacturers all have technical assistance available to service technicians via voicemail or e-mail.

Vehicle off-board diagnostic systems (whether they are expert systems or not) continue to be developed and refined as experience is gained with the various systems, as the diagnostic database expands, and as additional software is written. The evolution of such diagnostic systems is heading in the direction of fully automated, rapid, and efficient diagnoses of problems in cars equipped with modern digital control systems.

OCCUPANT PROTECTION SYSTEMS

Occupant protection during a crash has evolved dramatically since about the 1970s. Beginning with lap seat belts, and motivated partly by government regulation and partly by market demand, occupant protection has evolved to passive restraints and airbags. We will discuss only the latter since airbag deployment systems can be implemented electronically, whereas other schemes are largely mechanical.

Occupant protection by an airbag is conceptually quite straightforward. The airbag system has a means of detecting when a crash occurs that is essentially based on deceleration along the longitudinal car axis. A collision that is serious enough to injure car occupants involves deceleration in the range of tens of gs (i.e., multiples of 10 of the acceleration of gravity), whereas normal driving involves acceleration/deceleration on the order of 1 g.

Once a crash has been detected, a flexible bag is rapidly inflated with a gas that is released from a container by electrically igniting a chemical compound. Ideally, the airbag inflates in sufficient time to act as a cushion for the driver (or passenger) as he or she is thrown forward during the crash.

On the other hand, practical implementation of the airbag has proven to be technically challenging. Considering the timing involved in airbag deployment it is somewhat surprising that they work as well as they do. At car speeds that can cause injury to the occupants, the time interval for a crash into a rigid barrier from the moment the front bumper contacts the barrier until the final part of the car ceases forward motion is substantially less than a second. Table 10.4 lists required airbag deployment times for a variety of test crash conditions.

A typical airbag will require about 30 msec to inflate, meaning that the crash must be detected within about 20 msec. With respect to the speed of modern digital electronics, a 20 msec time interval is not considered to be short. The complicating factor for crash detection is the many crashlike accelerations experienced by a typical car that could be interpreted by airbag electronics as a crash, such as impact with a large pothole or driving over a curb.

The configuration for an airbag system has also evolved from electromechanical implementation using switches to electronic systems employing sophisticated signal processing. One of the early configurations employed a pair of acceleration switches SW1 and SW2 as depicted in Figure 10.18a. Each of these switches is in the form of a mass suspended in a tube with the tube axis aligned parallel to the longitudinal car axis. Figure 10.18b is a circuit diagram for the airbag system.

The two switches, which are normally open, must both be closed to complete the circuit for firing the airbag. When this circuit is complete, a current flows through the ignitor that activates the charge. A gas is produced (essentially explosively) that inflates the airbag.

**Table 10.4
Airbag Deployment
Times**

Test Library Event	Required Deployment Time (msec)
9 mph frontal barrier	ND
9 mph frontal barrier	ND
15 mph frontal barrier	50.0
30 mph frontal barrier	24.0
35 mph frontal barrier	18.0
12 mph left angle barrier	ND
30 mph right angle barrier	36.0
30 mph left angle barrier	36.0
10 mph center high pole	ND
14 mph center high pole	ND
18 mph center high pole	ND
30 mph center high pole	43.0
25 mph offset low pole	56.0
25 mph car-to-car	50.0
30 mph car-to-car	50.0
30 mph 550 hop road, panic stop	ND
30 mph 629 hop road, panic stop	ND
30 mph 550 tramp road, panic stop	ND
30 mph 629 tramp road, panic stop	ND
30 mph square block road, panic stop	ND
40 mph washboard road, medium braking	ND
25 mph left-side pothole	ND
25 mph right-side pothole	ND
60 mph chatter bumps, panic stop	ND
45 mph massoit bump	ND
5 mph curb impact	ND
20 mph curb dropoff	ND
35 mph belgian blocks	ND

Note: ND = nondeployment.

**Figure 10.18
Airbag Deployment
System**

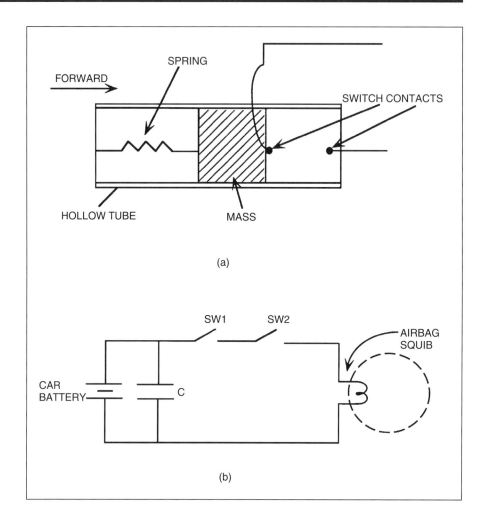

The switches SW1 and SW2 are placed in two separate locations in the car. Typically, one is located near the front of the car and one in or near the front of the passenger compartment (some automakers locate a switch under the driver's seat on the floor pan).

Referring to the sketch in Figure 10.18a, the operation of the acceleration-sensitive switch can be understood. Under normal driving conditions the spring holds the movable mass against a stop and the switch contacts remain open. During a crash the force of acceleration (actually deceleration of the car) acting on the mass is sufficient to overcome the spring force and move the mass. For sufficiently high car deceleration, the mass moves forward to close the switch contacts. In a real collision at sufficient speed, both switch masses

Figure 10.19
Accelerometer-Based Airbag System

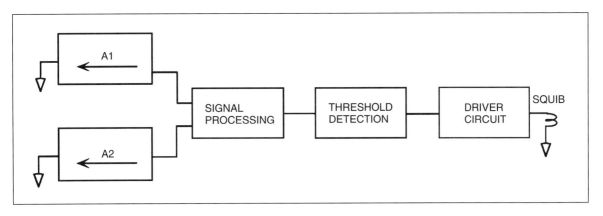

will move to close the switch contacts, thereby completing the circuit and igniting the chemical compound to inflate the airbag.

Figure 10.18b also shows a capacitor connected in parallel with the battery. This capacitor is typically located in the passenger compartment. It has sufficient capacity that in the event the car battery is destroyed early in the crash, it can supply enough current to ignite the squib.

In recent years, there has been a trend to implement electronic airbag systems. In such systems the role of the acceleration-sensitive switch is played by an analog accelerometer along with electronic signal processing, threshold detection, and electronic driver circuit to fire the squib. Figure 10.19 depicts a block diagram of such a system.

The accelerometers A1 and A2 are placed at locations similar to where the switches SW1 and SW2 described above are located. Each accelerometer outputs a signal that is proportional to acceleration (deceleration) along its sensitive axis.

Under normal driving conditions, the acceleration at the accelerometer locations is less than 1 g. However, during a collision at a sufficiently high speed the signal increases rapidly. Signal processing can be employed to enhance the collision signature in relation to the normal driving signal. Such signal processing must be carefully designed to minimize time delay of the output relative to the collision deceleration signal.

After being processed, the deceleration signal is compared with a threshold level. As long as the processed signal is less than this threshold the driver circuit remains deactivated. However, when this signal exceeds the threshold, the driver circuit sends a current of sufficient strength to activate the chemical and inflate the airbag.

Typically, the threshold is set so that airbag deployment occurs for a crash into a barrier at or above a specific speed. Depending on the system design, this speed can be anywhere between 8 and 12 mph. This speed range is chosen by the manufacturer to optimize the protection offered the car occupants while minimizing false deployment (that is, deployment when there is no crash).

In addition to airbags for protecting the driver and front seat passenger against frontal collision, airbags have become available for occupant protection against other types of collisions. Airbags now are available for protection against side impact. Conceptually, these occupant protection systems operate in ways similar to the type described above.

There will continue to be new developments in airbag technology in order to improve performance. Complicating this task is the fact that the signature of a crash differs depending on the crash configuration. For example, there is one class of signature for a crash into a rigid barrier (i.e., a nonmoving and incompressible object) and another for a crash between a pair of cars (particularly when vehicle curb weights are different). In spite of technical difficulties in implementation, the airbag is finding broad application for occupant protection and has achieved broad acceptance by the driving public.

Quiz for Chapter 10

1. In a microprocessor-based digital electronic engine control system, diagnosis
   a. is not really required
   b. can be accomplished with a voltmeter
   c. can be accomplished with a multimeter
   d. is best accomplished with a computer-based system

2. A timing light is useful for
   a. locating timing marks in the dark
   b. adjusting ignition timing
   c. checking dwell
   d. reading the clock on the instrument panel in the dark

3. An engine analyzer has been used to
   a. set ignition points in cars equipped with them
   b. measure intake fuel flow rate
   c. set the choke
   d. none of the above

4. In modern engines incorporating computer-based control systems, diagnosis is performed
   a. with a timing light only
   b. with a timing light and voltmeter
   c. in the digital control system
   d. none of the above

5. Diagnosis of intermittent failures
   a. is routinely accomplished with the on-board diagnostic capability of the engine control system
   b. is readily found using standard service bay equipment
   c. is accomplished by displaying fault codes to the driver at the time of the failure
   d. none of the above

6. A fault code is
   a. a numerical indication of failure in certain specific engine components
   b. displayed to the mechanic during diagnostic mode
   c. registered in memory whenever a failure in a component occurs
   d. all of the above

7. Failures can be detected by a computer-based control system in the following components:
   a. O_2 sensor
   b. MAP sensor
   c. brake switch on cars equipped with cruise control
   d. all of the above and more

8. An expert system is
   a. a computer program that incorporates human knowledge to solve problems normally solved by humans
   b. an organization of automotive engineers
   c. a digital computer
   d. none of the above

9. An expert system is applicable to automotive diagnosis because
   a. automobiles are designed by experts
   b. the diagnostic procedures used can be expressed in a set of rules or logical relationships
   c. modern automobiles incorporate complex digital computers
   d. all of the above

10. In addition to displaying fault codes, the example on-board diagnostic system explained in this chapter can
    a. tell the mechanic where to locate the faulty component on the engine
    b. measure certain engine parameters
    c. detect failures in the catalytic converter
    d. all of the above

Future Automotive Electronic Systems

Up to this point, this book has been discussing automotive electronic technology of the recent past or present. This chapter speculates about the future of automotive electronic systems. Some concepts are only in the laboratory stage and may not, at the time of this writing, have had any vehicle testing at all. Some of the system concepts have been or are currently being tested experimentally. Some are operating on a limited basis in automobiles. Some of the concepts that were included in the corresponding chapter of the previous editions of this book are now in production automobiles.

Whether or not any of the concepts discussed here ever reaches a production phase will depend largely on its technical feasibility and marketability. Some will simply be too costly to have sufficient customer appeal and will be abandoned by the major automobile manufacturers.

On the other hand, one or more of these ideas may become a major market success and be included in many models of automobiles. Some of these systems may even prove to be a significant selling point for one of the large automobile manufacturers.

The following is a summary of the major electronic systems that have been considered and that may be considered for future automotive application. For convenience, these ideas are separated into the following categories:

1. Engine and drivetrain
2. Safety
3. Instrumentation
4. Navigation
5. Communication
6. Information
7. Diagnosis

TELEMATICS

The latter three categories listed above fall under the term *telematics* whenever that function is performed partly off board the vehicle via a wireless link (e.g., cell phone). Future applications of telematics are described in greater detail later in this chapter.

ENGINE AND DRIVETRAIN

The first edition of this book described electronic engine control technology that had been developed up to about the 1981 model-year cars.

Considerable technical innovations have evolved in the interval since then. Some of these technological developments include

1. Knock control
2. Linear solenoid idle speed control
3. Sequential fuel injection
4. Distributorless ignition
5. Self-diagnosis for fail-safe operation
6. Back-up MPU
7. Crankshaft angular position measurement for ignition timing
8. Direct mass air flow sensor
9. Variable valve phasing
10. Hybrid vehicles

Although these technological changes have improved the performance and reliability of the electronically controlled engine, the fundamental control strategy for fuel metering has not changed. The fuel metering strategy has been and will probably continue to be (at least for the short term) to provide a stoichiometric mixture to the engine. This strategy will remain intact as long as a three-way catalytic converter is used to reduce undesirable tailpipe exhaust gas emissions. However, within the constraint of stoichiometric mixture control strategy, there will be some technological improvements in engine control. These improvements will occur in mechanical and electrical components as well as in software that is optimized for performance and efficiency.

In the area of mechanical components, research is being done in the area of variable parameter intake structures. New mechanisms and electromechanical actuators are being developed that will improve volumetric efficiency via:

1. Induction systems with variable geometry
2. Variable valve timing
3. Variable nozzle turbochargers
4. Throttle actuators

One important means for improved volumetric efficiency, which is in production at the time of this writing, is variable valve phasing. This technology was explained in Chapter 7. Future improvements to volumetric efficiency may well involve fully variable valve timing.

The performance and efficiency of any engine are markedly influenced by the intake system. The intake system configuration directly affects the volumetric efficiency of the engine, which is a measure of engine performance as an air pump. The design of an intake system in the past has involved many compromises and trade-offs that were made to enable high volumetric efficiency over the entire engine operating range. Variable geometry is achieved through the use of new electromechanical mechanisms or actuators that can change the shape and dimensions of intake system components.

**Figure 11.1
Configuration of
Variable-Geometry
Intake System**

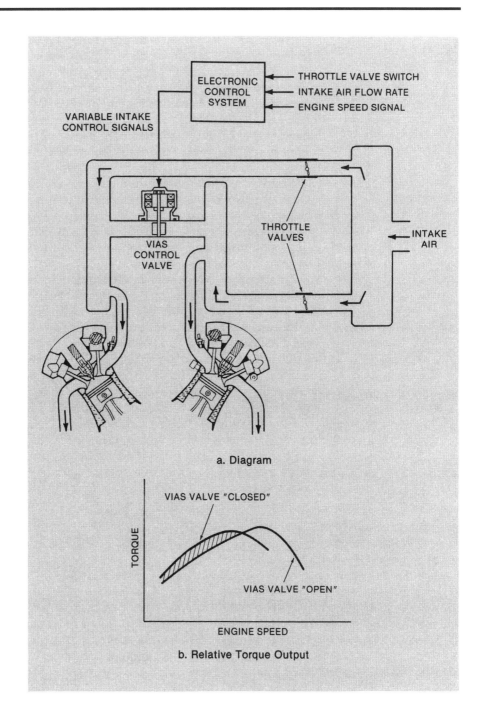

a. Diagram

b. Relative Torque Output

One such system is illustrated in Figure 11.1 for an experimental V-6 engine. This system has two separate intake systems, each of which has a throttle valve. In a traditional engine, the intake manifold is tuned to achieve maximum torque at a particular RPM. The system of Figure 11.1, which is known as a variable impedance aspiration system (VIAS), has two separate intake pipes leading from a plenum chamber to the cylinder banks, with a butterfly valve connecting the two sides. By suitable opening and closing of this valve, the effective dimensions of the intake pipes are changed, thereby tuning the intake. Figure 11.1b shows the relative torque output for an open and closed valve. Note the improved torque at low RPM.

An important aspect of volumetric efficiency is the valve timing (see Chapter 1). Valve timing and valve lift profile are designed with many constraints to ensure the best possible volumetric efficiency over a wide range of engine operations. In the future, valve timing opening and open duration will likely be electronically controlled and electrically activated. One scheme for this VVT concept uses electrohydraulically activated valves. Engine oil (under pressure) could be supplied through a solenoid operated valve to a hydraulic valve lifter such that the valve is forced open when the solenoid is activated.

Electrohydraulically activated valves have the potential to yield the long sought "camless engine." It is possible to improve vehicle fuel efficiency by leaving such valves closed during deceleration, thereby reducing pumping losses. For a hybrid vehicle, the energy absorbed by the engine during deceleration can be recovered via regeneration. In addition, it is possible to improve engine thermal efficiency by selectively disabling the valves on about one-half the cylinders of a multicylinder engine. In this scheme, pumping losses are reduced, thereby improving engine efficiency.

Variable intake components offer great potential for engine performance improvement. However, these components must be controlled by the engine's digital control system. A control system for optimal use of a variable intake system is currently under development and is, of course, equally as important as the components themselves. In addition, there is an increasing trend to apply modern control theory (i.e., adaptive learning systems) to automotive engine control.

Perhaps in the more distant future, technological improvements can be expected in the following areas:

1. Variable compression
2. Swirl control
3. Fuel atomization
4. Direct (in cylinder) fuel injection

Compression ratio directly affects the thermal efficiency and, hence, performance of the engine. It also affects knocking. A variable compression ratio has the potential for significant performance improvement when suitably controlled. The thermal efficiency of an engine is increased with increased compression ratio. However, excessively high compression ratio can lead to knocking. In a variable compression ratio engine the maximum compression ratio must be limited to prevent excessive knock. The development of actuator mechanisms and control strategies for variable compression are important future research areas.

Swirl is a term used to describe the motion of intake gases as they enter the combustion chamber. Swirl influences combustion speed and, thereby, thermal efficiency. Swirl control can theoretically be achieved by using a variable intake system. There is research currently being done in this area.

Efficient combustion of all of the energy that is available in the fuel is influenced by fuel atomization. When fuel is mixed with air, the droplets should be sized such that air and gasoline molecules can readily be combined. The atomization of fuel to optimally sized droplets is influenced by the fuel injector configuration. Research into new fuel injectors that can provide improved fuel atomization is under way. Also being researched is the use of ultrasonics to increase atomization after injection has occurred.

Moreover, direct injection of gasoline fuel into the cylinder similar to diesel engine fuel injection has thermal efficiencies relative to intake port injection. This technology is being evaluated for possible passenger car application.

In addition, fuel injectors based on the piezoelectric effect (see Chapter 6) have been developed. A voltage applied to a piezoelectric crystal causes a deflection that can be used to pump fuel. A piezoelectric fuel injector is a very high importance, fast-acting device that has many potential advantages for fuel injection.

Control Based on Cylinder Pressure Measurements

One of the more interesting control concepts currently under investigation is based on cylinder pressure measurements. Cylinder pressure developed during the power stroke has long been recognized as the most fundamental variable that can be monitored to determine the operating state of the engine. Cylinder pressure measurements provide real-time combustion process feedback that can be used for control of engine variables of individual cylinders.

Figure 11.2 is a block diagram of an engine control system that obtains the required feedback signal from a cylinder pressure sensor. An example of fuel control strategy using cylinder pressure is based on the relationship between air/fuel ratio and the cyclic fluctuation in cylinder pressure. Figure 11.3 is a graph of the fluctuation in peak cylinder pressure (θ_{pmax}) as a function of air/fuel ratio. This fluctuation remains relatively low for air/fuel ratios of approximately 13 to 20. For leaner mixtures, the random fluctuations in cylinder pressure increase. Such fluctuations are equivalent to rough engine operation and are undesirable. In the example fuel control strategy, the air/fuel ratio is maintained near 20 and is reduced whenever the measured cycle fluctuation in cylinder pressure exceeds a threshold value.

A corresponding spark-advance control strategy can be similarly derived from cylinder pressure measurements. In Chapter 7, a scheme for measuring

**Figure 11.2
Engine Control
System Based on
Cylinder Pressure
Measurements**

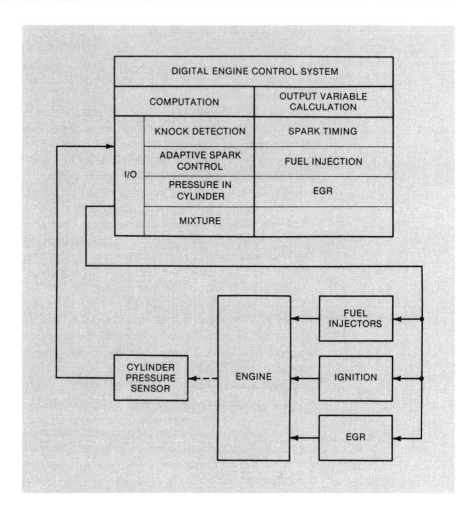

knock intensity from the rapid cylinder pressure fluctuations near TDC is explained. Thus, a measurement of cylinder pressure has the potential to provide fuel and spark control from a single sensor.

An experimental cylinder pressure sensor that uses a piezoelectric element has been developed (Figure 11.4a). The output voltage from the piezoelectric element is proportional to the applied pressure. Figure 11.4b is a sketch of the mounting configuration for this sensor in the cylinder head. Cylinder pressure is applied to the piezoelectric element, and an output voltage is generated that is suitable for closed-loop engine control.

Alternatively, a pressure can be implemented as a part of the cylinder head gasket (i.e., a "smart head gasket"). The measured pressure signal is sent to the controller via a wire harness that projects from the side of the gasket.

**Figure 11.3
Variation in Cylinder
Pressure with Air/Fuel
Ratio**

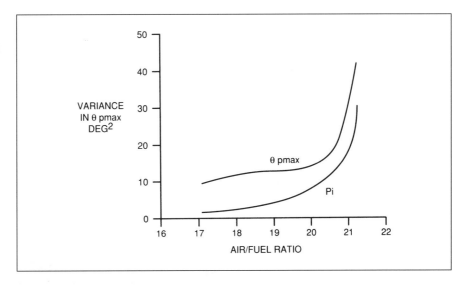

Wide Range Air/Fuel Sensor

There is another sensor that may influence the trend of future fuel control systems. This sensor is mounted in the engine exhaust pipe similarly to the presently used EGO sensor. However, this sensor generates an output that varies linearly with air/fuel ratio over a range of about 12 to 22. The importance of a control strategy based on air/fuel ratio measurements is illustrated in Figure 11.5, in which relative power, fuel consumption rate, and NO_x emissions as a function of equivalence ratio (see Chapter 5) are depicted. Note that engine power is reduced compared to stoichiometry ($\lambda = 1$) for relatively high values of λ, but that the reduction is smaller than the reduction in NO_x emission. The fuel consumption rate is minimum for $\lambda \cong 1.5$. In contrast, these variables are shown versus the output of a standard O_2 (EGO) sensor.

The sensor configuration is shown in Figure 11.6. This sensor uses yttria (Y_2O_3)-stabilized zirconia (ZrO_2) as a diffusion element that is preheated to a desired operating temperature. In actual operation, a voltage, V_s, is applied across this element, and a current, I_p, flows. The theory of operation is beyond the scope of this book, though it is based on the diffusion of various ions through the element. Nevertheless, current I_p varies linearly with λ, as shown in Figure 11.7. A measurement of the current (which is straightforward) yields a measurement of λ.

Whether this sensor concept will be broadly applied in engine control is yet to be determined. However, the control strategy based on air/fuel ratio measurements has the benefit of providing emission control without necessarily requiring a three-way catalytic converter, and at the same time achieves relatively good fuel economy.

**Figure 11.4
Cylinder Pressure
Sensor**

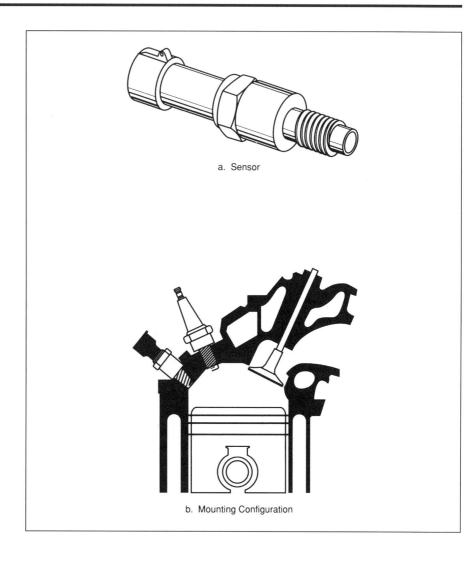

a. Sensor

b. Mounting Configuration

Alternative Engine

The engine that has been discussed in detail throughout this book is a
4-stroke/cycle, gasoline-fueled, spark-ignited (SI) engine (see Chapter 1). An
alternative gasoline engine is the 2-stroke/cycle engine. This type of engine
has been used for many years as a small marine engine, as motorcycle and
lawnmower engines, and briefly as a passenger car engine. Unlike the 4-
stroke/cycle engine, which requires two complete crankshaft revolutions
for each power stroke, the 2-stroke/cycle engine delivers power during each
crankshaft revolution. This engine has the potential to be more compact
and lightweight for a given power output and to require fewer parts than a

**Figure 11.5
Engine Performance
versus Equivalence
Ratio**

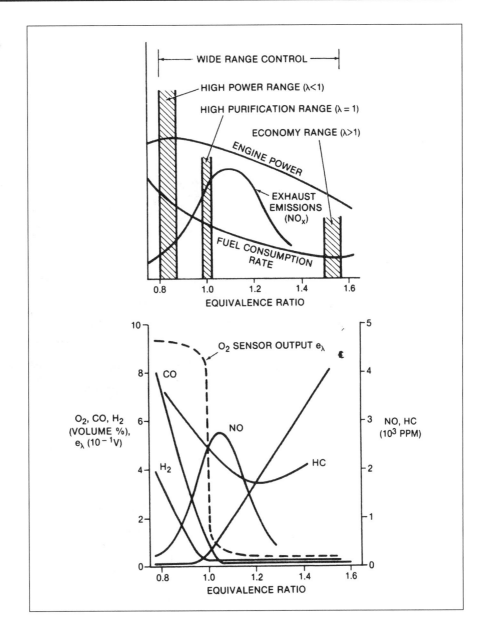

comparable 4-stroke/cycle engine. Great potential fuel economy benefits can be achieved using this engine compared with a 4-stroke/cycle engine due to reduced vehicle weight and improved vehicle shape for drag reduction.

In the past, the 2-stroke/cycle engine was virtually eliminated as a passenger car power plant due to the emission regulations of the Clean Air Act.

Figure 11.6
Linear Air/Fuel Sensor
Configuration

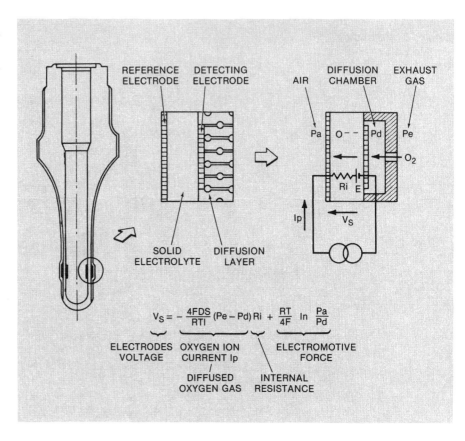

Poor emission performance results, in part, from less efficient combustion than the 4-stroke/cycle engine. In addition, the traditional 2-stroke/cycle engine requires mixing lubricating oil with gasoline, resulting in poor emissions.

The potential for this engine in cars may be returning due to recent developments in technology, including electronic fuel control. Figure 11.8 is a schematic cross-sectional drawing of a 2-stroke/cycle engine. Some of the new technology on this engine that is missing from the traditional 2-stroke/cycle engine includes the intake and exhaust valves, supercharger, direct fuel injection, and oil injector jet for lubrication. In at least one engine configuration under development, there are four valves per cylinder that assist in scavenging (i.e., removing exhaust and charging the cylinder with intake air). In addition, a Roots-type supercharger helps in scavenging and mixture distribution.

The direct fuel injection provides highly atomized fuel droplets. The control of fuel droplet size to very small droplets improves the surface/volume ratio of fuel, resulting in reduced emissions and improved fuel economy.

**Figure 11.7
Fuctional Operation of
Lambda Sensor**

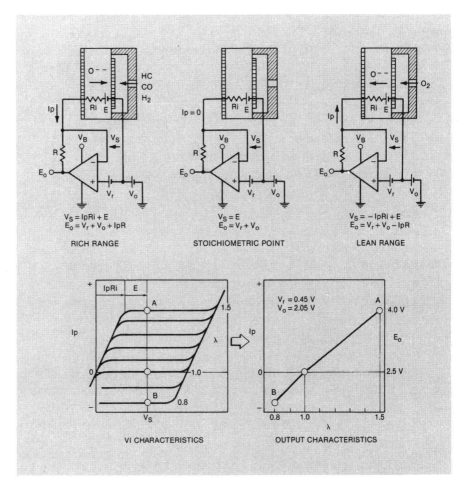

Other keys to optimal emission control include precise mixture distribution and ignition control. Mixture distribution is controlled by regulating (under electronic control) the fuel injection timing. Electronic controls have proved to be the only cost-effective means of mixture distribution and ignition timing control.

Should the highly sophisticated fuel control system for the 2-stroke/cycle engine meet all emissions and performance goals, the engine should have a great future in passenger car applications.

Alternative-Fuel Engines

In order to reduce dependence on imported oil, there has been a considerable development effort devoted to finding alternatives to gasoline fuels. The two leading candidates are natural gas and alcohol fuels (methanol

**Figure 11.8
2-Stroke/Cycle Engine
Configuration**

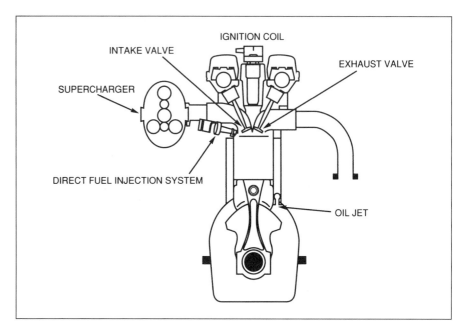

and ethanol). The latter fuel is made from grain and is a renewable fuel source. Ethanol is otherwise known as ethyl alcohol and is the alcoholic part of beer, wine, and liquor and is obviously nontoxic when consumed in reasonable amounts. Brazil has operated large fleets of ethanol-fueled cars for years, though at great government subsidy. For the foreseeable future, ethanol does not appear to be a practical alternative to completely replace gasoline as a motor fuel in the United States although it is often mixed with gasoline, forming so-called gasohol and as such can form at least a partial substitute for gasoline.

Methanol is an alcohol fuel that is potentially available at relatively low cost and can replace gasoline as a motor fuel. It can be manufactured from coal, which is in abundant supply in the United States. It is routinely used as a fuel for racing cars because it has a relatively high octane rating.

Unfortunately, methanol has a number of disadvantages for passenger use. For example, it has roughly half the energy of an equivalent amount of gasoline. Thus, for a given range, the fuel tank must be roughly double the size of a fuel tank for gasoline. In addition, methanol-fueled cars do not start readily in cold weather, which is an obvious disadvantage in the northern United States. Moreover, methanol is toxic and highly corrosive. The entire fuel system must be made from stainless steel in order to cope with the severe corrosion.

Yet another disadvantage of methanol is the lack of a distribution system (including gas stations equipped to sell this fuel). This latter problem can be potentially overcome with the advent of engines that can operate on either gasoline, methanol, or a mixture of the two. Vehicles that are so equipped are called *flexible fuel vehicles* (FFV).

Electronic fuel controls are vital to the success of any FFV. Fundamental to any FFV is a sensor that can measure the alcohol content of the fuel. There are two types of practical alcohol sensors available at the present time. One of these measures alcohol content optically by sensing the index of refraction for the mixture, which is a unique function of the alcohol content. The other senses alcohol with a capacitive sensor. This latter sensor is based on the differences in dielectric constant (see Chapter 5) of gasoline and methanol.

Once the alcohol content of fuel has been measured, the electronic fuel control system can properly regulate fuel delivery to stoichiometric mixture ratio. The quantity of fuel required for a given mass air flow rate increases as the alcohol content increases. For neat methanol (100% methanol), the fuel flow rate is roughly double that for neat gasoline.

The various problems associated with handling methanol mean that it is unlikely to play a role in passenger car fuel for the foreseeable future. Ethanol, on the other hand, is available in passenger car fuel in a mixture with gasoline at up to 15% ethanol in limited markets. At such a low concentration, it can be used to fuel cars without modification to the car. The future use of ethanol in car fuel is a complex function of many factors, including the cost and availability of petroleum and the relative cost of producing ethanol.

Electric and Hybrid Vehicles

Powering cars with electric motors has existed (in very limited numbers) since the earliest days. However, electric-powered cars have never competed practically with gasoline-fueled IC engine-powered cars. The most significant single factor limiting widespread application of electric cars has been and continues to be the relatively low-energy density of electric energy storage compared to gasoline. Energy density is the amount of stored energy per unit weight of the electrical storage means. At the time of this writing, the only practical means of storing electric energy is the chemical/electric cell or combination of cells commonly known as a battery. For a conventional automobile, the car battery is the familiar lead acid battery although NiMH batteries are being used in hybrid vehicles as suggested in Chapter 7. Although a car battery has ample energy storage to crank the engine for starting, if it were to be used to move the car, it has about enough energy to move a medium-size car less than a mile. A typical car battery weighs about as much as 5 gallons of gas, which can move the car at highway speeds 50 to 100 miles.

The few electric cars in existence have optimized powertrain and energy storage means. These cars are variably capable of moving a small car 50 to 100 miles before requiring a recharge. In spite of considerable expenditure in research and development, relatively little progress has been made in developing an electric car that competes strongly with existing gasoline-fueled cars in range and performance owing to the poor energy density of electric energy storage.

An alternative means of storing electrical energy to the car battery is the ultra high capacity capacitor (ultra-cap). This technology has very high specific power (i.e., power/unit weight), and it has very low specific energy. Ultra-cap technology will likely be used as a supplement to batteries for relatively short duration bursts of relatively high power. Such high power might be used to start a hybrid car engine and assist the engine in accelerating the car from a standing stop (e.g., in heavy traffic).

On the other hand, the hybrid electric car introduced in Chapter 1 (and discussed in some detail in Chapter 7) has made progress in matching the range and performance of gasoline-fueled cars. Operational efficiency of hybrid vehicles is improved by raising the voltage level of the vehicle electrical bus. This issue is one of the motivations for changing from 14-volt to 42-volt vehicle electrical systems. The future of these cars will be determined largely by cost of ownership and operation relative to conventional gasoline-fueled cars.

Fuel Cell-Powered Cars

There is a form of electrically powered car that may mitigate the energy density problem. The energy is stored in a chemical fuel that has the capability of great energy density, and electric power is created in a device known as a fuel cell. In its simplest form, a fuel cell converts energy stored in hydrogen (H_2) directly into electric power. Its only exhaust product is water (H_2O). A

**Figure 11.9
FFV System
Fuel Cell
Configuration**

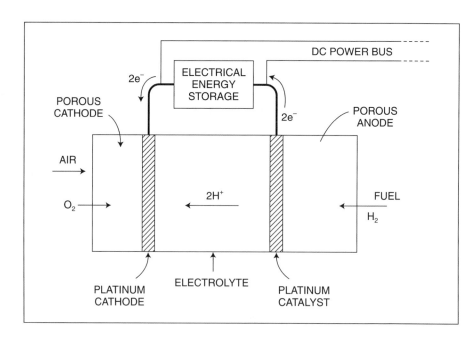

hydrogen-fueled fuel cell can theoretically produce electricity in amounts suitable to power a car (via an electric motor), with performance comparable to that of gasoline-fueled cars and with zero harmful exhaust emissions (i.e., only water). The great potential for fuel-cell-powered cars has motivated and will continue to motivate research and development aimed at solving a myriad of practical problems that pose obstacles to the practical fuel-cell-powered car.

For an understanding of some of those problems, it is instructive to briefly review the theory of the fuel cell. A fuel cell configuration is shown in Figure 11.9.

The fuel cell structure depicted here is known as a proton exchange membrane (PEM) cell. It consists of a pair of porous electrodes: an anode and a cathode separated by an electrolyte. Each electrode is coated on the electrolyte side with a platinum catalyst. The porous anode is supplied with hydrogen (H_2) which diffuses through the anode to the platinum-coated junction between the anode and the electrolyte. The platinum catalyst causes each hydrogen atom to separate into a free electron and a positively charged hydrogen ion (H^+) which is, in fact, a proton.

At the same time, the porous cathode is exposed to oxygen (O_2), which passes through the cathode to the corresponding platinum catalyst. The free electrons migrate from the anode to the cathode passing through an external circuit (including an energy storage device or battery). Owing to the catalytic action, the cathode chemical reaction is:

$$O_2 + 4H^+ + 4e^- \rightarrow 2H_2O$$

That is, the oxygen combines with free electrons and hydrogen ions to form water. There is no other exhaust product for this ideal reaction.

Unfortunately, a number of tough technical problems must be overcome before the fuel-cell-powered electric car can become a practical reality. Not the least of these problems is the storage of hydrogen, which can be achieved either directly as gaseous or liquid hydrogen or indirectly in a liquid hydrogen-rich fuel.

These storage methods have numerous advantages and disadvantages. The direct storage technique has the advantage that the hydrogen is available to be supplied from the storage means directly to the fuel cell. The disadvantage of direct storage is that the hydrogen must be stored at very high pressure or at very low temperatures. Another disadvantage of direct storage is the lack of an existing infrastructure to supply gaseous or liquid hydrogen to the customer. However, should the direct storage method prove to be practical, this infrastructure will develop rapidly.

The advantages of indirect storage include high-energy density for liquid fuel and a wide range of liquid fuels from gasoline through vegetable oil. Even methanol has great potential as a liquid fuel for fuel-cell-powered cars. The major disadvantage of indirect storage is the requirement to create hydrogen from the hydrogen-rich fuel. Creation of hydrogen from liquid fuel requires a catalytic device known as a reformer. The reformer chemically breaks down the liquid fuel into hydrogen and various compounds of carbon and other chemical elements, all of which must be separated from the hydrogen before it is supplied to the fuel cell. Even small amounts of impurities in the hydrogen can eventually degrade the fuel cell performance. Moreover, these other chemical compounds are released in the system exhaust and are potentially harmful.

Another practical problem limiting the application of fuel cells in electric cars is their relatively slow dynamic response. Performance of a fuel cell is enhanced by nearly steady-state operation. A practical fuel-cell-powered car will most likely require electrical storage cells, that can supply current as required at the widely varying power levels associated with driving an electric car. The fuel cell will mostly be used to replace electric energy taken from the storage cells, with the goal of maintaining a target state-of-charge.

The problem of maintaining the desired state-of-charge of the energy storage device requires electronic controls similar to those discussed with respect to a hybrid car (see Chapter 7). In fact, one can think of the fuel cell as a replacement for the engine/generator portion of a hybrid car. The benefits of the fuel cell include its potential for zero exhaust emission (i.e., a zero emission vehicle, ZEV) and the wide range of liquid fuels for which it can be designed.

Since fuel-cell-powered cars are electric cars, dynamic braking (using the motor as a generator) during deceleration/stopping can recover some kinetic energy, thereby improving the vehicle fuel efficiency.

The future of fuel-cell-powered cars is far from certain at the time of this writing. Numerous technical and infrastructure problems must be overcome before it will be a practical reality, although numerous automotive OEMs have plans to offer a fuel-cell-powered car for sale, one of which uses methanol for fuel. It just might be that after more than 100 years of automotive use of the Otto cycle IC engine, the fuel cell might be the "dark horse" replacement for it.

Transmission Control

Electronic control of an automotive transmission could provide maximum performance by matching engine controls and transmission gear ratios.

The automatic transmission is another important part of the drivetrain that must be controlled. Traditionally, the automatic transmission control system has been hydraulic and pneumatic. However, there are some potential benefits to the electronic control of the automatic transmission.

The engine and transmission work together as a unit to provide the variable torque needed to move the car. If the transmission were under control of the electronic engine control system, then optimum performance for the entire drivetrain could be obtained by coordinating the engine controls and transmission gear ratio.

Continuously Variable Transmission

One concept having great potential for integrated engine/powertrain control involves the use of a continuously variable transmission. Instead of being limited to three, four, or five gear ratios, this transmission configuration

**Figure 11.10
Continuously Variable
Transmission**

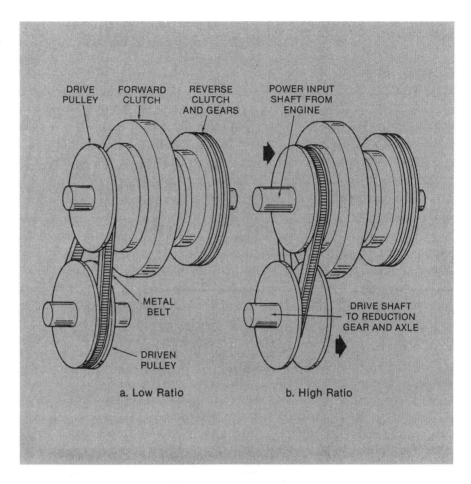

DRIVE
PULLEY

FORWARD
CLUTCH

REVERSE
CLUTCH
AND GEARS

POWER INPUT
SHAFT FROM
ENGINE

METAL
BELT

DRIVEN
PULLEY

DRIVE SHAFT
TO REDUCTION
GEAR AND AXLE

a. Low Ratio

b. High Ratio

has a continuous range of gear ratios from a minimum value to a maximum
value as determined by the design parameters for the transmission.

The continuously variable transmission (CVT) is an alternative to the
present automatic transmission. It is being developed presently and will likely
see considerable commercial use in production cars provided that certain
mechanical problems can be overcome.

The principle of the CVT is shown in Figure 11.10. Power is transmitted
from the driving shaft to the driven shaft by a belt that couples a pair of split
pulleys. The effective gear ratio is the ratio of pulley radii at the contact point
of the belt. The radii vary inversely with the spacings of the split pulleys. The
spacings are controlled by a pair of hydraulic cylinders that push the left half of
each pulley in or out.

The control strategy for an integrated engine and CVT system is
relatively complicated and involves measuring vehicle speed and load torque.

Considerable research effort has been and will continue to be expended to develop a suitable control system, the technology of which will, undoubtedly, be digital electronic controls.

SAFETY

Collision Avoidance Radar Warning System

Collision avoidance radar systems use low-power radar to sense objects and provide warnings of possible collisions.

An interesting safety-related electronic system with potential for future automotive application is the anticollision warning system. An on-board low-power radar system can be used as a sensor for an electronic collision avoidance system to provide warning of a potential collision with an object lying in the path of the vehicle. As early as 1976, at least one experimental system was developed that could accurately detect objects up to distances of about 100 yards. This system gave very few false alarms in actual highway tests.

For an anticollision warning application, the radar antenna should be mounted on the front of the car and should project a relatively narrow beam forward. Ideally, the antenna for such a system should be in as flat a package as possible, and should project a beam that has a width of about 2° to 3° horizontally and about 4° to 5° vertically. Large objects such as signs can reflect the radar beam, particularly on curves, and trigger a false alarm. If the beam is scanned horizontally for a few degrees, say 2.5° either side of center, false alarms from roadside objects can be reduced.

In order to test whether a detected object is in the same lane as the radar-equipped car traveling around a curve, the radius of the curve must be measured. This can be estimated closely from the front wheel steering angle for an unbanked curve. Given the scanning angle of the radar beam and the curve radius, a computer can quickly perform the calculations to determine whether or not a reflecting object is in the same lane as the protected car.

For the collision warning system, better results can be obtained if the radar transmitter is operated in a pulsed mode rather than in a continuous-wave mode. In this mode, the transmitter is switched on for a very short time, then it is switched off. During the off time, the receiver is set to receive a reflected signal. If a reflecting object is in the path of the transmitted microwave pulse, a corresponding pulse will be reflected to the receiver. The round trip time, t, from transmitter to object and back to receiver is proportional to the range, R, to the object, as illustrated in Figure 11.11 and expressed in the following equation:

$$t = \frac{2R}{c}$$

where c is the speed of light (186,000 miles per second). The radar system has the capability of accurately measuring this time to determine the range to the object.

**Figure 11.11
Range to Object for
Anticollision Warning
System**

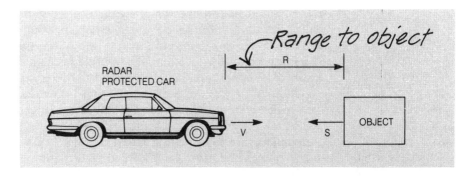

**Figure 11.12
Collision Avoidance
Warning System**

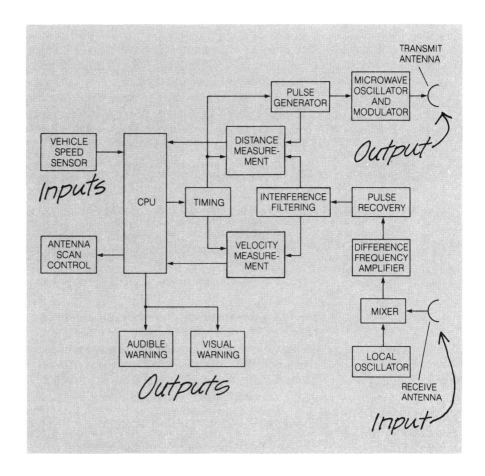

It is possible to measure the vehicle speed, *V*, by measuring the Doppler frequency shift of the pulsed signal reflected by the ground. (The Doppler frequency shift is proportional to the speed of the moving object. The Doppler shift is what causes the pitch of the whistle of a moving train to change as it passes.) This reflection can be discriminated from the object reflection because the ground reflection is at a low angle and a short, fixed range.

The reflection from an object will have a pulse shape that is very nearly identical to that of the transmitted pulse. As noted, the radar system can detect this object reflection and find *R* to determine the distance from the vehicle to the object. In addition, the relative speed of closure between the car and the object can be calculated by adding the vehicle speed, *V*, from the ground reflected pulses and the speed of the object, *S*, which can be determined from the change in range of the object's reflection pulses. A block diagram of an experimental collision warning system is shown in Figure 11.12. In this system, the range, *R*, to the object and the closing speed, *V* + *S*, are measured.

> A collision avoidance system compares the time needed for a microwave signal to be reflected from an object to the time needed for a signal to be reflected from the ground. By comparing these times with vehicle speed data, the computer can calculate a "time to impact" value and sound an alarm if necessary.

The computer can perform a number of calculations on these data. For example, the computer can calculate the time to collision, *T*. Whenever this time is less than a preset value, a visual and audible warning is generated. The system could also be programmed to release the throttle and apply the brakes, if automatic control were desired.

If the object is traveling at the same speed as the radar-equipped car and in the same direction, $S = -V$, and *T* is infinite. That is, a collision would never occur. If the object is stationary, $S = 0$ and the time to collision is:

$$T = \frac{R}{V}$$

Note that this system can give the vehicle speed, which is applicable for antilock braking systems. If the object is another moving car approaching the radar-equipped car head-on, the closing speed is the sum of the two car speeds. In this case, the time to closure is

$$T = \frac{R}{V + S}$$

This concept already has been considerably refined since its inception. However, there are still some technical problems that must be overcome before this system is ready for production use. Nevertheless, the performance of the experimental systems that have been tested is impressive. It will be interesting to watch this technology improve and to see which, if any, of the present system configurations becomes commercially available.

Low Tire Pressure Warning System

> Another potential application of electronics to automotive safety is a low tire pressure warning system.

Another interesting electronic system that is slowly finding use in automobiles is a warning system for low tire pressure that works while the car

**Figure 11.13
Low Tire Pressure
Warning System**

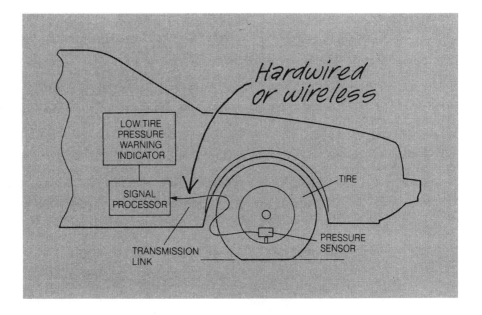

is in motion. This application is motivated in part by an act of Congress that among other things requires that new vehicles have tire pressure monitoring capability by the 2004 model year. A potentially dangerous situation could be avoided if the driver could be alerted to the fact that a tire has low pressure. For example, if a tire develops a leak, the driver could be warned in sufficient time to stop the car before control becomes difficult.

There are several pressure sensor concepts that can be used. A block diagram of a hypothetical system is shown in Figure 11.13. In this scheme, a tire pressure sensor continually measures the tire pressure. The signal from the sensor mounted on the rolling tire is coupled by a link to the electronic signal processor. Whenever the pressure drops below a critical limit, a warning signal is sent to a display on the instrument panel to indicate which tire has the low pressure.

A low tire pressure warning system utilizes a tire-mounted pressure sensor. The pressure sensor signals a loss in tire pressure.

The difficult part of this system is the link from the tire pressure sensor mounted on the rotating tire to the signal processor mounted on the body. Several concepts have the potential to provide this link. For example, slip rings, which are similar to the brushes on a dc motor, could be used. However, this would require a major modification to the wheel-axle assembly and does not appear to be an acceptable choice at the present time.

Another concept for providing this link is to use a small radio transmitter mounted on the tire. By using modern solid-state electronic technology, a low-power transmitter is mounted in the tire valves. The transmitter sends a signal to a receiver in the car body. The distance from the transmitter to the receiver is a few feet, so only very low power is required.

**Figure 11.14
Low-Pressure Sensor
Concept**

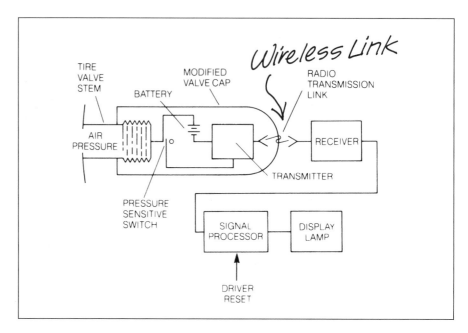

One problem with this method is that electrical power for the transmitter would have to be provided by a self-contained battery. However, the transmitter need only operate for a few seconds and only when the tire pressure falls below a critical level. Therefore, a tiny battery could theoretically provide enough power.

The scheme is illustrated schematically for a single tire in Figure 11.14. The sensor switch is usually held open by normal tire pressure on a diaphragm mechanically connected to the switch. Low tire pressure allows the spring-loaded switch to close, thereby switching on the microtransmitter. The receiver, which is directly powered by the car battery, receives the transmitted signal and passes it to the signal processor, also directly powered by the car battery. The signal processor then activates a warning lamp for the driver, and it remains on until the driver resets the warning system by operating a switch on the instrument panel.

One reason for using a signal processing unit is the relatively short life of the transmitter battery. The transmitter will remain on until the low-pressure condition is corrected or until the battery runs down. By using a signal processor, the low-pressure status can be stored in memory so the warning will still be given even if the transmitter quits operating. The need for this feature could arise if the pressure dropped while the car was parked. By storing the status, the system would warn the driver as soon as the ignition was turned on.

Still another scheme for monitoring tire pressure is to have a transmitter/receiver mounted on the car. In this scheme, the tire pressure sensor is a form of passive transponder that is interrogated by the transmitter/receiver system.

INSTRUMENTATION

The reduced cost of VLSI and microprocessor electronics is resulting in advanced instrumentation and the use of voice synthesis in warning systems.

It is very likely that some interesting advances in automotive instrumentation will be forthcoming, such as certain functions, new display forms including audible messages by synthesized speech, and interactive communication between the driver and the instrumentation. These advances will come about partly because of increased capability at reduced cost for modern solid-state circuits, particularly microprocessors and microcomputers.

The concept of a solid-state CRT-like display has great potential for future instrument panel (IP) display. It was shown in Chapter 9 that the solid-state display of this type can display alphanumeric or graphical data in a multicolor format. Multicolor liquid crystal display technology is likely to dominate for at least the near future (see Chapter 9). In a sense this technology has the capability of displaying on the IP information of the type commonly found on a PC screen. For example, electronic maps can form the basis of a navigational system depicting vehicle's present position, destination, and optimal route to the destination in the presence of known traffic problems. In effect, a solid-state CRT display has the capability of displaying essentially any important information the driver needs either for the particular trip or with respect to the vehicle status.

In addition, this type of display is potentially reconfigurable so that the IP can be custom tailored to the driver's needs. For example, one driver might prefer that only the minimum information be displayed (e.g., vehicle speed, transmission, gear selection, distance to empty fuel tank, turn signal indication, and light status). Another driver of the same car might wish to have various additional variables displayed (e.g., engine RPM, oil pressure, coolant temperature, fuel flow rate). It is possible that all future IP displays will be one form or other of liquid crystal multicolor CRT type display. Such an IP is similar in concept to the so-called glass cockpit of modern aircraft display, as discussed in Chapter 10.

One of the important functions that an all-electronic instrumentation system can have in future automobiles is continuous diagnosis of other on-board electronic systems. In particular, the future computer-based electronic instrumentation may perform diagnostic tests on the electronic engine control system. This instrumentation system might display major system faults and even recommend repair actions.

Another function that might be improved in the instrumentation system is the trip computer function. The system probably will be highly interactive; that is, the driver will communicate with the computer through a keyboard or maybe even by voice. By combining the vehicle instrumentation with telematics functions (discussed later), the entire system can be made to function online. In this way, trip-related information can be displayed optimally to the driver while he/she is driving.

Heads Up Display

In the first edition of this book, it was speculated that CRT displays or solid-state equivalents to a CRT would appear in production cars. This has, in fact, occurred, and there is a description of the CRT display in Chapter 9. It was also speculated that the CRT might be used in conjunction with a heads up display (HUD). There is no clear sign, however, that the basic display source will be a CRT. In fact, any light-emitting display device can be used with a HUD. A heads up display of the speed is now available on certain models of automobiles.

It is convenient to describe a HUD by presuming that the display source is a CRT-type display, keeping in mind that many other display sources can be substituted for the CRT. Figure 11.15 illustrates the concept of a HUD. In this scheme, the information that is to be displayed appears on a CRT that is mounted as shown. A partially reflecting mirror is positioned above the instrument panel in the driver's line of sight of the road. In normal driving, the driver looks through this mirror at the road. Information to be displayed appears on the face of the CRT upside down, and the image is reflected by the partially reflecting mirror to the driver right side up. The driver can read these data from the HUD without moving his or her head from the position for viewing the road. The brightness of this display would have to be adjusted so that it is compatible with ambient light. The brightness of this data image

The CRT-type display, when combined with a partially reflective mirror, results in a HUD. Information is displayed on the CRT in the form of a reversed image. The image is reflected by the mirror and viewed normally by the driver.

**Figure 11.15
Heads Up Display**

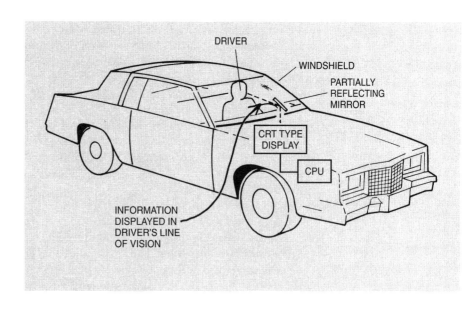

should never be so great that it inhibits the driver's view of the road, but it must be bright enough to be visible in all ambient lighting conditions. Fortunately, the display brightness can be automatically controlled by electronic circuits to accommodate a wide range of light levels.

Speech Synthesis

Speech synthesizers use phoneme synthesis, a method of imitating the basic sounds used to build speech. Computers rely on an inventory of phonemes to build the words for various automotive warning messages.

It is also possible to provide information to a driver by synthesized speech, which has great potential for future automotive electronic instrumentation. Important safety or trip-related messages could be given audibly so the driver doesn't have to look away from the road. In addition to its normal function of generating visual display outputs, the computer generates an electrical waveform that is approximately the same as a human voice speaking the appropriate message. The voice quality of some types of speech synthesis is often quite natural and similar to human speech.

The speech synthesis considered here must be distinguished from production voice message systems that have already appeared in production cars. In these latter systems only "canned," or preplanned, messages have been available. In the true speech synthesis system, relatively complex messages can be generated in response to outputs from various electronic subsystems. For example, the trip computer could give fuel status in relationship to the car's present position and known fueling stations (both of the latter being available from the navigation system). By combining information from several subsystems on board the car, it is possible to inform the driver of trip status at any required level of detail.

There are several major categories of speech synthesis that have been studied experimentally. Of these, phoneme synthesis is probably the most sophisticated. A *phoneme* is a basic sound that is used to build speech. By having an inventory of these sounds in computer memory and by having the capability to generate each phoneme sound, virtually any word can be constructed by the computer in a manner similar to the way the human voice does. Of course, the electrical signal produced by the computer is converted to sound by a loudspeaker.

Synthesized speech is being used to automatically provide data over the phone from computer-based systems and has potential application for data presentation cars. At the time of this writing, drivers in certain high-end cars can be in wireless communication with an information service operated by automotive OEMS. Synthesized speech could be used to supplement information from human operators for some routine messages or data.

MULTIPLEXING IN AUTOMOBILES

One of the high-cost items in building and servicing vehicles is the electrical wiring. Wires of varying length and diameter form the interconnection link between each electrical or electronic component in the vehicle. Virtually the entire electrical wiring for a car is in the form of a complex, expensive cable assembly called a *harness*. Building and installing the harness require manual assembly and are time consuming. The increased use of electrical and electronic devices has significantly increased the number of wires in the harness. Multiplexing already exists in one form or another in production automobiles. In the future, increased use of multiplexing can be anticipated to reduce wiring harness complexity and to reduce vehicle weight. Below we present a few candidate subsystems in which multiplexing can achieve these reductions.

Sensor Multiplexing

The use of microprocessors for computer engine control, instrumentation computers, etc., offers the possibility of significantly reducing the complexity of the harness. For example, consider the engine control system. In the present configuration, each sensor and actuator has a separate wire connection to the CPU. However, each sensor only communicates periodically with the computer for a short time interval during sampling.

It is possible to connect all the sensors to the CPU with only a single wire (with ground return, of course). This wire, which can be called a data bus, provides the communication link between all of the sensors and the CPU.

Sensor multiplexing can reduce the necessary wiring in an electrical harness by using time division multiplexing.

**Figure 11.16
Sensor Multiplexing
Block Diagram**

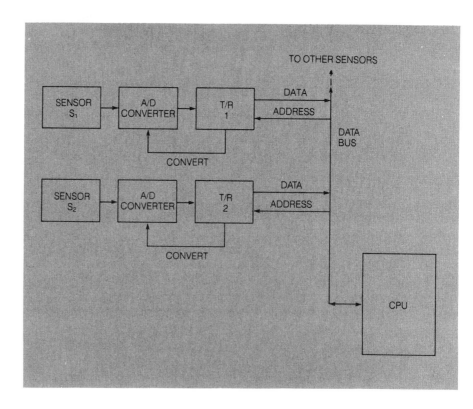

Each sensor would have exclusive use of this bus to send data (i.e., measurement of the associated engine variable or parameter) during its time slot. A separate time slot would be provided for each sensor.

This process of selectively assigning the data bus exclusively to a specific sensor during its time slot is called *time division multiplexing* (or sometimes just multiplexing—MUX). Recall that multiplexing was discussed as a data selector for the CPU input and output in a digital instrumentation system as described in Chapter 9. Limited use of multiplexing already exists in some production cars, but the concept considered here is for data flow throughout the entire car between all electronic subsystems.

To understand the operation of time division multiplexing of the data bus, refer to the system block diagram in Figure 11.16. The CPU controls the use of the data bus by signaling each sensor through a transmitter/receiver (T/R) unit. Whenever the CPU requires data from any sensor, it sends a coded message on the bus, which is connected to all T/R units. However, the message consists of a sequence of binary voltage pulses that are coded for the particular T/R unit. A T/R unit responds only to one particular sequence of pulses, which can be thought of as the address for that unit.

Each sensor in a multiplexing system sends its individual data over a common bus. The computer identifies the sensor by signaling each sensor with a unique address.

Whenever a T/R unit receives data corresponding to its address, it activates an analog-to-digital converter. The sensor's analog output at this instant is converted to a digital binary number as already discussed. This number and the T/R unit's address are included so that the CPU can identify the source of the data. Thus, the CPU interrogates a particular sensor and then receives the measurement data from the sensor on the data bus. The CPU then sends out the address of the next T/R unit whose sensor is to be sampled.

Control Signal Multiplexing

It also is possible to multiplex control signals to control switching of electrical power. Electrical power must be switched to lights, electric motors, solenoids, and other devices. The system for multiplexing electrical power control signals around the vehicle requires two buses—one carrying battery power and one carrying control signals. Figure 11.17 is a block diagram of such a multiplexing system. In a system of this type, a remote switch applies battery power to the component when activated by the receiver module (RM). The receiver module is activated by a command from the CPU that is transmitted along the control signal bus.

A multiplexed system can also control switching of electrical power for lights, motors, and similar devices. Each RM would switch power to the appropriate device in response to a CPU command.

This control signal bus operates very much like the sensor data bus described in the multiplexed engine control system. The particular component to be switched is initially selected by switches operated by the driver. (Of course, these switches can be multiplexed at the input of the CPU.) The CPU sends an RM address as a sequence of binary pulses along the control signal bus. Each receiver module responds only to one particular address. Whenever the CPU is to turn a given component on or off, it transmits the coded address

Figure 11.17
Control Signal Multiplexing Block Diagram

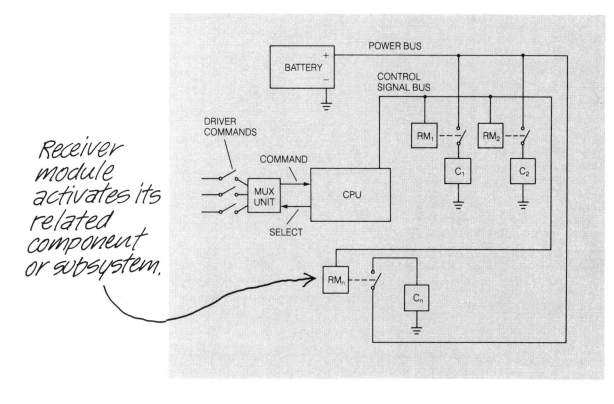

Receiver module activates its related component or subsystem.

and command to the corresponding RM. When the RM receives its particular code, it operates the corresponding switch, either applying battery power or removing battery power, depending on the command transmitted by the CPU.

Fiber Optics

Signal buses using fiber optics transmit data and control signals in the form of light pulses along thin fiber "wires." Such systems are relatively immune from noise interference.

It is possible, maybe even desirable, to use an optical fiber for the signal bus. For such a system, the address voltage pulses from the CPU are converted to corresponding pulses of light that are transmitted over an optical fiber. An *optical fiber*, which is also known as a *light pipe*, consists of a thin transparent cylinder of light-conducting glass about the size of a human hair. Light will follow the light pipe along its entire path, even around corners, just as electricity follows the path of wire. A big advantage of the optical fiber signal bus for automotive use is that external electrical noise doesn't interfere with the transmitted signal. The high-voltage pulses in the ignition circuit, which are a major potential source of interference in automotive electronic systems, will not affect the signals traveling on the optical signal bus.

For such a system, each component has an RM that has an optical detector coupled to the signal bus. Each detector receives the light pulses that are sent along the bus. Whenever the correct sequence (i.e., address) is received at the RM, the corresponding switch is either closed or opened.

A variety of multiplexing systems have been experimentally studied. It seems very likely that one form or another of multiplexing system will be used in the near future whenever the cost of such a system becomes less than that of the harness that it is to replace. It is possible that the move to multiplexing will occur in stages. For example, one existing system incorporates a multiplexing system for switches located in the door only.

NAVIGATION

One of the more interesting potential future developments in the application of electronics to automobiles is navigation. Every driver who has taken a trip to an unfamiliar location understands the problem of navigation. The driver must first obtain maps having sufficient detail to locate the destination. Along the trip the driver must be able to identify the car location in relationship to the map and make decisions at various road intersections about the route continuation.

On-board electronic navigation aids have been available for some time now in a form that includes a means for depicting an electronically generated map. Increasing use of such systems will occur in the near future. A brief review of this technology is given below. In addition, however, real-time off-board navigation systems are planned for future passenger car use. This off-board technology is discussed later in this chapter under "Telematics."

There has been considerable research done into the development of an electronic automatic navigation system, which may someday lead to the widespread commercial sale of such a system. Although stand-alone electronic navigation systems with multiscale electronic maps have been commercially

**Figure 11.18
Generic Automatic
Navigation System**

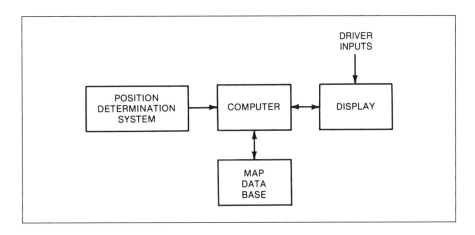

available for some time, these are somewhat less complex than the concept considered here. The present concept assumes a multisensor system that optimally integrates position and car motion data from the various sensors to obtain the best possible estimate of present position.

Figure 11.18 is a block diagram showing the major components of a generic automatic navigation system. The display portion of a research system is typically a solid-state CRT-type display. This display depicts one of many maps that are stored in memory.

Ideally, the display device should have the capability of displaying maps with various levels of magnification. As the car approaches its destination, the map detail should increase automatically until the driver can locate his or her position within an accuracy of about half a block.

The map database must be capable of storing sufficient data to construct a map of an entire region. For example, data could be stored on floppy disks (one for each region of the country) that are read into computer RAM as desired for a particular trip. Alternatively, a CD (compact disc) player could be used for large-scale data storage. In this case, the CD player would be part of the entertainment system. If the vehicle electronic system is integrated, the CD player can function as a large-scale memory for on-board navigation data.

The computer portion of the generic navigation system obtains signals from various position sensors and calculates the correct vehicle position in relationship to the map coordinates. The computer also controls the map display, accounting for magnification (called for by the driver) and displaying the vehicle position superimposed on the map. The correct vehicle position might, for example, be shown as a flashing bright spot.

Navigation Sensors

The most critical and costly component in the generic navigation system is the position-determining system, that is, the position sensor. Among the concepts presently being considered for automotive navigation are inertial navigation, radio navigation, signpost navigation, and dead reckoning navigation. Each of these has relative advantages in terms of cost and performance.

An inertial navigation sensor has been developed for aircraft navigation, but it is relatively expensive. The aircraft inertial navigation sensor consists of three gyros and accelerometers. Figure 11.19 is a block diagram of a typical navigation system using inertial navigation.

An inertial navigation system locates the vehicle position relative to a known starting point by integrating acceleration twice with respect to time. For example, along the x direction, vehicle position at time t is $x(t)$:

$$x(t) = x_0 + \int_0^t \int_0^r a(y)\,dy\,dr$$

**Figure 11.19
Automotive Inertial
Navigation System**

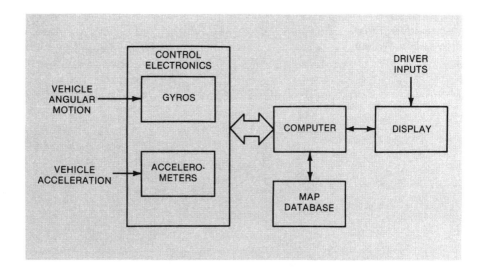

where

> x_0 is the initial x position
> a is the acceleration along x direction

A similar integration is performed along the two orthogonal directions.

An inertial navigation system has position errors due to initial gyro alignment errors, uncompensated gyro drift, and accelerometer errors. A typical high-quality commercial navigation system (e.g., Carousel IV) has a position error of about 3,000 feet for each hour of flight. Position errors generated at this rate in an automotive environment imply a trip of no more than a half-hour before the error exceeds the half-block limit. This error, in combination with the system's relatively high cost (about $120,000), renders the inertial navigation system unfeasible for automotive use for the foreseeable future. On the other hand, updated measurement of a car's present position can be obtained using radio navigation sensors.

Radio Navigation

A radio-based automotive navigation system uses either land- or satellite-based transmitters and automotive receivers for position location. Land-based transmitter systems that are potentially applicable include Decca, Loran-C, VOR, and Omega. The only satellite-based system that is potentially applicable is the Global Positioning System (GPS). The land-based systems are primarily intended for aircraft or ship navigation and have somewhat limited coverage. For example, Loran-C has no coverage for large portions of the southwestern United States. Nevertheless, research is being done on the applicability of these land-based systems to automotive navigation.

**Figure 11.20
Automotive GPS
Navigation System**

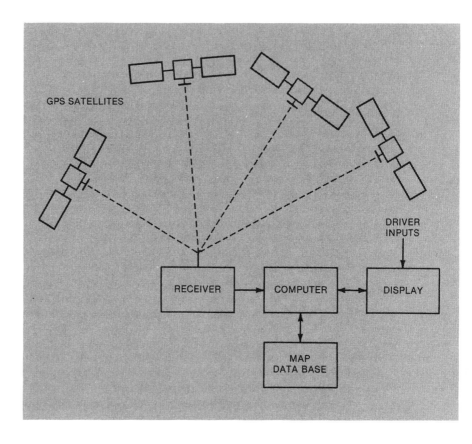

The GPS has 24 orbiting satellites, of which there are a minimum of four within line of sight of any location on earth. This is sufficient for position location. Figure 11.20 is a block diagram of a GPS-based automotive navigation system. Each satellite transmits clock pulses that give the time of transmission. The distance to any satellite is known by the relationship

$$R_i = c(t_i - t_r)$$

where

R_i is the distance to any satellite
c is the speed of light
t_i is the time that the clock pulse is transmitted from satellite to car
t_r is the time that the car receives the pulses

The measurement of the propagation time from satellite to receiver $(t_i - t_r)$ requires highly accurate (and expensive) clocks in both the satellite and the car. Position is determined (in three dimensions and time) by solving four equations involving the range to four satellites. In GPS service, an accuracy of

100 meters is quoted. In experiments, absolute accuracies of 30 meters have been achieved.

There are a number of problems associated with GPS-based navigation systems, including received signal strength, cost, time to fix position, and propagation considerations. The cost of a GPS receiver is determined partly by its precise clock. However, produced in sufficient quantities, the receiver cost could be brought into a commercially viable range. The time to fix initial position is on the order of two to three minutes, which is inconvenient but possibly acceptable. Once initial position is fixed, updated position is available in about two-second intervals. In addition, it is necessary to maintain a direct line of sight from the receiver to the satellite. This can be a problem in areas of tall buildings (where there are multiple propagation paths) or in mountainous terrain. Nevertheless, GPS is potentially viable for future automotive navigation and has many advocates.

Signpost Navigation

In signpost navigation, a number of information stations (signposts) are located throughout the road network. In one scheme, the signpost continuously transmits data concerning its geographic location. The on-board navigation system converts these data to map coordinates, which are displayed.

Figure 11.21 is a block diagram of a typical signpost navigation system. This system requires an augmented database to convert the transmitted data to map coordinates. This system has the capability to provide position to an accuracy of a few meters.

There are drawbacks to the signpost system, however, including an inability to determine position between signposts, inability to show a turn

**Figure 11.21
Signpost Navigation
System**

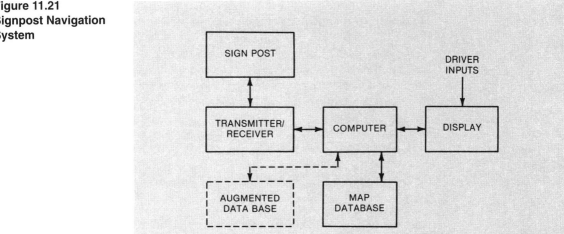

until the next signpost is reached, the need for signposts at every intersection, and the requirement for a large number of codes. Thus, in spite of the high accuracy of this system, it inherently requires a huge investment in infrastructure.

Dead Reckoning Navigation

Dead reckoning navigation is a method of determining present position from a known earlier position and information about vehicle motion. Figure 11.22 is a block diagram for such a system. The sensor components of this system include a heading sensor and a wheel speed sensor. Navigation systems of this type have been commercially available for some time. However, integration of this dead reckoning navigation system into a multisensor navigation system has not been available (the combined system being potentially a future electronic feature). The use of heading and speed information is illustrated in Figure 11.23. Experimental systems have used a form of magnetic compass sensor, known as a flux gate, to measure heading. Wheel speed sensors have already been explained in Chapter 8. Although this system is conceptually simple, it suffers from poor accuracy. It is estimated that a position error of about half a block would accrue for trips of less than six miles.

Typically, an electronic dead reckoning system employs a solid-state CRT-type screen (see Chapter 9) as a display device for presenting a map of the relevant geographic region. In at least one commercial system, there are eight different levels of resolution. The maps are generated from digital data that are stored on a compact disk (CD-ROM). Using the stored data, the electronic map is displayed on the screen, identifying the present position of the car as well as its destination. Using the present position (P_0 of Figure 11.23), the new position (P_1) is calculated.

Errors occur in any dead reckoning navigation system after a time. However, in automotive navigation systems, such errors can be readily bounded. It is presumed that the car is on a road (or in a driveway or parking lot) at all times. The coordinates of the road are known as part of the navigation database. Wherever the estimated position (P_1) is off the road, the computer adjusts the car position to the nearest point on the road. This correction procedure is known as *map matching* and results in extremely accurate navigation.

Voice Recognition Cell Phone Dialing

As beneficial as cellular phone systems are, they do have a potential safety disadvantage. For most people, dialing a number on a cell phone requires looking at the key pad while entering the digits. If the car is moving (and particularly if it is moving in heavy traffic), the momentary distraction of dialing the phone can potentially divert the driver's attention and an accident can occur.

**Figure 11.22
Dead Reckoning
Navigation System**

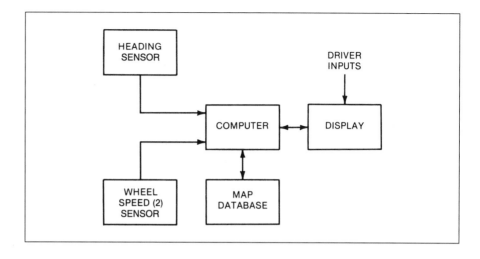

**Figure 11.23
Dead Reckoning
Navigation
Computation**

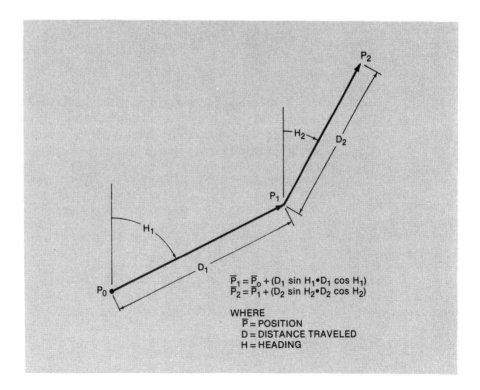

A scheme for dialing the phone without diverting the driver's attention from driving involves speech recognition technology. There are already cell phones available that can accept verbal dialing such that the driver simply speaks the telephone number to be dialed. When the connection is made the phone conversation can be completed without the driver having to physically hold the phone to his or her ear and mouth.

However, the majority of such hands-free cell phones can recognize only one or two individuals' voices. Normally such a system is trained to recognize the individual speakers. In the future it is likely that cell phone systems will be available that can recognize essentially any speaker. Using such systems, phone conversations can be completed without the driver ever having to divert his or her attention from the road.

TELEMATICS

Mobile communication via cell phone or satellite radio has great potential for advanced automotive communication and information retrieval. Communication of this type is generally called telematics, although the term is coming to have much broader meaning. Mobile Internet connectivity via such communication is possible for the automobile and in some sense already exists. In the near future, many believe that the automobile will become a portable Internet node. The types of information available to the automobile occupants are limited only by the Internet sources themselves.

Perhaps the only potentially serious issue/limitation to automotive Internet connectivity and its associated information is the issue of driver distraction. As long as a passenger is handling the Internet connection and information transfer, this should essentially be a nonissue. However, whenever the driver is the sole occupant, driver distraction, primarily visual distraction, is a potential safety issue.

One way to minimize driver distraction is to incorporate voice recognition and voice synthesis technology (see above) for all interactions with the telematics system. Such verbal interaction is potentially not much more distracting than ordinary conversation between the driver and passengers.

Given the Internet connectivity described here, the potential future information services available to a driver are virtually limitless. For example, at least one major electronics company has plans to provide real-time navigation to a car. The system, acting as a server, supplies information to the car, which in addition to navigation includes emergency calling, roadside assistance, routing, and, when available, traffic information. Server-based navigation permits arbitrarily complicated routing calculations and traffic information to be stored in various servers, enabling relevant trip information and guidance suggestions to be downloaded on demand to the vehicle via a wireless connection. Personalized traffic and weather information is available to the driver at any location where the wireless connection can be made. In urban and other high-population density areas, cell phone links are available. In remote areas, the digital link will be via satellite.

Although electronic maps will be well within the capabilities of any server-based system by use of solid-state CRT-type display, driver distraction can be minimized by voice maneuver prompting. Any server-based system having the complexity indicated above has much greater capability than navigation and traffic information. For example, it can search databases to locate best prices for fuel and lodging and can direct drivers to restaurants with preselected preferences. Essentially, any service or function available via Internet connectivity is potentially available to occupants of the car. The only significant limitation to such services is the need to avoid driver distraction.

Telematics applications will require on-board vehicle digital communications and some sort of control system for handling the information and data. There are many possible architectures for such communication systems in the future. One potential architecture having great promise is the embedded gateway model. A gateway is a networking module that can host many different telematics applications. For automotive (telematics) applications, a gateway should feature open standard interfaces to the various subsystems it serves. A gateway with open standard interfaces greatly enhances the ability to upgrade the system as technology and new applications evolve. The flexibility of such a system permits any telematics features to be added by a car owner at any time from purchase throughout the car's lifetime.

The gateway should be developed in the future having an interface capability to all other electronic subsystems. In addition to hands-free cell phone dialing and Internet connectivity, the telematics system can support entertainment for rear seat occupants. It can also provide a basis for a vehicle management system supporting diagnostics and maintenance functions as well

**Figure 11.24
Gateway Hardware
Architecture**

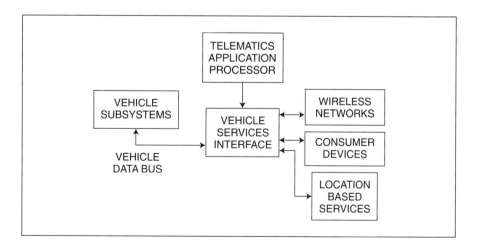

as real-time vehicle tracking. The diagnostic function is available from data supplied by each on-board electronic system. Whenever a problem or a potential future problem is present, the relevant data can be forwarded to a maintenance service via the telematics connectivity. The driver can then be warned of a potential problem to obtain preventative maintenance rather than waiting for a breakdown to occur.

Moreover, the driver can be reminded of scheduled maintenance in a timely fashion. Required oil changes, low windshield washer fluid and low tire pressure are examples of routine items to which the driver's attention can automatically be directed.

One example of the architecture for an automotive gateway that supports all telematics applications is shown in Figure 11.24. The vehicle subsystems depicted in Figure 11.24 include powertrain control, ABS/traction control, and cruise control, among other things. The wireless networks block includes cell phone and satellite links and in the future possibly other communication links. Consumer devices include PDA, video entertainment systems, video games, and even PC-like terminals (for passengers). The telematics applications processor reaches each of the other on-board systems via an interface hardware subsystem operating with its own software. The system depicted in Figure 11.24 is essentially "future proof" in the sense that it can be upgraded with hardware additions and software revisions at any future time. Some sort of system such as that shown in Figure 11.24 will yield a virtually limitless set of information services to the driver in the near future.

ADVANCED CRUISE CONTROL

The advanced cruise control (ACC) is a potential future extension of the cruise control system explained in Chapter 8. It will augment the hardware shown in Figure 8.8 with millimeter wave radar as well as with electrohydraulic brakes (also described in Chapter 8). In addition to regulating the throttle, this ACC system can regulate the brakes to achieve greater deceleration than is available with closed throttle.

The forward-looking radar can measure the difference to and speed of a lead vehicle. However, it can also detect other forward obstacles, including fixed obstacles at roadside.

An ACC can have many operating modes. Whenever the traffic density is low, the normal cruise control will regulate speed via throttle settings. When the radar system detects a forward, slower-moving vehicle it can adjust speed via throttle and/or brakes to maintain a fixed distance from own-car to forward car. Generally speaking, throttle control is sufficient if required deceleration is less than about 0.1 g. Any greater deceleration might require brake application. The smooth application of brakes to avoid jerky motion is one of the technical challenges that must be overcome before the ACC is ready for commercial use.

The addition of radar for measuring position and closing speed to forward obstacles has potential for collision avoidance. The major technical problem to be overcome for collision avoidance is discrimination of threatening from nonthreatening obstacles. For example, a car moving along a curve can have many obstacles along its forward instantaneous path that are nonthreatening as long as the car stays on the road. Any algorithm existing in the ACC that attempts to separate such nonthreatening obstacles from threatening obstacles (e.g., a vehicle stopped on the road) must take into account the vehicle motion and dynamics.

STABILITY AUGMENTATION

The existence of electronically controlled electric steering and electrohydraulic braking can yield improvements in vehicle stability in the future. In addition to electrohydraulic brakes, there is the possibility of pure electric brakes in which the brake pads are moved via an electric motor (known as brake-by-wire). There have been some experimental vehicles with electric brakes, and this technology may have a future.

A stability augmentation system would incorporate vehicle roll and yaw rate sensors that provide vehicle dynamic motion measurement to a control system that regulates brakes differentially and air suspension springs and dampers to minimize vehicle roll and to achieve optimal handling during certain maneuvers.

AUTOMATIC DRIVING CONTROL

Another rather interesting (but probably pretty far in the future) technology is the vehicle guideway system. This is a purely experimental system at the time of this writing that is envisaged as an automatic driving system. The concept involves automatic steering and automatic vehicle speed control. The concept leads to a system of multiple-vehicle automatic driving called *platooning*. In a platooning system a group of cars is automatically

**Figure 11.25
Automatic Driving
Control System**

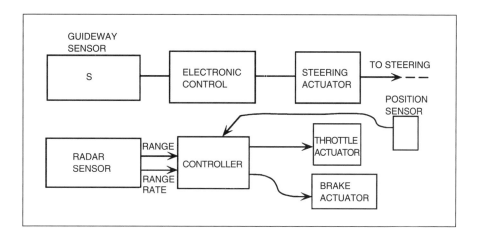

controlled to maintain a set highway cruise speed with a fixed nominal intercar spacing.

Steering control is via a signal radiated from a wire buried in the center of the roadway. Distances between cars and vehicle speeds are maintained with the aid of measurements made by an on-board radar system.

A simplified block diagram for automatic control is shown in Figure 11.25. In this figure, a sensor (S) is located on the bottom front of the car that picks up the signal radiated by the buried wire. This sensor signal is the input to a tracking controller that outputs a control signal to a steering actuator. Steering commands guide the vehicle to maintain the sensor over the guideway wire.

Vehicle speed control is accomplished using an on-board radar sensor. This sensor is located in front of the vehicle and directs a narrow radar beam forward. The radar sensor system obtains a measurement of the range to a car in front of the given car as well as the rate of change of that range. The sensor can also measure vehicle ground speed via Doppler shift of radar signals reflected from the ground.

The control system is a multiple-input/multiple-output controller that generates control signals for a throttle actuator and a braking actuator. Normally the controller will only activate the throttle; however, if the range to the vehicle is decreasing even with a closed throttle, then braking is required. The braking actuator pressurizes the brake lines automatically to slow the vehicle as required. This action could occur if the platoon of cars were driving down a long, relatively steep mountain or slope. It could also be required if an obstacle were encountered that was stationary (as in the case of a car with a breakdown). Panic-stop braking could actually be required in extreme cases.

Whenever manual control is required (e.g., when a given vehicle exits the highway in order to reach a given destination), the driver takes control by operating a control release switch.

There are many variations on the concept described above. Some will prove to be feasible; others will not. At this time the automatic vehicle guideway is an interesting experimental system with great potential for maintaining optimum traffic flow on otherwise busy or congested highways.

It should be emphasized that many of the topics included in this final chapter have an uncertain future in terms of production automobiles. Each idea discussed here has had at least an experimental confirmation of its technical feasibility. However, the final arbiter of the viability of each subsystem will be the automobile consumer, who will vote with his or her dollars on whether any given subsystem or feature is worth the incremental purchase price.

Quiz for Chapter 11

1. Engine performance may be improved in the future by
   a. tuning the intake manifold
   b. use of variable compression ratio
   c. variable valve timing
   d. all of the above

2. One potential engine control strategy based on a feedback signal from cylinder pressure may incorporate
   a. a piezoelectric cylinder pressure sensor
   b. a new MAP sensor
   c. an exhaust air/fuel sensor
   d. none of the above

3. An airbag is
   a. a mechanism for occupant protection in a car
   b. a container for use in case of airsickness
   c. an impact sensor
   d. all of the above

4. One concept for automotive collision avoidance involves
   a. braking rapidly in dangerous situations
   b. measuring the round-trip time of a radar pulse from protected car to collision object
   c. aircraft surveillance of highways
   d. wheel speed sensors

5. Doppler shift has potential automotive application for
   a. measuring the speed of passing trains
   b. automatic gear changing
   c. measuring vehicle speed over the road
   d. none of the above

6. A fuel-cell powered vehicle
   a. can be implemented using multiple proton exchange membrane cells
   b. is an electric vehicle
   c. can be fueled with hydrogen
   d. all of the above

7. A CRT-type display has potential automotive application for
   a. controlling vehicle motion
   b. recording vehicle transient motion
   c. monitoring entertainment systems
   d. displaying information to the driver

8. The term *HUD* refers to
   a. housing and urban development
   b. heads up display
   c. heads up driver
   d. none of the above

9. Speech synthesis is
   a. a system that automatically recognizes human speech
   b. an automatic checkbook balancing system
   c. a visual display of speech waveforms
   d. a means of electronically generating human speech

10. An optical fiber is
    a. a tiny beam of light
    b. an optical waveguide that is often called a light pipe
    c. an optical switch
    d. none of the above

11. An inertial navigation system incorporates the following sensors:
    a. radio receivers
    b. Doppler radar
    c. gyros and accelerometers
    d. none of the above

Glossary

Accumulator: The basic work register of a computer.

Actuator: A device which performs an action in response to an electrical signal.

A/D (also ADC): Analog-to-digital converter; a device which is proportional to the analog voltage level input.

A/F: *See* Air/Fuel Ratio.

Analog Circuits: Electronic circuits which amplify, reduce, or otherwise alter a voltage signal which is a smooth or continuous copy of some physical quantity.

Assembly Language: An abbreviated computer language which humans can use to program computers. Assembly language eventually is converted to machine language so that a computer can understand it.

BDC: Bottom dead center; the extreme lowest position of the piston during its stroke.

Bit: A binary digit; the smallest piece of data a computer can manipulate.

Block Diagram: A system diagram which shows all of the major parts and their interconnections.

BSCO: Brake specific fuel consumption; the ratio of the rate at which fuel is flowing into an engine to the brake horsepower being generated.

BSHC: Brake specific HC; the ratio of the rate at which hydrocarbons leave the exhaust pipe to the brake horsepower.

BSNO$_x$: Brake specific NO$_x$; the ratio of the rate at which oxides of nitrogen leave the exhaust pipe to the brake horsepower.

Byte: 8 bits dealt with together.

CAFE: Corporate-Average-Fuel-Economy. The government mandated fuel economy which is averaged over the production for a year for any given manufacturer.

Capacitor: An electronic device which stores charge.

Catalytic Converter: A device which enhances certain chemical reactions which help to reduce the levels of undesirable exhaust gases.

Closed-Loop Fuel Control: A mode where input air/fuel ratio is controlled by metering the fuel response to the rich-lean indications from an exhaust gas oxygen sensor.

CO: Carbon monoxide; an undesirable chemical combustion product due to imperfect combustion.

Combinational Logic: Logic circuits whose outputs depend only on the present logic inputs.

Combustion: The burning of the fuel-air mixture in the cylinder.

Comparator, Analog: An electronic device which compares the voltages applied to its inputs.

Compression Ratio: The ratio of the cylinder volume at BDC to the volume at TDC.

Control Variable: The plant inputs and outputs which a control system manipulates and measures to properly control it.

Conversion Efficiency (Catalytic Converter): The efficiency with which undesirable exhaust gases are reduced to acceptable levels or are converted to desirable gases.

CPU: Central processing unit; the calculator portion of a computer.

Cutoff: A transistor operating mode where very little current flows between the collector and emitter.

D/A (also DAC): Digital-to-analog converter; a device which produces a voltage which is proportional to the digit input number.

Damping Coefficient: A parameter which affects a system's time response by making it more or less sluggish.

DEMUX: Demultiplexer; a type of electronic switch used to select one of several output lines.

Diesel: A class of internal combustion engine in which combustion is initiated by the high temperature of the compressed air in the cylinder rather than an electrical spark.

Digital Circuits: Electronic circuits whose outputs can change only at specific instances and between a limited number of different voltages.

Diode: A semiconductor device which acts like a current check valve.

Display: Advice which indicates in human readable form the result of measurement of some variable.

Drivetrain: The combination of mechanisms connecting the engine to the driving wheels including transmission, driveshaft, and differential.

Dwell: The time that current flows through the primary circuit of the ignition coil for each spark generation.

Dynamometer: A device for loading the engine and measuring engine performance.

EGO: Exhaust gas oxygen; the concentration of oxygen in the exhaust of an engine. An EGO sensor is used in closed-loop fuel control systems to indicate rich or lean A/F.

EGR: Exhaust gas recirculation; a procedure in which a portion of exhaust is introduced into the intake of an engine.

Electronic Carburetor: A fuel metering actuator in which the air/fuel ratio is controlled by continual variations of the metering rod position in response to an electronic control signal.

Engine Calibration: The values for air/fuel, spark advance, and EGR at any operating condition.

Engine Crankshaft Position: The angular position of the crankshaft relative to a reference point.

Engine Mapping: A procedure of experimentally determining the performance of an engine at selected operating points and recording the results.

Equivalence Ratio: Actual air/fuel ratio divided by the air/fuel ratio at stoichiometry.

Evaporative Emissions: Evaporated fuel from the carburetor or fuel system which mixes with the surrounding air.

Foot-Pound: A unit of torque corresponding to a force of one pound acting on a one foot level arm.

Frequency Response: A graph of a system's response to different frequency input signals.

Gain: The ratio of a system's output magnitude to its input magnitude.

HC: Hydrocarbon chemicals, such as gasoline, formed by the union of carbon and hydrogen.

Ignition Timing: The time of occurrence of ignition measured in degrees of crankshaft rotation relative to TDC.

Inductor: A magnetic device which stores energy in a magnetic field produced by current flowing in it.

Instrumentation: Apparatus (often electronic) which is used for measurement or control, and for display of measurements or conditions.

Integral Amplifier: A control system component whose voltage output changes at a rate proportional to its input voltage.

Integrated Circuit: A semiconductor device which contains many circuit functions on a single chip.

Interrupts: An efficient method of quickly requesting a computer's attention to a particular external event.

Lead Term: A control system component which anticipates future inputs based on the current signal trend.

Limit Cycle: A mode of control system operation in which the controlled variable cycles between extreme limits with the average near the desired value.

Linear Region: A transistor operating mode where the collector current is proportional to the base current.

Logic Circuits: Digital electronic circuits which perform logical operations such as NOT, AND, OR, and combinations of these.

Lookup Table: A table in the computer memory which is used to convert an important value into a related value from the table.

MAP: Manifold absolute pressure; the absolute pressure in the intake manifold of an engine.

Mathematical Model: A mathematical equation which can be used to numerically compute a system's response to a particular input.

Microcomputer: A small computer which uses an integrated circuit which contains a central processing unit and other control electronics.

MUX: Multiplexer; a type of electronic switch used to select one of several input lines.

NO$_x$: The various oxides of nitrogen.

Op Code: A number which a computer recognizes as an instruction.

Open-Loop Fuel Control: A mode where engine input air/fuel ratio is controlled by measuring the mass of input air and adding the proper mass of fuel to obtain a 14.7 to 1 ratio.

Operational Amplifier: A standard analog building block with two inputs, one output, and a very high voltage gain.

Optimal Damping: The damping which produces the very best time response.

Peripheral: An external input-output device which is connected to a computer.

Phase Shift: A measure of the delay in degrees between the time a signal enters a system and the time it shows up at the output as a fraction of a full cycle of 360°.

Plant: A system which is to be controlled.

Proportional Amplifier: A control system component which produces a control output proportional to its input.

Qualitative Analysis: A study which reveals how a system works.

Quantitative Analysis: A study which determines how well a system performs.

RAM: Random access memory; read/write memory.

Random Error: A measurement error which is neither predictable nor correctable, but has some statistical nature to it.

ROM: Read only memory; permanent memory used to store permanent programs.

RPM: Revolutions per minute; the angular speed of rotation of the crankshaft of an engine or other rotating shaft.

Sample and Hold: The act of measuring a voltage at a particular time and storing that voltage until a new sample is taken.

Sampling: The act of periodically collecting or providing information about a particular process.

Semiconductor: A material which is neither a good conductor nor a good insulator.

Sensor: An energy conversion device which measures some physical quantity and converts it to an electrical quantity.

Sequential Logic: Logic circuits whose output depends on the particular sequence of the input logic signals.

SI Engine: Abbreviation for spark-ignited, gasoline-fueled, piston-type, internal-combustion engine.

Signal Processing: The alteration of an electrical signal by electronic circuitry; used to reduce the effects of systematic and random errors.

Skid: A condition in which the tires are sliding over the road surface rather thin rolling; usually associated with braking.

Slip: The ratio of the angular speed of the driving element to the angular speed of the driven element of a torque converter; also, the condition in which a driven tire loses traction so that the driving torque does not produce vehicle motion.

Software: The computer program instructions used to tell a computer what to do.

Spark Advance: The number of degrees of crankshaft rotation before TDC where the spark plug is fired. (*See* ignition timing.)

Spark Timing: The process of firing the spark plugs at the proper moment to ignite the combustible mixture in the engine cylinders.

Stoichiometry: The air/fuel ratio for perfect combustion; it enables exactly all of the fuel to burn using exactly all of the oxygen in the air.

System: A collection of interacting parts.

Systematic Error: A measurement error in instrumentation system which is predictable and correctable.

TBFI: Throttle-body-fuel-injector; a fuel metering actuator in which the air/fuel ratio is controlled by injecting precisely controlled spurts of fuel into the air stream entering the intake manifold.

TDC: Top dead center; the extreme highest point of the piston during its stroke.

Throttle Angle: The angle between the throttle plate and a reference line; engine speed increases as the angle increases.

Torque Converter: A form of fluid coupling used in an automatic transmission which acts like a torque amplifier.

Torque: The twisting force of the crankshaft or other driving shaft.

Transfer Function: A mathematical equation which, when graphed, produces a system's frequency response plot.

Transistor: An active semiconductor device which operates like a current valve.

Transport Delay: The time required for a given mass of fuel and air to travel from the intake manifold through the engine to the EGO sensor in the exhaust manifold.

Volumetric Efficiency: The pumping efficiency of the engine as air is drawn into the cylinders.

Answers to Quizzes

Chapter 1	Chapter 3	Chapter 4	Chapter 5
1. c	1. a	1. d	1. c
2. a	2. c	2. d	2. c
3. b	3. b	3. c	3. d
4. d	4. a	4. a	4. b
5. b	5. c	5. e	5. b
6. b	6. b	6. b	6. a
7. c	7. d	7. d	7. c
8. b	8. d	8. c	8. c
9. a	9. b	9. b	9. a
10. a	10. d	10. a	10. c
11. a	11. b	11. b	11. c
12. d	12. d	12. c	12. a
Chapter 2	13. b	13. d	13. c
	14. a	14. b	14. c
1. e	15. d	15. a	15. a
2. b	16. c	16. b	16. a
3. b	17. b	17. b	17. b
4. a	18. d	18. d	18. c
5. b	19. c	19. d	19. a
6. c	20. a		
7. b			
8. d			
9. d			
10. d			

Chapter 6

1. b
2. c
3. a
4. b
5. b
6. d
7. c
8. a
9. a
10. b
11. d
12. a
13. c
14. b
15. c

Chapter 7

1. d
2. a
3. b
4. d
5. b
6. b
7. c
8. c
9. d
10. b
11. d
12. c
13. d
14. a

Chapter 8

1. b
2. c
3. a
4. b
5. d
6. a
7. b
8. a
9. a
10. a

Chapter 9

1. a
2. c
3. c
4. c
5. a
6. c
7. c
8. a
9. d
10. a
11. a
12. a
13. b
14. b
15. a
16. c
17. c

Chapter 10

1. d
2. b
3. d
4. c
5. d
6. d
7. d
8. a
9. b
10. b

Chapter 11

1. d
2. a
3. a
4. b
5. c
6. d
7. d
8. b
9. d
10. b
11. c

Index

Page numbers followed by "t" denote tables; those followed by "f" denote figures.

Jump-to-subroutine instruction, 125–127

K

Knocking, 263
Knock level detector signal, 268f
Knock sensors, 226–227
Knock signal, 264
Knowledge engineer, 388

L

Lambda sensor, 220, 407, 411f
Large-scale integration integrated circuits, 103
Light-emitting diode, 217, 343
Light pipe, 428
Limit-cycle control, 73
Limit-cycle controller, 75, 149–151
Linear circuits, 87
Linear region, 86
Linear transfer characteristic, 57
Liquid crystal display
  advantages and disadvantages of, 345
  description of, 344
  illumination of, 345–346
  mechanism of operation, 344–345
  schematic diagram of, 344, 345f
  transflexive, 346–347
  transmissive, 346–347
  twisted pneumatic, 344
Loading errors, 54
Local area network, 371
Logic circuits
  adder circuits, 97–99, 98f
  description of, 94
  AND gate, 95, 96f, 127, 130, 132–135
  with memory, 99–102

NAND gate, 95–97, 96f
NOR gate, 95–97, 96f
NOT gate, 95, 96f, 130
OR gate, 95, 96f
XOR gates, 97–99, 98f
Lookup tables, 152–154
Lorentz force, 214
Low tire pressure warning system, 420–423

M

Magnetic circuit, 209
Magnetic field intensity, 209
Magnetic flux, 209–211
Magnetic focusing system, 350
Magnetic reluctance position sensors, 209–213
Magnetostriction, 226
Mainframe computers, 111
Manifold absolute pressure, 186–187, 250, 259, 277
Map matching, 434
Masking, 134
Mass air flow sensor
  circuit diagram, 207f
  concepts, 204
  description of, 180, 201, 243, 277
  strain gauge, 204–206
Master, 371
Master cylinder, 311
Maximum torque, 172
Mean best torque, 263
Measurement, 53
Mechanical rotary power, 8
Memory
  computer, 111–112
  definition of, 100
  logic circuits with, 99–102
  peripherals vs., 115
  RAM, 137, 145, 254
  ROM, 137, 145, 261, 298, 354

Q

R